A Global History of the Developing World

"Christopher White has written a stimulating book that will take the reader on a tour of three continents – Latin America, Asia and Africa. The book provides a comprehensive history of the developing world based on the author's profound knowledge of economic and social history over the last six centuries. The reader is not only provided with a new roadmap of World History but also with an alternative way of understanding key contemporary issues, such as global poverty or inequality. This book is highly recommended for students and their teachers in both social science and history."

Katsushi Imai, *University of Manchester, UK*

A Global History of the Developing World takes a sweeping look at the historical foundations of the problems of developing world society. Encompassing Asia, Latin America, and Africa, the book centralizes the struggle for self-determination in an attempt to understand how the current nation-states have been formed and what their future may hold. Although concentrating on the modern era, the book's scope is broad: It covers geography, ancient and modern history, economics, politics, and recent events.

The book features twelve chapters, organized into four thematic parts, each containing one chapter on each of the three continents. These parts cover different commonly experienced phenomena among the peoples of the developing world: imperialism, nationalism, globalization, and development. The first three are chronological, whereas the last surveys and analyzes the scholarly debates over the causes of development and underdevelopment. Through these chapters, Christopher M. White presents a wide-ranging study of the major themes in studies of the developing world, including slavery, imperialism, religion, free and fair trade, democratization, and economic development.

Including detailed profiles of key figures as well as maps and illustrations, *A Global History of the Developing World* vividly illustrates the culture, personalities, and histories of a key subject area. It is a perfect introduction for all students interested in the developing world in a historical context.

Christopher M. White is Associate Professor of history at Marshall University, Huntington, USA. His research interests include Latin American history, revolutionary movements, and US foreign policy. He is the author of *Creating a Third World: Mexico, Cuba, and the United States during the Castro Era and The History of El Salvador* (2007).

A Global History of the Developing World

Christopher M. White

Routledge
Taylor & Francis Group

LONDON AND NEW YORK

First published 2014
by Routledge
2 Park Square, Milton Park, Abingdon, Oxon OX14 4RN

and by Routledge
711 Third Avenue, New York, NY 10017

Routledge is an imprint of the Taylor & Francis Group, an informa business

British Library Cataloguing in Publication Data
A catalogue record for this book is available from the British Library

Library of Congress Cataloging in Publication Data
White, Christopher M., 1974–
A global history of the developing world / Chris White.
      pages cm
   1. Developing countries – History 2. Developing countries – History
   – Autonomy and independence movements. 3. Colonies – History.
   4. Imperialism – History. 5. Decolonization – History – 20th century.
   I. Title.
   D883.W55 2013
   909´.09724–dc23   2013013671

ISBN: 978-0-415-69210-6 (hbk)
ISBN: 978-0-415-69211-3 (pbk)
ISBN: 978-1-315-88563-6 (ebk)

Typeset in Sabon
by HWA Text and Data Management, London

MIX
Paper from
responsible sources
FSC® C013604
www.fsc.org

Printed and bound by CPI Group (UK) Ltd, Croydon, CR0 4YY

To Owen Moul, who loved his family, friends, and history.

Contents

Illustrations

Introduction: Overview of Latin America, Asia, and Africa

Reality and imagination

To begin our discussion of the developing world, it must be made clear that any description is a leap of imagination between the actual and the imagined worlds. That is to say that "reality" itself is elusive because it can be interpreted only by human beings observing their surroundings, with all of their known and unknown filters of perception. The use of language to depict what we *imagine* to be the "reality" of our observations only makes what we imagine seem more real. In other words, the more something is portrayed a certain way and the more that portrayal is heard by other people, the more it becomes a belief among the population. Language itself is a challenge to discern the reality of, precisely because it is a human-made *reaction* to what we observe and *not* a perfect reflection of that observation.

This is no mere philosophical play with words, nor is it simply a generalized statement. It applies directly to the history of the developing world because most of the depictions of this region (Latin America, Asia, and Africa) during the modern era (1500–present) have come from people in the Developed World (i.e., the West). This does not necessarily mean the portrayals are inaccurate, but it is important to ask questions such as the following:

- "How have Westernized depictions of the developing world served Western interests?"
- "What is missing from these Westernized accounts of the developing world?"
- "How has the history of the developing world as told from the Western lens shaped Western attitudes toward these three regions?"

We could continue asking questions such as these, but then we would risk entering into a very complex web of theoretical explanations that we have no space for in this Introduction. However, we will discuss theories of various stripes in the final part. This book is broken down into four parts, with three chapters each. The first three parts cover the fundamentals of the modern history of the developing world, ranging from the European conquests and colonizations of Latin America, Asia, and Africa of the sixteenth through nineteenth centuries, to the revolutions and market reforms of the twentieth and twenty-first centuries. These parts are designed to lay a foundation of important historical geography, events, figures, and trends for the reader. This leads to the fourth part, which evaluates the varying schools of thought on the causes of development and underdevelopment. The first three parts are meant to foment discussion and debate about the specifics and implications of historical events.

The last part hopes to create discussion and debate over the merits of different theoretical approaches of some of the most prominent authors of development theory. We are in luck as of late because there are a plethora of academic studies available to us that have sought to address this subject. Professors and activists from a wide array of backgrounds such as Jeffrey Sachs, Lawrence Harrison, Samuel Huntington, Jared Diamond, David Landes, Noam Chomsky, Paul Farmer, Paul Collier, David Korten, Muhammad Yunus, Thomas Sowell, Niall Ferguson, and others will be included in this discussion. I have not hesitated to include my own analysis throughout the book, which is informed by personal observations and honest scholarship. Not every reader will agree with the tone of the book at times, for I at times emphasize the barbarity, dishonesty, and meaning of events and historical figures to degrees that some will find unfair. However, I do this for all sides equally, as you will see when you read my portrayals of such disparate figures as Hernan Cortez and Robert Mugabe, Mahatma Gandhi and Joseph Sese Mobutu, and Mao Zedong and George W. Bush. In other words, liberals may be offended by my critiques of some of their heroes, but conservatives may also be offended by my critiques of theirs. This is part of honest scholarship from my own personal perspective. My approach is inspired by both radical scholars such as Howard Zinn, Edward Said, and Noam Chomsky and by pro-West/pro-capitalist scholars such as Niall Ferguson, Jared Diamond, and Thomas Sowell. These scholars, unlike most, do not consider their positions as simply "professorial" and do not write and teach simply for a "love of history" or for the sake of posterity. These authors have taken their research to the level of outreach, which involves exposing one's biases to an extent to be heard. It is in the same vein as these authors that I write this book.

Let us jump into this topic with both feet by really examining what we know about "the developing world." Even if the reader comes from Asia, Africa, or Latin America, has traveled there, has relatives or friends from there, or has read much about these places, it is important that we lay out what we know or think we know. To "think" one knows something means a lot in our modern world. It determines behavior. It determines attitude. It leads to vote outcomes. It leads to wars, peace, happiness, and sorrow. It has results that affect people's lives. How people in the Developed World (i.e., the West, the Industrialized World, the First World) think about the developing world determines whether people live or die there. The same could be said of how people of the developing world identify themselves. Just read the recent histories of India, Cuba, Vietnam, South Africa, and

China to see how post-colonialism and revolutionary ideas have drastically altered the lives of billions of people. To address the developing world in a manner conducive to critical analysis and depth of understanding, the reader may find it useful to engage in a four-step process based on the following questions:

1   What are your assumptions about this topic?
2   What sources inform your assumptions?
3   What level of legitimacy do you ascribe to those sources?
4   What do you gain from these assumptions?

These four questions will be ever present throughout the book in various forms. They are included to keep our thinking oriented toward confronting the extent of our own understanding of each chapter topic so that we may gauge in an honest manner what we do and do not know. The notion that much of what we believe we know about the world is based on mere assumptions should not insult the reader. In fact, this is more of an educational tool I use to promote discussion of the myriad topics we cover herein. If you start reading with the mindset that you indeed do possess many baseless assumptions, you have leapt out of the realm of closed-mindedness and into the realm of enlightenment, so to speak. This is a philosophical standpoint I value especially when dealing with the developing world because there are so many misconceptions disseminated by wholly uninformed figureheads, whose attitudes about the region often lead to disasters for which they are not held accountable. At the same time, when we see the actions of informed observers, their results may not always turn out favorable, but they tend to consider factors that are more closely consistent with reality to a greater degree than the uninformed, and they are less likely to stoke flames that burn out of control. As college students, you have a choice to make: do you prefer to make decisions based on preconceived notions or do you prefer to make informed decisions?

Let us use the image on the front cover as an example. I took the photograph in August 2005 while on the Uros Islands on Lake Titicaca in Peru. The Uros people live on a group of small man-made islands built from a thick layering of reeds. This particular group of Uros islanders makes most of their living through tourism. People pay to visit the islands and see how the Uros peoples have traditionally lived. Another group does not permit tourists to visit because they prefer to preserve their ancient culture. What are some of the possible moral questions that could arise from the effects of tourism on Indigenous cultures? Would it be better to remove the tourist presence from the Uros islands to allow the people to protect their culture? Does that question assume too much about the desires and agency of the Uros islanders? Is it possible that those islanders involved in tourism prefer that lifestyle just as much as those who have chosen to forsake tourism? Can you see benefits in each group's choices?

These questions are meant to help us explore, rather than conclude, to gain more texture in our understanding about the developing world. And that world is changing ever rapidly. The woman and child on the cover are not meant to convey a generalized image of the peoples of Asia, Latin America, and Africa. The picture is meant to raise questions. Do most Westerners believe that most people in the developing world live in huts? Does the fact that many Uros people live in huts mean their lives are inferior (or superior, depending on your perspective) in quality to those in the West? Does the fact that the people portray themselves as living in huts mean they actually do live in huts? Or are the islands merely a stage to present a show to tourists who wish to see "primitive," "authentic," "Indigenous" peoples? Does the image represent poverty or progress? Is the developing world as underdeveloped (i.e., "poor") as people in the West think?

Questions such as these should not lead to endless speculation; rather, they should encourage discussion based on observation and knowledge. There are many certainties in history, such as the proven existence of phenomena, the impact of leaders, the effects of wars, and environmental factors, to name a few. However, humans also view history in concrete ways that often lead to destructive behaviors. A large portion of the German population viewed Jews in a concretely negative way, and Hitler led the way toward their near elimination. The Hutus of Rwanda viewed the Tutsis this way, too, and their leaders facilitated the murder of most Tutsis. Countless other groups of people have carried out mass atrocities against other groups throughout history. In these cases, there was little room for analysis. The leaders did not encourage their followers to think critically about what they were doing. They were not confused about the cause when they killed unarmed men, women, and children. Though most of history is not made of genocide and war, these are poignant examples of the folly of unexamined ideas.

I have a saying in my classroom that aims to undermine my students' inclination to rush to judgment: "If you leave my class more confused than when you arrived, I have done my job." Of course, I do not wish for people to remain infinitely confused. The statement is intended to ask students to challenge their preconceived notions about the developing world. When we are humble in the face of information, abandoning nationalism, racism, sexism, classism, and all other prejudices aside from a belief in basic human rights and morality, we can use the study of history for the benefit of all mankind.

Geography

The landscape of the developing world and its usage has been the subject of much debate in the scholarship of the past century. Geographers are not alone in this endeavor, as biologists, geologists, anthropologists, historians, sociologists, and economists all must consider these factors as well. Although

Latin America, Asia, and Africa are physically separate, there are similarities in their geographical makeup.

1   The tropics (23 degrees north and south of the equator) make up an important part of all three regions.
2   Due to the lower level of industrialization in all three regions, land usage has been intimately tied to culture on a broader scale than in the West. In Western countries, 1 percent to 5 percent of the population works in agriculture, and in the developing world, this ranges from 12 percent to 90 percent, depending on the country.
3   Natural resources such as precious metals, wood, dyes, oil, and fertile soil in these three regions are what have traditionally drawn Western countries to seek to exploit them and, as such, many of their economies are still based on resource extraction and export.
4   Rapid urbanization in all three regions over the past century has unnaturally burdened many cities with the problems of overpopulation. Shantytowns, pollution, crime, housing shortages, price fluctuations, and unsafe buildings have emerged as crisis-producing ingredients in many cities. At the same time, cities have become the center of economic progress in all three regions.
5   The natural beauty of tropical, desert, and mountainous regions in Asia, Latin America, and Africa have been a huge source of revenue in the form of tourism from Westerners in the past two centuries in particular.

Still, the distinctions between the three regions are infinitely more important to the people who live there. That goes for each individual country, state, city, and ethnicity as well. Down to the smallest countries, such as Rwanda, El Salvador, and Laos, the people feel different than their neighboring countries, and even within each, the differences in tribe, ethnicity, or subcategory of governmental administration (state, department, county, city, hamlet, village, etc.), the people feel distinct. Therefore, any treatment of these regions as a whole must keep in mind the smaller entities that will be inevitably overlooked at times for the sake of space in this book.

Latin America

There are hundreds of Indigenous languages and dialects that have been preserved since the time of the conquest of the Americas. Recent research indicates that people have inhabited Mexico for anywhere between 13,000 and 50,000 years. Corn was first domesticated in Mexico approximately 8,000 to 6,000 years ago, or approximately 3,000 to 5,000 years after domestication of wheat and barley in the Fertile Crescent of the Middle East. The history of the Indigenous peoples of Mexico and the rest of Latin America prior to the arrival of Christopher Columbus is mostly lost due to the fact that the

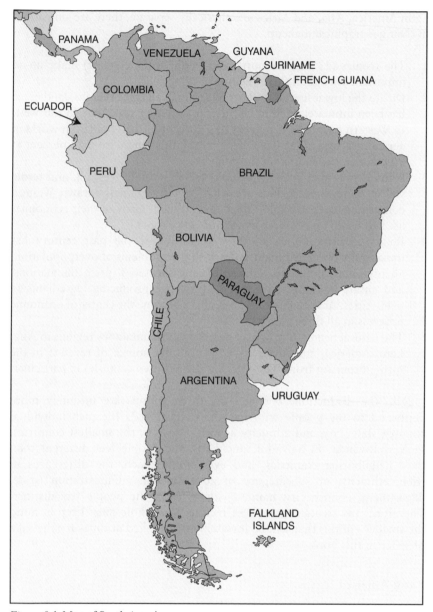

Figure 0.1 Map of South America

Spanish conquistadors systematically destroyed nearly all the written records they found. At the same time, most of the Americas never produced writing systems before Columbus. Much of what we know of this period comes from Spanish chroniclers during the colonial era and the work of archeologists and historians beginning in the nineteenth century and continuing to this day.

For the past five centuries, the main image people received about Latin America was Eurocentric, but the five decades of progressive scholarship has yielded a rich record detailing the advancements of Indigenous society the likes of which most outsiders could not imagine precisely because it contradicted the narrative handed down for generations before. Now, it is clear that the Nahua, Maya, Arawak, Quechua, Aymara, Tupi, Guarani, and Mapuche, to name only the dominant groups, lived in complex societies with technological and governmental advancements that rivaled those of the Old World.

Unlike Africa and Asia, Latin America is not a continent. It is a region that spans North America and South America. Mexico, Central America, and the Caribbean are considered part of North America and the continent of South America begins at the border between Panama and Colombia. Much of the land is mountainous, with many mostly dormant volcanoes, with the dominant mountain chain being the Sierra Madre that runs south from Canada through the United States, Mexico, Central America, and the Andes down to the tip of Chile and Argentina (Tierra del Fuego).

The north of Mexico is mostly desert with semi-arid lands as well, with tropical forests running south along the east and southwest coasts and northeast through the Yucatan, then down through all of Central America. Environmental degradation has been a major problem over the past century due to overuse of the land, increased population density, and urbanization; thus, the natural forest has disappeared in most places. With the exception of Belize, which speaks English primarily, Spanish is the main language of Mexico and Central America.

The Caribbean is more diverse per capita than the rest of Latin America due to the many different European countries that colonized and fought over the islands during the colonial era. Spanish is the dominant language by far, and both French, with its Creole variations, and English and Dutch are also spoken. Cuba is the most prominent feature due to its size by comparison to the rest. Hispaniola is the second largest island, and it is divided by two bitter enemies, Haiti and the Dominican Republic. Jamaica and Trinidad and Tobago (one country despite the "and") are also major players in the Caribbean, while the smaller countries of the Bahamas, Curacao, Martinique, Guadeloupe, and others cannot be left out.

South America is quite diverse as well, with Spanish and Portuguese spoken by an almost equal number of people, myriad Indigenous languages (new ones are still being discovered), and record-setting starkly different geographical features side by side. The Amazon River is the largest river in the world, and Brazils' Patanal region is the world's largest wetlands. There is more rainforest territory in South America than any place on Earth. Not far from the rainforest is the driest region on the planet, Chile's Atacama Desert, and it is right next to the world's longest mountain chain, the Andes, which are also the second highest in the world. This geography has proved to be an impediment to unity throughout history but, in recent years, the leaders of South America have sought to overcome these obstacles through regional trade agreements and political solidarity on a level never seen before.

There are 33 countries and territories in Latin America and the Caribbean, only one of which is still a dictatorship. Dictatorship was the norm in the region until the rise of democratic systems in the past three decades, and although right-wing governments were the norm into the 1980s, the left has come to power in the past decade in nearly every Latin American country, with some exceptions (Mexico and Colombia, especially). This has a lot to do with the left's belief in the malfunctioning of the U.S.-style capitalist model (referred to as "The Washington Consensus" or "neo-liberalism") implemented in the 1980s, and although figures such as Hugo Chavez and Raul Castro (Fidel stepped down in 2006) have some influence, in general, Latin Americans have shifted away from the revolutionary politics of the Cold War era and toward a more moderate progressivism. Left-leaning leaders such as Luis Ignacio da Silva (Lula) of Brazil, Michelle Bachelet of Chile, and Mauricio Funes of El Salvador are much more the norm. However, as the history of the past century has demonstrated time and again, Latin American politics can shift in an instant. Witness the revolutions in Mexico, Cuba, and Nicaragua that took observers by surprise with the magnitude of the change they installed, not to mention the rapid reduction of the military's power in government throughout the region after the 1980s (despite its role in the Drug War, no small matter). We will address these recent events more fully in Part III.

Asia

The largest continent, containing half the planet's population, Asia stands out as a giant on the global scene and especially by comparison to its western neighbor, Europe. Asia is the only continent of the three we will be studying that has an east-west orientation, but its width from north to south is also considerable. Asia's western border technically begins with the Ural Mountains in Russia in the northwest and stretches southwest to the Arabian Peninsula. Turkey is Asia's westernmost country, and from there, one travels 6,000 miles east through forty-seven countries, two of which have the largest populations on Earth (China and India), and at least four of which have reached "Developed World" status (Japan, South Korea, Taiwan, and Singapore). Hong Kong could be on that list of countries as well, but it has never had the status of a country. It was under British control until 1997, when it was consumed by China. Going eastward from Turkey, one crosses south into the Arabian Desert on the Arabian Peninsula, then crosses the Persian Gulf to Ancient Persia and modern-day Iran before heading north and east into the "seven stans" (Afghanistan, Pakistan, Kazakhstan, Kyrgyzstan, Uzbekistan, Turkmenistan, and Tajikistan) of Central Asia, with the Himalayan Mountains on the eastern side.

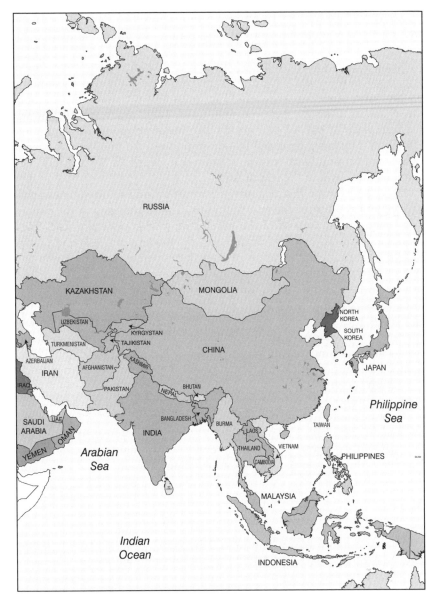

Figure 0.2 Map of Asia

Once into the Himalayas (the highest mountains on the planet), the
culture, climate, and terrain alter dramatically. The Himalayan villages in
Bhutan, India, Afghanistan, Nepal, Tibet, and Pakistan have a different way
of life from their lowland neighbors. They have more ancient attributes and
have adapted to their environment in physical ways unlike anyone except in
the Andes. The Tibetans do not technically have their own country because

the Chinese Communists carried out a war of annexation there in the 1950s, and Tibet has become the focus of international attention and debate ever since.

Next, we go south from the Himalayas to India, the second largest population in the world. At 1.2 billion people, India has been a major player on the Asian scene for millennia. The Indus Valley civilization flourished there (and in Pakistan) between 5,000 and 3,000 years ago, and it was the birthplace of two of the world's five major religions, Buddhism and Hinduism. Hinduism preceded Buddhism (indeed, the Buddha was born in India), and yet Buddhism was the religion that spread far beyond India east and north throughout the rest of Asia.

Yet, it was Europe that conquered the world, industrialized, and set the pace of global life over the past 500 years. This is changing in the twenty-first century, with the rise of the developing world, especially Asia. What should not surprise readers is that before the modern era, Asia and Europe were not that different in terms of their development. Indeed, it was only in the past 2,500 years that Europeans have created advanced civilizations; whereas Asians have a 5,000-year history of advancement. Asians invented farming more than 11,000 years ago, the first on the planet. The ancient Sumerians, the Egyptians, the Persians, the Indus Valley civilization, the Chinese, and others have traditions dating back thousands of years before the Greeks and Romans. And yet, Asia's longer history of civilization did not signify economic, political, and social progress above that of Europe by the nineteenth century.

Asian history could not possibly be covered anywhere near what it merits in this book due to its size, population, and rich history. China, India, Japan, the Middle East, and Indonesia alone are individually significant enough to merit entire chapters here and more, but we will have to accept general pictures of them under the regional designation of "Asia."

Africa

The continent with the longest history of human inhabitance, Africa is the homeland of us all. Australopithecus lived there between 4 and 2 million years ago, then came *Homo habilis*, *Homo erectus*, and *Homo sapiens*, as countless laboratories full of their remains show us with overwhelming evidence. Humans migrated out of Africa some 50,000 years ago to inhabit Europe and Asia, later traveling to the Americas and all tracing their roots back to the motherland. In addition, most languages can be traced to their African roots, and today, there are more than 1,500 languages spoken there.

Africa is the longest continent from north to south and has a tremendous range of climate, terrain, resources, and peoples in fifty-two countries. North Africa comprises Morocco, Algeria, Tunisia, Libya, Egypt, and Sudan, with all except the latter having Mediterranean coastlines. These countries

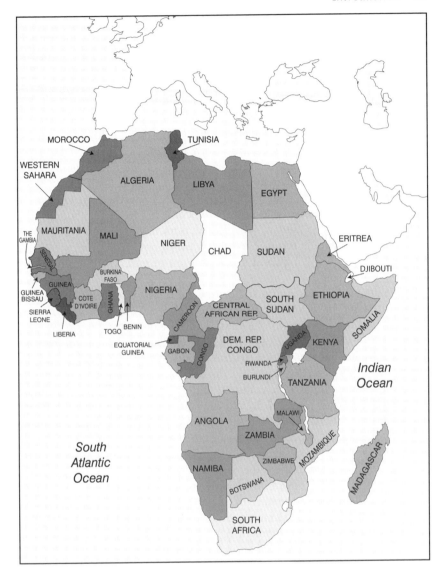

Figure 0.3 Map of Africa

are inhabited by descendants of Arabs, Berbers, whites and blacks who speak Arabic and French, while the vast majority south of North Africa (Sub-Saharan Africa) are black and speak a variety of native and European languages. Sedentary agriculture and advanced civilization arrived in this area much earlier than Sub-Saharan Africa due to contact with the Middle East and Europe.

The most significant point in time for them came with the rise of Islam in the seventh century. Arab traders, diplomats, and invaders extending their influence west from the Arabian Peninsula embarked on the largest religious conversion in world history. The Muslim World includes more than 1 billion people today, and this includes North Africa and the northern half of Sub-Saharan Africa and the Middle East, Malaysia, and Indonesia. The Ottoman Empire dominated much of North Africa from the sixteenth to the early twentieth centuries, and European conquest in the nineteenth century later altered their racial and cultural makeup.

The Sahara Desert is the largest desert in the world and extends unrelentingly from east to west and south through the northern halves of Sudan, Chad, Niger, Mali, Mauritania, and all of Western Sahara. Their racial makeup is a combination of Arabic and black, with black more prevalent, and they are religiously similar to their northern neighbors. In fact, this region has long been known for conflict between Christians and Muslims, especially in Sudan, where civil wars have claimed the lives of over 2.5 million people recently. While Ottoman power did not extend this far south, Europeans conquered nearly this entire region in the nineteenth century.

Sub-Saharan Africa is a term to describe the largest poor region on Earth. Books often use the term in contrast to the higher economic development of northern and southern part of the continent. There is truth in this statement, but it overlooks the complexity of the region. Though half of the world's poor live in Sub-Saharan Africa, with a population of 700 million, and the region has been beset by wars and disease over the past two decades in particular, it also contains rich cultural and environmental value. The most significant historical phenomenon to hit this region came with the Bantu migrations that lasted between 1500 BCE and 1000 CE. The Bantus make up the largest ethnic group in Africa, and they all share a common language group. Great kingdoms, smaller city-states, and tribal communities arose throughout this region in the wake of the migrations, only to suffer conquest and subjugation by European invaders during the modern era.

A central geographical feature of Sub-Saharan Africa is the Congo River basin. This contains vast stretches of verdant, lush land in central Africa that has nurtured the development of a wide variety of tribal groups. The Portuguese first entered the Congo in the fifteenth century to extract slaves bound for Europe and later the Americas. The Belgians, French, and Germans conquered this area for its resources in the nineteenth century. Endeavors by outsiders such as these have caused environmental and cultural devastation, and much of the forested areas have become barren as a result. The amount of natural resources such as rubber, ivory, palm, uranium, gold, coltan, and oil have long lured both outsiders and locals to seek control over the region. Today, they are used in part by armed groups who extract their wealth to finance wars. The eastern Congo, comprising the Democratic Republic of Congo (DRC), Rwanda, Burundi, and Uganda, is perhaps the most war-torn region of the past two decades on the planet, with a drastic reduction in the past several years.

Southern Africa is geographically quite different from most of Sub-Saharan Africa due to its distance from the equator. It is outside of the tropics and, in fact, some places have climates similar to that of Europe. South Africa became particularly welcoming for Europeans who eased into settlement there more easily than any place else on the continent beginning in the seventeenth century. Southern Africa is also a zone with a wide mixture of cultures: Native Africans, Europeans, and Indians of the Subcontinent have mixed there for centuries. In addition, Germany, England, and Portugal all had colonies in the region between the nineteenth and twentieth centuries.

Africa's most recent history should be seen as a conflict between reality and imagination, and though this is the truth with all three regions covered in this book, it matters most for Africa. The reason is because Africa is the poorest continent on the planet, and yet the image of Africa as simply "impoverished" obscures the reality that Africa is also prospering rapidly. Economically, politically, and socially, the continent has excelled in leaps and bounds in the short period of time since Independence from Europe began only fifty years ago. They have elected female heads of state, something the United States has never done in 230 years of independence. Their market capacity has drawn many new investors to the region recently, as cities have exploded in size, and farmers in many regions are able to gain greater harvest yields due to microcredits, native innovations, and financial and technical assistance. The scourge of the continent is the spread of HIV/AIDS, tuberculosis, and malaria in particular, which take millions of lives every year. Without these threats, there is no telling what Africa could accomplish, and images of the destitute continent should not dominate our thoughts about its 900 million diverse peoples.

The last note of this Introduction is this: Though it is my hope that readers walk away informed, it is also my hope to confuse, for if we believe we are fully informed, we risk becoming complacent. To avoid this, we must always realize that we are involved in a dialogue with the material we read. Books are not like food, which can be ingested and are fully understood in their capacity to fuel us. Books are an author's attempt to contribute toward humanity's knowledge and, as such, students should take what they learn from the book to the next level by reading even more. I have provided a list of further readings, films, and online content at the end of each chapter to facilitate this. Good luck and enjoy.

Part I
Imperialism

1 Latin America and the Caribbean (1492–1898)

Timeline

1492	Columbus "discovers" the Americas
1500	Pedro Cabral "discovers" Brazil
1519	Hernan Cortez arrives in Mexico
1532	Francisco Pizarro arrives in Peru
1542	The New Laws pass, forbidding Indian slavery
1697	Treaty of Ryswick gives Haiti to French
1791–1804	Haitian war of Independence
1810–1826	Wars of Independence in all Spanish territories except the Dominican Republic, Cuba, and Puerto Rico
1822	Brazilian Independence achieved
1823	Monroe Doctrine declared
1846–1848	The Mexican American War
1868–1898	Cuban wars of Independence
1888	Slavery abolished in Brazil
1898	Spanish American War

1492 and the legacy of Christopher Columbus

Before embarking on the material from this chapter, take some time to consider the following questions:

1   What are your assumptions about Columbus's role in history?
2   What sources inform your assumptions about him?
3   What level of legitimacy do you ascribe to those sources?
4   What do you gain from believing in these sources?

When Christopher Columbus secured funding for his expedition across the Atlantic Ocean in search of a westward route to Asia, he knew his name would go down in history as one of its greatest discoverers. Indeed, Columbus is considered *the* greatest discoverer in history by most observers, especially when one considers how often his name is accompanied by the words "discovered America," but how much do we know about his actions and their consequences? The foregoing set of four questions serves the purpose of prompting students to think about Columbus as an agent of historical change in as many ways as possible. Did he actually "discover" the Americas, or would you use a different verb to describe what he did? Should he be admired for his accomplishments, or should he be vilified? Do you know how answers to these questions might vary within different ethnic groups in the Americas? Or, can you only *assume* what those answers might be?

October 12, 1992 was the 500th anniversary of Columbus's arrival, and there were two major camps dedicated to recognizing this event. Anti-Columbus groups pointed to the near depopulation of the native peoples of the Americas and their displacement with Europeans, Africans, and an entire host of people of mixed races, whereas those who championed his legacy chose to focus on what his actions meant for "civilization" and "progress."

If we examine what we know or think we know about Columbus, the answers are sure to range across the spectrum from positive to negative in a manner unlike many other historical figures whose actions also led to the deaths of millions. People such as Adolf Hitler and Joseph Stalin are less "controversial" than Columbus because it is next to impossible to make positive arguments about *their* legacies. The technological and economic advances they oversaw were dwarfed by the tens of millions of people they killed in such a short period of time. In the case of Columbus, we have a figure responsible for bringing the Western and Eastern hemispheres into permanent future contact, which has led to myriad results. Many see this single act as the beginning of the largest scale of human suffering to ever hit the planet. The near extinction of Native Americans and the enslavement of millions of Africans for European profit on the sugar and tobacco plantations, not to mention the silver, diamond, and gold mines of the Americas, is enough fodder for Columbus's detractors. However, many also see Columbus representing the pinnacle of human progress during Europe's surge toward global prominence, and they believe he deserves to be among the most celebrated people in history.

This chapter covers 400 years of what resulted from Columbus's discovery. October 12, 1492, the Italian navigational expert believed he had finally spotted Asia. If he had, the planet would have been nearly half its actual circumference, and Columbus would have fulfilled his initial goal of establishing a trade route benefiting his benefactors, King Ferdinand and Queen Isabella of Spain. Trade had flourished across the Eastern hemisphere for thousands of years, but the 8,000 mile overland distance from the Iberian Peninsula on the westernmost tip of Europe to the east coast of China has forever been a mountainous obstacle to trade and communication. Columbus did not know it even on his death bed in 1506, after four trips to the New World, but he had failed to complete his mission.

He had, in fact, found a route to an unknown continent (except that the Vikings had settled in modern-day Newfoundland about 500 years prior and then left). Columbus's letters to Spain spoke of the abundance of gold and the docility of the people he found in the Caribbean islands, which he assumed to be islands just off the coast of Asia. Gold was especially important because it served as currency in the Old World. Elated at the prospect of acquiring both large gold deposits and new souls for conversion to the Catholic faith, the Spanish Crown felt a compulsion to exploit Columbus' discovery by supporting further voyages. As is well known by now, the resulting influx of European settlers led to armed conflict with the Indigenous peoples of the Caribbean (the Arawaks, Caribs, and Tainos). Though the Europeans held the advantage, this was not due to mere superiority of weapons, intelligence, or military tactics; in fact, 90 percent to 95 percent of all Indigenous peoples died as a result of communicable diseases against which they possessed virtually no immunities. This experience was unique to the colonization of the Americas, for when Europeans conquered much of Africa in the nineteenth century, it was not the Indigenous Africans who died due to European diseases but the other way around.

Pre-Columbian history

The most well-known Latin American civilization was the Olmec, which thrived from approximately 1500 BC to 400 BC in Mexico. The Olmecs also influenced future generations of Mexican and Central American civilizations for centuries to come. The first recorded use of the zero occurred in the Olmec region of influence, known as Mesoamerica in 32 BC and, by this time, the Olmec had faded, and the Maya had risen in its place. The Europeans who later deemed Native Americans inferior failed to see the thousands of examples of the Indigenous peoples, many of which are readily available for observation in archeological sites, museums and books today.

The Olmec cities such as Tres Zapotes and the rest were abandoned in last centuries BC, giving rise to the Maya (in southern Mexico, Yucatan, and northern Central America) and the Teotihuacanos of the Central Valley of Mexico. Large city-states containing enormous pyramids were used for religious and political purposes, demonstrating the intricacies of these new civilizations. The Maya and the Teotihuacanos in particular were known for their trade networks (with Teotihuacan at the center until the seventh century AD), art, and literacy. Teotihuacan is one of the most visited archeological sites in the world today. Just situated outside of Mexico City, it boasted a population of more than 200,000 in the first centuries AD. The Maya had many more cities, however, with a wide variety of structures still intact in Palenque (Mexico), Tikal (Guatemala), and Copan (Honduras), which are visited every day by tourists and researchers. The period in which Teotihuacan and the Maya city states thrived was 300 to 900 AD (the Classic era), and when these cities were abandoned between the eighth and ninth centuries, there began a new era, the Post-Classic Era (1000–1450 AD).

Were these the only major city complexes to speak of in Latin America, they would indeed stand out as exceptional for their uniqueness alone; however, the vast array of ruins left behind by the Inca and pre-Inca peoples of the Andes shatters that notion entirely. One has only to glimpse the stone aqueducts created by the Chavin de Huantar civilization in northern Peru more than 2,900 years ago to understand this. These peoples harnessed the power of hydraulics as they tapped into the water sources of the Andes at heights of up to 14,000 ft. above sea level to divert water for irrigation to the valleys below.

The Chavin peoples ruled northern Peru from 900 BC to 200 BC and included a wide variety of city complexes that helped set in motion a wave of civilization, which was augmented in the south and west by other groups. Eventually, the Inca Empire came to dominate Peru, along with most of Bolivia, Ecuador, and parts of Chile, Colombia, and Argentina. They expanded their reach over the course of one century (1435–1532) and produced such architectural marvels as Cuzco, Sacsayhuaman, Pisac, Ollantaytambo, Machu Picchu, and many others. These were a combination of urban and rural peoples who had adapted extremely well to a harsh environment, again demonstrating how far Native Americans had climbed on the eve of Columbus's arrival.

The Conquest of the Americas

Hernan Cortez became the most well-known conquistador of his day. A conquistador could be either praised or hated, depending on those whose story was heard the loudest. In the case of Cortez, a strong commander seeking glory for Spain and for himself, the year 1519 would place him in the history books. His 1519–1521 expedition to Mexico by way of Cuba quickly brought down the Aztec Empire so that Spain could enhance its own imperial domain and status within Europe. Cortez and his 500 conquistadors arrived in Mexico in 1519 and soon followed a path through the dense mountain passes and jungles between Veracruz and Mexico City, finally arriving in 1520 at the Aztec capital of Tenochtitlan. Along the way, Cortez acquired more Indian assistance from people seeking to resist the rule of the Triple Alliance (Aztecs). Most important among them were the fierce Tlaxcalans, who fought Cortez initially and then decided to join forces, adding thousands to the conquistador's cause. Upon arrival in Tenochtitlan, the Spaniards quickly kidnapped the Triple Alliance ruler, Moctezuma, and used him as a puppet king until fighting broke out between both sides. Moctezuma was killed either by the Spanish or by his own people. Soon, the people of Tenochtitlan drove out the Spanish occupants, killing two-thirds of them in the process.

The Spaniards had left behind an unseen and silent killer. Smallpox spread throughout the city over the course of the next few months, killing one-third of the city's population. As the epidemic progressed, Cortez recovered his army's strength by recruiting thousands of Indigenous enemies of the Triple Alliance and building ships. The great battle for Tenochtitlan lasted throughout the summer of 1521 until the Spanish captured the last emperor, Cuauhtemoc, and the city with him. He was tortured and executed soon after.

History is almost always told by the victors but, in this case, we have records from both sides. One of Cortez's men, Bernal Diaz del Castillo, chronicled his perspective in his book, *The Discovery and Conquest of Mexico, 1517–1521*. From the Triple Alliance side, we have the Mexican scholar Miguel Leon-Portilla's rendition of the conquest through his use of native documents and accounts given to sixteenth century Spanish chroniclers. His book, *The Broken Spears: The Aztec Account of the Conquest of Mexico*, should be read as a companion piece to Castillo's.

There were several key differences between the conquests and subsequent colonization efforts carried out against the Aztecs and the Maya. After completing the conquest of Tenochtitlan, the conquistadors had a foothold for conquering the rest of Mexico and Central America. The conquest of the Maya of the Yucatan Peninsula and Central America, however, differed from that of the Triple Alliance because the Maya lived in small city-states and hunter-gatherer tribes. Thus, one definitive battle against a centralized authority would not take place outside of Tenochtitlan. As a result, Spanish control was limited in the Yucatan and, therefore, concentrated much more on the subjugation of Central American and central Mexican Indigenous peoples, and the conquest of the Maya took all of the 1520s to complete.

Cortez's example was quickly followed in the conquest of the Incas in South America. South America's greatest civilizations cropped up in the Andes mountains. The Incas were only the latest empire to dominate a large region of the Andes by the time of the arrival of the conquistadors in 1532. The Incas, however, set the bar higher than all of the other Indigenous empires before. Their control stretched more than 3,000 miles from Colombia to Chile along the spine of the Andes. An 18,000-mile road system connected all regions of the Empire to the capital of Cuzco, Peru.

It was not until the arrival of the smallpox epidemic in the 1520s, which had begun in Mexico and made its way south through Central America and finally to South America, that the beginning of the end was signaled. This epidemic killed untold numbers of Incas in the decade prior to Pizarro's arrival. Both the Inca king and his heir apparent died in quick succession from the epidemic, and the ensuing battle over succession between the brothers Huascar and Atahualpa provided an opportunity for the newly arrived conquistadors serving under Francisco Pizarro to exploit.

Pizarro's 1532 entrance in the midst of the Inca civil war was one of history's precipitous moments. Atahualpa, fresh from victory over his brother, no doubt was at the height of his confidence when Pizarro challenged his authority. Atahualpa agreed to meet with the Spaniard in Cajamarca on November 16. There, the Inca lost thousands of men and his own freedom to a Spanish surprise attack. Pizarro had only 165 men, but he had the element of surprise and firearms.

Atahualpa was taken captive, much as Cortez had done with Montezuma in Mexico, and the following year had him executed. With the Inca gone, the Spanish quickly established authority over the former empire. As disease spread throughout the land at a quickening pace throughout the sixteenth century, 90 percent to 95 percent of the Inca's former subjects perished. The Spanish also forcibly took Inca lands for themselves, often enslaving the Indians to be used for mining and agriculture as they had done in the Caribbean, Mexico, and Central America. By the 1540s, the Spanish had explored and conquered lands throughout the Andes and the west coast of South America, and the Portuguese had control over the east coast of Brazil.

The conquest of the Americas set in motion the Christianization of the native peoples, further empowering the Catholic Church. It also initiated the widespread loss of native lives and territories. The conquest also gained a foothold for Spanish and Portuguese power in former strongholds of native empires. Mexico's name under Spanish colonial rule was New Spain, and the former Inca Empire became Peru. The conquest also kick-started the "Columbian Exchange," a term made popular by Alfred Crosby to describe the interwoven process of New World and Old World exchanges in foods, maps, disease, culture, economies, environment, and other elements. The Columbian Exchange theory posits that an understanding of the effect of European contact with the Americas can best be understood as an environmental, economic, and biological interaction. The landscape of the Americas, with its new germs, plants, animals, goods, and people, were forever altered as a result of European conquest and colonization. The *mestizo* race (mixture of European and Indigenous blood) also resulted from this exchange. This new race, along with a wide number of other racial mixtures resulting from African arrivals, helped create a variety of hybrid cultures across the Americas that comprise the majority of today's population there.

Another result was cultural. The Europeans who arrived in the sixteenth century set in motion a pattern of framing the Americas in Eurocentric terms. By portraying the Indigenous people as "simple," "childlike," "savage," or "uncivilized" and the land as "virgin" in need of exploitation, the Americas were seen as in need of European rectification. It is important to note that although European culture supplanted Indigenous culture in many ways, the Indigenous culture has remained in many ways as well.

Colonization

Spanish and Portuguese colonization followed on the heels of conquest. This process disrupted and altered the lives of the Native peoples rather quickly as the Europeans sought to control their labor and religion. Indigenous peoples were forced to relocate to Spanish-style cities and towns, where their behavior could be monitored and their labor exploited. As the distance to the Iberian Peninsula was a year-round trip, the Crown's edicts often went by the wayside as colonial administrators governed with relative autonomy, yet in a highly centralized manner. Therefore, much corruption took place while the Spanish authorities kept up their loyalty to the Crown at all costs for nearly three centuries. The term "obedezco pero no cumplo" (I obey but do not comply) emerged during this era to illustrate the difficulty of colonial administrators' adhering too strictly to the Crown's demands.

The Spanish Crown's hierarchy of control over its colonies was indeed elaborate. Atop sat the Royal Court Council, followed by the Council of the Indies, the Viceroy, and the Audiencia, and four more levels down was the Cabildo at the bottom. Throughout most of the colonial era, it was essential for the top administrators to be born in Spain (Peninsular) to maintain the purity of the office. Being born in the Americas meant one was partly tainted with non-European exposure. Creoles were Europeans born in the Americas, a status that kept them just below the status of the Peninsulars.

The era of the Hapsburg monarchy (1500–1700) was an era of experimentation in the colonies. The crown did not have experience in colonialism over such a vast territory, which included most of the Western Hemisphere but also extended its reach into the Pacific and Atlantic Oceans. Centralized control over such a system was impossible and, as such, corruption ran rampant. The cases of the *repartimiento* system and the Manila Galleons illustrate this well. The *repartimiento* was a forced labor draft of Indians that benefited Spanish colonial officials financially and politically. In the case of Central America, the *repartimiento* helped to fuel the growth of a monopolistic economy controlled by the colonial authorities who were beholden to no one above them. The Manila Galleons were the largest ships in the world during the colonial era, and they made annual trips between the Americas and the Philippines. They left the port of Acapulco, Mexico loaded with gold and silver and returned with silk, porcelain, ivory, and spices. Those involved in the trade consistently deceived the colonial authorities as to the amount of goods being traded and, therefore, cheated the Spanish Crown out of massive profits. With the arrival of the Bourbon dynasty in 1700 on the throne in Spain, centralized control was asserted but not effective.

Brazil

Portuguese Brazil was comparatively more relaxed than Spanish America. The Portuguese were also spread throughout the world, but their attention was distributed between Africa, East Asia, and the Americas. Brazil was unimportant until the French, English, and Dutch began encroaching into the Caribbean and northern South America in the mid-1500s and beyond. As such, the Portuguese made an effort to solidify their hold over Brazil by doling out large parcels of land to be controlled by slaveholders who exploited the territory initially for its brazil wood (used for red dye) and then later for sugar, gold mining, shipping, construction, and all manner of labor. The Portuguese did put a Viceroy in charge of Brazil but instead used a governor-general whose interest it was to oversee the growth of Portuguese wealth there.

As opposed to the Spanish conquest, the conquest of Brazil was gradual. In fact, in some ways, it continues to this day in Brazil. Ever since the first Portuguese arrived, there have been clashes with Indigenous peoples. Of course, for most of the colonial era, the Portuguese saw little reason to venture inland and instead stayed close to the coast. The coastal Tupi-Guarani tribes were largely conquered in the first two centuries of colonization, and in the eighteenth and nineteenth centuries, settlers pushed into the interior to gain control over the Amazon River Basin. A phenomenon that emerged in Brazil during the colonial era was regionalism, whereby the people felt more tied to their regions than to the central colonial or Crown authorities. This continues to this day, albeit Brazilians have become more nationalistic with the rise of modernization and, in particular, now that they are competitive with the other powerful economies of the world. Brazil's enormous size and its sparse population also meant that its coasts still largely defined its colonial character, despite the fact that the bulk of Brazil was on the frontier. In addition, Brazilians were less beholden to their colonial masters than were the Spanish and, to this day, Brazil is decisively more relaxed and open than Spanish Latin America as a whole.

The Catholic Church

More so than any other factor in colonial Latin America, the Catholic Church's connection to the Iberian Crowns signified a deep control over both society and government. The Church and the State were essentially the same institution. Evangelization and conversion were of the utmost importance for controlling the new Indigenous population, whose beliefs were in stark contrast to the Europeans'. Conversion did not just happen. It was carried out by force. The Indigenous peoples were tortured, murdered, kidnapped and, in some cases, persuaded to convert in the initial decades after the conquest until the entirety of Latin America was covered. After the foundation was laid, future generations of Indigenous peoples perpetuated the Catholic beliefs handed down to them, sometimes maintaining some of their pre-Columbian beliefs as well.

To be sure, in the sixteenth century, conversion took on a more draconian form than in later centuries. The case of Bishop Diego de Landa of the Yucatan instituted some of the harshest measures against idolatry enacted during the colonial period. He ordered burnt more than 20,000 Indigenous religious objects and killed many Mayan Indians and tortured many more.

The colonial Church arrived in the Americas during its Inquisition era. The Inquisition was composed of several aspects and had several goals, notably the punishment of heresy. The heretics were difficult to weed out, however, and thus there are many cases of torture, imprisonment, and execution in which the "guilty" never received anything resembling a modern-day version of a fair trial. There has also been much debate about the extent of the Inquisition's oppression, and the truth is not certain to this day. However, what is certain is that the tortures and executions were of the most barbarous types that readers could surely investigate on their own if they so chose. However, the Inquisition was also used as a political tool and as a means of controlling societal behavior. For example, women's behavior often came under the control of the Inquisition.

Women were expected to maintain the home, raise the children, be subservient to men in general, and lead a pious life. This meant chastity until marriage because the punishment for deviating from this norm was public shame. Of course, there were exceptions, and these illustrate the general ways in which all members of colonial society to varying degrees learned to negotiate through the draconian structures that sought to limit their daily choices. Women often had sex before marriage, as did men, and as long as this was kept secret, there was little danger to either party. When knowledge of a woman's behaving outside societal norms became public, the situation changed because society members then became aware that the woman's parents, husband, brothers, and priests were not keeping the woman in line. The issue then turns to one's "honor," which is dependent on class, gender, and race intertwined. Parents had to deal harshly with their daughters who engaged in acts deemed unruly for women for fear of having their honor publicly tarnished, and women in turn sought to preserve and indeed improve their honor by adhering to these rules.

At the same time, women in colonial society found opportunities for autonomy and agency. The case of Sor Juana Ines de la Cruz (1651–1695) is important. Sor Juana was a Mexico City nun known for her prolific writing that challenged the status quo. She helped disprove traditional notions about the subordinate abilities of women in society and, for this, the Church punished her by taking away all of her possessions, including her writings, and forbidding her to write any more. She died at the age of 43 after tending to sick patients during an epidemic. A film made about her life entitled *I, the Worst of All* illuminates her significance particularly for audiences unfamiliar with her work, despite its overemphasis on a possible love affair between her and the Viceroy's wife. She is one of the pinnacle authors of the Spanish Golden Age of writing, which includes other such giants as Miguel de Cervantes, author of *Don Quixote de la Mancha*. Her case demonstrates both the opportunities for women and their limitations. She could not have become the prolific author she became without the convent because she could not appear to be that independent of the Church. Inside the Church, she was controllable and, therefore, less of a threat to the status quo. Her accomplishments were celebrated by the Church authorities until she challenged them. There were indeed many other women who contributed to colonial Latin American history in a variety of public and private ways and, but for the space limitations of this book, we could address more of them.

Slavery

The tragedy of slavery in the Americas begins with the Conquest of the Caribbean carried out by the Spanish in the first decades after Columbus's arrival. The nearly complete decimation of the Indians that resulted caused Europeans to seek other forced laborers as replacements. Father Bartolome de las Casas, a Dominican friar who had taken part in the Conquest and later repented, became the greatest defender of the Indians as their numbers dwindled. His book, *A Brief Account of the Destruction of the Indies* (1542), is still a classic telling of the actions of the conquistadors in determining the course of New World history through bloodshed. However, de las Casas also widely proposed the enslavement of Africans for labor in the Americas as a suitable replacement for the Indians, and eventually 20 million Africans were stolen from their homelands as commodities to be used for the benefit of whites in the Americas. Of course, only 10 to 12 million made it across the Middle Passage alive due to the horrific conditions of the slave ships. Only 4 percent of these arrived in the U.S. South, while upward of 40 percent went to the Caribbean, and 50 percent went to Brazil. The Spanish mainland had African slavery but comparatively little in contrast to the sugar plantations of the Caribbean and Brazil.

The slave population also carried out a wide range of work in colonial society. Slaves were integral to mining, agriculture, construction, domestic service, and many other areas, all of which contributed to the growth of colonial economies. However, life expectancy was as low as seven years at times due to the extremely harsh conditions in which they were forced to work. Slavery in the Americas is perhaps the single largest academic category of colonial studies, and thus there are a number of good sources students can seek out to learn more about this topic.

This race-based system of exploitation and profit was part of the racial hierarchy of privilege that placed those born in Spain or Portugal (Peninsulars) at the top, followed in order by Creoles, Mestizos, Mulattos, free people of color, and enslaved people of color. Being black or Indian was seen as inferior, and those living free held the privilege of owning property along with other legal rights such as right to own their labor. The African slaves and Indians forced into labor obligation systems bore the brunt of colonial oppression because they lacked most freedoms and led a precarious existence at best. This racial hierarchy goes a long way toward explaining the socioeconomic divisions still plaguing Latin America today.

Profits

Spain and Portugal used the colonies for the enhancement of their political and economic strength. These two extracted profits from mining and sugar primarily, which elicited attacks from English pirates primarily. Gold and silver leaving the Americas soon filled the coffers of northern European banks that eventually helped to finance the Industrial Revolution that began in the late eighteenth century. Mexico and Peru were the Spanish Empire's principal gold and silver mining locations, and Brazil produced considerable quantities of gold, silver, and diamonds. In each case, the labor force consisted largely of Indians and African slaves, with high levels of danger in all mining operations. The miners would often spend half the day underground, often months away from their families. The Indians working in the mines at Potosi, in modern day Bolivia, like many others, developed a habit of chewing large quantities of coca leaves to alleviate their hunger and to provide a mild stimulant for their long and harsh workdays.

However, despite mountainous profits for some, this dependence on a few products for export developed into a sometimes unstable economic system dictated by booms and busts. As large quantities of bullion were extracted, profits were high, which meant that standards of living increased. However, when profits dropped, as they must from time to time, standards of living dropped, subjecting large groups of workers and their dependents to deprivation. This boom-bust cycle continues in all monoculture countries or countries that place a heavy dependence on the production or extraction of one or a few products.

With an abundance of bullion and commodities being transported through ports and boats, these two became the targets of pirates often working for European governments (English, French, Dutch). Perhaps most famous among these was the English pirate Sir Francis Drake, whose voyages in the Americas in the 1560s and 1570s were the stuff of legend. He was even knighted in 1581 by Queen Elizabeth I. The threat of piracy and enemy invasion led to a substantial effort on the part of the Spanish to defend their ports with fortresses such as El Morro at Havana harbor and San Juan de Ulua at the port of Veracruz, Mexico, which are still preserved to this day.

Independence

The Hapsburg family ruled Spain and its colonies between 1500 and 1700. Their rule was characterized by a decentralized yet hierarchical style. By 1700, the death of Charles II led to the War of Spanish Succession that resulted in the crowning of Philip V of the Bourbon family in 1713. Bourbon rulers set out to professionalize and centralize control over the colonies with a series of reforms aimed at maximizing profits and limiting corruption. Just as modern trade concepts were implemented, political and social ideas took hold in Europe in the form of the Enlightenment. Latin American elites started studying considerably more often in Europe, where Enlightenment philosophers such as Descartes, Locke, Hume, Rousseau, and other notables had gained ground in their ideas that challenged traditional authority. Many of these students returned to Latin America to work for subversive forms of change that sought to undermine Spanish and Portuguese authority, eventually leading to the wars for Independence.

First, however, a few matters to get out of the way about world events: The British capture of Havana in 1762, the Peace of Paris of 1763, the American Revolution of 1775, the French Revolution of 1789, and the Haitian Revolution of 1791 signified the massive changes occurring in the world that would affect the Americas quickly and violently. The British presence in Havana was brief, but it led to the expansion of slavery in Cuba, which lasted for the next 124 years in an area where slavery had represented a much smaller level of importance for nearly 300 years thus far. The Peace of Paris ended the Seven Years War between the French and the English and helped shape the factors that led to the American Revolution. The American Revolution then helped inspire the French Revolution, which in turn inspired the Haitian Revolution, which helped inspire revolutionary movements across the Americas by the 1810s.

In 1775, the American Revolution began as a movement led by mostly white slaveholding men who sought independence from England. The French colony of Saint Domingue (Haiti) witnessed a slave uprising just sixteen years later. It was the first and only case where a slave uprising led to national independence in human history. That year, 1791, signified the beginning of the end of France's control over their most lucrative colony. The leader of the revolt, Toussaint L'Ouverture, was captured by the French and imprisoned and died in 1803. However, his successor, Jean Jacques Dessalines, consolidated the Independence movement, becoming Haiti's first president. Dessalines was killed shortly thereafter, and thus followed a succession of heroes and tyrants that suffered similar fates over the course of the next 200 years. It could be argued that Haiti has never been accepted as an equal among the nations of the world because not only did they suffer ostracism for being a "Black Republic" but the number of French, German, and U.S. interventions in Haiti have left the island reeling. Today, it is the poorest country in the hemisphere.

The mainland Latin American colonies rose against the Spanish from 1810 to 1826 amid significant trials of Spanish and Portuguese power in Europe. The Bourbons had imposed reforms that reduced the economic and political power of the Creole elite, which caused a widespread Creole dissent by the early 1800s. Once Napoleon invaded Portugal in 1807 and Spain in 1808, both crowns exited the peninsula for temporary exiles. The Portuguese King Joao established his court in Brazil, and the new Spanish king, Ferdinand VII, was replaced by Napoleon's brother, Joseph.

In 1810, a group of liberal Spaniards formed the Cortes de Cadiz to initiate the Spanish resistance to French rule. They wrote their famous liberal constitution in 1812. Meanwhile, independence uprisings from Argentina to Venezuela and Mexico surged across Latin America with leaders such as Juan de San Martin (Argentina), Simon Bolivar (Venezuela), and Miguel Hidalgo y Costilla (Mexico). The Spanish colonial authorities were weak at this time, which gave temporary advantage to the rebels until 1814, when the French left the Iberian Peninsula. Ferdinand VII immediately organized the resistance to independence. When a liberal revolt threatened Ferdinand's rule in 1820, he reinstituted the 1812 liberal constitution, which threatened the privileges and power of Peninsular elites defending the Crown in Latin America.

Many of these Peninsulars saw no point in continuing the fight to preserve the Empire and agreed to a truce with the rebels. Mexico stands out as an example of how difficult it was to consolidate independence. The revolts lasted eleven years there and were initiated by Father Miguel Hidalgo y Costilla in 1810. He was executed the following year by the Inquisition. Then, Father Jose Maria Morelos took up Hidalgo's cause, only to be executed by the Inquisition in 1815. By 1821, the newest rebel leader, Vicente Guerrero (1820–1821), was prepared to compromise with the Royalists, who now saw little need in defending the new liberal constitution of Spain. The leader of the Royalist cause, Agustin de Iturbide, became the first monarch of Mexico (1822–1823), and the new country suffered almost continuous dictatorship over the next three decades, with one leader in particular (Antonio Lopez de Santa Anna) ruling eleven times between 1833 and 1855. It would take another uprising ninety years later to address the problems unfixed in 1821.

In Argentina, a pro-Ferdinand VII junta aimed at independence rose to power in 1810. The Creole-Peninsular rivalry quickly caused divisions within this movement, even after it adopted the 1812 liberal constitution of the Cortes de Cadiz. In 1816, Argentine Independence became official despite the growing number of strongmen (such as Jose de San Martin and Juan Pueyrredon) competing for centralized power. This lack of centralized power was eventually filled by Juan Manuel de Rosas from 1829 to 1852.

The story of Chilean Independence is along similar lines. A pro-Ferdinand VII liberal junta took power in 1812 and eventually defeated the Spanish after Bernardo O'Higgins and Jose de San Martin crossed over the Andes from Argentina to Chile between 1817 and 1818. O'Higgins became Chile's first president (1818–1823) and thus established a pattern of democracy in Chile that lasted until the coup that overthrew Salvador Allende in 1973.

Although the independence fights of the Southern Cone were indeed significant, the struggles that took place in northern South America yielded the number-one liberator of them all. In fact, the wealthy Venezuelan-born Creole Simon Bolivar was known as "The Liberator" for leading the charge to crush Spanish authority in five future countries—Venezuela, Colombia, Ecuador, Peru, and Bolivia—between 1812 and 1825, dwarfing the accomplishments of all the rest. The country of Bolivia is named after Simon Bolivar.

Bolivar served as president of the newly created country of Gran Colombia, which unified Colombia, Venezuela, and Ecuador, from 1819 to 1830, when he died. However, this union did not last past his death. Bolivar's vision extended to a unified Latin American nation of unlimited possibilities; however, the great chasms between races, classes, genders, and regions that had become entrenched during the colonial period made this

Figure 1.1 Simon Bolivar (1783–1830) (World History Archive/Alamy)

dream impossible. Still, the size of Gran Colombia was close to the current size of the continental United States today, and yet even the new nation of the United States contained only thirteen small colonies on the east coast upon its Independence. The South Americans were dealing with a much more complex and geographically spread out situation, and soon Gran Colombia divided into the nations of Ecuador, Colombia, and Venezuela.

Brazil's Independence followed a completely different trajectory from that of the Spanish colonies. The Portuguese royal court fled the Iberian Peninsula in 1807 in the wake of Napoleon's invasion. In 1816, King Joao IV ended Brazil's colonial status, making it a kingdom equal with Portugal. The king returned to Portugal in 1821, leaving his son Pedro I in charge. Pedro I declared Brazil independent from Portugal the following year, and as such, there was no war for Independence such as what happened in all the major Spanish colonies. The Republic of Brazil was finally proclaimed in 1889, the year after slavery was abolished there, making Brazil the colony most associated with slavery in the Americas.

When compared to the majority of Latin American countries politically and economically, Brazil stagnated throughout the nineteenth century. It eventually forged ahead toward the end of the century with a boom in coffee production and some modernization as a result. However, the rule of Pedro II (1831–1889) is seen as relatively benevolent and should be considered as yet another example of Brazil's uniqueness within Latin America. Today, Brazil leads Latin America economically. The level of misery in some sectors of Brazil still surpasses that of any other country in Latin America, however, with a fourth of its population of 200 million living in poverty.

The rise of U.S. influence: 1846 and 1898

The United States was busy expanding its territory through various wars and diplomacy as Latin Americans gradually recovered from their wars of independence. The "Colossus to the North," as it is referred to in Latin America, shifted its focus south in 1846 when it declared war on Mexico on the false claim that the latter had invaded U.S. territory. After many bloody battles, the Mexican dictator Santa Anna signed over a third of Mexico's territory to the United States in the Treaty of Guadalupe Hidalgo in 1848. This intervention set a precedent for the future, both in the eyes of Latin Americans and the United States that has loomed over U.S.–Latin American relations for the past century and a half.

Cuban Independence took place in an era different from that of the other mainland movements of 1810–1826. When the Cubans rose up against the Spanish in 1868, the United States was a rising power on the world stage despite its entanglement in its own Civil War (1861–1865). By the end of the Cuban Independence movement in 1898, the United States was the sole hegemony in the Americas. The war began when a plantation and slave owner named Carlos Manuel de Cespedes freed his slaves and rose in rebellion against the Spanish in 1868. The Ten Years War resulted in countless lost lives, no independence, but some slavery reforms. Slavery was abolished only in 1886.

More battles took place over the next two decades, but it was relatively calm, during which time the famous independence leader Jose Marti organized the independence movement largely from abroad. He returned to Cuba to lead the revolt in 1895, where he was killed during his first battle. His mantel was taken up by tens of thousands of his followers, many of whom have statues dedicated to them across Cuba today. It was almost expected that the independence movement would be snatched from the jaws of victory in 1898, when the U.S. military invaded Cuba and Puerto Rico, striking the final blow against the Spanish Empire.

The age of Latin American Independence can be seen as both a boon and a burden for these new countries. Places such as Mexico and Brazil were able to eventually move away from European direct domination, but they were still subject to the whims of the market as underdeveloped nations, whose political systems were often times mere reflections of the old colonial style hierarchies that oppressed the majority of the population. It was not until the twentieth century, however, that true revolutionary changes were implemented through revolutions of even wider implications than the Independence movements.

The national period

The post-independence republics of the 1820s suffered political conflict and disorder amid the rising conservative and liberal philosophies. There arose in importance the *caudillo* (strongman), a phenomenon in which militaristic men stepped into the power vacuum left by the Spanish. The age of the *caudillo* has not disappeared from Latin American politics, as we shall see in later chapters; however, it did wane considerably toward the middle of the nineteenth century when liberalism gained in importance. From approximately 1850 to 1930, liberals who looked to the West for guidance in economics and politics tended to push aside the conservatives bound to the traditionalism that many hoped had disappeared with Independence from Spain and Portugal.

The major economic consequence of liberalism was the massive increase in exports and imports that worked to incorporate Latin America into the world market. During the latter half of the nineteenth century, Auguste Comte's positivism, which held that society should be conducted based on scientific observation, influenced Latin American leadership across the hemisphere. Latin American positivist leaders in turn aimed to restructure society on the grounds of free trade, education, anti-clericalism, scientific principles, and European immigration to modernize. Racism also pervaded many Latin American positivist policies, which included efforts to "whiten" the population through encouraging European immigration, especially in the Southern Cone. On the one hand, liberal efforts to advance economically succeeded: the upper crust of society became exceedingly wealthier as they dominated export industries and cooperated with foreign companies to maintain and increase access to resources.

On the other hand, the concentration of wealth into the hands of the oligarchy that had existed under colonialism made the upper class even more powerful than before. Through exports of coffee in El Salvador, for example, dictatorships were able to purchase weapons from the United States, which reinforced their power whenever the peasantry demanded a voice in national affairs. Uprisings in the west of that country in the late nineteenth century resulted from the government's seizure of all available lands for coffee cultivation. This act meant that previously owned small plots that produced subsistence crops would be dedicated to coffee, which was exported almost exclusively to enrich the oligarchy. This happened to varying degrees across the region. Some posit that this period of liberalization provided a net gain for Latin Americans, while others posit the opposite. It will take further reading to understand this debate, particularly when we enter the twentieth century.

Discussion questions

1   Speculate on how the Americas would be now if Columbus had never arrived. Encourage students to explore their options on multiple levels: They can experiment with time, place, action, and the like.
2   How much of the dominance of Latin America and the Caribbean by Europeans was due to cultural factors, and how much of this was due to disease?
3   How does colonialism explain Simon de Bolivar's difficulties in uniting South America into one large and powerful country?

Historical figures

Atahualpa (1497–1533)

He was the "Inca" or king of the people known as the Incas. However, the term *Inca* refers only to the king himself. However, his reign was short-lived because when he was captured by Pizarro in November 1532, he had only just completed the war of succession against his brother, Huascar. Atahualpa is a tragic figure in Inca history; however, unlike Montezuma, he is not considered to be a fool or a coward. More so, history treats him with an aura of nostalgia, as if his ascendency represented the last hope of the Incas, and his downfall signified the end of a once great civilization. Atahualpa's capture was punctuated by his infamous "ransom" in which he had two rooms filled with silver and one with gold to secure his release from Spanish custody. After the ransom demands were filled, the Spanish executed him with the garrote in July 1533, upon suspicion that he was leading an insurrection.

Aztecs

There were no Aztecs. There never was a group of people, anywhere in Mexico or otherwise, called the "Aztecs," except for sports teams at San Diego State University in California. This makes sense when we consider that the term *Aztec* was never used until the English usage of the Spanish word "Azteca," which in itself was never used by the people of Mexico prior to the arrival of the Spanish in the sixteenth century! In fact, the empire referred to as "Aztec" was an alliance of three cities on Lake Texcoco, with Tenochtitlan (founded in 1325) as its capital. The "Mexica" is a more apt term for the people who made up what we refer to as the Aztecs, giving rise to the eventual name of the country, "Mexico."

Simon Bolivar (1783–1830)

Highest among all Latin American "heroes," Bolivar was known simply as "The Liberator." Venezuelan by birth, he led the independence movements of five future South American countries (Venezuela, Colombia, Ecuador, Peru, and Bolivia) between 1810 and 1826. His companion, Manuela Saenz, was instrumental in assisting Bolivar, and she was known for having saved the Liberator's life at least twice. He is especially famous for promoting his vision of a united Latin America that sought to overcome the imposition of Spanish colonial boundaries on the region as a whole. Despite his failure to do this, his vision has been a common thread among revolutionary leaders ever since Bolivar's time.

Friar Bartolome de las Casas (1484–1566)

He is known simply as "Protector of the Indians" to many, and yet history also records him as the earliest proponent of African slavery in the Americas. His life's work was to illuminate the atrocities committed by the Spanish during their conquest of the Americas. In the process, he advocated that Africans should replace the dead and dying Indigenous peoples as an enslaved labor class. He pleaded with Spanish colonial and royal authorities to halt the devastation wrought against the Indigenous peoples and produced the book entitled *A Brief Account of the Destruction of the Indies*. His work led to the official abolition of Indigenous slavery; however, in practice, there were enough loopholes in the Spanish colonial administration that de facto slavery continued to exist throughout the colonial period.

Hernan Cortez (1485–1547)

Perhaps the most famous and archetypal conquistador, Hernan Cortez is most well known for his conquest of Mexico in 1521. As legend told it for centuries, Cortez took the Aztec capital with just a few hundred Spaniards, along with horses, canons, firearms and, most important, disease. The real story is much more complex and includes the assistance of tens of thousands of Indigenous peoples, mainly the Tlaxcaltecas, the long-time enemies of the Aztecs. Today, Cortez is vilified in Mexican history for displacing Indigenous rule with European rule and bringing about the subsequent devastation that led to the near annihilation of the Indigenous people.

Father Miguel Hidalgo y Costilla (1753–1811)

A Jesuit trained priest from Valladolid, Mexico, Father Hidalgo initiated the Mexican war of Independence on September 16, 1810 with his Grito de Dolores. Tens of thousands of mostly Indigenous followers took up his call of "Death to Spaniards!" and their rebellion spread across central Mexico until succumbing to defeat at the hands of the Spanish royal military. Hidalgo was tried by the Inquisition and executed in 1811; however, his mantel was taken up by many others, who continued the fight for ten years until a compromise led to Independence in September 1821.

Toussaint L'Ouverture (1743–1803)

A former slave, L'Ouverture led what became the only successful slave uprising that ended in national independence in world history. Haitian slave conditions were among the harshest recorded in the Americas, and this fact helps explain L'Ouverture's ability to garner such widespread support. He was captured and imprisoned in a French prison, where he died in 1803. Haiti gained its Independence in 1804, the first Latin American or Caribbean nation to do so.

La Malinche (1496–1550)

The most controversial woman in Mexican history for her role in assisting Hernan Cortez in bringing down the Aztec Empire, La Malinche is largely considered to be a traitor. She spoke Nahuatl and a Mayan dialect because she lived in southern and central Mexico growing up. She was given as a gift to Cortez in what is now the modern state of Tabasco, and she and Cortez are said to have produced the first *mestizo* (mixed-race) child in Mexico. La Malinche is used derisively both as a noun and as a verb to describe a Mexican who has betrayed others of his or her kind. For many Mexicans, La Malinche represents a stain on Mexican heritage because she willingly allowed herself to be used by the invading Europeans who destroyed most of native society.

Jose Marti (1853–1895)

The undisputed leader of the Cuban Independence movement, Jose Marti nonetheless died in 1895, at the beginning of the military campaign that ultimately led to Spain's exit from the island in 1898. He is most known for his decades of work to rally together the Cuban people to carry out the overthrow of the Spanish, spending many years abroad where he also garnered considerable political and financial support for the cause. He is especially well known for his call for Latin American solidarity, a call initiated by Bolivar in the 1810s, and later taken up by Fidel Castro and Ernesto "Che" Guevara, the leaders of the Cuban Revolution.

Jose de San Martin (1778–1850)

This Independence leader rivaled Bolivar in his volume of exploits in the wars of independence. However, he did not have Bolivar's staying power or his dominant leadership presence. He helped lead the charge for Argentine Independence in 1812, then took command of his own army and, with the assistance of Chilean Bernardo O'Higgins, crossed the Andes to Chile, where they defeated the Spanish in 1818. He then sailed to Peru, where he helped initiate the war for Independence there in 1821. After meeting with Bolivar in Guayaquil, Ecuador in 1822, San Martin left the Independence movement entirely.

Moctezuma II (1466–1520)

Known as Moctezuma (with a *c* in Mexico), he is commonly known by Western tourists for striking victims with "Montezuma's Revenge," or traveler's diarrhea. These are both linguistic alterations to the Nahuatl (Aztec language) name for the third-to-last Aztec ruler, pronounced "Motecuzona." This powerful tlatoani (emperor) ruled from 1502 to 1520 and is perhaps the most tragic figure in Mexican history for his alleged cowardice in the face of the conquistadors, led by Hernan Cortez. A year after his mysterious death in 1520 (killed by his own people or the Spanish?), the Aztec Empire was in the hands of the Spanish.

Francisco Pizarro (1478–1541)

Although Cortez has more name recognition as a conquistador, Francisco Pizarro's conquest of the Inca Empire is of equal historical importance. Unlike Cortez, however, Pizarro, who had made three trips to South America over the course of nearly a decade to reconnoiter the region, overthrew the Inca Atahualpa in one fell swoop. In November 1532, Pizarro and 165 men ambushed the Inca and his 6,000 unarmed men in the northern Peruvian town of Cajamarca. They captured Atahualpa, held him for ransom, and executed him eight months later. The full consolidation of Spanish rule over Peru took several years to complete and, in the process, Pizarro was killed as part of a family feud in 1541.

Further readings

Castillo, Bernal Diaz del. *The Discovery and Conquest of Mexico, 1517–1521.*

Coe, Michael. *The Maya.* New York: Thames and Hudson, 1999.

Crosby, Alfred W. Jr. *The Columbian Exchange: Biological and Cultural Consequences of 1492.* Westport, CT: Greenwood Press, 1972.

De las Casas, Bartolome. *The Devastation of the Indies: a Brief Account.* Multiple Editions.

Freyre, Gilberto. *The Masters and the Slaves.* New York: Alfred A. Knopf, 1946.

Galeano, Eduardo. *The Open Veins of Latin America: Five Centuries of the Pillage of a Continent.* New York: Monthly Review, 1997.

Hemming, John. *Red Gold: The Conquest of the Brazilian Indians, 1500–1760.* Cambridge, MA: Harvard, 1978.

Leon-Portilla, Miguel. *The Broken Spears: the Aztec Account of the Conquest of Mexico.* Boston, MA: Beacon, 1962.

Lynch, John. *The Spanish American Revolutions 1808–1826.* New York: Norton, 1986.

Mann, Charles. *1491: New Revelations of the Americas before Columbus.* New York: Vintage, 2006.

Mattoso, Katia M. de Queiros. *To Be a Slave in Brazil, 1550-1888.* New Brunswick, NJ: Rutgers, 1996.

Stein, Stanley J., and Barbara H. Stein. *The Colonial Heritage of Latin America: Essays on Economic Dependence in Perspective.* New York: Oxford, 1970.

Films

Guns, Germs, and Steel, part 2. Dir. Cassian Harrison and Tim Lambert. National Geographic, 2005.

The Mission. Dir. Roland Joffe. Warner Bros, 2003.

I, the Worst of All (Yo, la Peor de Todas). Dir. Maria Luisa Bemberg. First Run Features, 2003.

The Last Supper (La Ultima Cena). Dir. Tomas Gutierrez Alea. New Yorker, 2007.

The Conquistadors, four part series. Dir. David Wallace. PBS, 2006.

The Other Conquest (La Otra Conquista). Dir. Salvador Carrasco. Starz/Anchor Bay, 2007.

Cabeza de Vaca. Dir. Nicolas Echeverria. New Concorde, 2001.

Aguirre, Wrath of God. Dir. Werner Herzog. Starz/Anchor Bay, 2000.

Quilombo. Dir. Carlos Diegues. New Yorker, 2005.

Online content

Museo Nacional de Antropologia de Mexico: www.gobiernodigital.inah.gob.mx/mener/index.php?id=33

The Mayan Popol Vuh: http://library.osu.edu/projects/popolwuj/

Asociacion Popol No'j: http://popnoj.redmaya.org/

Ghosts of Machu Picchu (PBS video): http://video.pbs.org/video/1392958573/

1491 author Charles Mann's website: www.charlesmann.org/Book-index.htm

Discovery Channel: Who Owns Machu Picchu? http://video.nationalgeographic.com/video/player/specials/treasure-wars/machu-picchu-tw.html

Mexico: Aztec City: http://dsc.discovery.com/tv-shows/other-shows/videos/assignment-discovery-mexico-aztec-city.htm

Museo Larco: www.museolarco.org/

Palenque Red Queen: http://dsc.discovery.com/tv-shows/other-shows/videos/assignment-discovery-palenque-red-queen.htm

2   Asia (1492–1945)

Timeline

1492	Expulsion of Moors from Iberian Peninsula
1511	First Portuguese Catholic missionaries arrive in Southeast Asia
1526	The Mughals take over India
1756–1763	7-Years War
1840–1842	Opium War
1854–1856	Crimean War
1857	Sepoy Rebellion
1850–1864	Taiping Rebellion
1868	The Meiji Restoration
1885	Founding of the Indian National Congress
1911	Xinhai Revolution
1915	Armenian Genocide
1921	Founding of the Chinese Communist Party
1923	Ataturk founds Republic of Turkey
1931–1945	Japanese occupation of China
1945	United States drops nuclear bombs on Hiroshima and Nagasaki, Japan

Assumptions

1   What do you know about pre-1945 Asia?
2   Is this true knowledge? Are there concrete sources you can point to on Asia that have informed your thoughts about the region?
3   How do you weigh the legitimacy of those sources?
4   If those sources are less than accurate portrayals of Asia, what effect do you think they have had on your ideas?

Many Westerners have seen films such as *Lawrence of Arabia, Gandhi, The King and I*, and others familiar to movie viewers over the past six decades. We should start with these films because they help us to flesh out some concrete examples stemming from the preceding assumptions-based questions about Asia. *Lawrence of Arabia*'s title conveys that the significance of the events of the film rests on the British official T. E. Lawrence; so, how accurate can the film be in conveying the significance of the local Arabs who did the bulk of the fighting and dying during those years? What effect do you think this film, which places a British official center stage in the struggle for Arab nationalism in the 1910s, must have had on Western audiences' ideas about the level of agency exerted by the Arabs themselves? This line of questions could apply to Central, South, Southeast, and East Asia as well. Though Bruce Lee and Jackie Chan represent Chinese culture to Western audiences, Japan's shift away from the Shogunate to modernization under the Meiji Restoration is seen through Tom Cruise's eyes in *The Last Samurai*. That Asia's ancient traditions provide substantial information pointing the way toward more deeply understanding modern Asia is lost in these films despite what may be sincere efforts by directors to honor Asian culture.

In a way unlike Latin America and Africa, the people of Asia have a stronger connection to their ancient civilizations. The inventions of writing, agriculture, animal domestication, monotheism, and the most important advancements in education and technology prior to the Industrial Revolution originated in Asia. Both Latin America and Africa were conquered and colonized by Europeans who replaced native regimes and diminished and outright eliminated much of the old cultural, social, and economic foundations of these regions. In contrast, although most of Asia was in fact colonized by Europeans in the past few centuries, and indeed the term *Asia* is a European invention, the continent has near-uninterrupted civilizational roots dating back thousands of years. Though the African and Latin American civilizations of Zimbabwe and Peru, respectively, represent incredible advancements in civilization, not to mention the dozens of others throughout both continents dating back thousands of years, these were subdued by outsiders and were less integral in the creation of the current nations in which they reside than were nearly all of Asia's civilizations. Egypt is an exception in Africa mostly because its connections are more pertinent to the Middle East, which spans between North Africa and Central Asia.

Arab peoples were the first to invent agriculture and animal domestication 11,000 years ago, and there have been myriad empires that have encompassed these peoples for the past 5,000 years. Indians celebrate their five-millennia-old Harappa roots as well as the literature dating from the Aryans 3,500 years back. Hinduism and Islam also meet here. Iranians, despite being Muslim for the past thirteen centuries, still feel an intimate connection to their pre-Islamic history dating back to Darius the Great 2,500 years ago. Turkish people are also largely Islamic, yet they have been at the crossroads of manifold cultures for thousands of years, including those from the Far East, Europe, and the Middle East. The Chinese civilization dates back 4,000 years, and the nation has experienced varying degrees of unification under a number of dynasties from different parts of the country going back 2,500 years, when Buddhism, Taoism, and Confucianism first took root. These three forms of cultural guidelines still influence most Chinese.

Pre-modern history

The Middle East

The Fertile Crescent is the region of modern Iraq mostly, between the Tigris and Euphrates Rivers. It was here that the first known domestication of crops took place approximately 11,000 years ago. This led gradually to the rise of sedentary life, which allowed for hierarchical systems of civilization: Fewer people were needed for food acquisition (as was the case during the 99 percent of human history of hunter-gathering), and as such, more people could concentrate on matters such as philosophy, governance, art, architecture, and the like. The ancient Sumerians in modern Iraq are considered the world's oldest civilization, dating back more than 5,000 years, and 1,000 years later, the Egyptians, Indus Valley peoples (modern India and Pakistan), and China developed beyond them. The Egyptians stand head and shoulders above the rest in part due to the monuments left behind and especially because they were the first unified nation in the ancient world, and that unity has continued in Egyptian culture to this day.

By the third millennium BCE, Asia saw the rise of major changes in religion and philosophy.

The only two monotheistic religions of the time were Judaism and Zoroastrianism (Iran), and these two came into contact with the Persian (Iranian) invasion of Judah (Israel) in the sixth century BCE. The following 300-year period is known as the "axial age." Great classical philosophers from ancient Greece (Socrates, Plato, Aristotle); China (Lao Tse, Confucius); and India (the Buddha) became centerpieces of their respective regions' societies. When the Greek General Alexander the Great (356–323 BCE) extended his armies from Greece through Egypt, Syria, Iran, and Central Asia, he left the legacy of Greek culture. These lands soon encompassed what is referred to as the "Hellenic" world, in which many cultures intermingled, and the three religions of the region spread over the next two millennia (Judaism, Christianity, and Islam). At the same time, a vibrant trade was established with East and Central Asia via the Silk Road and the Indian Ocean trade. These connections were essential for the exchange of goods and ideas and would permanently connect both ends of the continent in the thirteenth century AD with the Mongol invasions. The division of the Roman Empire into west and east in 395 AD led to the gradual demise of the western half, but the new capital at Constantinople endured for another millennium in the east in modern Turkey.

Islam arrived with the Prophet Mohammad (571 AD–632 AD), whose message in the Arabian Peninsula spread rapidly throughout the Middle East in the seventh and eighth centuries. Soon, North Africa, parts of Central

Africa, the Iberian Peninsula, and West and Central Asia were under Islamic rulers known as *caliphs*. The rivalry between Christianity and Islam clashed when the Crusades hit the Middle East between 1095 and 1291, leaving an imprint that lasts to this day. This paled by comparison to the effect of the Mongol invasions that conquered most of Asia and parts of Europe in the thirteenth century, culminating in the sack of Sunni Islam's capital of Baghdad in 1258. The Mongols preserved the caliphate system in Muslim lands, however, and the Ottoman Empire gradually replaced the caliphate with the sultanate beginning in the fourteenth century. The Ottomans then conquered the remnants of the Roman Empire (referred to as the Byzantine Empire) when they sacked its capital at Constantinople (modern Istanbul) in 1453 and slowly acquired territories under Roman and caliph control thereafter.

India

India before 1948 includes modern India, Pakistan, and Bangladesh. The roots of its partition (which took place in 1948 and 1971) can be found in the thousands of years' worth of migrations, conquests, and cultural developments of a wide variety of peoples. India in its longest-running form is more of a continent than a single united, semi-homogenous country. If it were united today it would have 1.5 billion people and would surpass China by 200 million. The first civilization to arise there was the Harappa, which originated in the Indus River Valley, in the western coastal region. Although there is no certainty to the date in which cities were first built, the time frame archeologists play with is between 3100 BC and 1700 BC. India's ancient and sacred story of the *Mahabharata* is believed to explain the Bharata war, whose date ranges from 3102 BC to 950 BC.

Archeologists believe the first cities of the Indus Valley were developed independently, as opposed to influenced by the ancient Sumerians and Egyptians, at least before 2000 BC. Researchers also believe the Harappa to be the first to develop organized cities as far back as 2300 BC, and they may have been the first to use the ox-drawn wagon and to spin and weave cotton. Their writing system remains unintelligible, but the twentieth-century excavations of Harappa and Mohenjo-Daro demonstrate distinct, common Indian roots in the long-standing literary classics such as the Vedas and the *Mahabharata*. There, Harappa had some contact with Mesopotamia; however, in contrast to their fellow ancient civilizations, the Harappa did not evolve into the future Indian civilization, and its disappearance 3700 years ago is still a mystery.

Hinduism is central to Indian culture and Indians still take immense pride in the ancient stories known as the Vedas, which are believed to derive from the Aryans. This is in dispute as of late; however, Indian tradition follows that immigrants known as Aryans entered the north of India some 3,500 years ago and became the central focus of India's most famous epic, the

Mahabharata. Whether the Aryans conquered or gradually settled India over the course of several centuries, it has become associated with some of the great pillars of Indian culture. These are Sanskrit, the *Brahman* priesthood, and the infamous hierarchical caste system that has divided the Indian people into more than 5,000 categories, with the Brahman class on top and the Untouchables on the bottom.

Buddhism originated in India and contributed significantly to Indian culture and world history with beginnings dating to the life of Gautama Buddha approximately 2500 years ago. The Buddha taught not of a deity but of the search for enlightenment that acknowledged the human existence as a state of suffering that could be overcome through Buddhist practices too complex to describe here. Buddhism spread from India west, south, north, and east to influence India, Afghanistan, Sri Lanka, Tibet, China, Southeast Asia, and Japan in the following centuries, making it the dominant religion of Asia. The Indian political landscape ebbed and flowed according to differing regional power players during the two millennia after the rise of Buddhism. The end of the first millennium AD witnessed the rise of Islam in West and Central Asia, including India, and the Delhi Sultanate emerged in India in 1206. This lasted until 1526, when the Mughals took their place.

China

One great question about Chinese civilization is whether it developed independently or as a result of influence from other places, such as the Middle East. It is unknown whether agriculture developed independently in China, although research is increasingly pointing that way. Millet in the dry and cold north and rice in the humid and hot south began at least 7,000 years ago, if not much earlier, along with animal domestication. Unlike the Middle East and India, Chinese civilization does not derive its fundamentals from deities but from legendary humans considered responsible for major innovations. Fu Xi brought the domestication of animals and developed the concept of the family. The Emperor Yao created the bow and arrow, silk, writing, boats, and other inventions. Yu dredged canals to tame the floods, thus creating many of the rivers still used in China today, and he initiated China's dynastic tradition 4,000 years ago. This was the Xia dynasty, which was followed by the Shang (1600–1050 BC), significant for developing strong government, temples, chariots, bows, bronze-tip spears and, especially, writing. The Zhou era (1050–256 BC) witnessed great changes associated with expansion, warfare, and the rise of the classic philosophers, especially Confucius (551–479 BC). Confucianism promotes firmly rooting Chinese society in traditional notions of hierarchy and learning to promote harmony. The other *isms* of Daoism and Legalism also took root during the Zhou period.

The Qin dynasty (221–206 BC) is credited with unifying China within the southeastern third of what is modern-day China. They initiated the strong centralized state, which was then taken up by the Han (202 BC–220 AD), who consolidated the gains of the Qin under an increasingly militaristic emperor dealing with nomadic tribes in the north and the west. The Silk Road became significant during this period as Chinese silk made its way west through Asia as far as Rome. This connected China economically and culturally with most of Eurasia. The fall of the Han in 220 was followed by two-and-a-half centuries of fragmentation and decentralized control, which came to an end with the Sui (581–617 AD), who reunified China. The Tang (618–907) followed with an expansionist policy that overextended the empire's reach, and the less expansionist Song (907–1276) retracted and sought to maintain and defend their existing boundaries. The Chinese population was at 100 million by 1102, which was the U.S. population by 1915.

The Song period witnessed the gradual encroachment of independent states from all over China, culminating in the Mongol conquest in 1276. The Mongols' brief rule through the Yuan Dynasty from 1276 to 1368 changed the face of Asia. Genghis Khan (1162–1227) began the Mongol invasions, and his successors brought all of China under Mongol rule and extended their power under divided states into West Asia. The Mongol era forced China into global power status, and this was further enhanced by the Ming Dynasty (1368–1644), who ironically first decided to increase its reach, then decided to reduce it. The Ming's investment in sea exploration demonstrated its ability to dominate the world. Its vessels were the largest in the world, and they sailed as far as Africa and throughout the Indian and western Pacific Oceans. However, the Ming were concerned about foreign penetration and, therefore, ended China's naval program in the fifteenth century, just as southern Europeans (Portuguese, Spanish, and Italian) began to develop theirs.

Post-1453 Middle East

The Ottoman conquest of Constantinople in 1453 signaled the fall of the Roman Empire, and in the following century their rule expanded further into the Muslim world. The rise of the Ottoman Empire was swift but rocky. Within a century of taking Constantinople in 1453, Ottoman armies conquered the Arabia Peninsula, Egypt, Syria, Iraq, and North Africa and defeated Iran in battle. This last war (1514) reinvigorated the Sunni-Shiite (Ottoman-Iran) divisions within the Islamic world that still play a role in Middle East conflicts today. Christian Europe was on the rise at this time as well, and the Ottoman military would do battle on land and sea with northern and western rivals over the course of the next four centuries. The Ottoman Empire's attempts to meet the needs of such military expenditures led to declining infrastructure development, and its overextension led to a lowering of troop morale and trust. Setbacks also represented decline just as the empire ascended: The Moors were expelled from the Iberian Peninsula in 1492, the Ottoman Navy lost at the Battle of Lepanto in 1571, and their military lost a great battle in Vienna in 1683.

The rise and decline of the Ottoman Empire must be understood in the context of its geography and its competition with Christian Europe. Islam was able to flourish for 1,000 years in part due to its relative isolation from powerful state-sponsored religions in the Middle East, and Christian Europe was highly fragmented after the separation of the Roman Empire into east and west in the late fourth century, thus posing little difficulty for the rise of an Islamic empire. However, after the Italians, Portuguese, Spanish, Dutch, French, and English expanded their power through sea exploration and conquest and colonization of new lands, their wealth rose relative to the Ottomans. This mattered most when Napoleon used French Revolutionary fervor to expand Christian Europe's power into the Ottoman domain of Egypt in 1798. This occurred in the midst of the Enlightenment and the Industrial Revolution, both of which were connected to the broader Scientific Revolution sweeping the West since the sixteenth century.

Napoleon's occupation of Egypt thus began French and later English colonialism in the Middle East. They would stay and expand over the next century and a half. The Russians presented another problem, as they took Ottoman lands throughout the nineteenth century. The Crimean War (1854–1856) resulted from this conflict, and France and Britain sided with the Ottomans against Russia. This initiated Turkish connections with Europe that eventually had a long-lasting influence in both places. The British helped the Ottomans again in 1878 to block a Russian attempt to conquer Turkey, but the Russians would not be deterred and took Ottoman lands into Central Asia. By the late nineteenth century, the British and the French had taken most of North Africa, and by 1911, the Russians had taken Iran (principal Islamic rival to the Ottomans), and the Italians were poised to take Libya.

By the outbreak of WWI in 1914, the Ottoman Empire hitched its wagon to the Central Powers just as it was dealing with massive fragmentation from within its borders. Independence movements had been erupting over the past century from Serbs, Greeks, Albanians, and Armenians, and the Turkish authorities exacted mass repression against the Greeks and Armenians in particular. The first genocide of the twentieth century was perpetrated against the Armenians in 1915. Upward of 1.5 million Armenians were killed through a combination of outright executions and forced marches.

The genocide of the Armenians represents a conundrum for international politics in the post-WWI era for a number of intertwined reasons. The Ottoman Empire dissolved after its defeat in WWI, and though much of the former Empire was divided among the British and the French, the two principal Islamic world rivals, Turkey and Iran, remained independent. Iran witnessed a nationalist coup led by Reza Khan against the shah in 1921, and he ruled as shah until 1941. His son, Reza Shah Pahlavi, ruled from 1953 to 1979. Rather differently and unique in the Islamic world, the new Turkish republic was created by the famous Mustafa Kemal "Ataturk" (1923–1938), who expelled all foreign interlopers, secularized the government, and pushed for modernizing the economy. This new direction for Turkey has been encouraging for Western powers, in particular during the Cold War and the War on Terror, as the governments in Istanbul have worked closely with the United States in particular to provide assistance in combating Communism and Islamic extremism. This alliance has made it politically inexpedient for the government in Washington, DC to pressure Istanbul to recognize its actions against the Armenians in 1915 as "genocide," as this declaration could undermine the strategic relationship between the United States and Turkey.

The post-WWI era was one of great change in the Middle East. The British and the French increased their power as a result of the Ottoman Empire's fall as each took over former Ottoman territories both as a result of the Sikes-Picot treaty of 1916 and in "mandates" dictated by the Paris Peace Conference of 1919. The British mandate included Iraq and Palestine, whereas the French held control over Lebanon, Syria, and Transjordan (which later became Jordan). The Arabian Peninsula was largely outside European control while witnessing a guerrilla war of conquest by abd al-Aziz ibn Saud, who won control by 1926, naming his realm Saudi Arabia in 1932. Since then, the power of Saudi oil has played a tremendous role in shaping both Middle East and international geopolitics.

Some Middle East countries sought alliances with the Axis while others lined up with the Allies. It was during the war that King Ibn Saud forged an enduring friendship with the United States through the efforts of the Franklin Delano Roosevelt (1933–1945) administration that has lasted to this day. The North Africa campaign fought mostly in modern-day Libya also placed the Middle East center stage in the early days of the war, and the Allies met for the famous Tehran Conference in Iran in 1943, but by and large the region played a minor role in WWII. The most significant aspect of the Middle East during the war was the effect of the genocide perpetrated against the European Jewish population. Hitler's systematic murder of 6 million Jews caused a great influx of Jewish refugees to their traditional homeland in the British mandate of Palestine, which became the State of Israel in 1947. The following seven decades have witnessed intermittent war, general unrest, and countless UN debates and resolutions.

Post-1500 India

Between 1526 and 1947, India initiated its road toward cohesion, which of course ruptured in the years thereafter. The Mughals were responsible for this beginning with the first of their emperors, Babur, a descendant of Genghis Khan. The Islamic Mughals tapped into the now-centuries-old roots of Islam that had been developing in India and its neighbors and that eventually led to the division of India in 1948 and that of Pakistan itself in 1971. Babur rose to power during fortuitous times, when firearms were starting to replace most other weapons. Babur initially conquered Afghanistan between

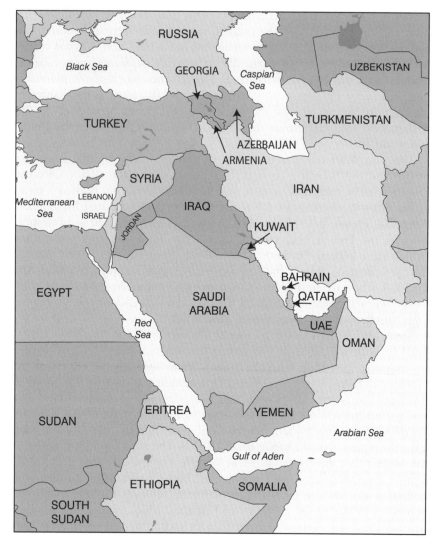

Figure 2.1 Map of the Middle East

1504 and 1519 while simultaneously setting the stage to conquer India from the Lodis, who were already warring among themselves, in 1525. Babur's Mughal warriors and the Panjabi regional ruler Ibrahim's Lodis fought at Panipat in 1526 in a battle that should have favored the Lodis. In the end, Babur's forces won out, but they and the future Mughals had to contend with various Afghan and Indian factions for the next three decades as Mughal power gradually consolidated over most of India. Great monuments such as the Taj Mahal were built during the Mughal period, which lasted officially from 1526 to 1857.

   The British East India Company challenged Mughal control beginning in 1757 by expanding trade in India on behalf of the Crown. This was enabled by the British defeat of the French in the Seven Years War from 1756 to 1763, and yet it was not until a mutiny against British control broke out in 1857 that the Mughals lost their empire. The Sepoy Rebellion of that year was the result of both simmering resentment over British rule and anger within the military over the new Enfield rifle cartridges they were given, which contained tallow. Because it was possible for this tallow to come either from pigs or cattle, its usage offended the religious sensitivities of both Muslims and Hindus in the ranks. The soldiers killed many British civilians in heinous ways, but the British ended the rebellion with killings on a far larger scale with the intention of crushing all future dissent over British rule. This was by no means the only revolt experienced during the Raj (British colonial rule) in India, but the Sepoy example laid the foundation for much of the discontent against the British that continued throughout the next ninety years until Independence. In fact, the Indian National Congress (INC), the organization composed of both Hindus and Muslims that eventually toppled the Raj in 1947 began in 1885, just twenty-eight years after the rebellion.

   The INC was a powerful organization for Indian national consciousness from its beginning. The rise of famous INC figures such as Mahatma Gandhi and Jawaharlal Nehru would solidify the INC's name in history. Gandhi, born in Gujarat in 1869 to Brahman caste parents, rose to prominence on the world stage even before leading the INC. He went to law school in England from 1888 to 1891, an experience that changed his worldview considerably. In fact, despite his reputation for bringing down the British Empire in India, Gandhi was a life-long Anglophile who appreciated the British cultural contribution to the world if not its military and economic dominance of India. Gandhi spent most of 1893 to 1915 in South Africa both as a lawyer and as a leader of the nonviolent civil disobedience campaign representing the Indian community there. He made a name for himself in South Africa for his philosophy of *Satyagraha* (pursuit for truth, soul truth, etc.) that served as a spiritual foundation for his rights campaigns.

   The incident that motivated Gandhi to action occurred upon his initial arrival in South Africa. He was told to leave a train car reserved for white passengers and, in this situation, Gandhi saw a contradiction in the legitimacy of British colonial authority, for on the one hand, the British claimed to spread "civilization," while on the other, it treated its non-white subjects as inferiors. Gandhi saw himself as a citizen of the British Empire, entitled to all of the same rights as anyone else within the Empire, except its black members, whose cause he never championed. His main achievement in South Africa was the Indian Relief Act in 1914, which provided protections for Indians within the new Union of South Africa (South Africa became semi-autonomous under this Union in 1910, while still remaining a British colony). Gandhi also established two *satyagraha*-based farms there (Phoenix Farm and Tolstoy Farm), where followers converged to study Gandhi's teachings.

Figure 2.2 Mohandas Gandhi (1869–1948) (Dinodia Photos/Alamy)

Indian Independence took place gradually under Gandhi's leadership between 1920 and 1947. Although it could be argued that the INC's founding in 1888 laid its foundations, it was not until Gandhi initiated his non-cooperation movement in 1920 that the movement began to grow. Gandhi became the INC's leader in 1921 (although he would lose it later to other, younger members) and was promptly arrested and imprisoned between 1922 and 1924. In 1930, the movement officially declared Indian Independence, and Gandhi led his famous Salt March to the sea that challenged British monopoly control over sea salt production. This led directly to negotiations between Gandhi and the British Viceroy in India, Lord Irwin, resulting in the Gandhi-Irwin Pact. This act provided the INC with legal protections and paved the way toward Indian dominion status. Gandhi's direct participation waned over the course of the next sixteen years as followers with more energy (much of Gandhi's strength had been sapped with extensive hunger strikes) such as Jawaharlal Nehru and Muhammad Ali Jinnah led the struggle for Indian Independence. It was during this period that Jinnah rose to prominence as the future founder of the Muslim nation, Pakistan, even as India and the British Crown worked assiduously to defeat the Axis threat during WWII.

The Crown's representative during the war years was the indomitable Prime Minister Winston Churchill, a man whose life paralleled Gandhi's in many ways. Not only were the two born only five years apart (Gandhi was Churchill's elder) but both got their political feet wet in South Africa, both participated (in differing ways) in the Great Boer War (1899–1902) and WWI (1914–1918), and both would represent their respective sides in a battle for the identity of their nations. After this struggle, the British Empire was a shell of its former self, maintaining mostly a few scattered colonies in the Caribbean and Africa, and India was its own sovereign nation. Many suffered on the road to 1947, however, chief among them the residents of East Bengal, who lost upward of 1.5 million people to starvation in 1943 due to the British government's policy of diverting resources to the war effort and away from this already-poor region. This was only one example of intensive damage, which must be added to the list of hundreds of thousands of imprisonments and cases of public abuses of Indians by British authorities, including the occasional massacre of unarmed civilians, such as the 1919 Massacre at Amritsar.

By 1947, Churchill had been voted out of office as Prime Minister in favor of Clement Atlee, and the Indian people were free to choose their own future path. Peace, however, appeared to have been held together only by the British, for the country's religious cleavages between Muslims and Hindus (primarily, as there were many others) quickly led to one of modern history's most intensive slaughters. Known simply as "Partition," Hindus and Muslims engaged in a year-long blood-letting campaign from 1947 to 1948 that eventually led most Indian Muslims to flee westward to Pakistan and east to East Pakistan (the future country of Bangladesh). Gandhi was himself assassinated in 1948 by Hindu extremists, but his legacy as the standard bearer for non-violence was later taken up by various movements around the world, including the U.S. civil rights movement of the 1950s and 1960s led by Dr. Martin Luther King, Jr. and the Liberian women-led peace movement of the 2000s, to name only two.

Post-1492 China

Columbus's voyage to the New World set the globe down a path from which it has not returned since 1492, and China was his actual goal. The post-1492 era that brought the Old and the New World together has been referred to as the age of the "Columbian Exchange." This included Europe-Africa-Latin America trade and travel and the cultivation of everlasting connections between East Asia, particularly China, and the West. By the sixteenth century, Chinese merchants were trading silk and porcelain for silver and gold brought over on the Spanish Galleons from the Americas. The Spanish desired porcelain, silk, and spices while the Chinese needed precious metals for money. The Ming soon had to contend with other European goods entering the region and treated much of it as contraband, but eventually the amount of exchange overwhelmed even their most diligent administrators' ability to thwart the massive influx of American and, eventually, European goods and money. This trade eventually altered the face of China's agriculture, geography, and economy. Food such as corn, chilies, peanuts, and cacao became popular in China, and soon farmland acreage expanded, much of it on previously unused plots, many on unstable slopes. This caused both an increase in population and increased landslides, flooding, and disease.

Science and philosophy advances went both ways between East and West during this period. The Chinese invention of gunpowder had reached Europe and the Middle East already to great effect by the fifteenth century. Those who utilized it proved adept at conquering their rivals. From the opposite direction, the European Enlightenment came first via Portuguese, Italian, and Spanish missionaries in the sixteenth century who established missions mostly along the East Asian Pacific coastal areas in places such as Macao and the Philippines and Southeast Asia. European encroachments coincided with mass protests against Ming rule in the sixteenth century over corruption, abuse of power, and financial crises, which were suppressed with deadly effect. Indeed, the Ming were faced with myriad difficulties in the last century of its rule, including wars with Japan, famine, drastic fluctuations in population growth, natural disasters, disease, floods, and the suicide of the last Ming emperor in 1644. Although history has judged the Ming often in a negative light, they proved adept at maintaining relative stability for two centuries amid great changes.

The Qing Dynasty (1644–1911) witnessed the rise of Manchu rule. Thus, non-Chinese ruled China again, but this was accepted as relatively normal. The Manchus, like the Mongols, were an ethnic group from the north who ruled through a dynasty under a different name. The Mongols ruled under the Yuan, and the Manchus ruled under the Qing. It was under the Manchus that the modern boundaries of China were solidified through force as they also expanded to envelop Mongolia and Indochina, the latter of which was taken by the French in the nineteenth century.

By the nineteenth century, China had ceased to be the world's dominant power. Europe was decisively on top, with the United States gaining considerable momentum throughout the century. There were many differences between China and the West, but the main reason for the dichotomy was there was no Industrial Revolution in China. In addition, the Qing were non-Chinese rulers less interested in what Western advancements could offer China, unlike those pushing for the reforms of the Meiji Restoration in Japan, for example, which surpassed its Asian neighbors in rapid succession in the last decades of the nineteenth century.

These divergences occurred in a climate of rapid industrialization taking place mostly in Western Europe and the United States that had begun with the Industrial Revolution in the late eighteenth century. Advancements in science and philosophy in the wake of the Renaissance catapulted the West beyond the material achievements of the rest of the globe and provided the foundations for much of the modern world as we know it today. However, Western advancements were not the result of European innovations alone: Asian, African, and American (Western Hemispheric) ideas, products, and peoples contributed greatly to this rise. Wheat, barley, rice, pigs, sheep, goats, cattle, and horses had all arrived from Asia and Africa, where dedication to agricultural techniques and animal domestication developed for thousands of years prior to their arrival in Europe. Alexander the Great's conquests in the fourth century BC from the Mediterranean to Central Asia (that created the Hellenic World) increased the extent of Europe's contact with foreign cultures to the east. This helped connect the West with Asian trade routes, most notably, the Silk Road from China. The rise of the Islamic caliphate after the Islamic Invasions of the seventh and eighth centuries only increased these connections further, and Islamic scholarly innovations in mathematics, geography, medicine, and philosophy provided a foundation for European learning centuries later. Gunpowder, paper, and the compass all arrived in Europe as a result of the Mongol Invasions of the thirteenth century, and it was this key series of events that knitted the East and the West together more fully than any other in history. The world changed dramatically as a result, and it has never looked back.

China and Japan compared

In the early nineteenth century, China and Japan appeared to have a similar level of economic development. By the end of that century, the two had diverged, as Japan had reached a level of power similar to the strongest in Europe while China lagged behind. How did this divergence take place? One way of understanding this is by examining the Chinese versus the Japanese reactions to the arrival of Western envoys. A 1793 visit to the Qing court by the gift-bearing British diplomat Lord George McCartney was viewed as insulting to the Chinese emperor, who saw little use in an increase in the trade that had already developed between Asia and the West. The British joint-stock venture of the British East India Company worked to link China to India during this time as the crown acquired more control over India. By 1840, the company no longer existed, but British merchants sought a huge payoff from selling Indian opium in exchange for Chinese tea.

The Opium War of 1840 to 1842 was the result. The Qing court had worked tirelessly to prevent the arrival of opium to China due to the ill effects on public health, but British naval superiority forced the Chinese to accept Indian opium, and Chinese capitulation in 1842 illustrated how far its power had declined in relation to the new dominant country, Great Britain. The British thereafter purchased large quantities of tea, which changed the face of traditional British and Indian culture, but the Chinese silver used to purchase Indian opium created British wealth at the expense of the Chinese economy. The Opium War was followed by further British and French interventions in 1858 to 1860 and 1883 to 1885, leading to the creation of European enclaves in coastal China where Chinese laws did not apply.

The pressures on the Qing dynasty increased further with the Taiping Rebellion from 1850 to 1864. Perhaps the deadliest war in global history aside from WWII, with as many as 30 million deaths, the war began with the rise of the Taiping rebel leader, the Christian fundamentalist Hong Xinquan, who propagated the view the Manchus were under the devil's control. Hong influenced his followers to carry out indiscriminate violence against unarmed men, women, and children for years unabated before the Qing's General Zeng Guofan crushed the revolt in 1864. Despite these internal and external conflicts, the 1860s and 1870s witnessed China's gradual industrialization along Western lines, assisted by the arrival of European advisors and, most important, loans to finance these projects.

Japan is one of the wealthiest countries in the world today, but it was not so two centuries ago. This change came about in a number of ways. Historians often point to the arrival in 1852 of a U.S. fleet led by Commodore Mathew Perry as the jumping off point for Japan's rise. Perry's displays demonstrated the potential for scientific, political, economic and, especially, military advancements offered by Westernization. The Japanese have a history of taking pieces of wisdom from other cultures while preserving their own distinct heritage and, in this spirit, they worked to end the era of dominance by shogun rulers in the 1860s and restored the Meiji emperor in 1868. The Meiji Restoration, as it has come to be known, signaled the beginning of Japanese economic, political, and military reforms that eventually led to Japan's imperialist ventures in East Asia and the Pacific in the twentieth century.

This played out initially with a series of wars with China and Russia in 1894 to 1895 and 1904 to 1905, respectively. Japan was victorious in both. Meanwhile, despite some Chinese advances, the political scene was dominated by the anti-modernization Empress Dowager Cixi, who held near-total power from 1861 to 1908. The Boxer Rebellion of 1898 to 1901 further weakened Qing rule as xenophobic Chinese rebels attacked foreigners across the country, eliciting armed intervention from the United States, Russia, and other nations and resulting in increased debt for the Chinese government.

The dawn of the twentieth century witnessed the divergence of Asia's two most powerful nations. Just after Japan conquered Korea in 1910, China began its road to revolution under the founding father of the Republic of China, Dr. Sun Yat-sen (1866–1925). Sun was a revolutionary leader who had spent most of his life abroad, mostly in the West, and had been inspired by progressive ideals. He organized the Xinhai Revolution of 1911 that eventually overthrew the Qing Dynasty, but his Revolutionary Alliance was not able to successfully fill the power vacuum afterward. Sun served as the first president of the Republic under his new political party, the Kuomintang (KMT), for four months before stepping down in favor of Yuan Shikai, who ruled as an authoritarian dictator until 1916. The following twelve years plunged China into an era of competing warlords.

The Chinese Communist Party (CCP) was founded with the assistance of the Soviet Union (USSR) in 1920. Although Mao had to wait until 1934 to lead the CCP, he joined in the early days of 1921 and gradually rose within the ranks of the party. He had rivals from within the CCP, but his

Figure 2.3 Mao Tse Tung (1893–1976) Pictorial Press Ltd./Alamy

opponent was the leader of the KMT (also referred to as the "Nationalists"), General Jiang Jieshi (1887–1975), also known as Chiang Kai Shek. After an initial period of cooperation between the CCP and the KMT, which Moscow encouraged through its financial support of both groups, Jiang used force to suppress the CCP beginning in 1927 and officially seized control of the government in 1928. The CCP-KMT conflict grew over the next nine years, with the climax occurring with the Long March of 1934 to 1935.

The Long March is at the center of Mao's legendary rise to prominence within the CCP. The story follows that Mao led his troops in a series of marches and battles throughout China over the course of one year, losing 90 percent of his 80,000 followers in the process. The maintenance of the CCP army in the face of such odds is what has gone down in history as the example of Mao's fortitude. While some have disputed the idea that Mao should be elevated for what is mostly a series of losses, this remains as a central "truth" in Mao's status as the most important icon in China's history. After hundreds of thousands of deaths resulting from a decade of civil war, both would cooperate against the Japanese invasion.

Although the two had played only marginal roles on the side of the Allies in WWI, Japan succeeded in acquiring Chinese territory at the Paris Peace Conference in 1919 after WWI, further upsetting the already-stung Chinese. The Japanese then invaded and occupied Manchuria in 1931 and began taking over the rest of China in 1937. This was part of a broader Japanese imperial effort to conquer East Asia and the Pacific in general that included a chain of islands from Japan southward through the Philippines and Indonesia and Southeast Asia. The Chinese suffered 20 million deaths resisting the Japanese from 1937 to 1945, a few million less than the Russians lost resisting the Nazi invasion of 1941 to 1945. Nevertheless, perhaps the worst single atrocity against a civilian population perpetrated during WWII took place when the Japanese destroyed Nanking in 1937. This event, in which the Japanese slaughtered 200,000 people, still serves as a source of tension between China and Japan. The occupation as a whole served as a humiliation and an atrocity writ large, but the "Rape of Nanking" represented the epitome of Japanese treachery against the innocent.

Japan's downfall came in 1945 due to both Chinese and U.S. military action. Both Jiang's and Mao's forces resisted the Japanese in China for eight long and bloody years, while the United States won a series of battles against Japan in the Island Hopping Campaign that culminated in the sacking of Okinawa in 1945. Finally, U.S. President Harry S. Truman (1945–1953) ordered the nuclear destruction of Hiroshima and Nagasaki in August 1945, which led to Japan's official surrender and, as such, the end of the Japanese Empire. The Chinese Civil War continued immediately afterward.

Discussion questions

1   How would you compare the differences in significance of the genocide of the Armenians in the Ottoman Empire to that of the Jews of Europe?
2   What do you think explains Japan's unique rise to economic and military dominance in Asia prior to 1945?
3   Do you believe the United States was justified in dropping the atomic bombs on Japan in 1945?
4   Of the three regional/national groupings covered in this chapter (the Middle East, India, and China), which is the most important on the global stage in 1945?

Historical figures

Mustafa Kemal "Ataturk" (1881–1938)

This famous military officer of the Ottoman Empire became even more famous for becoming the nationalist father of the modern nation of Turkey. He was especially well known for building a secular state that allowed for both Islamic devotion throughout the country while promoting secular politics, laws, and education. Ataturk's rise to power in the wake of the breakup of the Ottoman Empire after WWI came at an auspicious time for the new nation, and he chose to take advantage of the opportunity to both reduce the risk of plunging into economic and political doldrums and to modernize Turkey. He was president under a one-party regime from 1923 to 1938. Ataturk's policies have made Turkey stand out among nations of the former Ottoman Empire for its consistent political stability, separation of mosque and state, and professionalization of the military, to name a few results of his programs.

Empress Dowager Cixi (ruled 1861–1908)

This concubine of Qing Emperor Xianfeng rose quickly through the ranks of Chinese imperial power first through mothering a son for the emperor. She held the real power behind her young son, Emperor Tongzhi, from 1861 to 1875, and after Tongzhi died at 18 in 1875, she held power behind her three-year-old nephew, Guangxu. Although never technically the monarch, the Empress Dowager held absolute power, which she exercised ruthlessly whenever challenged. She presided over the crushing of the Taiping Rebellion and is known for resisting much of the Western-style technological and cultural advances that China's rival, Japan, took full advantage of during her reign. It was during her tenure that Japan rose to prominence in East Asia, and the anti-imperial sentiment within China began building up that led to the 1911 Xinhai Revolution. She died in 1908, the last true symbol of Chinese monarchical rule. She was succeeded by yet another child emperor, the two-year-old Pu Yi, the last emperor of China, overthrown in 1911.

Mohandas Gandhi (1869–1948)

His name is the most associated with the words "peace" and "nonviolence" in the history of the world. He was the philosophical leader of India's independence movement from 1916 until his death in 1948, using *Satyagraha* (the search for, or demand for, truth) as a means of demonstrating how non-violent civil disobedience could undermine British colonialism.

Jiang Jieshi (1887–1975)

Popularly known as Chiang Kai-Shek in the West, this leader of the KMT (also known as the Nationalists) and military general in charge of the Chinese government from 1927 to 1949 rose to international prominence during and after WWII. He was especially known as Mao's principal rival during the Chinese Revolution. His defeat at the hands of Mao's forces in 1949 caused him and his followers to retreat to the island of Formosa, renamed Taiwan, and there he continued to rule as head of the Kuomintang until his death in 1975.

Genghis Khan (1162–1227)

Arguably one of history's most important figures, Genghis Khan's legacy cannot be summarized easily. Born Temujin, he changed his named to Genghis Khan as an adult and was responsible for uniting the Mongol tribes of China's northern region known as Mongolia today and for his and his descendants' conquest of most of the known world of the thirteenth century, extending Mongol dominance throughout most of Asia, Eastern Europe, and into the far reaches of the Middle East. In a manner similar to that of Christopher Columbus, Genghis Khan set in motion the events that brought the Eastern hemisphere together forever. Trade routes, political connections, religion, technology, and many other elements were shared across Asia, Europe, and Africa as a result of the Mongol invasions, which happened in part as a result of their overwhelming ability for military destruction over nearly every foe encountered.

The Prophet Mohammad (570–632)

The founder of the religion of Islam and the man responsible for uniting the Arabian tribes, he is known as "The Prophet Mohammad" by his followers. Mohammad is by far the most important person historically in the Muslim world in a manner similar to and different from the significance of Jesus for the Christian world. Though Mohammad was confirmed as an historical person and was not considered divine, Jesus is not considered a factual, historical "person" universally, and Christians believe him to be the son of God and, thus, divine. Also unlike Jesus, Mohammad's influence spread rapidly both during and immediately after his life throughout the Arabian Peninsula, North Africa, Eastern Europe, and Western and Central Asia. Today, Islam and Christianity compete as the two biggest religions.

Sun Yat-sen (1866–1925)

A somewhat tragic figure while still maintaining his heroic status in Chinese history, Sun Yat-sen was the leader of the Xinhai Revolution that toppled the Qing Dynasty in 1911. He began his revolutionary activities by founding the Revive China Society in Hawaii in 1894 and from there expanded to Hong Kong. He spent considerable time learning from Westerners and the Japanese about progressive alternatives to the status quo in China and much of his efforts were used raising money for the revolution. After military officers loyal to Sun toppled the Qing emperor in 1911, Sun wrote a constitution for republican government in 1912, but the following four decades were plagued with civil war and Japanese occupation.

Further readings

Gandhi, Mohandas K. *An Autobiography: the Story of my Experiments with Truth*. Boston, MA: Beacon, 1993.

Goldschmidt. Arthur, and Lawrence Davidson. *A Concise History of the Middle East: Ninth Edition*. Boulder, CO: Westview, 2007.

Herman, Arthur. *Gandhi and Churchill: The Epic Rivalry that Destroyed an Empire and Forged our Age*. New York: Bantam, 2009.

Keay, John. *India: A History*. New York: Grove, 2000.
Mann, Charles. *1493: Uncovering the New World Columbus Created*. New York: Vintage, 2012.
Mango, Andrew. *Ataturk: the Biography of the Founder of Modern Turkey*. London: John Murray, 1999.
Mukerjee, Madhusree. *Churchill's Secret War: The British Empire and the Ravaging of India during WWII*. New York: Basic Books, 2010.
Oren, Michael. *Power, Faith, and Fantasy: America in the Middle East, 1776-Present*. New York: Norton, 2007.
Said, Edward. *Orientalism*. New York: Random House, 1978.
Shuyun, Sun. *The Long March: The True History of Communist China's Founding Myth*. New York: Anchor, 2008.

Films

The Seven Samurai. Dir. Akira Kurosawa. Criterion, 2005.
City of Life and Death. Dir. Chuan Lu. Kino International, 2011.
Amigo. Dir. John Sayles. Warner Bros, 2011.
Mongol. Dir. Sergei Bodrov. New Line, 2008.
1911 (Xinhai Geming). Dir. Jackie Chan and Li Zhang. Well Go USA, 2012.
Gandhi. Dir. Richard Attenborough. Sony, 2007.
Lawrence of Arabia. Dir. David Lean. Sony, 2012.
The King and I. Dir. Walter Lang. 20th Century Fox, 2006.

Online content

Guns, Germs, and Steel Episode One Transcript, Out of Eden: www.pbs.org/gunsgermssteel/show/transcript1.html
The British Museum, Mesopotamia: www.mesopotamia.co.uk/
The British Museum, Ancient China: www.ancientchina.co.uk/menu.html
TED Talks: Rajesh Rao, A Rosetta Stone for the Indus Script: www.ted.com/talks/rajesh_rao_computing_a_rosetta_stone_for_the_indus_script.html
The University of Chicago, Ancient Mesopotamia: http://mesopotamia.lib.uchicago.edu/
National Geographic, Mohenjo Daro: http://science.nationalgeographic.com/science/archaeology/mohenjo-daro/
Indian National Congress: www.aicc.org.in/new/
Japan National Geographic: http://travel.nationalgeographic.com/travel/countries/japan-guide/
PBS Secrets of the Dead: China's Terracotta Warriors: http://video.pbs.org/video/1907176069/

3 Africa (1415–1952)

Timeline

1415	Henry the Navigator takes Ceuta
1488	Bartolomeu Dias sails around Cape of Good Hope
1517	Ottoman conquest of Egypt
1652	Dutch colonizers arrive on the Cape of Good Hope
1798	Napoleon invades Egypt
1805	British settle Cape Colony
1807	British Slave Trade Act passed, ending slave trade in British Empire
1838–1879	Zulu Wars
1867	Suez Canal built
1880–1903	Boer Wars
1884–1885	Conference of Berlin
1885–1908	King Leopold II's ownership of the Congo Free State
1899	Battle of Omdurman in Sudan
1912	African National Congress (ANC) founded
1930	Haile Selassie crowned King of Ethiopia
1948	Afrikaner Nationalists institute apartheid in South Africa

The African continent's history prior to the arrival of Europeans in the fifteenth century is a topic rarely discussed by Westerners outside the natural sciences and Egyptology circles. It is a well-established fact within the scientific community that humans originated in Africa, with our hominid ancestors evolving over the course of some 4 to 6 million years there, culminating in the emergence of *homo sapiens* approximately 160,000 to 200,000 years ago. The first modern humans left Africa around 50,000 to 60,000 years ago and began the great trek that spread our species throughout the globe. Egypt has been the focus of much popular and academic attention for thousands of years, dating back to the rise of an Egyptian kingdom itself 5,000 years ago. Its monumental pyramids and artistic relics still dazzle both scholar and tourist alike. More recently, Western historians and archeologists have ventured south from Egypt to places such as Sudan,

Ethiopia, Zimbabwe, the Congo, South Africa, and West Africa to research the great African civilizations that flourished for thousands of years before Europeans arrived. These societies were, of course, already known by Africans themselves, but they were largely unknown to non-Africans until recently.

- What images come to mind when you think about what Africa was like prior to the twentieth century?
- What are the sources that inform your ideas about Africa during this period?
- Are they legitimate or fictitious sources?

Try to use this time to take note of the images and sources of those images to fully examine the extent of your knowledge about Africa during this period prior to reading further.

Ancient Africa

Egypt no doubt sets a standard far above any other civilization of its time, creating a definitive Egyptian culture that spans the past five millennia. The Egyptians created solid foundations in art, literature, governance, construction, labor management, and agriculture (with the reliable Nile River Valley as its source) that influenced future civilizations. The Pharaohs (kings) ruled from 2700 BC to 1070 BC during the Old and New Kingdoms, overseeing the development of great structures, such as the famous pyramids and Sphinx at Giza that have symbolized ancient Egypt to the world more than anything else Egyptian. However, the last 2,300 years have largely been dominated by non-Egyptian rulers, resulting in a series of outside cultural influences such as Persian, Greek, and Turkish.

This began with the Persian conquest of Egypt in 343 BC and was later followed by Greek ruler Alexander the Great's conquest of Egypt in 332 BC. Greek civilization flourished within Egypt for 300 years until the fall of Cleopatra VII at the hands of the Romans in 30 BC. Egypt was then under Roman (and Byzantine) control until the Persians took Egypt in 621 AD. This was overturned through a series of battles between recently converted Islamic armies of Arabia (the Rashidun) and the Roman (Byzantine) Empire from 639 to 646, ending in Roman defeat and, as such, the introduction of Arab control and influence.

Since then, Egypt has been largely a Muslim country. In the wake of the Arab conquest, Egypt maintained a degree of autonomy within the caliphate. The Mamluks from Turkey conquered Egypt in 1174 and controlled the country until the Ottoman conquest of 1517, and these two empires signified Turkish dominance of Egyptian political life for six centuries. This would be overturned in the nineteenth century, which also opened the era of European imperialism there.

Portugal opens Africa: The fifteenth century

The Egyptian story sets the stage for understanding the gradual merging of Africa with the rest of the world. Of course, the first humans were Africans to begin with, but the European incursions into Africa beginning in the fifteenth century set in motion events that eventually brought all of the continents together, creating the modern world we know today. The Portuguese prince, Henry the Navigator (1394–1460), initiated the European incursion into Africa in 1415 after leading the effort to take the North African port town of Ceuta, just across the Straits of Gibraltar from the Iberian Peninsula. Just as Columbus attempted eight decades later, Prince Henry was enchanted with the prospects of Portugal's gaining further access to trade with the Orient. The main obstacle to trade was the geographical barrier of Africa itself. It would take until the French engineer Ferdinand de Lesseps finished building the Suez Canal in 1869 that this rather large continent would cease standing in the way of trade between Europe and Asia. In the meantime, finding a route between Europe and Asia proved elusive even though they had developed contacts, which included North Africa, for more than two millennia via the Mediterranean and various overland routes as well. The Portuguese prince saw the value in risking everything to find a sustainable method of transit, and his acquisition of Ceuta began the process. By 1488, the Portuguese were the most experienced sailors in the world, and one of their own, Bartolomeu Dias, became the first European to sail around the Cape of Good Hope.

This established a reliable, albeit dangerous route to Asia (due to the storms on the Cape), which began a period of heavy trading and competition among European states to extend their power through acquiring trading partners abroad and, eventually, colonies. The Portuguese were the main Europeans for the first two centuries as they explored the coasts from Morocco to the Cape and up the east coast of Africa, establishing colonies at Guinea-Bissau, Angola, and Mozambique and trading posts in other places, most notably in the Congo. Diogo Cao found the mouth of the Congo River for Portugal in 1482, which began European exchange with, and often oppression of, the Congo. Christianity always came part and parcel with Iberian (Portuguese and Spanish) colonialism, and the Portuguese contact with the Kingdom of the Kongo was no exception. Quickly after Cao's arrival, the Kongo royalty were baptized Christians. Aside from the introduction and expansion of European religion, the slave trade in particular became central to the Portuguese presence in this region for the next four centuries.

Slavery

Slavery itself was well-entrenched in Africa and the Mediterranean prior to the Portuguese arrival. This history dates back several thousand years to the Greeks and the Romans. Roman slavery is more closely related to modern slavery as they utilized slaves for agricultural production that was linked to international trade. This resulted from the widespread Roman conquests that incorporated tens of millions of new subjects and added more than one million slaves just under Julius Caesar's reign alone. Italy itself had between two and three million slaves.

Slavery as an institution flourished even with the decline of the Roman Empire, especially in North Africa. Sugar production by slaves took off, beginning in the twelfth century, and expanded rapidly in places such as Palestine, Cyprus, and Spain. By the time of Spain's and Portugal's incursions into the Americas in the fifteenth and sixteenth centuries, sugar and slavery were already closely tied. However, slavery was not deeply entrenched as essential to African society during this period, with a few exceptions. There was a trans-Sahara Islamic slave trade with roots dating back to the Islamic invasions of the region in the eighth century. Still most of Africa did not have large slave populations; instead, slaves performed small functions tied to religion, housework, military service, and agriculture. Slaves were essential in the power structure of the Songhay Empire in the Niger River Valley in the fifteenth century, and this region would eventually supply large numbers of slaves to the Americas. While slavery had been present in Africa for hundreds of years before the Portuguese arrival, its character was different. Whereas slavery as a status automatically passed to one's kin under European slavery, this was not the case in Africa, and slaves were not uniformly treated as subhuman.

The Portuguese began trading gold for African slaves to work as servants in Europe in 1444 and continued to do so at a small annual rate of several hundred until colonization of the Americas boosted this trade in the early sixteenth century to several thousand per year. They first did this by purchasing slaves from established Muslim traders on Africa's west coast and then created their own slave trading posts at Sao Tome, an island off the West African coast, and through their support for the King of the Kongo, they were able to secure slave trading rights in the region known as the Congo (today) in the 1560s as well. The Portuguese quickly established a permanent station in Luanda (the future capital of Angola) to the south of the mouth of the Congo, and this city eventually surpassed Sao Tome as the primary slave trading port. Ten to twelve million slaves arrived in the Americas, but up to half of those who were bought and sold in Africa never made it, making the total number of people taken from Africa by force approximately 20 million.

It is obvious that slavery enhanced the wealth of Europeans at the expense of Africans during this period. As European goods were traded in exchange for African slaves, Europeans benefited twice in a situation where only some Africans benefited (those who sold the slaves), and many more not only lost everything but established a pattern of loss that extended from them to their families and descendants both in Africa and in the Americas. Conversely, many people in Europe, Africa, the Caribbean, the U.S. South, and mainland Latin America believed they benefited from industries linked to slavery. This included merchants in Europe, slave traders in Africa, ship captains and employees on the Atlantic, and traders, plantation owners, mine owners, and consumers throughout the Americas. There is an opposing argument that rests on the notion that slavery was not cost-efficient and in fact slowed growth. There are others still who argue that the descendants of African slaves living in the Americas are in fact better off as a result of being brought to the Americas, given the condition of Africa in the past five centuries. This argument seems twisted in a sense because it offers to validate slavery. The abolition of slavery in the Americas in the nineteenth century only brought to an end the institution in the Western Hemisphere, however, and not in Africa, where it rejuvenated as a result of European colonialism, particularly that of the Belgians in the Congo.

Southern Africa

Nearly two centuries after Dias sailed around the Cape of Good Hope, the Dutch began their penetration of southern Africa. The Cape climate resembles much of southern Europe due to its location between thirty and forty-five degrees south of the Equator. As opposed to the rest of Africa, which has both tropical and desert climate, southern Africa has appealed to European settlers for four centuries. The Portuguese, who preceded all other Europeans in exploration, were the first to pass along the African coast southward and find a route around the Cape of Good Hope. Bartholomeu Dias did just that in 1488 and, soon afterward, the Portuguese, Dutch, French, and English were engaged in explorations and eventually conquests and colonization schemes in Asia. Thus, the Cape became the ideal way station between Europe and her Asian colonies. The Dutch in particular wanted a small colony on the Cape of Good Hope to be used to grow vegetables and produce meat to feed sailors and colonists traveling between the Netherlands and the Dutch East Indies. Scurvy was a treacherous cause of much death and incapacitation for sea travelers, and these foods helped to stave off this threat at an apt location. The initial Dutch settlers were mandated by their government in Amsterdam not to disturb or mingle with the native inhabitants, of whom there were many, and to simply set up a post to supply their countrymen with nutrient-rich food.

This task went to Jan van Riebeeck, who settled on the Cape in 1652 along with a hundred other Dutch citizens. Dutch wine producers were the next to arrive in the 1670s, followed by French Huguenots (Protestants who had fled French Catholic repression for the Netherlands) where they received assistance for settlement in the Cape in 1688. Over the next century, the colony prospered, and Asian and European immigration and African slaves increased the population. By 1805, the British had established an official military garrison in the Cape Colony as a result of various European conflicts and to serve as a way station between Britain and India. As the population increased along with tensions between Europeans vying for control over southern Africa, some settlers decided to head further inland to acquire more land and autonomy, which brought them into conflict with African tribes. This voyage came to be known as the "Great Trek."

The first major clashes took place in the 1830s between the Voertrekkers (nomadic farmers largely of Dutch descent) and the Zulu nation, which was created by the famous Shaka Zulu, who died in 1828. The Voertrekkers, whose legend gave rise to the name *Boers*, were a combination of Dutch Calvinists, French Huguenots, and Germans with a long history of migration that held to deeply entrenched traditions and a new language they had created as a result of their shared history, particularly linked to the travails of the so-called Great Trek. On the Zulu side, Shaka had developed an empire that encompassed a vast territory within southern Africa. He also inculcated a martial spirit in his people that participated in a uniquely effective form of warfare with its enemies. The Zulus were experts at using their own terrain to their advantage, but the Voertrekkers had firearms, a technological innovation centuries ahead of the spears and shields used by the Africans. Still, the first engagement with the Zulus in 1838 came with a surprise attack on the Voertrekkers, which killed more than 200 men, women, and children who had no chance to defend themselves. This attack laid the foundation of the Great Trek myth, for the response would demonstrate the Voertrekkers' character.

At the Battle of Blood River in 1838, a few more than 400 armed Voertrekkers defeated a band of more than 10,000 Zulus, killing hundreds of their enemy and suffering little losses. This battle entered the lexicon of Boer history to prove God had chosen the Boers to dominate southern Africa. The trek had been initiated in the 1830s as a result of new British laws that constrained the traditional Boer way of life, namely the abolition of slavery. The Boers living in the Cape Colony depended on slaves to cultivate their farms and, thus, the British laws drove them north to seek their own republic to continue this way of life. The Boers eventually created the Orange Free State and the Transvaal and, between the 1830s and 1870s, they thrived in these two Boer Republics.

By 1877, the British decided to take the Boer republic of the Transvaal with just twenty-five troops who did not fire a shot, thus initiating the British conquest of the Boer republics and Zululand that continued on and off until the conclusion of the so-called Boer Wars in 1902. The purpose was to unite South Africa under the British flag. This was met with considerable resistance from both the Boers and the Zulus. Neither the Boers nor the Zulus were going to simply allow the British to remove their sovereignty. Diamonds had been discovered near the famous De Beers farm in 1868 in the Cape Colony, and the subsequent diamond and gold rush of the 1880s made South Africa all the more valuable. The British also desired complete control over the entire region to ensure a secure coaling station for ships flowing between Europe and India.

The divisions in the Transvaal were too numerous to deal with all at once and, luckily for the British, the Boers supported their efforts in 1879 to crush the Zulus in the Transvaal. However, 20,000 Zulus launched a surprise attack at the infamous battle of Isandlwana that killed 800 British troops. The British soon subdued the Zulus entirely later that year, ending the Anglo-Zulu War, and Zululand was officially annexed into British territory. However, the Boers opposed outright British control of the Transvaal and soon revolted.

The Boer leader of utmost importance was Paul Kruger (1825–1904). In December 1880, he initiated the effort to retake the Transvaal for the Boers by launching an ambush on the British that killed fully one-eighth of all the Empire's troops in South Africa. After more Boer defeats of the British, both sides signed the Convention of Pretoria in August 1881, which gave the Boers virtual autonomy in the Transvaal and ended the First Boer War, also known as the Transvaal War. The Second Boer War of 1899 to 1902 exceeded the brutality of the first by many times.

On the other side of the Anglo-Boer divide was Britain's most important colonial leader in southern Africa, Cecil Rhodes (1853–1902). Originally seeking fortune in mining, he also had a vision of British imperialism in the region. He would be largely responsible for British expansionism over the whole of Southern Africa. The colonies of Northern and Southern Rhodesia were named after him, he was prime minister of the Cape Colony from 1890 to 1896, and he was the president of the De Beers diamond company. It was largely because of his efforts that South Africa eventually fell under complete British dominion, and these efforts led the Boers to revolt as well. The First Boer War was minor by comparison to the second, and the revolt was led by the same man, Paul Kruger, whose guerrilla tactics proved decisive in many battles. However, after a few initial victories beginning in 1899, Kruger's troops were soon routed when British reinforcements arrived and, by 1902, the British had consolidated control over the former Boer republics (Transvaal and Orange Free State). The treaty ending the Second Boer War promised the Boers more autonomy eventually and, by 1910, this was accomplished under the Union of South Africa. By this time, the British controlled Egypt, Sudan, Southern Africa, and much of East and West Africa.

The Union of South Africa granted the colony self-governance, which meant white Afrikaner control over the black, colored (mixed race), and Indian population, which made up 80 percent of South Africa. The government quickly established discriminatory laws based on race that exceeded those under British mandate. These laws were met with stiff resistance by a new organization founded by Pixley Ka Isaka Seme in 1912 called the African National Congress (ANC). This organization was led by mostly well-educated non-whites protesting their marginalization by the white minority, and it eventually became the main organization opposing apartheid from 1948–1994. However, much would happen between 1912 and 1948, namely, the rising influence and increasing radicalism of the conservative and racist Afrikaner Nationalist party.

In the 1920s and 1930s, several future Afrikaner Nationalists studied in Germany under National Socialist (Nazi) teachers and became impressed with Adolf Hitler's ideology, eventually returning to South Africa infused with these values. The leaders of the Afrikaner Nationalists agreed in 1948 that Hitler's segregation of the population into different races would succeed in South Africa. However, unlike the Jews of Europe, the non-whites in South Africa made up a considerable majority of the population; therefore, extermination was not possible (or desirable). Instead, the Afrikaner Nationalists, who came to power in 1948, instituted apartheid, which means "separateness" in Afrikaans. Chapter 6 will address how this all played out through 1994.

Napoleon's legacy in Egypt

Just prior to the British incursions on the Cape, the French Revolution threw a wrench into the international system that cannot be overlooked. Napoleon's invasion of Egypt in 1798 was a watershed event. It was the first time a European power had taken over an African or Middle Eastern country, and although it represented a significant departure in foreign policy terms, it also signified the beginning of wider Africa's and the Middle East's opening to European influence that continues to this day. Napoleon's stated intention was to take power away from the militaristic Mameluke beys controlling Egypt so as to transfer power back to the Sultan of Turkey. By 1801, the French had been expelled by the British, and soon began a French-British rivalry over Egypt that lasted for the next 150 years.

For the first seven decades of the nineteenth century, Egypt proved malleable to European interests, and the Egyptian rulers seemed only too happy to go along. The most important leader (Khedive) of this period was Muhammad Ali (1805–1848), made famous and infamous for both his progressive reforms and his ruthless elimination of political enemies both real and perceived. Following in Napoleon's style, he annexed territory beyond Egypt's traditional boundaries, extending into the Sudan and Syria between 1823 and 1833. When Ali's grandson Ismael took over in 1863, the British and French presence proved to be a bane and a benefit to varying degrees. On the one hand, the two European powers sponsored the Suez Canal project run by Ferdinand de Lesseps in 1867 that finally linked the Indian Ocean to the Mediterranean. On the other hand, the Khedive was totally dependent upon European financing to run his country and, in particular, French and English bondholders held a tremendous share of power over his future. Eventually, Ismael's overspending earned him the wrath of these bondholders, and the two governments conspired to have him replaced by his son, Tewfik, in 1880. It was this sort of imperialist meddling that led to a nationalist coup seeking autonomy from European and Turkish control. The

British responded with brute force and crushed the rebellion in two days, restoring Tewfik to power.

The British and French would continue to hold ultimate power of the affairs of the Egyptian state due to its economic and strategic interests ultimately tied to the Suez Canal. Another coup in 1952, that of the future President, Gamal Abdul Nasser (1952–1970), against the interests of these two would prove just how far the merits of imperialism as a method of international relations had sunk. By the time of the 1952 Revolution, Egyptians had endured nearly two-and-a-half millennia of outside rule emanating from a wide variety of sources. Therefore, Egypt's national identity has been the source of much negotiation and conflict throughout its history and in particular during the political changes occurring during the Arab Spring since 2011.

Not Egypt: Sudan

Much of the Sudan had been annexed by Muhammad Ali in 1823 when he founded the modern capital of Khartoum, and this gain was later consolidated under his grandson, Ismael. However, the Sudanese proved difficult to bring completely under control given their distance from Cairo, which was where British and Egyptian authorities collaborated to control Khartoum. In 1885, Islamists bent on overthrowing this authority took up arms and initiated a rebellion that lasted until 1899, when the British and Egyptian armies finally crushed it. The story itself is the stuff of legends, not only because of the scale of the battles that led to tens of thousands of deaths but also due to the power of the Sudanese rebels to defeat the British at times. The first battles took place in 1885 when British reinforcements failed to reach a garrison in Khartoum under the famous commander there by the name of General Charles George Gordon. The rebels were led by Muhammad Ahmad (the Mahdi leader) who aimed to expel the non-Muslims from both Sudan and Egypt as part of a larger holy war. After capturing and decapitating General Gordon, the Ahmad instituted sharia law and died of typhus shortly thereafter in 1885.

His successor, Abdullah Ibn Mohammad (1885–1899), carried on the fight under the title of Khalifa, and the British resumed their counterinsurgency in 1896. This time, the joint British-Egyptian military effort had the benefit of significant planning, which paid off handsomely when they confronted the rebel forces between 1896 and 1899. The most important battle took place at the Khalifa's capital in Omdurman in 1898. The British used heavy machine guns to their advantage against ancient weaponry possessed by the rebels, ending with 10,000 dead on the Khalifa's side to forty-seven dead on the British-Egyptian side. The Khalifa himself was deposed finally in the following year, which solidified British rule over Sudan until independence in 1956.

The Berlin Conference, 1884–1885

A somewhat different form of imperialism led to the so-called Scramble for Africa that created literal European colonies in Africa, as opposed to the type of control exercised by the French and the British in Egypt. The series of meetings between November 1884 and February 1885 that came to be known as the Berlin Conference (but were called the West Africa Conference at the time) have considerable symbolic importance. It was not the event that officially decided the boundaries of the European colonies in Africa that many still believe, but it was where the major European colonial powers—France, Britain, Germany, and the newcomer Belgium (and some others such as the United States and the Ottoman Empire)—finally came together on diplomatic terms. The reason why this conference has been overstated in importance is perhaps for the purposes of simplification in history books. It would be much more difficult to explain what actually happened in a matter of sentences because it inevitably must include the decades of European-backed explorations of lakes, rivers, and other territories and the trade treaties established during this period, not to mention the myriad African kingdoms they contended with, the strange role of the Boers in South Africa, and many other factors. Therefore, the conference serves the purpose of summarizing the intentions of European colonialists during this era, but it does not encompass the actual history beyond that fact.

For years prior, competition between Britain and France had reached a fever pitch, but lately, Germany and Belgium, with their headstrong leaders Otto von Bismarck and King Leopold II, sought to expand their own nation's power through the acquisition of colonies as well, and France and Britain had little choice but to accept this. The host of the conference, Bismarck was playing a game in which he saw acquiring colonies in Africa as a means of expanding Germany's strength in relation to France and Britain. 1883 and 1884 witnessed key events in the Scramble for Africa, as Germany sought colonies that lay within the British sphere of influence mainly as a way of demonstrating their defiance of British presumed supremacy. Bismarck deliberately sent out emissaries in the early 1880s to West, South, and East Africa to wedge themselves into the British dominion, to which the British responded with equal parts conciliation and determination. For example, the Germans sought to solidify their dominance of Southwest Africa in 1884, which the British allowed, but then the British sent 4,000 troops to secure Bechuanaland (modern Botswana) on Southwest Africa's eastern border as a means of minimizing any future possibility of German encroachment on British control over Southern Africa.

The single person most involved in paving the way toward recognition of his colonial rights in Africa was King Leopold II. Henry Morton Stanley's five years of work in the Congo had secured him the rights to the territories of 450 tribal zones, and his emissaries secured official recognition of Leopold's rights to the Congo from most of the important players of that age: the United

States, Britain, France, and Germany. The French had carved out the largest amount of territory, mostly in West and North Africa, with the British perhaps in equal parts in all four of the cardinal directions and Germany in all but the north. Thus, this conference served as a jumping off point for entrenching European rule over Africa. The continent has not been the same since.

West Africa

Until the 1880s, British involvement in West Africa was tentative and informal. The Oil Rivers region, as much of Nigeria was known, offered a lucrative trade in palm oil in particular, which was used as an industrial lubricant and for soap products, but the competition was fierce. Not only the British but the French, the Germans, and Africans themselves were formidable opponents in this area. The British colonial official Edward Hewett argued in 1883 for the British to transition from unofficial or informal imperialism in West Africa to the acquisition of actual colonies between Sierra Leone in the northwest all the way to the Congo. The purpose behind this was twofold: (1) to seal the French out of West Africa and (2) to enable the British to have a legal justification for utilizing the military to enforce a British monopoly on trade in the region. Prior to this, the British military had used force numerous times against helpless villages and armed opponents, often leaving many dead and destitute—all for the defense of British companies.

The British thought they were in luck, as two Cameroon kings named Acqua and Bell had openly requested British annexation and received a visit by an impressed Hewett in 1883. Hewett assumed that if anyone were to challenge Britain's aspirations there, it would be the French, whose famous explorer de Brazza might snatch up Cameroon for France. However, the German Chancellor Otto von Bismarck also entered the fray in 1883 by pursuing control over Cameroon, Togo, and Southwest Africa to establish German imperialism in Africa. The Germans succeeded in all three cases and in Ruanda-Urundi and Tanganyika as a result of the Berlin Conference of 1884–1885, only to lose all of them after WWI. In the end, the British did gain and consolidate imperial control over the Oil Rivers (Nigeria) and the Gold Coast (Ghana), Sierra Leone, and Gambia, while the French acquired Senegal, French West Africa (Mauritania, Mali, Niger, Benin, Burkina Faso, and the Ivory Coast), and French Equatorial Africa (Gabon, Chad, Central African Republic, the Republic of Congo).

East Africa

Zanzibar is an island off the east coast of Africa that long dominated the slave trade under the Sultan of Zanzibar. The British anti-slavery crusade began before the abolition of slavery in the Empire in 1834 and extended to patrols in East Africa that threatened the Sultan's reliance on slave labor. The Sultan's slaves produced cloves, the main source of income in his empire, which included both the island and some of mainland East Africa (parts of Uganda, Tanzania, and Kenya). The British had held considerable sway for several decades prior to their final demand on Sultan Sayid Barghash-bin-Sayid in 1873 to end the slave trade once and for all. Barghash's acquiescence signified more British influence in the region, but both the French and the Germans also represented challenges, which caused the British government to lean toward a complete takeover of the Sultan's territory from 1884 to 1885. In 1885, the German government announced it was casting a protectorate over part of Barghash's mainland territory. By 1886, the Sultan had lost most of his land as a result of a German-British agreement to divide his lands with the former in the south and the latter in the north but including further lands as far west as Lake Victoria. This paved the way toward British control over Kenya and Uganda and German control over Tanganyika and Ruanda-Urundi.

The Belgian spear of civilization

Belgium is a colony the size of the U.S. state of West Virginia or a little more than twice the size of El Salvador, which is the smallest country in mainland Latin America. By comparison to its European neighbors, Belgium felt rather weak and isolated, but this was acceptable to most Belgians in the 1880s. King Leopold II (1865–1909) desired greatness beyond his predecessors, and he knew the expansion of the country's power was in imperialism, as it had been for the other powerful European states. The difficulty was in finding a justification for a sudden costly venture into the unknown. It could not be simply for profit or glory in this post-Enlightenment era of progressivism. Imperialism in the guise of morality would do the job.

African slavery was gradually abolished in the Americas between 1807 and 1888 as a moral cause led mostly by liberal Europeans, Latin Americans, and U.S. citizens but, to the chagrin of many in Europe, it had continued in Africa under the tutelage of Islamic slave traders. The arrival and expansion of the steamboat and the railroad in the nineteenth century made transportation costs less expensive as well, reducing the economic utility of slave labor. The steamboat in particular made exploration into unchartered territory less expensive and most feasible. Science also helped the explorers travel through Africa with less fear of death from tropical diseases, a major deterrent to exploration prior to the discovery of quinine, which prevented (and prevents) malaria.

The greatest friend to Africa among Europeans was the English explorer and doctor David Livingstone. He was considered a gentleman explorer who respected and even loved the native inhabitants more so than his European counterparts. Livingstone made great discoveries in Africa, mostly of rivers and lakes, between 1849 and 1871 before dying in 1873. Africa's beauty and diversity of cultures and environment captivated him as it has so many others throughout history, but he also found that slavery had grown rampant there under the control of Africans themselves, and he sought to expose this scourge to the world to bring it to an end with the help of "civilization," which for him meant, primarily, Christianity.

In 1876, Verney Cameron, a member of Livingstone's crew, stated to the Royal Geographical Society (the premier exploration and scientific organization on the planet at the time) that in his travels across Africa, the continent was full of "unspeakable riches" just ripe for European plucking. This statement caught the attention of the Belgian king, who invited several of the world's most famous explorers to Brussels that year for a conference to discuss the contemporary state of knowledge on Africa. The conference whetted Leopold's appetite for acquiring an African colony, and he would soon have it.

Unlike Livingstone, although a close friend of his nonetheless, the U.S. journalist-turned-explorer Henry Morton Stanley did not share the doctor's appreciation for Africa on a personal level. Stanley ended up becoming the most famous explorer of Africa for his exploits that shattered Livingstone's. His first expedition to Africa was to find Livingstone after the doctor had vanished from the world scene for a number of years. Stanley's famous remark upon finding the elderly Livingstone in 1871 remains etched into the lore of discovery: "Doctor Livingstone, I presume?" Stanley was an explorer by trade, not for emotional or spiritual reasons such as those of Livingstone, and his behavior with the Africans soon earned him the nickname "Breaker of Rocks," for not only was he a stern leader who rarely failed to succeed despite the great physical and mental obstacles, but he routinely used force over his own men as well as the natives. Not only are there numerous eyewitness accounts of his abuses but Stanley himself admitted to carrying out a massacre of thirty-seven villagers after a harmless affront on at least one occasion.

From 1874 to 1877, Stanley undertook one of the boldest explorations yet, traveling from Zanzibar on the east coast to the mouth of the Congo on the east coast, even circumnavigating Lake Victoria on the way. It proved difficult due to disease, attacks by natives, and the vegetation. At the same time, the famous French explorer Pierre Savorghan de Brazza was exploring the Ogowe River, which branches west from the Congo River. De Brazza was known for his respect for the Africans, and he and Stanley were competitors in the power game taking place in Europe.

It was Stanley who made the headlines after his 1877 success in reaching the mouth of the Congo after 999 days and nearly 7,100 miles, which nearly killed him several times. Upon hearing of this, Leopold met with Stanley in 1878, and Stanley signed a five-year contract in which he agreed to bring the Congo under Belgian control. This was to take place behind the façade of the International African Association, an organization essentially under Leopold's control but with the appearance of an African aid organization. By the end of Stanley's five years in the Congo, he had convinced 450 tribal chieftains to sign away their sovereignty to the Belgian king, who soon became the owner of what was called "the Congo Free State." Leopold's initial desire was to use the Congo for acquiring ivory, but with the rise of bicycle and automobile sales and electricity lines that required rubber, both resources became highly lucrative. In 1890, rubber exports from the Congo stood at 100 tons and, in 1901, they hit 6,000 tons.

The Belgian authorities spared no violence in enforcing the rubber quotas set for each village across the Congo. The hated and feared *Force Publique* was staffed with white officers and black soldiers (a common practice across Africa during the colonial period) who would destroy entire villages, pillage communities of their food and water, kill and maim at will and, especially, sever the limbs of those who did not come through with the amount of rubber Leopold demanded to increase his wealth. The barbarity witnessed in the Belgian Congo elicited the rise of the first human rights campaign in African history, mostly led by journalists and missionaries who produced extensive photographic and testimonial evidence of Belgian misdeeds to the point where international pressure clamped down on Leopold so thoroughly that the Belgian parliament took control over the colony itself in 1908. It was no longer his sole possession, but it would become the possession of the Belgian government, which allowed private companies to exploit its diamond, gold, rubber, and uranium resources, to name a few, while maintaining a draconian dictatorship over the Congolese peoples. When the independence movement came about in the 1950s, the Congo had no preparation to become a unified country, a topic to which we return in Chapters Six and Nine.

German imperialism in Africa: Short-lived, long felt

Chancellor Otto von Bismarck played an important yet confusing role in Europe's Scramble for Africa. He is known as the host of the Berlin Conference of 1884 to 1885 that carved Africa into its respective colonies, yet he had claimed to despise the thought of German colonialism, especially in Africa. That is, until 1884, when he sent out emissaries to secure trading and protectorate rights in West, East, and Southwest Africa. Germany's moves in Africa that year accelerated the already heated race to take over Africa by France, Britain, and Belgium. France and Britain were the two main states openly competing for access to Africa's riches (Belgium was doing so behind the scenes so as to seize the Congo out from the beneath the French and the British), yet Germany was the most powerful economic and military power in Europe, and its incursions into Africa illustrated to France and Britain just how quickly they would need to move to gain and preserve their piece of the pie. This mad dash among these three would ultimately increase the stakes on the global stage as well, for when WWI broke out in 1914, European wealth in Africa made each state that much more powerful and, as a result, more coveted by the others.

Germany's loss in that war would mean the end of a short, three-decade imperialist venture in Africa that had left countless dead, chief among them the Nama and Herero of Southwest Africa. The future country of Namibia did not possess much wealth in the 1890s when the German war against its native peoples began. Germany wanted its land primarily for its livestock potential. Rebellion broke out in 1893 when a Nama chief named Hendrick Witbooi (at age sixty-six) took up arms against the German authorities as part of a wider campaign to control the entire territory. German Southwest Africa was made up of a number of tribes that had mixed over the years as a result of Bantu migrations from the north (the Bantu Migrations had populated much of West, Central, East, and Southern Africa over the course of more than 1,000 years) and migrations from the south by Khoisan bushmen, leaving the ever-increasing encroachment of white settlers orchestrating the takeover of the future state of South Africa.

The ethnic differences present in the German colony worked to Germany's advantage. Some natives had even been educated by German missionaries and were pro-Western in outlook, whereas others looked to the Germans to fight their own domestic enemies. Despite Witboois' lively and sometimes successful guerrilla warfare against the Germans, he was initially defeated in 1894 by Governor Theodor Leutwein's field commanders. However, this victory would prove only the beginning of a fourteen-year war that eventually included both the Nama and the Herero, the latter of which were much larger in population. The opportunity for division seemed to come with the rise to power of a pro-West, Christian-educated Herero chief named Samuel Maharero, whom the Germans felt they could count on for support against his rival Nikodemus. The latter was shot in 1896 for leading a Herero revolt against the Germans, who had both Maharero and Witbooi on their side. However, these two eventually rose against the Germans after Leutwein began taking large parcels of native lands as a punishment for their revolts. By 1904, Maharero took up arms to lead a colony-wide revolt. Initial attacks resulted in great victories for the Herero, including the acquisition of most of the colony's farm animals.

However, on August 13, 1904, at a place called Omaheke, the German General Lothar von Trotha scored a decisive victory for German colonialism when he surrounded a Herero settlement and guerrilla contingent and ordered its destruction. His order was to kill every man there, which was carried out, and the women and children taken as prisoners were also subject to rape, beatings, and murder. The Herero who escaped the massacre at Omeheke (untold hundreds or more were killed) were also subject to death from thirst and starvation and toxicity due to von Trotha's order to poison all water holes in the area.

On October 1, 1904, von Trotha issued his "Extermination Order" to the Herero people, which explained that they were no longer allowed to live in the colony upon pain of death. This eventually led to an expanded war against the Nama and the Herero ending in 1907, which left the majority of these two tribes dead or displaced. By 1919, the end of WWI left Germany without colonies and, as a result, Britain gained control over Southwest Africa, which was then taken over by South Africa upon its independence in 1948. Southwest Africa became Namibia upon its independence from South

Africa in 1980. In addition, the Germans established colonies in Ruanda-Urundi (Rwanda and Burundi) and Tanganyika (Tanzania), which they were forced to abandon after WWI to the Belgians and the English respectively.

French Africa

The French presence was mostly felt in North, Central, and West Africa, with Algeria standing out as the most important. Algeria's role in the French Empire stemmed initially from its proximity to France, just across the Mediterranean, which also made it a strategic location. Louis XIV sent troops to retrieve captives from Barbary pirates there in 1684, and there was fighting there during the Napoleonic Wars. The French began their conquest of Algeria in 1830 and continued to battle rebellious elements throughout the colony during their occupation until forced out by the Algerian Revolution in 1962. Like all of its non-African colonies, the French considered its colonies in Africa as states within the French nation, thus making it very difficult for the French to conceive of letting them go during upheavals. The endurance of dozens of French colonies as of this writing, largely in the Caribbean, South America, and the Pacific, illustrates this well. Other regions such as Senegal, Mali, Niger, the Ivory Coast, and the Republic of Congo (Brazzaville) were conquered gradually as French merchant interests expanded in West and Central Africa between the 1840s and 1880s.

One man in particular deserves French accolades for his work in exploring Africa for France in a manner similar to Henry Morton Stanley's work for King Leopold II. His name was Pietro Paolo Savorgnan di Brazza (1852–1905), of Italian origin but French by choice. Known for his kinder treatment and general respect for the Africans, di Brazza competed with Henry Morton Stanley for access to the Congo and, to this day, his name is memorialized in the name of the capital of the Republic of Congo, Brazzaville, which resides on the side of the Congo River opposite from the capital of the Democratic Republic of Congo, Kinshasa (which was Leopoldville until Independence in 1960). Di Brazza, later named De Brazza, explored the Congo River region between 1875 and 1882 for the French, ending in his crowning achievement, coaxing chief Makoko into agreeing to French protection over his realm on the Congo River. French rule was deemed less brutal in general than that of the Belgians, who instituted a slave state in the Congo Free State and divided the Tutsis and Hutus into separate spheres in Ruanda-Urundi. The Belgian actions led not only to impoverishment but to genocidal wars, the effects of which are felt as of this writing. The French, conversely, were certainly exploitative economically, but were also less violent and cultivated a sense of Francophone cultural pride within its African colonies, which is not witnessed to the same degree in the non-French African colonies. This becomes apparent in the Cold War and post–Cold War era, when observers can see France competing for influence in Africa with the United States, England, and the Anglophone African countries of East and Central Africa.

Discussion questions

1   Which region of Africa stands out as the most compelling as an area of study for you? Explain with details, comparing your chosen region to the others.
2   Do you consider European colonialism in Africa to be more positive than negative? Elaborate with examples.
3   Which continent was affected more profoundly by European contact: Africa, Asia, or Latin America? Provide details to explain your answer.
4   What factors explain Europe's conquest of Africa? Consider the elements discussed above and your own interpretations from outside this book.

Historical figures

Pierre di Brazza (1852–1905)

Known as Henry Morton Stanley's rival explorer, this Italian Frenchman was also considered Stanley's moral superior for his better treatment of the Africans during his exploits. Di Brazza was France's principal explorer responsible for assisting the French in its acquisition of large swathes of central Africa, including the country whose capital is named after him (Republic of Congo).

Shaka Zulu (1787–1828)

Although he never led his men into battle against Europeans, he is most well known for his successors' combat with the Boers who entered Zulu territory in the 1830s. After his death, Shaka unified the tribes of southern Africa under a martial spirit that remains within millions of southern Africans to this day. It was Shaka's military and political genius that set his legacy in stone. Zulu attacks on Europeans have gone down in military history as legendary, whether successful or not. The attack on the Voertrekkers at Blood River in 1838 and on the English military at Isandlwana in 1879 are the two most infamous Zulu successes, known for their efficiency and ruthlessness in eliminating their victims with utter surprise.

King Leopold II (1835–1909)

His name is synonymous with "The Scramble for Africa" more than any other European ruler for both his behind-the-scenes rallying of interests to secure the Congo for Belgium and for the revealed brutality that resulted in his ownership of the colony upon which he never set foot, the Congo Free State (1885–1908). King Leopold II is still a hero in Belgian history for elevating Belgium's status into the ranks of the other European imperial states, whereas he is considered a villain not only to the Congolese but to outsiders concerned with human rights history and the effects of European colonialism in Africa in general.

Cecil Rhodes (1853–1902)

Perhaps the most well-known European imperialist in Africa, Cecil Rhodes arrived in South Africa at the age of eighteen on the cusp of the mining boom and later became the governor of the Cape Colony and the president of the De Beers diamond company. His failed Cape-to-Cairo railway plan exemplified his ambition to bring most of Africa under British influence, and although this was not completed, he was responsible for conquering most of southern Africa beyond the Cape colony at the turn of the century, and the country of Rhodesia bore his name until 1980, when it became Zimbabwe.

Muhammad Ali Pasha (1769–1847)

Considered the founding father of modern Egypt, this former Ottoman officer of Albanian origin shook the Ottoman Empire to its core by taking over both Egypt and Sudan beginning in 1805. He oversaw a series of reforms that extricated Egypt from Turkish control and established autonomy for Egyptians and Sudanese while paving the way toward French and English imperialism there. His successors ruled until the 1952 Revolution led by Gamal Abdul Nasser.

Henry Morton Stanley (1841–1904)

The greatest explorer of Africa, his name became synonymous with European imperialism for his assistance to King Leopold II in the Belgian king's conquest of the Congo. Stanley first made his name as the man who found Dr. David Livingstone, a famous explorer in his own right and medical doctor who lived in Africa most of his life. Unlike Livingstone, Stanley developed a reputation for cruelty in his quest to make African geographical discoveries for his own personal glory and profit, the result of his benefactors in Europe, and his book sales and speaking fees. The nickname "Breaker of Rocks" was given to him by the Africans who knew his temperament in the face of both physical obstacles and the native peoples who opposed him.

Emperor Haile Selassie (1892–1975)

This Ethiopian monarch ruled from 1930 to 1974 and came to symbolize two contrasting elements of Africa to the world. Selassie first became admired by Westerners and Africans for his resistance to the Italian invasion of 1935 to 1936. He established long-lasting cultural, business, and political ties to the United States in particular. In addition, he is considered to be a deity incarnate to Rastafarians.

Further readings

Cocker, Mark. *Rivers of Blood, Rivers of Gold: Europe's Conquest of Indigenous Peoples.* New York: Grove, 1998.

Farwell, Byron. *The Great Anglo-Boer War.* New York: Norton, 1990.

Hochschild, Adam. *King Leopold's Ghost: A Story of Greed, Terror, and Heroism in Colonial Africa.* Boston, MA: Mariner, 1999.

Klein, Herbert. *African Slavery in Latin America and the Caribbean.* New York: Oxford, 1986.

Lapierre, Dominique. *A Rainbow in the Night: The Tumultuous Birth of South Africa.* Cambridge, MA: Da Capo, 1999.

Pakenham, Thomas. *The Scramble for Africa, 1876–1912.* London: Abacus, 1991.

Rediker, Marcus. *The Slave Ship: A Human History.* New York: Penguin, 2007.

Films

Lost Kingdoms of Africa. Dir. Sarah Howitt, Ian Lilley, and Mark Bates. BBC, 2010.

Shaka Zulu (1987 Television Series). Dir. William C. Faure. A & E, 2012.

Roots, Episode 1 (Television Series). Dir. David Greene, Marvin J. Chomsky, John Erman, and Gilbert Moses. Warner, 2011.

Guns, Germs, and Steel, part 3. Dir. Cassian Harrison and Tim Lambert. National Geographic, 2005.

Congo: White King, Red Rubber, Black Death. Dir. Peter Bate. Art Mattan, 2006.

King Leopold's Ghost. Dir. Pippa Scott and Oreet Rees. Linden, 2006.

Zulu. Dir. Cy Enfield. Studio Canal, 2000.

Breaker Morant. Dir. Bruce Beresford. Image, 2008.

Online content

Africa Federation: www.africafederation.net

The Voertrekkers: www.voortrekker-history.co.za/

The British Museum: Ancient Egypt: www.ancientegypt.co.uk/menu.html

Zimbabwe National Geographic: travel.nationalgeographic.com/travel/countries/zimbabwe-guide/

East African Slave Trade, BBC: www.bbc.co.uk/worldservice/africa/features/storyofafrica/9chapter3.shtml

TED talk: Human Origins in Africa:
   1. www.ted.com/talks/zeresenay_alemseged_looks_for_humanity_s_roots.html
   2. www.ted.com/talks/louise_leakey_digs_for_humanity_s_origins.html
   3. www.ted.com/talks/spencer_wells_is_building_a_family_tree_for_all_humanity.html

Royal Museum for Central Africa (Belgium): www.africamuseum.be/collections

National Museum of African Art (Smithsonian): http://africa.si.edu/

Museum of the African Diaspora (MoAD): www.moadsf.org/

Museum Africa: www.museumafrica.org/

Discovery Channel: 7 Part Series on Africa: http://dsc.discovery.com/tv-shows/africa/episodes/episodes.htm

Part II
Nationalism

4 Latin America and the Caribbean (1898–1992)

Timeline

1898	Cuban Independence achieved
1903	U.S. secures rights to build Panama Canal
1910–1920	The Mexican Revolution
1912–1933	Marine Occupation of Nicaragua
1932	La Matanza (massacre of 10,000–30,000) in El Salvador
1948–1958	La Violencia (Era of Violence) in Colombia
1954	CIA overthrows Guatemalan president Jacobo Arbenz
1959	Cuban Revolution triumphs
1962	Cuban Missile Crisis
1965	U.S. invasion of the Dominican Republic
1967	Che Guevara killed in Bolivia
1973	Salvador Allende overthrown in Chile
1973–1985	"Dirty Wars" in Brazil, Argentina, Chile, Uruguay, Paraguay
1979	Nicaraguan Revolution triumphs
1989	Caracazo in Venezuela
1992	Salvadoran Civil War ends

Beginning with Cuban Independence, this chapter will follow the theme of "the struggle for nationalism" by examining the rivalries that shaped politics and society over most of the twentieth century. The revolutionary movements in Mexico, Central America, Bolivia, Cuba, Chile, Colombia, and Peru form a major part of this chapter, as will the many U.S. interventions and the various U.S.-backed governments that aimed to shape political and economic life during the century. The century also witnessed dramatic changes in the economy, which will also play a large role in this chapter. The culmination will deal primarily with the economic crisis of the 1980s, U.S. interventions and revolutions in Central America and Peru (civil wars in El Salvador and Peru end in 1992), and the impact of the end of the Cold War.

Before we start, let's see what we think we know about Latin America in this era:

1   What concrete ideas, examples, and images come to mind when you think of Latin America in the twentieth century?
2   What are the sources of these? How did they get into your head?
3   Do you trust the legitimacy of these sources?
4   Thinking psychologically, why do you maintain these ideas, examples, and images in your mind? Do you benefit from them in any way?

We return to the preceding types of questions in every chapter for a very simple reason, which is to become ever more mindful of the way our preconceived notions can shape our views of new historical material. If certain events damage one's view of his or her country, ethnicity, region, and so on, how does that person think about those events differently than someone else? Is it possible that two people viewing the same event will develop entirely different memories of that event? I think we can all agree that this happens all the time.

If we apply this perspective to Latin America in the twentieth century we can see how important the struggle for nationalism becomes. All Latin American and most Caribbean countries (some are so small in population as to barely reach the size of a small town) experienced upheaval on a grand scale due to nationalistic conflicts over the future direction of the country. Though Independence movements that took place in the nineteenth century engulfed entire countries, it was not until the twentieth century that *nationalism* took hold broadly. This can be seen in the politics, economics, and culture of each country and, unfortunately for the reader, all of these elements were always intertwined, making it impossible to make simple cause-and-effect assumptions.

Political economy

Latin America followed an export-led growth economic model from 1850 to 1930. This brought both modernization and an ever-increasing disparity of wealth between the upper and lower classes. Examples of the backlash against this are the Mexican Revolution (1910–1920), the Salvadoran Communist uprising (1932), and widespread labor unrest throughout the region. The Great Depression of the 1930s caused economists to abandon this nineteenth-century liberal positivist principle of growth because terms of trade for primary products had fallen to an all-time low. This caused Latin American economists to theorize that the long years of export-led growth had made Latin America dependent on the industrialized world to the detriment of Latin American economic development. Import substitution industrialization (ISI) was the new economic model. This involved a protectionist approach to industrialization, which, in theory, aimed to benefit the masses.

ISI itself had two phases. The first phase began with the rise of economic nationalism in the 1930s and 1940s and continued through the 1960s as a means toward economic independence. The second phase began in the 1960s with a tremendous increase in industrialization and exports and actually led to the neo-liberalism (also referred to as "free trade" and "globalization") that has become so contentious since the 1980s and 1990s. The initial phase of ISI consolidation involved the nationalization of many businesses to produce goods and services for the public and to reduce imports to a minimum, with the benefits supposedly going to the public. Examples of this are Brazil's and Mexico's nationalization of the oil industries. This phase had mixed results, with booms in economic growth and the expansion of industrial infrastructure, yet without the balance of export-led growth to supplement inward-looking development.

The second phase of ISI that began in the 1960s was dedicated to the manufacture of durable goods. This required enormous increases of foreign loans, which were predicated on the assumption that growth would continue. However, the protective nature of ISI-facilitated corruption, inefficiency, and gross mismanagement of funds, which, when combined with hundreds of billions of dollars of foreign loans, caused the debt crisis of the 1980s. In addition, the interest rates were low in the 1970s, and commodity prices were high, motivating Latin American nations to borrow heavily against a backdrop of promising returns for lenders and borrowers alike. However, when interest rates became high and commodity prices dropped in the early 1980s, debt servicing became burdensome to the point that, when combined with the foregoing problems, an enormous debt crisis resulted. Mexico's default in 1982 ignited the flame that spread across Latin America, revealing debt problems in most other nations.

Soon, the International Monetary Fund and the World Bank restructured Latin America's debt, which involved the rapid reduction of public spending, value-added taxes (VAT), inflation, and privatization. Privatization is perhaps the most important factor for the implementation of neo-liberalist policies. Subsequently, the 1980s warranted the label of the "Lost Decade" for the tremendous drop in growth rates from the level of the 1970s. Therefore, when the term *free trade* came to be used frequently to describe the future of economic growth in the 1980s and 1990s, it must be understood that this came about as a result of the destruction of ISI. Still debated is the extent to which the fault of this destruction can be laid on ISI itself, but economists almost universally view that model as defunct due to its fundamental problems. Regardless, when North American Free Trade Agreement (NAFTA) was signed in 1991 the future seemed tied to eliminating trade barriers in favor of European Union-style economic integration, which when applied to Latin America and the Caribbean present a whole new host of challenges, which will be discussed later.

With this backdrop of political and economic forces at work, let us look at some individual country histories.

Cuba

After Cuban Independence, the United States established itself as protectorate over the island through a series of actions. The Platt Amendment of 1901 stood out as most important among these, which gave the United States the right to intervene in Cuban affairs at will. Although it could be argued that the United States used the right sparingly, most Cubans resented U.S. authority there. U.S. business interests were higher on a per capita basis in Cuba than in all other Latin American countries by the time Fidel Castro took power in 1959. The U.S. hand was seen in coffee, sugar, oil, nickel, and tourism, with the last being the sorest spot for 1950s revolutionaries due to the Mafia's role in controlling gambling, prostitution, and hotels.

As was common throughout twentieth-century Latin America, the United States supported a series of Cuban dictators and provided some of the essentials for public works, including education and medical facilities. However, it was U.S. support for Fulgencio Batista that Cubans remember with the most hostility. Batista had taken power briefly in 1933, only to hand it over quickly, and he remained influential behind the scenes until taking power in a coup in 1952. He made deals with Mafia bosses such as Santos Traficante and Meyer Lanske to run the casinos in Cuba, and they in turn gave him millions of dollars in tribute. The U.S. government provided him with military assistance that he used unsparingly against Cuban dissidents.

On July 26, 1953, a young lawyer named Fidel Castro led the failed raid on the Moncada Barracks in Santiago de Cuba. After serving less than two years in prison, Castro rebuilt his army in Mexico with the assistance of the future revolutionary icon, the Argentine physician Ernesto "Che" Guevara. From Mexico, the Castros, Guevara, and eighty others set sail for Cuba in late November 1956. Over the next two years, they slowly built the revolution into a grass-roots movement that eventually engulfed the island and caused Batista to depart on December 31, 1958.

The Cuban Revolution is the most important event to take place in Latin America during the twentieth century for a multitude of reasons. It represented a successful revolution on the doorstep of the United States against a U.S.-backed ally who defended U.S. economic interests that were also threatened by the revolutionaries. It also represented a direct threat to the future of U.S. influence in the hemisphere due to the example Castro set for other revolutionaries. It also eventually became a Soviet ally, which represented a threat to U.S. national security, especially during the Cuban Missile Crisis of 1962. However, that security threat was highly exaggerated during most of the Cold War, as direct Cuban threats against the United States outside those thirteen days are nonexistent. The death toll from Castro's "revolutionary justice" is unknown due to the government's refusal to cooperate with independent and international observers. Credible estimates range between 700 and 7,500. However, Batista has been cited generally as killing upward of 20,000 or more, and the numbers for the U.S.-backed

Figure 4.1 Fidel Castro (1926–) (Nik Wheeler/Alamy)

dictatorships in Guatemala, Haiti, the Dominican Republic, El Salvador, and Nicaragua far exceed Castro's.

Aside from the deaths, Cuban families have suffered tremendously from the cataclysm of the Revolution. It has meant a five-decades-old wedge between those living in the United States (primarily in Miami) and Cuba. Families in many cases have been permanently divided, shattered by the uncompromising nature of Castro's policies and those of the United States toward Cuba. In Cuba itself, the U.S. embargo imposed since 1961 has meant vastly diminished access to consumer goods, which increased Cuba's dependency on the Communist Bloc countries during the Cold War. Freedoms have been severely limited in Cuba despite the benefits of universal health care, employment, and education. In fact, those three are often not considered much of a benefit to people who can only aspire to the bare minimum. However, culturally speaking, Cuba has flourished with the assistance of the Cuban state. Art, music, dance, poetry, and literature all receive ample governmental support. However, the freedom of expression has been limited, and this diminishes the overall positive effect of cultural innovations.

A discussion of Cuba cannot leave out the most dangerous moment in human history: the Cuban Missile Crisis. Because the United States had sponsored the Bay of Pigs invasion in April of 1961 and other acts aimed at overthrowing and assassinating Castro, the Cuban leader agreed to allow Soviet nuclear-tipped intercontinental missiles to be stationed on the island. In October 1962 the United States discovered the weapons and demanded their removal and, after several days of negotiating, the Russians agreed to

Figure 4.2 Ernesto "Che" Guevara (1928–1967) (Salas Archive Photos/Alamy)

do so with several conditions, without consulting the Cubans. This case demonstrates both the increasing level of Cuba's power on the global stage and its limitations.

Throughout the Cold War, Castro would maintain a balance between allegiance to the Communist Bloc countries and Cuban autonomy. In fact, his military and humanitarian ventures in Africa (tens of thousands of health professionals were sent there and hundreds of thousands of troops) were largely of his own initiative independent of the Soviets. By 1991, the Soviet Union had dissolved, and Cuba was left without their billions of dollars in annual support, forced to completely restructure their economy and military.

Haiti

The slave rebellion that brought about Haitian Independence gained Haiti little benefit aside from the end of slavery and outright French dominion, for a country benefits from sovereignty only to the extent that it can control its own destiny. Ever since 1804, Haiti has suffered despotism, foreign intervention, environmental devastation, natural disasters, and endemic poverty on a level that surpasses nearly every country on Earth. Despite these problems, Haiti's rich cultural mix of African, Indigenous, and European traits still enchants many foreign visitors.

Events in 1915 shook Haiti to its core much as did the 1791 rebellion that overthrew French colonialism. That year, U.S. marines invaded Haiti to restore order after a revolt led to the assassination of President Guillaume Sam. Or so the United States claimed. President Woodrow Wilson (1913–

1921) ordered the intervention, and quickly the mission transformed into one of preserving financial assets and nation building. The marines remained for nineteen years. During this time, the United States rewrote the Haitian Constitution to allow foreigners to own land and resources; they instituted the *corvée*, a system of forced labor for public works projects, built up the education and medical infrastructure, and made the country "safe" for foreign investors. In the process, more emphasis was placed on the importance of the capital Port Au Prince, a city without the geography to sustain a large population. This set in motion a growth in the city that eventually set the stage for the massive devastation wrought by the earthquake of 2010 that killed 300,000 people, mostly in Port Au Prince.

Many Haitians resented the U.S. occupation and took up arms in the 1919 Cacos rebellion to drive the marines out. The marines swiftly put the rebellion down, killing thousands of civilians in the process. Despite continuous confusion among politicians and military officials over the purpose of staying in Haiti, the marines stayed until 1934, when the new doctrine of U.S. foreign policy in Latin America came into effect: the Good Neighbor Policy.

The Good Neighbor Policy was a replacement for the more interventionist Roosevelt Corollary to the Monroe Doctrine. The 1823 Monroe Doctrine simply made clear the U.S. intention to prevent further European meddling in Western Hemisphere affairs. The Roosevelt Corollary lived strong from 1898–1933, during which time the United States intervened militarily fifty times in Latin American affairs. However, the Good Neighbor Policy represented a shift away from direct intervention toward U.S. support for existing rulers.

Haiti became an example of the double-edged sword of this new U.S. policy after the marines departed. By 1957, a country doctor by the name of Francois "Papa Doc" Duvalier (1957–1971) had taken control of Haiti with promises of strong economic development and Black Nationalism.

Papa Doc and his son, Jean Claude "Baby Doc" Duvalier (1971–1986), killed thousands during their three-decade reign, with nearly complete support of the U.S. government. Their Tonton Macoutes private security force intimidated the population, as the Haitian elite became wealthier and the poor became poorer. Baby Doc was overthrown in 1986 in a popular rebellion that eventually brought to power Haiti's first democratically elected president, the Catholic priest, Jean Bertrand Aristide (1991, 1994–1996, 2000–2004). He was elected with 67 percent of the vote and served seven months before a military coup overthrew him in September 1991.

The Dominican Republic

The island of Hispaniola is shared by two rival nations. The Dominican Republic occupies the eastern two-thirds, and Haiti occupies the western third. Both have about 10 million inhabitants, which means the population density of the Dominican Republic is much less than Haiti's. On top of this advantage, the Dominican Republic has done wonders with its environmental protection efforts by comparison to Haiti's nonexistent programs. This contrast is visible from aerial photos of the border, which show desertification on the Haitian side versus lush green tropical lands on the Dominican side.

Part of this can be attributed to a Dominican dictator with a mixed legacy on the island. Rafael Trujillo (1930–1961) ruled the country with an iron fist and an interest in placating the poor. As opposed to the Duvaliers of Haiti, Trujillo is remembered for providing land, jobs, and public works for the poor and the rich. Trujillo was inspired by the work of the marines during the U.S. occupation of his country, which lasted from 1914 to 1924. He viewed the United States as an example to be imitated, and, after the occupation, he invited U.S. entrepreneurs and military officials to stay on as consultants. The U.S. government enjoyed working with Trujillo despite his despotism because he could be counted on to provide order internally and to protect U.S. interests. Unfortunately for some, this meant the United States would look the other way during repressive stages. For example, in 1937, Trujillo stoked anti-Haitian immigrant hatred and instigated a massacre of 18,000 Haitians working in the country. The United States continued its support for the dictator into the John F. Kennedy administration (1961–1963). However, it was Kennedy who authorized the Central Intelligence Agency (CIA) to overthrow Trujillo. Despite this support, when Trujillo was assassinated in 1961, it was unclear whether it was the CIA's doing.

Joaquin Balaguer rose to power just before Trujillo's assassination, serving as a figurehead president in the last year of Trujillo's life and for a year afterward (1960–1962). In 1963, populist candidate Juan Bosch was elected president and then was quickly overthrown that same year. Two years later, the populace rose up to restore Bosch to power, which caused U.S. president Lyndon B. Johnson (1963–1969) to send 20,000 marines to the island in 1965 for fear the rebellion was Communist. It was not, and after the invasion, Balaguer served as president from 1966 to 1978 and again from 1986 to 1996, thoroughly controlling Dominican political life in the post-Trujillo years. Today, most outsiders know the Dominican Republic for its tourist resorts and talented baseball players. Unlike the bulk of Latin America, whose national sport is soccer, baseball is the national sport in the Dominican Republic, as it is in Cuba, Nicaragua, and Venezuela.

Mexico

Mexico in the twentieth century experienced unexpected extremes, unexpected because at the beginning of this period, the country was in the midst of unprecedented economic growth and political stability only to be plunged into the bloodiest civil war to hit Latin America for the next hundred years. The dictator Porfirio Diaz (1876–1911) had ruled Mexico with a carrot-and-stick approach, rewarding his followers and punishing his detractors. In 1910, the wealthy landowner and politician Francisco Madero led a rebellion against Diaz that quickly engulfed the country, empowering a multitude of previously-marginal regional strongmen. Men such as Pancho Villa, Emiliano Zapata, Venustiano Carranza, and Alvaro Obregon soon rose to prominence as the dominant revolutionaries after Madero's assassination in 1913. For the next seven years, those four would battle with and against one another for the soul of Mexico. Carranza and Obregon served as president (1915–1920 and 1920–1924, respectively), whereas Zapata and Villa were largely marginalized after 1915. All four would be assassinated between 1919 and 1928 but, interestingly, that seemed to end the era of instability in Mexican politics, for there would be no assassinations of presidents and no crises of succession between 1928 and 2006, making Mexico the most stable Latin American country (politically) during this period.

The political life of Mexico was dominated by the party that emerged from the Revolution, known simply as the PRI (Institutional Revolutionary Party). Although it went under different names at times, the PRI controlled the presidency from 1929 to 2000. It was known as an umbrella organization that tended toward the center of the political spectrum while including elements of both the left and the right. Under the PRI's watch, Mexico experienced 6 percent growth rates between the 1940s and 1970s, leading observers to coin the term "The Mexican Miracle." However, by 1968, discontent among the population led to a nonviolent uprising in the streets of Mexico City that the military put down on October 2 with extreme force in a zone of the city known as Tlatelolco. At least 500 people were killed that day, but the evidence was removed from the streets in time for the Olympics to go off without a hitch ten days later. The massacre at Tlatelolco was the first chink in the PRI's armor, for their power slowly eroded over the next three decades as opposition parties gradually emerged from the darkness in the 1980s, a decade that proved decisive for the future of Mexican political, economic, and social life.

In 1982, miscalculations in Mexico's oil industry (under the state-run oil company, Pemex) led to a massive debt crisis. By the end of the summer, Mexico owed $80 billion to international banks that it could not pay back, setting off a debt crisis that soon rippled through all of Latin America and even beyond. The debt-restructuring process forced Mexico to devalue its peso and sell off state-run businesses (privatize), and millions were put out of work. On top of this, an 8.1 earthquake hit Mexico in 1985 and destroyed much of the capital, causing billions of dollars in damages. By 1991, Mexico had privatized most state-run businesses to finance its massive debt and ushered in the era of neo-liberalism with the signing of NAFTA between the United States, Canada, and Mexico. NAFTA would not take effect until 1994 but, by 1991, the Mexican government and economy had almost completely reoriented themselves away from the Revolution's foundations, despite what was being taught in Mexican schools.

Central America

The history of Central America is both exciting and sad, depending on the observer: Exciting because of its variety, and sad because of its war and poverty. It is composed of seven countries geographically (Belize, Guatemala, El Salvador, Honduras, Nicaragua, Costa Rica, and Panama) and five traditionally (all but Belize and Panama), for reasons we do not have time to discuss here. Suffice it to say that this region, the size of only one medium-size country if it united, is divided mostly due to historical circumstances. From the colonial era to Independence in 1821, the modern day Central American countries were governed separately, and although they experimented with unification several times over the next century, these efforts failed, leaving the isthmus eternally fragmented.

However, the fate of each is tied to the rest whenever an economic or political crisis occurs. The U.S. presence looms larger in Central America than the rest of Latin America, in part due to this fragmentation and in part due to its poverty and geography. British and French interests were gradually pushed out by the twentieth century, especially after the United States secured the rights to build the Panama Canal in 1903 and large U.S. corporations such as the United Fruit Company (UFCo) came to hold tremendous economic and political influence even earlier. U.S. corporations cooperated with national governments in Guatemala, Honduras, Nicaragua,

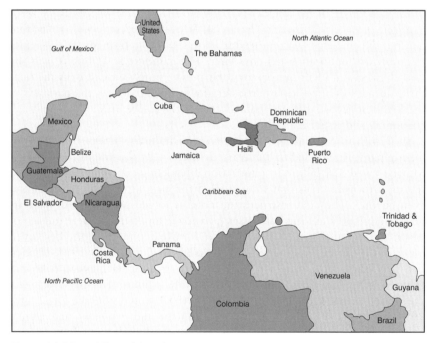

Figure 4.3 Map of Central America

and Costa Rica to develop transportation and communication systems and provide jobs for hundreds of thousands of people. This meant that domestic political interests were tied with foreign economic interests and, as a result, any potential challenge to either would elicit a response from the other. In all cases, democracy was severely curtailed as a result of this foreign influence.

A perfect example of this took place in Guatemala in 1954 when President Jacobo Arbenz (1951–1954) expropriated a large swathe of UFCo land for distribution to thousands of poor Guatemalans. As foreign companies such as UFCo had been given favorable treatment under the dictator Jorge Ubico (1920–1944) and his predecessors, its treatment by Arbenz came as a shock, and as a result the company enlisted the support of the U.S. presidency, the State Department, and the CIA to overthrow Arbenz in 1954. Codenamed "Operation Success," this coup shattered Guatemalan democracy and plunged the country into dictatorship and an intermittent civil war over the course of the next four decades. The U.S.-backed Guatemalan military slaughtered upward of 200,000 mostly unarmed peasants, students, teachers, union workers, and other activists seeking to end this genocide, and the price of this policy can be seen today in Guatemala and the United States, as Guatemala is one of the most crime-ridden countries in the world, and many of its citizens fled to the United States to seek refuge from the very governments the United States supported. This occurred in Central America in general, and this set off a trend of out migration to the United States that continues to this day.

However, it would be inaccurate to characterize Central America as dominated by U.S. interests.

In El Salvador, a country the size of the U.S. state of Massachusetts, the Salvadoran coffee oligarchy (also referred to as "the fourteen families") controlled political life into the 1980s. In 1932, a several-thousand-strong Communist-inspired uprising in the west of the country was put down within three days, after which ensued the largest-scale massacre of unarmed civilians in the history of Latin America. Over the course of less than a month, the Salvadoran military executed upward of 10,000 to 30,000 people, virtually wiping out the Pipil Indian population. The dictator who carried out this massacre, General Maximiliano Hernandez Martinez (1932–1944) was supported by the U.S. government, which had supplied the Salvadoran military with weapons since the 1870s and continued to do so after *La Matanza* (as the massacre of 1932 came to be known).

The next four decades saw the perpetuation of dictatorship and the rise of a grass-roots democracy movement that eventually splintered and gave birth to five armed rebel movements in the 1970s. The FMLN (Farabundo Marti National Liberation front) encompassed those five groups and became the largest rebel movement (15,000 strong) in Latin America during the entire Cold War. The military and its death squads killed upward of 70,000 people, almost all of them unarmed, to crush the FMLN. The worst massacre took place in December 1981 at the village of El Mozote, where the Salvadoran military systematically killed 900 unarmed people. Most of them were women and children. However, the civil war ended in a manner that has been noted as a model for future conflict resolution. Most of the military units disbanded permanently, as did all rebel units, and democracy took root for the first time in Salvadoran history. El Salvador has lived without war for the past two decades; yet, the gang violence has caused a tremendous surge in murders and drug trafficking.

Nicaragua has also suffered greatly over the course of the twentieth century, often due to U.S. interventions. As with Haiti and the Dominican Republic, the U.S. marines occupied Nicaragua from 1912 to 1933 with the stated intention of stabilizing the country and assisting with developing an infrastructure for a stable future. They intervened first in 1909, and then returned in 1910 and 1912, each time to combat Nicaraguan leaders deemed hostile to U.S. interests. They fought the rebels led by Augusto Cesar Sandino from 1927–1933 and left without capturing him or stopping the rebel campaign. Sandino was executed the following year upon the command of the head of the U.S.-trained National Guard. His name was General Anasastio "Tacho" Somoza Garcia, and he and his sons ruled Nicaragua until the Sandinista uprising toppled the last Somoza (Anastasio "Tachito" Somoza Debayle) in 1979.

The subsequent decade witnessed only a two-year period of relative peace, because once U.S. president Ronald Reagan (1981–1989) took office, the Sandinistas became his prime target. The Reagan administration dispatched the CIA, along with the Argentine military, to train and equip a counter-revolutionary force known as the Contras to fight the Sandinistas from bases in Honduras and Costa Rica. The Contras killed thousands of civilians and soldiers with bombs, bullets, and landmines supplied by the United States and other countries, and these acts became entwined in the Iran/Contra Scandal that broke in the United States in 1986 to 1987. By 1990, the Contra War was over, and the Sandinista president, Daniel Ortega was voted out of office in favor of the first elected female president in Latin American history, Violeta Chamorro (1990–1997). Still, Nicaraguans had little to celebrate. Not only had they lost 30,000 people to the Contra War, but Somoza had killed 50,000 during the late 1970s, and even after all of these losses, Nicaragua was among the poorest countries in the hemisphere, along with Haiti, Bolivia, and Honduras.

The jewel of Central America is Costa Rica. No army, no military dictatorships, a beacon for ecotourism, beautiful beaches and jungles, and fruit and coffee plantations as far as the eye can see. The Costa Ricans love to greet each other and foreign visitors (except Nicaraguans) with the phrase "mi amor," and this greeting is symbolic of the different flavor of Costa Rican culture by comparison to the rest of Central America. Unlike Guatemala, Honduras, Nicaragua, and El Salvador, Costa Rica has prospered politically and economically over the past two centuries since independence without the shackles of militarism to hold it back. And while it is by no means without its problems, poverty chief among them, Costa Ricans are decisively more united in their nationalism than the rest. However, it did have a civil war in 1948 that killed 2,000 people, but the Costa Ricans abhorred war so much that they abolished the army that year.

Although geographically part of Central America, Panama is more connected historically to Colombia and the United States. Still, the history of Central America would be incomplete without discussion of the significance of Panama, especially because of the Panama Canal. Panama was part of Colombia until Panamanian Independence severed the new country from the old in 1903. The United States assisted in this effort because it wanted the rights to build what became the world's most important canal. The engineering feat alone surpassed anything done in world history to that point. The canal opened in 1914 and, until 2000, it was U.S. property, as was the Canal Zone, a ten-mile wide swath of land in the middle of the country. Tensions rose several times between Panamanians and U.S. troops over the course of the century, and Panama eventually became a haven for drug smugglers and money laundering. In 1989, President George H. W. Bush (1989–1993) sent 20,000 soldiers and marines to Panama to overthrow and capture the dictator, Manuel Noriega. He had been convicted of drug trafficking-related crimes, and he had killed, tortured, and imprisoned thousands of Panamanians. In the process of capturing Noriega, U.S. troops killed between 2,000 and 4,000 people, according to a variety of human rights organizations.

Colombia

As with many Central American and Caribbean countries in the beginning of the twentieth century, Colombia dedicated a tremendous amount of resources to banana and coffee cultivation and export mostly for U.S. and European consumption. A strike of banana workers and their families against the UFCo in Santa Marta led to a massacre by the Colombian military in 1928 that shook the continent but only forty years later. At the time, as with the massacre of unarmed civilians in El Salvador in 1932, slaughters of this sort did not cause much outcry inside or outside Latin America. The hundreds or thousands who died (nobody knows for sure) at Santa Marta simply served as a reminder to those who would attempt to seek higher standards of living at that time. However, Colombia's favorite son, Gabriel Garcia Marquez, wrote about the massacre in his *One Hundred Years of Solitude* in 1967. Readers were captivated by his ability to tell the history of Latin America in matter-of-fact terms that demonstrated the depths of suffering and richness of culture in the region.

Despite its violent history (civil wars, massacres, drug wars, etc.), Colombia is among a few others (Costa Rica, Chile, and Uruguay) with a long history of relative democracy. The population has rarely tolerated outright dictatorship, with some exceptions. The darkest episode in its history came twenty years after Santa Marta. Populist left-wing candidate Jorge Eliecer Gaitan had promised major reforms that challenged the Colombian elite. His widespread popularity was evident during his speeches, when thousands of supporters cheered as he spoke of the new direction Colombia would take. When he was assassinated in April 1948 in Bogota, his followers rioted. The streets were scenes of carnage for the next week and, in the end, 3,000 lay dead. This kicked off *La Violencia* (the Era of Violence), a ten-year civil war that caused another 200,000 deaths by 1958.

The end of *La Violencia* ushered in a power-sharing arrangement between liberals and conservatives for the next decade and, since then, presidential elections have been nonviolent struggles between these two. However, the war also produced the FARC rebel group (Revolutionary Armed Forces of Colombia), a Marxist organization living mostly in the jungles that has subsidized its struggle through kidnapping and drug trafficking. Other rebel groups have emerged in FARC's wake, committing the same crimes but on a smaller scale. In the 1980s, FARC helped create a political party that would participate non-violently in Colombian politics. By the end of this experiment, 3,000 of its members had been killed by death squads linked to the Colombia government.

Cocaine trafficking surged in importance in the 1970s and 1980s with Pablo Escobar of the Medellin Cartel at the helm. Escobar's infamy as the world's most powerful cocaine kingpin was deserved: He killed thousands of people, with other traffickers and law enforcement his main targets; he controlled a large portion of the cocaine being smuggled into U.S. cities; and he nearly reached billionaire status. By 1992, he had escaped from a prison of his own making with the connivance of Colombian military officials on his payroll. His story continues in a later chapter.

Chile

As one of Latin America's longest-lasting democracies (with the exception of 1973–1990), one of its wealthiest countries per capita, and the most earthquake-prone South American country, Chile stands out as a unique specimen of analysis. Its main export has been copper for the past century. This mineral has been "Chile's life blood," as stated by former president Salvador Allende (1970–1973) at first due to the tax revenues from the U.S. corporations that owned the mines and later due to revenues gained by Chilean state-owned mines.

Ownership over the copper industry has always been at the heart of Chilean politics. They came to a head in 1970 when Marxist presidential candidate Allende won on a platform that included nationalization of the mines. He won with only slightly more than 36 percent of the vote, while the two conservative candidates split the rest. Allende's presidency was confirmed by parliament, but the U.S. government and Chilean conservatives worked tirelessly for the next three years to bring him down.

Allende nationalized thousands of businesses, including the copper mines, and moved Chile closer to a command economy than most Chileans were prepared to support. The 1973 midterm elections actually placed Allende's UP (Popular Unity) party above the rest, but his own popularity had waned considerably. On September 11, 1973, the U.S. supported a coup against Allende led by General Augusto Pinochet.

The Pinochet era lasted seventeen years and had mixed results, depending on the side one took. In the first weeks after the coup, the military rounded up thousands of Allende supporters and suspected subversives, including some foreigners, and held them incommunicado in the National Stadium in Santiago. With U.S. support, at least 3,000 people were killed, or, "disappeared," a term invented in South America during this era. It usually meant that the military killed someone and left no trace of their fate. Thousands more were tortured, imprisoned, and eventually set free. Pinochet is considered the embodiment of dictatorship in South America by his opponents, but his supporters uphold his image as next to saintly. They consider him the savior of Chile for preventing the rise of Communism and a deterrent to Communists in other Latin American countries. He also presided over great economic growth in the 1980s as the rest of Latin America dealt with a devastating debt crisis and currency devaluation. By 1988, the writing was on the wall that Pinochet's repressive methods were indefensible despite the possible benefits of his rule, and he agreed to a referendum in 1989. His opponents won out, and he stepped down in 1990, still reserving his right to Senator for Life status. Thus opened a new era in Chilean politics whereby moderate socialists governed for the next two decades.

Argentina

Argentina was once one of the top ten wealthiest countries in the world. Its wheat and beef sales and its foreign investments exceeded all other Latin American countries. As with the United States, Argentina was a prime entry point for European immigrants, especially from Italy, Spain, England, Germany, and Portugal in the late nineteenth and early twentieth century. Just as oil exploration began to yield hopeful results in the early twentieth century, depression hit in 1913 and lasted until 1917. The economy bounced back somewhat afterward but then depression hit again from 1921 to 1924.

Political turmoil added to Argentina's economic ebb and flow throughout the next seven decades. The Radical president Hipolito Yrigoyen (1916–1922, 1928–1930) made a definitive stamp on Argentine history with his pro-union bent. However, this proved problematic when the president allowed right-wing military and vigilante groups to massacre and intimidate strikers between 1919 and 1922. By 1946, a new popular president rose to power with his even-more-popular wife. Juan Peron (1946–1955) and his

Figure 4.4 Evita (1919–1952) (Pictorial Press Ltd./Alamy)

wife, Evita, are the most popular president and first lady in Latin American history. The fervor surrounding their reign epitomizes the meaning of the political term *populism*. Argentine pride and nationalism were restored under their watch, and yet three years after Evita's untimely death at age thirty-three, Peron was overthrown and exiled for the next two decades.

During that time, the military worked hand in hand with most governments until Peron returned in 1973. By this time, pro-Peronist youth groups had been causing chaos in the streets, clamoring for his return. Peron used the military and police to put down this movement, which caused many to join the rebel group, the Montoneros. Peron died in 1974, and his wife, Isabela, took over the presidency. She in turn handed power over to a military junta in 1976, and the junta initiated a seven year "Dirty War" that led to the forced disappearance of up to 30,000 people. The case of Chile was severe enough, but Argentina gave new meaning to the word *disappear*. As with Chile, many Argentine children were born to female prisoners whose babies were then adopted by Argentines connected to the military. In 1982, Argentina invaded the Falkland Islands, a territory claimed by the British, who quickly took them back in a humiliating defeat for the Argentines. This accelerated the downfall of the junta, which disbanded in 1983 in favor of democratic elections. The president who followed the junta's reign attempted to strike a balance between healing the wounds of the past and building a better future. President Raul Alfonsin (1983–1989) first presided over an effort to prosecute the worst criminals from the Dirty War era and then backtracked by providing amnesty for those still untried.

Brazil

We must be reminded that Brazil's history does not always follow the trends of the rest of Latin America. Not only did it achieve independence without firing a shot (after all, the prince of the crown of Portugal declared Brazilian Independence in 1822), but monarchy and slavery lasted decades longer as well. In addition, the wave of European-style liberalism of the nineteenth century did not hit Brazil until the tail end of the century: Universities, elections, and modernization principals were rushed into the system only with the overthrow of the emperor Pedro II (1831–1889). Soon after the Republic of Brazil was declared in 1889, the country adopted the slogan "Ordem e Progresso" (Order and Progress) for its flag, and the words remain there to this day. The term comes from the father of positivism, the French philosopher Auguste Comte (1798–1857) who advocated a scientific approach to government, society, and economy. To modernize, the Brazilians took up Comte's ideas, as did most other Latin American countries at that time.

Coffee was king in Brazil at the turn of the century and indeed, it is still the world's number-one coffee producer. The country's economic planners used the export of coffee to drive modernization (i.e., export-led growth). However, they quickly realized that diversification and industrialization were necessary to sustain growth, and in the 1930s, the government of Getulio Vargas did just that. The populist Brazilian president (1930–1945, 1951–1954) is quite an enigma to all observers. At times a brutal dictator and at others a reformer, he took his own life rather than be overthrown. Vargas instituted the "New State," which supposedly broke with the "Old Republic" that lasted from the end of Pedro II's rule until 1930. His achievements were similar to those of Cardenas in Mexico: He nationalized the oil, mining, steel, and automobile industries. However, unlike Cardenas, who was open to leftist politics in general, Vargas was a staunch anti-communist. Vargas was instrumental in acquiring U.S. assistance during World War II, which brought Brazil and the U.S. ever closer. His suicide took place in the midst of internal discord surrounding financial and political matters still unclear to this day.

The year 1964 began a new era of dictatorship for Brazil after President Joao Goulart (1961–1964) was overthrown in a CIA-sponsored coup. As was fitting of the profiles of Latin American presidents targeted for CIA operations (Arbenz in Guatemala, Castro in Cuba, and Allende in Chile), Goulart was a leftist bent on redirecting some of the nation's highly concentrated wealth into the hands of the vast numbers of poor people living in shantytowns and the countryside. The military probably did not need much CIA assistance to topple Goulart because of the elite's hatred of him and his policies. After his overthrow, the country was run by a military junta (group) until 1985, during which time thousands of suspected and real opponents of the junta were "disappeared," tortured, executed, and imprisoned. The term "to disappear" someone became particularly infamous in the case of Argentina, as discussed earlier, but it actually began in Brazil a decade earlier. The scale of repression in Brazil did not approach Argentina's, however, and it should be noted that, as was the case in Argentina, there was a small rebel force opposing the junta that carried out violence.

Unlike Argentina or Chile, the Brazilian junta undid itself without waiting for a public backlash. It initiated the *abertura* (political opening) in 1974 and, by 1985, a president unshackled to the military sat as head of state. In the meantime, however, the generals had begun a process of economic liberalism that undid the economic nationalism begun under Vargas. President Jose Sarney (1985–1990) presided over a debt crisis that shook Brazil to its core, and his successor, Fernando Collor (1990–1992) left office in a scandal resulting from corruption charges that almost led to his impeachment.

Conclusions

To cover the history of Latin America and the Caribbean from 1898 to 1992 in one chapter is to scratch the surface of a very complicated mixture of events, causes, effects, people, and places. The major difference between the beginning of this era and the end is the level of agency Latin Americans began to have in their daily lives in 1992 by comparison. In 1898, virtually all of Latin America lived under dictatorship, and by 1992, only Cuba remained. However, even though Latin Americans prefer democracy, not all would agree that the price of achieving it was worth it. So many had to suffer to arrive at what many feel is a bitter sweet end to the era of outright dictatorship, only to find that their economic prospects were only slightly, if at all, lifted. The population of Mexico increased tenfold during this time, and the rest of Latin America is only slightly behind in its growth rate. Although the economies of all improved, the benefits are often outweighed by the added burdens of population growth, environmental pressures, wars, crime, drugs, and U.S. interventions. The fact that populist leaders rose to prominence during this period illustrates something very important to Latin Americans that in the West cannot be comprehended because it goes against their own experiences. Populists respond to the desperation of people who yearn to be equals with those considered above them. U.S. interventions tell Latin Americans that they do not matter as much as the citizens of the United States. This is the same message Latin Americans received when they lived under Spanish rule, and it is precisely why the people of Latin America see the actions of the United States as "imperialist." Their struggle for nationalism during the twentieth century was a struggle to achieve equal status in relation to each other and to be considered above the intervention of the United States.

Discussion questions

1   What should be the legacy of Che Guevara and Fidel Castro? Were they liberators or scourges on Latin American society? Explain your answer with examples.

2   Was U.S. interventionism justified in Latin America during the period discussed? Provide both a pro and a con answer with examples.
3   Compare and contrast the way in which natural resources factored into the politics of Latin American countries covered in this chapter.

Key historical figures

Salvador Allende (1903–1973)

The only Marxist presidential candidate to ever be elected in Latin America, Allende was the president of Chile from 1970 to 1973. A large portion of the Chilean population opposed Allende from the start and in fact welcomed the military coup that overthrew him on September 11, 1973. The U.S. role in overthrowing Allende has been misunderstood by most observers. The CIA was largely involved in supporting opposition candidates prior to Allende's election and attempting a variety of "dirty tricks" aimed at undermining his legitimacy both before and after he took office.

Oscar Arias (1940–)

This former Costa Rican president (1986–1990, 2006–2010) is most well known for winning the Nobel Peace Prize in 1987 for helping to bring an end to the Central American civil wars of the 1970s and 1980s that killed upward of 300,000 and displaced 3 million people. Arias' ideology of demilitarization is a compelling continuation of the legacy begun by the other famous former Costa Rican president, Jose "Pepe" Figueres, who disbanded the Costa Rican military in 1948. Costa Rica's example of demilitarization has been followed by Haiti and Panama, and nations from around the world consult with Arias to this day.

Lazaro Cardenas (1895–1970)

He was known to the Mexican people as "Tata Cardenas" for his populist reforms and personalist style of running the Mexican government from 1934 to 1940. A traditional populist who used radio, television, newspapers, and advanced forms of transportation to communicate with as many sectors of the population as possible, president Cardenas represented the highest form of revolutionary politics. The Mexican Revolution (1910–1920) took the lives of one-tenth of the Mexican population, and in the post-war years, people needed to feel as though the sacrifice was worth it. After fourteen years of fits and starts under previous presidents, Cardenas took control and decreed major reforms aimed at alleviating the massive problems suffered by most of the Mexican population. He is most well known for redistributing 50 million acres of land to landless and land-poor families and nationalizing the petroleum industry.

Fidel Castro (1926–)

The most recognizable and longest-running ruler in Latin American in history, Fidel Castro Ruz is best known for leading the Cuban Revolution. After suffering failure at the Moncada Barracks on July 26, 1953, he named his movement after that date as a symbol of his determination to turn defeat into triumph. By 1959, the revolution had succeeded in overthrowing the old system, and he was on his way toward implementing a socialist system. By 1968, Castro had driven out most of the wealthy and middle class Cuban businessmen and professionals, helped bring the world to the brink of nuclear holocaust (Cuban Missile Crisis, 1962), and thrown his lot in completely with the Soviet Union. He had also presided over mass executions that numbered into the hundreds if not thousands. The Communist Republic of Cuba, as it came to be known, represented both defiance against U.S. hegemony in the Americas, which for many meant hope for more autonomous versions of nationalism, and the depths to which Communism could plunge unwitting populations. Castro's presence has shaped relations between the United States and Latin America more so than any other by far, precisely because what he represents is the extent to which leaders south of the border can defy the United States when pressed.

Pablo Escobar (1949–1993)

Colombia's *La Violencia* (1948–1958) caused the deaths of 200,000 people in the wake of the assassination of the populist presidential candidate Jorge Eliecer Gaitan. The generation who came of age during this era learned to use violence to survive, and Pablo Escobar was no exception. Escobar started out with petty dealing in the 1960s, eventually making his way up to running the infamous Medellin Cartel and becoming one of the wealthiest men on the planet. He used extortion, murder, kidnapping, bribes, and so on to maintain his cocaine empire until his death at the hands of the Colombian military and the U.S. Army's Delta Force in 1993.

Evita (1919–1952)

Eva Duarte was born in relative obscurity for someone who would become perhaps one of the most famous women in politics in world history. The future first lady to Juan Domingo Peron (1946–1955) worked as a radio actress and eventually met Colonel Peron, whose popularity almost matched Eva's. When they married and Juan became president, the two mutually benefited the other and the nation with their populist styles. He gave jobs to the poor and promoted Argentine pride in the wake of the country's massive economic downfall, and she cultivated a following among "los descamisados" (the shirtless ones), handing out bread and silver pesos to her throngs of admirers as she rode through the countryside by train. "Evita" died of cervical cancer at the young age of 33.

Ernesto "Che" Guevara (1928–1967)

Che achieved fame (or infamy, if you prefer) due to his actions in the Cuban Revolution. Yet even Castro has not reached the historical significance of Che. Only Jesus Christ's likeness has been reproduced more often than that of Che, who died less than five decades ago. Che was born in 1928 in Argentina and soon developed chronic asthma, a condition that would plague him throughout his life. He became a doctor in part due to this illness, but his greatest passion was social justice. After fleeing Guatemala in 1954 in the midst of a CIA coup, Che ended up in Mexico City, where he met Fidel Castro the following year. His social justice bent evolved into revolutionary militancy as he joined with the Cubans, and he eventually developed a reputation for ruthlessness and intelligence both on and off the battlefield. In 1965, he left to fight against the U.S.-backed dictator of Zaire, Joseph Sese Mobutu, only to return to Cuba in 1966. He then mounted his last expedition to foment rebellion in Bolivia, where he was captured and executed on October 9, 1967 by U.S.-backed Bolivian rangers.

Gabriel Garcia Marquez (1928–)

Born in Colombia, this Nobel Prize in Literature laureate is the most well-known Latin American novelist. He is particularly famous for his timeless classic, *One Hundred Years of Solitude,* and other books such as *Love in the Time of Cholera*, and *News of a Kidnapping*. He is considered one of the pinnacle contributors to the Latin American genre of magical realism, characterized by the duality of humanity's interpretation of existence. The magical realist imagines life as a struggle between fact and fiction, traditional and modern, Indigenous and European, and many more elements of Latin American life in particular. "Gabo," as he is affectionately known to his friends and admirers, is also openly socialist, as are many other Latin American writers and artists.

Rigoberta Menchu (1959–)

Another Nobel Peace Prize laureate, this Quiche Mayan Indian woman from Guatemala was honored for her work in calling attention to the atrocities carried out by the Guatemalan military against the unarmed civilian Indian population during the 1970s and 1980s. According to the UN Truth Commission results, the Guatemalan military murdered upward of 200,000 mostly unarmed men, women, and children in their efforts to destroy the various rebel groups that numbered no more than 7,000. However, Rigoberta's fame is also overshadowed by the fact that much of her testimony as recorded in the book, *I...Rigoberta Menchu: an Indian Woman in Guatemala*, has been challenged by Guatemala scholar David Stoll, who still recommended her for the Peace Prize. That said, two Truth Commissions report the same kinds of atrocities described by Rigoberta, and they gathered their data from many thousands of witnesses.

Diego Rivera (1886–1957)

The most famous muralist in Latin America, possibly the world, Diego Rivera is another example of a Latin American socialist who has given expression to the voiceless. He and Marquez, although from different eras, spent lifetimes devoted to publicly revealing the burden of European and U.S. influence on Latin America. Themes such as the conquest, colonialism, the Catholic Church's conversion of Native Americans, the role of U.S. capitalism, and U.S. military and CIA interventions are all present in Rivera's murals. He was married to the famous Mexican artist of extraordinary talent, Frida Kahlo, and the two of them were and still are international names that bring great pride to Mexicans.

The Somoza Dynasty (1936–1979)

Anastasio (Tacho), Luis, and Anastasio (Tachito) ran Nicaragua from 1936 to 1979 without seeking much to improve the lot of the average Nicaraguan. It would be incorrect to say that they all ruled the same. Tacho (1936–1956) ruled the longest and was generally understood to be corrupt but less brutal than his Dominican counterpart, Rafael Trujillo. The poet Rigoberto Lopez assassinated Tacho at a dinner party in Leon in 1956, ushering in the era of Tacho's son Luis. Luis (1956–1963) was the most benign of the three, believed to be less inclined toward brutality despite the hundreds of people rounded up and imprisoned upon suspicion of participating in his father's assassination. Tachito (1967–1979) was the most hated of the Somozas. His brutality took on proportions comparable to that of Trujillo and the Duvaliers, especially between 1977 and 1979, when he ordered the bombing of cities involved in the Nicaraguan Revolution that succeeded on July 19, 1979. However, Tachito's fate was not sealed until the following year, when Argentine revolutionaries assassinated him in Asuncion, Paraguay.

Further readings

Anderson, Jon Lee. *Che Guevara: A Revolutionary Life*. New York: Grove Press, 1997.
Farmer, Paul. *The Uses of Haiti*. Monroe, ME: Common Courage, 2006.
Galeano, Eduardo. Translated by Cedric Belfrage. *Century of the Wind*. New York: Norton, 1988.

Knight, Alan. *The Mexican Revolution*. 2 Volumes. Lincoln, NE: University of Nebraska, 1990.

Kornbluh, Peter, *The Pinochet File: A Declassified Dossier on Atrocity and Accountability*. New York: The New Press, 2003.

LaFeber, Walter. *Inevitable Revolutions: The United States in Central America*. New York: Norton, 1993.

Marquez, Gabriel Garcia. *One Hundred Years of Solitude*. New York: Harper Perennial, 2006.

Martinez, Tomas Eloy. *Santa Evita*. New York: Vintage, 1997.

Paz, Octavio. *The Labyrinth of Solitude*. New York: Penguin, 1999.

Thomas, Hugh. *The Cuban Revolution*. New York: Harper Torchbooks, 1977.

Films

Salvador. Dir. Oliver Stone. MGM, 2001.

Men with Guns. Dir. John Sayles. Sony, 2003.

Innocent Voices. Dir. Luis Mandoki. Lightyear, 2008.

Cover Up: the Iran/Contra Affair. Dir. Elizabeth Montgomery. Mpi, 2001.

The Motorcycle Diaries. Dir. Walter Salles. Universal Studios, 2005.

Rojo Amanecer. Dir. Jorge Fons. Grupo Nuevo Imagen, 2005.

In the Time of the Butterflies. Dir. Mariano Barroso. MGM, 2002.

Tango. Dir. Carlos Saura. Sony, 1999.

Fidel. Dir. David Attwood. Lion's Gate, 2002.

Che. Dir. Steven Soderbergh. Image, 2008.

The Official Story (La Historia Oficial). Dir. Luis Puenzo. Koch Lorber, 2004.

City of God (Cidade de Deus). Dir. Fernando Meirelles and Katia Lund. Miramax Lionsgatc, 2011.

Cautiva. Dir. Gaston Biraben. Koch Lorber, 2007.

Machuca. Dir. Andres Wood. Passion River, 2007.

Rodrigo D: No Future. Dir. Victor Manuel Gaviria. FACETS, 2004.

Maria's Story. Dir. Monona Wali and Pamela Cohen. PM Press, 2010.

Missing. Dir. Costa-Gavras. Universal, 2004.

Online content

Latin American Network Information Center: http://lanic.utexas.edu/

The Virtual Diego Rivera Museum: www.diegorivera.com/

The Mothers of the Plaza de Mayo: www.madres.org/navegar/nav.php

Museum of the Word and the Image: http://museo.com.sv/

Havana Journal: http://havanajournal.com/

Center for International Policy: www.ciponline.org/

Council on Foreign Relations: www.cfr.org

CIA World Factbook: www.cia.gov/library/publications/the-world-factbook/

5   Asia (1945–1989)

Timeline

1945	Division of North and South Korea, North and South Vietnam
1947	Indian Independence
1947–1948	Partition: Indo-Pakistan War
1948	Arab-Israeli War, State of Israel created
1949	Chinese Revolution, Indonesian Independence
1950–1953	Korean Conflict
1953	CIA overthrow of Iran Prime Minister Mohammad Mossadegh
1955	Bandung Conference (also known as the Asia-Africa Conference) in Indonesia
1967	Six Day War
1967–1976	Cultural Revolution in China
1971	Pakistan-orchestrated genocide in East Pakistan (Bangladesh)
1973	Yom Kippur War
1975	South Vietnam, Cambodia, and Laos fall to Communists.
1975–1979	Khmer Rouge–orchestrated genocide in Cambodia, Indonesia-orchestrated genocide in East Timor
1979	Iranian Revolution
1979–1989	Soviet invasion and occupation of Afghanistan
1980–1988	Iran-Iraq War
1989	Tiananmen Square massacre in China

The foregoing timeline only scratches the surface of the important events taking place in Asia in the period between WWII and the Tiananmen Square massacre. Considering that, what can we presume to understand about Asia during those years?

1   More specifically, what ideas come to mind when we discuss Asia during this period?

2   What sources inform our ideas? Who or what informed us? When did
    we learn these things?
3   How well informed were those people or other sources that informed
    us? Why should we listen to them?
4   If we entertain notions about post-war Asia based on sources with shaky
    foundations, why do we maintain these as legitimate in our minds? What
    do we gain from thinking this way?

1945: The end and the beginning

The end of World War II brought a sense of relief and sorrow to hundreds
of millions of people around the globe. They mourned their 50 million dead
and tens of thousands of destroyed cities and towns across Europe, Asia, and
North Africa. The two atom bombs dropped on Hiroshima and Nagasaki,
Japan were seen by most as isolated events, used to crush the indomitable
Japanese will to fight. Most would not have considered that these bombs
would be a new beginning, not the end, of globalized warfare.

No more German dominance of Europe. No more Japanese dominance
of East Asia. However, the post-war period proved more difficult than most
expected due to the rise of the East-West conflict, also referred to as the
Cold War, whose battle lines were drawn in the closing days of WWII. The
Potsdam conference among Winston Churchill, Harry Truman, and Josef
Stalin from July 16 to August 2, 1945 provided for the division of Korea
at the 38th parallel, with a Soviet-backed Communist north and a U.S.-
backed south. Vietnam was divided at the 16th parallel, with the U.S.-backed
Chinese Nationalists in charge of the north and the British in charge of the
south, after which the French attempted to retake all of Indochina (Vietnam,
Laos, and Cambodia).

This was a period of widespread revolutionary movements across the
developing world, ranging from moderate anti-colonialist to Communist
in orientation. These were not always mutually exclusive either, as was
the case with Ho Chi Minh's revolt against the French in Vietnam. There
was no mistaking the wave of tumult spreading: The Philippines gained
independence from the United States in 1946; India gained independence
from the British in 1947; Israel was created through a UN mandate in 1948;
Indonesia gained independence from the Dutch in 1949; Egypt gained
its independence in 1952; and, the most significant of all, the Chinese
Communists came to power under the leadership of Mao Tse Tung in China
in 1949. Thus, this chapter deals with a flurry of divergent and convergent
movements that do not always follow a neat timeline or fit into a fixed
pattern but do catapult Asia onto the forefront of global events.

More than anything, the Cold War in Asia was a period of divided lands
and peoples struggling over the future. To the prominent non-Asian Cold
War divisions of Germany and Cuba can be added Asian divisions in Israel,
India, Vietnam, Korea, the Persian Gulf, and China. In all of these cases,

divided peoples both played the role of pawns in the rivalries between Cold Warriors and exerted their own agency in shaping the future of their countries. The causes of these divisions were largely political and religious but were always accompanied by violence and international efforts to both halt and continue the fighting. It is to these divisions that we now turn.

China

There are three "T" words that evoke great controversy in China: Taiwan, Tibet, and Tiananmen. All three symbolize the divisions resulting from the massive foundational changes arising from Communism in China.

Taiwan

Taiwan must be understood as an extension of China for those who have lived there since 1949. The post-WWII fighting between Jiang's Nationalists (KMT) and Mao's Communists picked up where they had left off before the Japanese occupation. Jiang received $3 billion in U.S. assistance to combat Mao's rebels. After two decades of fighting that witnessed hundreds of thousands of deaths, not to mention the millions displaced and injured, all aside from the millions killed under Japanese occupation, the Chinese Revolution came to an end in October 1949 with Mao's Red Army as victorious. Jiang's KMT then fled to the island of Formosa, later called Taiwan, where they regrouped to resume their war against Mao. The United States quickly came to the KMT's aid there, sending military and economic assistance and CIA officers who organized anti-Mao units to infiltrate the mainland. All efforts to retake China failed, and after tremendous U.S. support, Taiwan became a country unto itself. However, even this is a controversial issue, as China, known as the People's Republic of China (PRC) since 1949, does not recognize Taiwan's independence, nor does Taiwan recognize the Communist government's legitimacy in the PRC.

Tibet

The western province of Tibet was not part of China until Mao's government began annexation efforts there. Tibet is culturally distinct from the rest of China, even with China's great diversity. The Tibetan monks under the leadership of Dalai Lamas have traditionally governed its affairs, and it was the followers of the fourteenth Dalai Lama (Nobel Peace Prize laureate, 1989) who have resisted Chinese encroachment since 1949. The Dalai Lama engaged in peace talks with the Chinese government in 1954 to no avail and, by 1959, left for exile in India, still seeking to maintain leadership of Tibet. The Chinese have killed upward of 1 million Tibetans and consider irrelevant the arguments of human rights advocates calling for Tibetan autonomy. At times, it has been illegal to fly the Tibetan flag, and this ties in with the broader failures of the government to maintain the myth that Communism unites the country under a singular vision dictated by Mao and his legacy to China.

Tibet thus fits into the broader role of myth-making in promoting Mao's image as savior and father of the Chinese people. The Long March itself is the central myth promoting Mao's leadership, which we covered in Chapter 2, but the Great Leap Forward represents another. This took place between 1958 and 1961 as a plan for rapid industrialization to "leap" into the modern world. The famine that killed 23–38 million resulted from drought, government ineptitude, and the exportation of food in exchange for advanced weaponry from the Soviet Union. The myth began in its promotion stage, when people were encouraged to follow the Community Party's instructions to turn in iron tools that could then be used in industrial production. Peasants handed over their farming implements, essential for growing crops and, thus, feeding the Chinese population. People were also informed that with Communism, the bounty of the harvest would expand beyond their wildest expectations. The famine was also mythologized.

For Mao's defenders, it was not Communism's fault that so many died but that of the famine. For Mao's opponents, the famine was his fault entirely. The late 1950s also witnessed divisions between the USSR and China, termed the Sino-Soviet Split. Ideological divisions and territorial disputes along the border between the two countries created conditions not unlike the hostilities between Pakistan and India, and in fact China supported Pakistan while the USSR supported India. Ideological divisions soon revealed themselves within China itself, culminating in the so-called Cultural Revolution that lasted from 1967 to Mao's death in 1976.

The Cultural Revolution has been given even more scrutiny in China than the Great Leap Forward due to the widespread nature of the upheaval. Rather than carry out an outright Stalinist purge within the Party, Mao sought to indoctrinate the youth to cleanse the country of dissent. This had the same effect as a purge, for many of the old-line Communists were in fact imprisoned, tortured, expelled from office, and executed after being accused of counter-revolutionary activities and thoughts. The death toll was much lower (400,000) than expected, but it was the level of intimidation experienced by older people and all perceived non-conformists at the hands of the youth brigades carrying Mao's *Little Red Book* that left an indelible stain on China. It was only with Mao's death that people breathed a sigh of relief at the end of this stage of Mao's power consolidation.

Tiananmen Square

Beijing's Tiananmen Square rivals Moscow's Red Square as the largest central square in the world. Mao's enormous portrait presides over this most important Chinese space to this day. Most outside of China would not readily conjure up a concrete image of the square before 1989. Ever since, the world knows it as the place where hundreds of young people were gunned down by the Chinese military. The road leading to Tiananmen is paved with many events that both span Mao's reign and the thirteen years after.

In 1972, U.S. President Richard Nixon (1969–1974) made his historic visit to China to meet with Mao and his advisors. The meetings opened the chapter that led the country down the path toward international political and economic integration. However, it would take internal Chinese governmental leadership to make this happen from within the country. Deng Xiaoping (1904–1997) filled that role. Although never officially China's head of state, his position on the Central Advisory Commission of the Communist Party after Mao's death helped him influence the country's future in a way most Chinese have appreciated. The capitalism-under-socialism model he implemented allows for relative economic freedoms through the assistance of state power and under the ultimate arbitration of the totalitarian Communist government.

By 1989, the economy had grown substantially, and yet the government would not yield to calls for a pluralistic economic opening. Students who had been educated in the post–Cultural Revolution environment felt themselves part of a broader political wave of changes sweeping the rest of the Communist world, particularly in Eastern Europe and the Soviet Union, where Mikhail Gorbachev's (1985–1991) reforms of Glasnost and Perestroika were taking effect. In addition, a new philosophical movement founded by Li Hongzhi known as Falun Gong started to grow during this period. Not only were political and economic changes occurring within China but new philosophical trends were emerging. It was little surprise when protestors mostly looking for dialogue with the government over possible democratic changes began occupying Tiananmen Square on April 15. Their numbers swelled into the hundreds of thousands over time as they sought discussions with the Chinese government run by the Central Advisory Commission of the Communist Party, whose principal leaders were Zhao Ziyang and Deng Xiaoping. Gorbachev visited Beijing in May to meet with the Chinese leadership and reestablish relations after thirty years of hostilities. The protests continued during the visit and into early June, when the military was given orders to empty the square by force. On June 4, the military opened fire on the students, killing untold hundreds. The matter was whitewashed afterward and has become a source of criticism toward China by insiders and outsiders ever since, as the world watched the protests and the shootings on television.

These three "T" issues go to the heart of China's struggle on the world stage in the wake of Mao's rise to power. Taiwan symbolized the political divisions that emerged after the Revolution of 1911: Those following Jiang represented traditional Chinese nationalism albeit while receiving substantial support from the USSR in the 1920s and 1930s and the United States after 1945, while those staying behind represented Maoist revolutionary doctrine that evolved into Communist capitalism. The dividing lines established during the war between the Nationalists and the Communists that lasted for more than two decades and carried over after 1949 forged divergent identities among the Chinese peoples on the island and on the mainland, that shape definitions of these two now-mutually distinct nationalist identities today.

Tibet is a symptom of the two-sided nature of Communist programs instituted under Mao's leadership. On the one hand, Tibet was absorbed into China, and the average Chinese deems this as just, whereas on the other hand, it led to 1 million deaths and international condemnation of China. This issue can be linked to the Great Leap Forward and the Cultural Revolution because they, too, fall under the mythology promoted by Mao as necessary for China's growth and unity. Finally, Tiananmen represents the broader conundrum of the legitimacy of the post-Mao Chinese leadership. Prosperity under Deng Xiaoping's guidance must be measured against his role in putting down the students seeking political opening, for example, and the world's outrage at the massacre was not matched by its will to sanction China's leaders, which it completely lacked. Indeed, China's status as an economic powerhouse with one of the world's most powerful militaries provides it with privileges afforded to a limited group of countries, including the United States. One in five of us live there as well, and another one in five lives in the region we cover next.

India, Pakistan, and Afghanistan

The great icon of Indian history, Mohandas Gandhi, began leading the push for independence in 1916 during the peak of European imperialism. The rest of the European colonial territories in Africa and Asia were not on their way toward self-governance, so how would India buck the trend? Indeed, it was not until the 1950s that Europe's other colonies would begin to achieve independence. It was India that led the way. Gandhi's philosophy of non-violence and non-cooperation represented a distinctly Indian philosophical approach to the problem of foreign dominance. Instead of taking up arms against the British, they would cause the economic and political foundations of the imperial power structure to crumble from within through a challenge to London's moral authority.

Gandhi's non-violent revolutionary philosophy was called *Satyagraha*, which grew out of his reading of both Jainism and Henry David Thoreau's essay, *Civil Disobedience*, written in 1849 to articulate a vision of how citizens could assert their rights through non-violent protest. Gandhi and the Indian National Congress trained followers to resist the urge to fight back when faced with British force during Indian sit-ins, marches, protests, and fasts. Even as colonial authorities killed, tortured, and imprisoned their Indian subjects for two decades during this struggle, Gandhi's followers eschewed violence as a response and, as a result, removed any legitimacy for the British to use force against the revolutionary movement. In other revolutions, rebels using violence elicited what could be portrayed as a legitimate resort to violence on the part of the state.

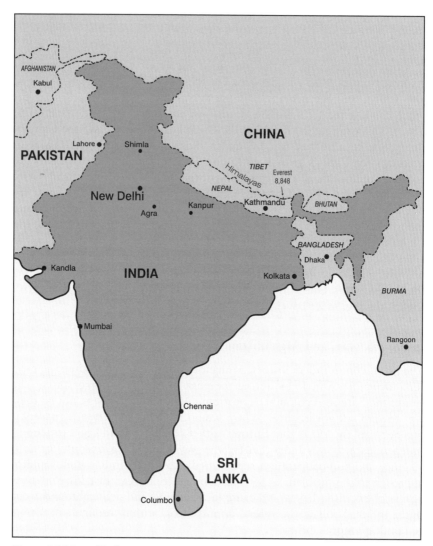

Figure 5.1 Map of India

However, in India, this was difficult for the British to sustain, in particular after WWII. This was in part due to the Atlantic Charter, a Western-powers pronouncement advocating the end of colonialism in the developing world. Gandhi (and Jawaharlal Nehru's) Indian National Congress led India to independence in 1947, but there were far too many problems left behind by the British for the newly independent to solve. Religious and political differences that had been percolating since the rise of the independence movement itself brought the rise of both Hindu and Muslim leaders whose visions for India diverged. The Muslim League leader, and future founder of Pakistan, Muhammad Ali Jinnah (1876–1948), had seen the Nazi threat during WWII as an opportunity to push for his vision of a Muslim nation separate from India called PAKISTAN. This was an acronym that linked each desired region to be incorporated into the new nation to a letter: Punjab, Aghania, Kashmir, Iran, Sind, Turkharistan, Afghanistan, and Baluchistan. This vision of course did not play out exactly, and to the group was added Bengal, which became the province of East Pakistan until 1971, when it became the independent nation of Bangladesh.

Muslims and Hindus fought one another almost immediately over the future of India between 1947 and 1948 in what has been referred to simply as "Partition" ever since. This war killed perhaps 1 million people and led to the division of India into Muslim and Hindu states. Pakistan was initially divided into West and East Pakistan, with current-day Pakistan on the west side of India and current-day Bangladesh on the east side. Kashmir was left to be fought over for the next six decades or more (as of this writing), as it has been occupied by the Indian military, which battles Pakistani-backed insurgents, as both Pakistan and India claim it. The two also fought wars in 1965 and 1971, with the latter leading to the Pakistani genocide of between 300,000 and 3 million Bengalis and Bangladeshi Independence.

The Indo-Pakistani wars were also linked to the Cold War. India received assistance from the Soviet Union while Pakistan allied itself with the United States and China. As such, these two relatively impoverished countries elevated their own strategic importance on the global stage while they increased their individual capacities to destroy their neighbor. Both eventually acquired nuclear weapons (India in the 1970s and Pakistan in the 1980s) and developed militaries far beyond what could have been achieved outside the context of the Cold War due to their allegiances with superpowers.

The politics of India and Pakistan have also represented distinct tendencies. India is often referred to as "the world's largest democracy" and Pakistan's political history is mostly authoritarian. India's gift to the world was Gandhi, and his assassination on January 30, 1948 by the Hindu extremist Nathuram Godse bequeathed an uncertain legacy to India's future. His successor, Jawaharlal Nehru (1889–1964) had impeccable leadership and intellectual credentials, and his family would dominate Indian politics for the next half century. Nehru would lead on a global stage as well but would come to represent a decisively more leftward political bent. He was Prime Minister from 1947 to 1964 and, with brief exceptions, was succeeded by his kin, such as his daughter Indira (1966–1977, 1980–1984) and her son, Rajiv Gandhi (1984–1989). The INC as a political party has been under the Nehru-Gandhi family's sway and those connected to the Independence movement's founders. This has made the INC particularly nepotistic since 1947; however, many formidable opposition parties such as the BJP and the VHP have been created, and these have added new dimensions to the Indian democratic process. Despite this, assassinations have also plagued Indian politics. Not only was India's beloved Gandhi assassinated, but so were Indira and Rajiv (in 1980 and 1991, respectively). In addition, violence has broken out quite often throughout the country, leading to the deaths of thousands and political imprisonment of hundreds of thousands. Much of this is due to regional, ethnic, political, and religious conflicts that illustrate India's extreme diversity.

Pakistani politics, conversely, have been shaped largely by strong men and strong allies. Unlike India, military generals have played a large role in political life, and many have served as head of state since 1947. The formidable creator of Pakistan, Jinnah, held control only briefly in the beginning before dying of an illness in 1948 and was succeeded by Liaquat Ali Khan, who also died quickly, in 1951. Generals Ayub Khan (1958–1969) and Yahya Khan (1969–1971) ruled during a particularly tumultuous period. They presided over two wars with India (1965 and 1971), and Yahya carried out the genocide in East Pakistan in 1971. Out of the genocide was born the newly independent nation of Bangladesh. Indira Gandhi sent troops to assist in this effort as it fit into the broader war between India and Pakistan.

Within two years of the genocide in Bangladesh, Pakistan's most influential national and international figure rose to prominence. Zulficar Ali Bhutto (1973–1977) held the presidency as the first civilian to rule in many years and set the tone for the conflict between civilian and military rule for decades to come. His presidency ended when General Zia Ul Haq (1978–1988) overthrew and executed him. General Zia was a fundamentalist Muslim with aspirations of expanding the military's power and Pakistan's role on the international stage. The U.S. administrations of Jimmy Carter (1977–1981) and Ronald Reagan (1981–1989) became instrumental in both of these aspects.

Afghanistan interlude: 1973–1989

Zia's rule coincided with the rise of Communist control over Afghanistan that began in 1978 with a coup led by the People's Democratic Party of Afghanistan. Also known as the Saur Revolution, the revolt brought down a five-year period of relative progress led by Mohammad Daoud Khan, who had led a bloodless coup against Mohammad Zahir Shah in 1973. The newly established Communist government was led by Nur Muhammad Taraki from 1978 until 1979 when he was overthrown by Hafizullah Amin. The Communists instituted social and economic reforms that threatened the Islamic customs of traditional Afghans. Reforms aimed at equal rights for women (such as educational and political openings) were not well received by traditionalists. At the same time, Taraki and Amin used brute force to crush all opposition, which largely came out of an Islamic fundamentalist movement that became known as the "mujahedeen."

The National Security Advisor to President Jimmy Carter came up with an idea in 1979 to support the mujahedeen as a means of combating communism in Afghanistan. Zbigniew Brzezinski's notion followed from the logic that the Soviets would intervene in Afghanistan and thus suffer the same fate as that of the United States in Vietnam: an unwinnable war or a quagmire. His goal was not to provide the mujahedeen with the means to defeat the Soviets militarily but to bleed the Soviets dry. U.S. support began that summer and continued throughout the 1980s and reached $3 billion by the time of the Soviet withdrawal in 1989.

Moscow's invasion of Afghanistan in December 1979 was not unlike its invasions of Hungary in 1956 and Czechoslovakia in 1968. Punishing its client states for deviations in behavior was common, if not acceptable to the West or the suffering people of those countries. Most government offices and military command posts were run directly by the Soviets as they propped up the Afghan Communist dictatorship. The Soviet occupation of Afghanistan differed from their actions in Hungary and Czechoslovakia in one respect though: The troops who remained systematically terrorized the civilian population for a decade, killing 1 million and displacing millions.

However, the Soviets failed to force outright submission. The mujahedeen received support from the United States, Saudi Arabia, and Pakistan, not to mention the large numbers of Islamic fighters who flowed to the country from surrounding nations. By the time of the Soviet withdrawal from Afghanistan in 1989, the Islamic fundamentalist base had become fully galvanized across Afghanistan, Pakistan, and Saudi Arabia, to name a few places, and the battles over Afghanistan in the 1990s and into the twenty-first century find their roots in this initial conflict.

As all United States aid to Afghanistan passed through Pakistan and the United States aided Pakistan outright as well, the Pakistani military's coffers expanded nearly tenfold, and Zia developed the first atomic bomb in the Muslim world, thus heightening the dangers of the Indo-Pakistan conflict over Kashmir. The Zia years were seen by fundamentalists as glorious, but there was a surge of liberalism developing there as well. Shortly after Zia died in a plane crash in 1988, Zulficar Ali Bhutto's daughter, Benazir, took the political stage by storm and was soon elected prime minister in 1988 as Pakistan's first female head of state. The daughter proved as significant as the father due to her charisma and the fact that a woman had been elected to the top political seat in a Muslim country. With a population of 150 million (the second largest Muslim population in the world), this was no small feat.

Aside from war and politics, India and Pakistan (and, outside Asia, in Mexico) became a testing ground for the philosophy of the *Green Revolution* (implemented between the 1940s and 1970s), a technological breakthrough in agricultural production that relied on the use of pesticides, fertilizers, and genetically engineered seeds to create high-yield, mostly cereal, crops. This method, credited to U.S. agronomist Norman Borlaug (Nobel Peace Prize laureate), has been seen as both a blessing and a curse. It both helped create the conditions for high yields, which fed more people, but increased the populations of all three of these countries, thus creating more mouths to feed in poor countries and soil erosion and a dependence on fertilizers, pesticides, and specialized seeds. Between 1960 and 2012, the populations of Mexico and India tripled, while Pakistan's quadrupled. This conundrum has spawned countless conferences, books, and informal discussions that fit into the broader topics of development aid to underdeveloped nations, environmental management, and agro-business in general.

Korea

North and South Korea did not exist as independent countries prior to WWII. Korea was unified before and during the Japanese occupation (1910–1945). The Potsdam conference divided Korea at the 38th parallel. The North was controlled by a Moscow-backed Stalinist dictator named Kim Il Sung (1948–1994), and the South was controlled by a U.S.-backed dictator named Syngman Rhee (1948–1960). In both cases, widespread repression by the dictatorships sought to cleanse the new countries of dissidents. North and South Korean support from their respective superpower allies made this possible on a grand scale.

On June 25, 1950, the North launched a drive across the border to take over all of South Korea. Almost immediately, the United States gained the support of the UN to send troops to stop the North's advance. By June 29, the North had captured the capital at Seoul and, by June 30, U.S. President Harry Truman (1945–1953) began sending U.S. troops led by the famous WWII commander, General Douglas MacArthur, as head of the UN force.

The war was costly in blood and treasure. The United States relied both on heavy bombing of the North and even crossed the border and dropped bombs on Chinese soil. The Chinese sent 300,000 troops into North Korea in October and quickly proved that the war could not be won outright by either side. The war lasted for three more years until a ceasefire was signed on July 27, 1953. Although often overlooked, the Korean War proved an important lesson: that Cold War battles were difficult to win outright. Two to four million people died in three years of fighting, with no clear winner. Israel presents another such divided nation that proves this point further.

Israel and the Middle East

Adolf Hitler's genocidal policies killed upward of 6 million Jews, or approximately three-fourths of the global Jewish population. The famous British-authorized Balfour Declaration of 1917 has often been cited as the document legitimizing the creation of the Jewish homeland. However, the Jewish people themselves point to this region as their traditional lands and their God-given right. The British mandate over Palestine had lasted since the fall of the Ottoman Empire after WWI, and the British revoked this mandate in 1948 as the UN provided a resolution dividing Palestine into three sections: Arab, Jewish, and international (Jerusalem). The Arab League, an organization representing the interests of Arab countries, refused to accept this while the Jewish independence movement in Palestine led by David Ben-Gurian vowed to resist Arab hostility.

The resulting Arab-Israeli War lasted from 1948 to 1949 and ended with Israel asserting its right to the boundaries set by the UN. Another result was the internal displacement of Palestinian Arabs living in lands claimed by Israel and the exit of many Arabs to neighboring countries, where many lived for decades afterward. The plight of the Palestinians stirred up resentment toward Israel over the course of the twentieth century.

Egyptian leader Gamal Abdul Nasser's (1952–1970) call to Pan-Arabism included an anti-Israel ideological foundation with which most surrounding Arab countries identified. When he nationalized the Suez Canal in 1956, Prime Minister Ben-Gurion (1948–1954, 1955–1963) followed Britain and France's lead by sending Israeli troops to Egypt for a short time, where the Israelis achieved a swift victory, before U.S. pressure convinced them to retreat. However, the conflict between Israel and its Arab neighbors increased over the years, and Nasser's antagonism, accompanied by Syria especially, and his ability to rally Jordan and Iraq to the anti-Israel cause made tensions rise throughout the Middle East. Both sides supported and carried out small-scale attacks against the other between 1956 and 1967 and, by May of that year, there was no turning back.

The Soviets had initially supported Israel but this changed in the 1960s as the United States threw its support behind Israel for political and Cold War strategic reasons and began to support Israel's military buildup. Soviet weapons, spies, and advisors poured into Egypt and Syria, and Soviet advisors falsely claimed that Israel had amassed its troops on its northern border with Syria, causing both Syria and Egypt to prepare for war. At the same time, Israeli Chief of Staff Yitzak Rabin ordered the activation of Israeli Defense Force reserves in a show of strength toward Syria and Egypt, albeit they did not move to the border with either Syria or Egypt. Rabin's move has been judged hasty by credible observers, for it provided Egypt's Nasser with a reason to put his troops on alert. Nasser then closed the Straits of Tiran, provoking Israel to request U.S. President Lyndon Johnson (1963–1969) to back Israel in the event of war. Johnson's response was unequivocal: only if Israel did not fire the first shot.

Believing itself in need to ward off an imminent Egyptian and Syrian attack, Israel struck first, targeting Nasser's air force on June 5, 1967. Israeli Prime Minister Levi Eshkol (1963–1969) aimed to destroy Nasser's air warfare capacity to prevent the primary Arab nation from leading an assault on Israel. Jordan, Iraq, and Syria quickly entered the war as well, and all three failed along with Egypt. In what has been dubbed the Six Day War, it took Israel less than a week to invade and take territory claimed by Egypt (Gaza, Sinai Peninsula), Jordan (West Bank, East Jerusalem), and Syria (Golan Heights). These six days had implications that reached far beyond the founding of the State of Israel, for since then the world has been forced to deal with the ups and downs of Arab-Israeli tensions, warfare, terrorism, and negotiations on a scale unmatched by any other international relations situation since WWII.

Nasser died three years later and was replaced by Anwar Sadat (1970–1981), another antagonist toward Israel at the time (he would become a peace broker later in his rule). He was particularly known for starting the Yom Kippur War against Israel with its ally Syria on October 6, 1973 in an effort to take back the Sinai Peninsula and the Golan Heights. The fighting was much more serious than that in 1967. Israeli Prime Minister Gold Meir (1969–1974), Israel's first female head of state, committed all of Israel's resources to the war, and in the end was able to prevent Israel from being consumed by the invading armies. The UN and the United States gradually brokered peace between Egypt and Israel over the course of the following year. The Camp David Accords of 1978 were signed by Sadat and Israeli Prime Minister Menachem Begin (1977–1983). These provided for future peace between the two principal rivals in the region, and peace talks in 1979 provided for the return of the Sinai to Egypt. Sadat's assassination on October 8, 1981 on the eighth anniversary of the Yom Kippur War was the result of Muslim extremists bent on punishing him for negotiating with Israel.

Despite peace with principal rival Egypt, Israel's internal conflict with the Palestinian Liberation Organization (PLO) has held much of its attention since the Arab League created it in 1964. Its leader between 1969 and 2004 was Yasser Arafat (1929–2004), who rose to international celebrity status among revolutionaries and symbolized terrorism for Israelis and many in the West. The PLO was known for its attacks on Israeli targets but also for raising awareness about the plight of the Palestinians. After three decades of operating from bases outside Israel (Jordan, Lebanon, Tunisia), the PLO convinced Israel in 1993 to allow the Palestinians their own police force in the Occupied Territories and thus returned there after thirty years of exile.

The civil war in Lebanon from 1975 to 1991 brought the Palestinian problem to world attention due to the tensions brought to Lebanon from upward of 400,000 Palestinian refugees living there in the wake of the wars in Israel. The divisions inherent within Lebanon go back to the stipulations of its independence from France in 1943. The country is divided among Maronite Christians and Shiite and Sunni Muslims, and despite constitutional provisions legally dividing power among the three, political and cultural influence between these groups has caused much turmoil down the years. The outbreak of war began in 1975 with the killing of four Maronites in an assassination attempt against a Phalangist (Maronite) party founder Pierre Gemayel. Maronites then attacked Palestinians, which led to a cycle of violence that eventually brought Syria, Israel, and the United States into Lebanon's orbit. When Israel invaded in 1982 to support its Phalangist allies against Syria-backed Sunni militias (the PLO, the Palestinian Liberation Army, and others), Iran and Syria supported the emergence of the now-formidable enemy of Israel, the Shiite extremist group known as Hezbollah. The United States intervened in 1982 to assist the Israeli/Phalangist side in expelling the Syrians and their allies and suffered numerous terrorist attacks as a result, most notably the 1983 Marine barracks bombing. The United

States pulled out in 1984, and the fighting continued between the Israeli/ Phalangist units and the Muslim units into the late 1980s, culminating in a series of agreements that ended the war officially in 1991.

Southeast Asia

As WWII ended, Jiang Jieshi's troops held control over the northern half of Vietnam until France asserted its desire to reconquer their territory lost during WWII in Indochina (Vietnam, Laos, Cambodia) between 1946 and 1954 in what was referred to as the French War in Indochina. The French had a formidable foe in the resistance. A famine that killed possibly 2 million

Figure 5.2 Map of Southeast Asia

people between 1944 and 1945 caused widespread suffering and discontent and anti-imperialism among the Vietnamese. The Indochinese were in no mood to accept further colonialism. Ho Chi Minh's Viet Minh rebels, who had helped defeat the Japanese already, were well versed in the methods of guerrilla warfare, and the now-eminent military strategist General Vo Nguyen Giap (1911–) was their top commander. After eight years of war, the Viet Minh humiliated the French military with a resounding defeat at Dien Bien Phu in 1954.

After Dien Bien Phu, the French pulled out of Southeast Asia entirely, and the United States effectively took its place as the primary Western influence in the region for the next two decades. The Geneva Conference on May 8 of that year concluded with an agreement on national elections for 1955 and also moved the division between North and South to the 17th parallel. The United States later replaced South Vietnamese Prime Minister Bao Dai with Ngo Dinh Diem (1955–1963), an anti-communist pro–United States dictator. The United States also reneged on its Geneva Conference commitment to support national elections, fearing a win by the popular Ho Chi Minh. U.S. President Dwight Eisenhower (1953–1961) pushed for a separate election in the South to provide Diem with a victory there, thus ensuring the separation of the two Vietnams.

U.S. political and military officials gave Diem enormous support in the interest of preventing the fall of South Vietnam to the Communists. This was part of the Eisenhower administration's "domino theory," which envisioned Communism as an evil force that would take over the world quite easily unless the United States and its allies stood firm against its spread. Diem's authoritarianism appealed to the United States and his anti-communist Vietnamese countrymen. As a Catholic himself, he received tens of thousands of refugees from the North who had felt the persecution of the anti-Catholic Communist government there.

The North's new government under Ho Chi Minh instituted reforms advertised as beneficial to the masses that also demanded complete conformity to the Communist line. Land reforms targeted middle- and upper-income families, many of whom suffered from imprisonment, torture, starvation, and death as their resources were redistributed by the Hanoi government. Those deemed enemies of the people without the means to flee the country were often put into reeducation camps. Some of these prisoners sent out messages to the outside world pleading for assistance and, in the absence of that, cyanide capsules so as to have the means to commit suicide. The reality of these conditions was broadcast to the South Vietnamese peoples by the Diem government and his U.S. advisors, but many South Vietnamese people suffered from their own persecution by Diem himself, who killed and tortured many as well.

By 1960, Diem's repression coincided with the infiltration of Northern operatives into the South via the Ho Chi Minh Trail, which ran through Laos and Cambodia to the west. With ever-increasing Soviet and Chinese support,

Figure 5.3 Ho Chi Minh (1890–1969) (Bettmann/Corbis)

the Northerners coordinated with Southerners disillusioned with Diem to form the insurgency known as the Northern Liberation Front (NLF). In 1961, Eisenhower left office advising the new president, John F. Kennedy (1961–1963) to send troops to Southeast Asia. Kennedy stepped up the U.S. advisory role there and began bombing Southern pockets of NLF resistance in 1962. In November 1963, both Diem and Kennedy were assassinated. In addition, Ho Chi Minh's role in the war was reduced to figurehead by the early 1960s with the rise of the primary Communist Party leaders Le Duan and Le Duc Tho. These two represented an even more radical element within the North Vietnamese government, for they advocated all-out war in the South at the expense of socialist development in the North. Thus, instead of consolidating the foregone conclusion of Communist victory in the North, Duan and Tho pushed for Vietnamese unification. This effort would push the United States further into the war, which then brought increased Chinese and Soviet support to the North.

The new U.S. president, Lyndon B. Johnson (1963–1969) soon took the war to a new level. On July 31, 1964, the U.S. Navy provided support for South Vietnamese raids on Northern coastal positions in the Gulf of Tonkin. Johnson then falsely claimed that U.S. ships had been attacked without provocation "on the high seas" by the North on August 3. The attacks did not take place on August 3 (although they had on August 2), and the August 2 attacks were in retaliation for the U.S.-backed raids by the South Vietnamese. Johnson then ordered U.S. air attacks on the North on August 4. "The Gulf of Tonkin" became a punch line during Johnson's presidency as journalists quickly realized this to be a false pretext for expanding the war in

Vietnam. This ratcheted up U.S. military engagement in Vietnam almost to the point of no return. Actual attacks on U.S. military advisors in 1965 led to full-fledged U.S. involvement in the war. The United States also began its intervention in Laos in 1964 to fight the Communist Pathet Lao forces there.

By 1968, the U.S. and Vietnamese casualties mounted at an unprecedented rate. Newspapers in the United States told of more than 1,000 U.S. troop deaths every month, while the death toll for the Vietnamese in the North and the South was many times more. The average Vietnamese citizen on either side of the Demilitarized Zone (DMZ) at the 17th parallel separating the two countries suffered a fate worse than the troops. In the South, citizens were in an impossible position, with two armies forcing their allegiance in opposite directions. They were expected to side with the U.S.-backed Army of the Republic of Vietnam upon pain of imprisonment or death, but if they refused the NLF's allegiance, they suffered the same fate. Thus, when U.S. troops murdered more than 500 unarmed men, women, and children at the hamlet of My Lai in 1968, the soldiers claimed they were carrying out their mission to weaken the enemy. The Tet Offensive earlier that year witnessed the enduring power of that insurgency and signaled to the U.S. public that the war was far from over, despite the glowing assurances of the Johnson administration that the United States was in fact winning the war.

The war would continue through another U.S. administration. President Richard M. Nixon (1969–1974) initiated the process of "Vietnamization" that provided an end to the military draft and the gradual withdrawal of troops. However, Nixon also extended the war into Cambodia beginning in 1969, with bombing raids and then, eventually, troop deployments to that country. The Paris Peace Talks in 1973 ended with a U.S. agreement to pull out of Southeast Asia. Less than a year into the Gerald Ford (1974–1977) administration, in April 1975, the NVA took over the South Vietnamese capital of Saigon, causing the largest refugee crisis on the planet since WWII and driving the U.S. presence from Vietnam entirely. In the end, though a few more than 58,000 U.S. troops died, the United States killed 2 million Vietnamese civilians. The extent of U.S. atrocities against Vietnamese civilians has been the subject of increasing scholarship since the war, with a 2013 account being the most damning. *Kill Anything that Moves: The Real American War in Vietnam* by Nick Turse demonstrates that massacres such as My Lai were commonplace and that the U.S. military leadership in fact sanctioned the atrocities and only punished a few over the course of the entire war.

The story of Cambodia is even more intense than that of Vietnam, albeit on a much smaller scale (Vietnam had 30 million people, Cambodia had 7 million). Cambodia's destiny was tied to that of Vietnam once the NLF and NVA began setting up bases there from which to launch attacks against South Vietnam. The leader of Cambodia, Prince Norodom Sihanouk, presided as head of state virtually unopposed from 1941 to 1970 and took a neutralist stance in the war, which allowed for the growth of Communist penetration there and dissent from within his own administration.

Sihanouk's overthrow in 1970 by Prime Minister Lon Nol (1970–1975) was followed by the continued devastation of Cambodia under the U.S./ South Vietnamese invasion and the rise of the Communist insurgent group known as the Khmer Rouge. The United States dropped 500,000 tons of bombs on the Cambodian countryside between 1969 and 1973, which led to the deaths of possibly hundreds of thousands of people due to the bombs themselves, to the internal refugee crisis that ensued, to the destruction of the economy, and to the disruption of the food supply. The majority of the refugees eventually descended on the capital city, Phnom Penh, exacerbating the crisis further. These trends coincided with Lon Nol's increasing isolation in the capital as the Khmer Rouge gained popularity with the population ravaged by the war.

The Khmer Rouge overthrew the last remnants of Lon Nol's government in April 1975 and quickly plunged Cambodia into a genocide that rivaled that of the Nazis, albeit under different circumstances. Phnom Penh had swelled in population due to the high influx of refugees resulting from the U.S./South Vietnamese invasion to a total of 3 million by 1975. The Khmer Rouge, led by Pol Pot, emptied the city's inhabitants by force to the countryside, turning the country into one large collective farm. Virtually the entire country lived under concentration camp conditions. Family ties were severed. Dissidents were starved to death, tortured, and executed. It is estimated that one-third of the population of 7 million perished under Pol Pot's rule, which ended only after the Vietnamese invasion of 1978 and 1979. Both the United States and the USSR condemned the Khmer Rouge. The United States used it as an example of Communist atrocities in general, and its newspapers flooded readers with stories to such an extent that Pol Pot became synonymous with Adolf Hitler. The USSR used Cambodia's example to further legitimate its enmity toward China, as the Khmer Rouge was inspired by Mao's teachings.

The small country of Laos also became embroiled in the wider wars of Southeast Asia, beginning with the French attempt to reconquer Indochina from 1946 to 1954. Laotian Communists organized resistance to the French and the Laotian monarchy under the banner of the Pathet Lao, which worked in conjunction with Ho Chi Minh's Viet Minh resistance in Vietnam. Once the French were expelled in 1954, the Pathet Lao acquired some political power in the north and quickly spread an insurgent movement from the small northern region known as the Plain of Jars that then emanated throughout the country. The U.S. government assisted the Laotian military's counterinsurgency campaign against the Pathet Lao with massive aerial bombardment and CIA cooperation from the 1960s through 1975, when the Pathet Lao took over.

The Communist government plunged Laos into deep despair in the years to come. At the same time, the U.S. involvement in Vietnam, Laos, and Cambodia exacted a toll that not only led to the deaths of millions at the time but lasts to this day. U.S. landmines continued to kill thousands of people in the decades after leaving Southeast Asia in 1975, and the defoliants the United States sprayed to eliminate the insurgents' ground cover have caused widespread birth defects that have been passed down through the bloodstream from generation to generation. The overall significance of the wars in Southeast Asia is complex and has been covered in many books and articles that readers should consult if they wish to learn more.

The Cold War also raged in neighboring Indonesia during this time period. Indonesia's independence leader, Sukarno (1949–1965), hosted a summit of developing world leaders in 1955 in the city of Bandung. The conference is often credited with leading to the rise of the term *Third World* to depict the interests of those people residing outside of the First (the West) and the Second (the Communist Bloc) Worlds. Sukarno himself was a nationalist who sought to include all nationalist movements under one anti-colonial banner in his fight for independence against the Dutch since his creation of the Indonesian National Party (PNI) in 1927. His anti-colonialist credentials established, he was thus a natural leader of the emerging post-colonialist movements of Asia, Africa, and Latin America. The conference brought together leftist leaders from Asia and Africa to discuss future visions of what came to be called "Third World" development.

Bandung was soon overshadowed by the Chinese Communists who had recently succeeded in taking control of the most populous country on Earth. The Chinese example that violence was necessary for independence was being followed in places such as Laos and Vietnam, whereas the Indian and Indonesian examples of non-violence represented an alternative path followed from Ghana to South Africa to El Salvador and many more. Both examples served as practical methods of achieving the ultimate goal of "liberation," but the leadership characteristics and power structures of each country determined how much of each to use. Vietnam and Ghana were quite different from one another, for example, as were Indonesia and Iran, and these disparities would serve to divide revolutionary leaders not only across national boundaries, as exemplified at the Bandung discussions, but within the movements themselves.

Bandung also set in motion several concrete and long-lasting ideas with international resonance. The confluence of ideals there during that week in April 1955 helped galvanize an awakening among developing world countries that they constituted a strong force on the international stage and that the recent creation of the UN and the Cold War conflict itself could be used to increase the power of Asia, Africa, and Latin America if these regions worked together. This has worked at the UN in the form of the Afro-Asia-Latin America group and in a broader, less official capacity as the Non-Aligned Movement. Peaceful international relations and disarmament also took center stage at the conference through a series of pronouncements that eventually led to the creation of the International Atomic Energy

Agency at the UN. However, nations such as China, India, and Pakistan soon worked feverishly to develop their own nuclear weapons arsenals, and the post-colonialist leaders of Egypt, Iraq, Syria, North Vietnam, and many others systematically grew their military budgets through Chinese and Soviet assistance programs to carry out their post-colonialist visions.

Shortly after Bandung, Sukarno's leftist sympathies eventually drew the CIA to orchestrate his overthrow. The CIA's first attempt in 1958 failed, but they succeeded in 1965 in helping bring to power General Suharto, who systematically murdered all suspected dissidents, particularly those of the Chinese-backed, Indonesian Communist Party (PKI). The death toll from Suharto's consolidation of power ranges from 500,000 to 1 million. Suharto's invasion and occupation of the tiny island nation of East Timor starting on December 7, 1975 also led to the deaths of up to 200,000 East Timorese (one-third of the population) from 1975 to 1979, an act that has been condemned as genocide. Suharto's support from multiple U.S. governments for his anti-communism helped uphold his regime through 1997, when civilian control was restored.

The Persian Gulf

Post-war Iran witnessed the rise of a nationalist movement bent on extricating itself from outside control over its vast oil resources. Saudi Arabia had developed a strong relationship with the U.S. government, and oil companies during and after WWII and in the process negotiated a deal that allowed for a 50-50 division of oil wealth between the Saudis and the U.S. companies. The Iranians had no such deal and, in fact, viewed the British as exploiting Iranian oil wealth. The British-owned Anglo-Iranian Oil Company (now British Petroleum) held a contract over all of Iran's oil until the Majlis (Iranian parliament) voted to nationalize Iran's oil, thus expelling the British. Iranian Prime Minister Mohammad Mossadegh (1951–1953) stood out as the figurehead of nationalization, and thus the British sought his overthrow. As with Indonesia, the first attempt failed, but then they called on the CIA.

The Eisenhower administration was concerned about the growing influence of the Communist Tudeh party in Iran, and therefore viewed Mossadegh's overthrow as a way to "stabilize" the region. The CIA hired protestors to foment public dissent in the streets of Tehran and convinced military officers to overthrow Mossadegh in 1953. This all rested on Shah Reza Pahlavi's cooperation, however, and initially he was not willing to exercise his right to take power. After acceding to the CIA's pressure (which included putting pressure on the Shah's twin sister), the Shah was installed and supported with military, economic, and political assistance from the United States for the next 26 years (1953–1979).

Iran's history changed markedly after the 1953 CIA coup, named Operation Ajax. The Shah's rule placed Iran center stage within the Cold

War struggle between East and West and led to the surge of Shiite Islamic fundamentalism that set off the rise of Islamic movements in the late 1970s and 1980s. These, of course, planted the seeds for the latest global conflict, the so-called War on Terror. The Shah ruled Iran as an authoritarian supported with U.S. military, political, and economic support in part because he provided U.S. companies with access to Iranian oil fields and in part because he represented a bulwark against Communism on the USSR's doorstep. The Shah's secret police, known as the SAVAK, helped suppress political dissent within the kingdom through intimidation, imprisonment, torture, and execution in an effort to maintain economic and political stability within Iran and to enrich himself with oil wealth in a manner not unlike the royalty of the Arabian Peninsula.

The Shah's rule came to an end in 1979 when revolutionaries inspired by the exiled religious leader Ayatollah Khomeini overthrew him in a popular rebellion infused with Islamic fundamentalism and anti-U.S. sentiment. The revolt's energy helped inspire other Islamic uprisings in traditional Sunni strongholds such as Pakistan, Afghanistan, and Saudi Arabia that same year. The world took additional notice of the Iranian Revolution when students loyal to Khomeini took the U.S. embassy staff hostage in Tehran between 1979 and 1981. U.S. President Jimmy Carter (1977–1981) failed to obtain the hostages' release, and this aided in his opponent's (Ronald Reagan's) election in November 1980. Soon the changing political landscapes of the United States and Iran would affect Iran's western neighbor, Iraq.

Iraq was under Ottoman rule until 1918 and British rule until 1932, after which its political landscape shifted a number of times under military coups until it joined the Arab League in 1945. The British decided to place a Hashemite king in Iraq during its mandate in an attempt to unify the country politically. However, generals inspired by Nasser gained international attention with their own post-colonialist revolutionary movement in 1958 when the nationalist and left-leaning General Abd al-Karim Kassem (1958–1963) overthrew the Iraqi monarchy.

The West feared that Kassem's act would inspire similar disruptions in Middle East politics, and a U.S. Marine contingent was sent to Lebanon to prevent an revolt that was in fact ensuing there. Kassem ruled Iraq as a reformist with relative popularity, albeit not on Nasser's scale in Egypt, until a rebel group with Pan-Arabist inclinations overthrew and assassinated him in 1963. The Ba'ath Party was one group among the coup plotters, and it was Pan-Arabist, secular, and socialist. The Ba'athists were marginalized initially but then took full control in 1968 under the leadership of Ahmad Al-Bakr (1968–1979). Al-Bakr's socialist reforms were supported by the USSR for a decade until he stepped down due to illness, paving the way for his vice president, Saddam Hussein.

Hussein (1979–2003) envisioned Iraq as the major power in the Middle East and sought to realize this initially with the takeover of western Iran in

1980. Iraq's invasion sought also to crush the rise of Shiite power on his eastern border and within his own country. Despite Iran's and Iraq's large Shiite majority population, Hussein's Ba'ath Party was made up of the Sunni minority, which comprised 20 percent of Iraq. Hussein's Soviet support seemed to ensure an easy victory against Iran, whose number-one ally until the revolution, the United States, had just become its number-one enemy. In addition, the United States soon decided to ally itself with Hussein in an effort to help him crush the Khomeini regime. The Iranians supported the rise of Hezbollah in Lebanon to resist the 1982 Israeli invasion of that country, and soon Iran's Lebanese allies were taking U.S. citizens hostage in Beirut, including at least one CIA officer. Iranian-linked groups were also involved in an array of terrorist actions across Europe and the Middle East during the 1980s; thus, the United States sought friends in dictators such as Iraq's Hussein, Pakistan's Zia Ul Hak, and others.

Khomeini's Iran quickly turned into a virtual police state that enforced strict Sharia law. Many thousands were executed for suspected disloyalty and failure to adhere to the new statutes, and the repression was only enhanced in response to the Iraqi invasion. Despite their technical disadvantage on the battlefield, Iranians had a population three times larger, and Iranian generals sent "human waves" of tens of thousands of young Koran-carrying men against Hussein's tank divisions and machine gun nests. Iran made significant progress in thwarting Hussein's advance across the border, but his Russian-made tanks proved especially difficult to counter.

By 1985, Iran had found a way to obtain U.S.-made TOW anti-tank missiles. Iranian, Israeli, and U.S. middlemen coordinated a covert operation later dubbed "Arms for Hostages" as a means of selling Iran U.S. weapons to use against Iraq (which was backed by the U.S. and the USSR) in exchange for Iran convincing Hezbollah to release five U.S. hostages held in Lebanon (they were quickly replaced with five more U.S. hostages). This covert operation became public in late 1986 when it was discovered that the United States had significantly marked up the prices for the weapons and diverted the profits to a Swiss bank account that was then used to purchase weapons for the U.S.-backed "Contras" in Central America. "Arms for Hostages" then became the "Iran/Contra" scandal and brought to light the extent of covert operations in U.S., Israeli, Iranian, and Central American wars and politics. The Iran-Iraq War ended in 1988 in a stalemate. Nearly 1 million had died in the process, and neither side gained a hint of success. Hussein used poison gas against the Iranians and his own Kurdish population in addition to devastating the Marsh Arabs in the south. The late Cold War battles in the Persian Gulf region and the broader Middle East would set the stage for the post–Cold War conflicts.

Emerging trends: Japan points the way forward

Japan clearly holds a special place as the first Asian country to achieve developed nation status. The Meiji Restoration that began in 1868 was responsible for the pre-WWII economic growth that catapulted a previously backward nation into modernization. The postwar period was initially assisted by the U.S. occupation forces led by General Douglas MacArthur, who set up a protectionist economic state. The decades thereafter witnessed tremendous growth under the auspices of both the protectionist apparatus and the ingenuity of the Japanese people. The nation's mission was to compete with the West in the global market place of products and ideas. Japan's formula for growth rested on a balance between government oversight and private initiative, and this set the platform for the rest of Asia to follow. This was not Communism, which used totalitarian control over a planned economy that operated within a protectionist, state-directed economic model. Although there were massive gains in production in some Communist countries, namely the Soviet Union, these gains were in labor and resource-intensive areas such as heavy industry associated with national defense, which did little to alleviate the poor living and working conditions of the average Russian. The Soviet state also used slave labor and maintained a police state throughout its existence between 1917 and 1991, leading to the death of 25 million people and imprisoning of tens of millions more.

Under the Japanese model, a government ministry both held an advisory role and controlled business financing. It served the industries as opposed to the other way around and helped build up the war-torn economy in the wake of WWII. This was the MITI (Ministry of International Trade and Industry) model and, in Japan, it did not serve to make the economy revolve around militarization, as was the case of many Communist countries. Instead, the MITI supported the emergence of companies such as Sony, Mitsubishi, Toyota, Honda, and many others that have been competitive internationally for decades. Although some Japanese companies have complained that the MITI was unduly bureaucratic and often biased, the MITI is considered by many observers to be the epitome of the cause of Asia's economic "miracle." By the 1980s, many U.S. companies were being overtaken by Japanese companies, and Americans began complaining that the MITI gave the Japanese an unfair advantage. This complaint continues today against the other East Asian economic powerhouses that have surged to prominence in the post–Cold War era. The MITI was problematic, however, when it came to predicting the future of technological innovations because its managers were not trained in these areas. The software, hardware, engineering, and manufacturing innovators knew what was possible and what was not, and the MITI managers did not always have their finger on the pulse of the market. By the mid to late 1990s, it had become apparent that the MITI model was not a panacea. In fact, Japan's growth has stagnated in the past two decades as China has surpassed it in output. Japan's example set the stage for the most important change occurring in the world in the past two decades since the end of the Cold War, which is the rise of Asia, to which we turn in Chapter 8.

Discussion questions

1 How should history judge Mao Tse Tung? Is he a savior or a monster? Although this has been much debated ever since he first rose to power in 1949, is this even important now, given the different direction China has taken away from his ideology?
2 With the benefit of hindsight, is it possible to make the case that the U.S. wars in Southeast Asia benefited the people of the region?
3 The Green Revolution has provided food to untold millions of people, but do you think this is the answer to the problems of the developing world, given that it also led to uncontrollable population growth and dependence on pesticides, fertilizers, and specialized seeds (i.e., a move away from traditional farming)?
4 Which method for successful revolution do you believe provided better results: violent or non-violent change? Use the examples of China versus India, Indonesia versus Vietnam, or any others to illustrate your points.

Historical figures

Sirimavo Bandaranaike (1916–2000)

The first female prime minister in the world, she served Sri Lanka from 1960 to 1964 and then again from 1970 to 1977 and 1994 to 2000. Her first term was the result of the assassination of her husband, Prime Minister Solomon Bandaranaike, in 1959. Her close alliance with China and India helped her develop and defend socialist programs, and she changed the name of the country from Ceylon to Sri Lanka in 1972. Her daughter would later serve as president, and she would serve as her daughter's prime minister until her death in 2000.

Indira Gandhi (1917–1984)

The daughter of the first prime minister of India and India's first female prime minister, Indira Gandhi left an indelible imprint on the political culture during her terms (1966–1977, 1980–1984) in office. She was known for presiding over much of the Green Revolution, establishing relations with the USSR to maintain its defenses against Pakistan, the development of a nuclear weapons program, and her assassination at the hands of her own bodyguards in 1984.

Muhammad Jinnah (1876–1948)

He was the leader of the Muslim League during British rule of India and the founder of Pakistan. Jinnah was considered among the great political leaders of the twentieth century. History points mostly to Jinnah's activism in the two decades leading up to independence in 1947, which divided India from within among Hindus and Muslims. Illness prevented him from ruling more than one year into Pakistani independence, but he is still considered the father of the nation.

The Fourteenth Dalai Lama (1935–)

At the age of two, this son of a Tibet farming family was revered as the reincarnation of the thirteenth Dalai Lama. From that time on, his life has centered on the leadership of the Tibetan peoples. At the age of twenty-one, in his capacity as representative of all Tibetans, he attempted to reverse the onslaught of Chinese military dominance by meeting with Mao and his advisors. His exile in India since 1959 has in fact elevated his profile to human rights advocacy leadership, not just for Tibetans but for oppressed peoples around the world. He won the Nobel Peace Prize in 1989.

Golda Meir (1898–1978)

The fourth Prime Minister of Israel (1969–1974) and the only female to hold that post as of this writing, Golda Meir was decisive in reinforcing Israel's international influence and national pride. She was born in the Ukraine in 1898 and spent much of her early years in the United States before joining a kibbutz in Palestine in the 1920s. She was also instrumental in pushing for Jewish statehood in the 1940s and was among the signatories of the Israeli Declaration of Independence in 1948. She is known for her strong demeanor, her stalwart defense of Israel in the face of Arab hostility, and her leadership during the Yom Kippur War of 1973.

Ho Chi Minh (1890–1969)

The founder of independent Vietnam and the Communist political leader of North Vietnam, Ho Chi Minh soon became both the hero and the villain of millions around the world. His initial work in fighting the Japanese occupation of Vietnam (1941–1945) fostered his development as a military and political leader, which was only enhanced by his leadership in defeating the French effort to retake Indochina (1946–1954) and especially through his success at leading the war against the United States until his death in 1969.

Jawaharlal Nehru (1889–1964)

This first prime minister of India was also Gandhi's co-leader of the Indian Independence movement between the 1920s and 1947 and the father of a political legacy bequeathed to India in the wake of his terms (1947–1964). He was known for his leftist tendencies, which were seen during his terms and those of his daughter and grandson. The Nehru family represented the most important political family in India since Independence.

Deng Xiaoping (1904–1997)

Despite never serving as head of state of China, he is known as the key leader in China's capitalist reform movement after Mao's death in 1976. China remained Communist politically but moved decisively into the world capitalist system and even maintained 11 percent growth rates into the first decade of the twenty-first century.

Muhammad Suharto (1921–2008)

He was the former dictator of Indonesia (1965–1997). He is known for his CIA-backed coup overthrowing independence leader Sukarno and for his brutal effectiveness in crushing the Communist PKI movement in 1965 and the East Timorese independence movement in 1975.

Mao Tse Tung (1893–1976)

Known as "Chairman Mao" to his followers, he led the Chinese Revolution to victory in October 1949, then ruled China until his death in 1976. He was known for leading the Long March (1934–1935), resisting the Nationalists and the Japanese, instituting the failed Great Leap Forward (1958–1961), and fomenting the Cultural Revolution (1967–1976). Proponents point out his successes in making China a powerful, united country, whereas opponents accuse him of the genocide of up to 70 million people.

Further readings

Chang, Jung, and Jon Halliday. *Mao: the Unknown Story*. New York: Anchor, 2005.
Coll, Steve. *Ghost Wars*. New York: Penguin, 2004.
Fisk, Robert. *The Great War for Civilization*. New York: Vintage, 2005.
Karnov, Stanley. *Vietnam: A History*. New York: Penguin, 1997.
Kramer, Mark, ed. *The Black Book of Communism*. Cambridge, MA: Harvard, 1999.
Kuper, Leo. *Genocide: Its Political Use in the Twentieth Century*. New Haven, CT: Yale, 1981.
Lewis, Bernard. *The Middle East: A Brief History of the Last 2,000 Years*. New York: Scribner, 1995.
Nguyen, Lien-Hang T. *Hanoi's War: An International History of the War for Peace in Vietnam*. Chappell Hill, NC: University of North Carolina, 2012.
Oren, Michael. *Six Days of War: June 1967 and the Making of the Modern Middle East*. New York: Random House, 2002.
Prashad, Vijay. *The Darker Nations: A People's History of the Third World*. New York: New Press, 2007.

Shawcross, William. *Sideshow: Kissinger, Nixon and the Destruction of Cambodia.* 1979.

Turse, Nick. *Kill Anything that Moves: The Real American War in Vietnam.* New York: Metropolitan Books, 2013.

Vogel, Ezra. *Deng Xiaoping and the Transformation of China.* Cambridge, MA: Belknap Press of Harvard, 2011.

Films

Mr. Jinnah: The Making of Pakistan. Dir. Christopher Mitchell. 2003.

The Last Emperor. Dir. Bernardo Bertolucci. Criterion, 2008.

Heaven and Earth. Dir. Oliver Stone. Warner, 2004.

The Killing Fields. Dir. Roland Joffe. Warner, 2001.

TV Series: Traffik. Dir. Alastair Reid. Acorn, 2001.

Charlie Wilson's War. Dir. Mike Nichols. Universal, 2008.

The Sun behind the Clouds. Dir. Ritu Sarin and Tenzing Sonam. Zeigeist, 2010.

Online content

The National Security Archive: www.gwu.edu/~nsarchiv/

The Parallel History Project on Security Cooperation: www.php.isn.ethz.ch/

The Cold War International History Project: www.wilsoncenter.org/program/cold-war-international-history-project

6   Africa (1952–1994)

Timeline

1952	Egyptian Revolution
1952–1960	Mau Mau Rebellion in Kenya
1954–1962	Algerian Revolution
1956	Suez Crisis
1957	Ghana Independence
1958	All African People's Conference in Ghana
1961	Congo Prime Minister Patrice Lumumba assassinated
1964–1990	Nelson Mandela imprisoned
1965–1997	Joseph Sese Mobutu's dictatorship in Zaire
1967–1970	Genocide in Biafra, Nigeria
1974	Portuguese Revolution ends its colonialism in the developing world
1975–2002	Angolan Civil War
1974	Ethiopian Revolution
1981	Egyptian president Anwar Sadat assassinated
1983–1984	Ethiopia Famine
1990	Nelson Mandela released from prison
1992–1994	Operation Restore Hope in Somalia
1983–2002	Sudanese Civil War

Africa from colonies to countries

1   How much do you know about the transition from African colonialism to independence? What names, places, or events come to mind?
2   Where do your ideas about this come from?
3   How legitimate are the sources of your information?
4   Do you gain anything from thinking this way?

The foregoing questions attempt to elicit a gut reaction and an intellectual reflection from the reader. These are important to consider because they help us lay out what we know and think we know about a presumably obscure series of topics for most people in the West. Depth of knowledge itself is incredibly hard to come by, even among the most worthy of scholars, journalists, activists, politicians, and so on and, therefore, these questions are valid points of reflection and reference for anyone, especially introductory students. The era of this chapter is the next stage after colonialism. It examines the details of how Africans shed the chains of their imperial masters in the hopes of achieving self-determination, and yet, so many, indeed, most were not much better off at the end of the century than they were upon independence a mere two generations before.

Why is this? Can it be explained by the horrors of European colonialism? Or is it, as some think, in spite of the benefits of European colonialism? That is, is it the fault of outsiders or insiders? Should Africans have adhered to European values or to those of their own? Is Western capitalism (which has extracted wealth from Africa) the cause of their poverty, or has their lack of pluralistic democracy and free market capitalism from within caused their poverty? The individual histories of the 1952–1994 period shed considerable light on the differences and similarities experienced across the continent, and the reader should pay close attention to and perhaps even categorize them into groups according to political trajectories and results to better understand them.

The issue of development in particular, to which we return on a theoretical level in Part IV of this book, can be viewed systematically in Africa during this period. Like Latin American countries from the 1930s to 1980s, African countries relied on the ideology of economic nationalism from the 1960s to 1980s to assert their own agency as new nations and to accelerate growth during their post-colonial era. In particular, they used import substitution industrialization (ISI), hoping to leap into the industrialized world much the way hoped by Latin American countries. However, Latin America had more than a century of independence from Spain and Portugal by the time it began ISI, whereas Africa started with ISI almost immediately after independence. Latin America was more stable than Africa as well, with a longer history of building up the necessary infrastructure to build and maintain economic and political systems. In addition, it had a relatively solid class of intellectuals, business leaders, and political connections with the West as sovereign, albeit to varying degrees dependent, governments and borders. If Latin American progress turned out as it did, with all of its problems, how could Africa fare any better?

The trend across Africa was decisively more socialist than capitalist during this period, with Zaire and South Africa standing out as more friendly to the West, and Angola, Egypt (under Nasser), Algeria, Ghana, Tanzania, Zimbabwe, Libya, and many others more socialist for long periods of time. However, African traditions mitigated any dogmatic leaning toward the left or the right, and almost no leaders pushed for complete nationalization along Communist Bloc lines. This is understandable considering the low literacy rates, the high unemployment, the high rates of infant mortality and infectious disease, and the virtual absence of preparation for self-governance. In 1960, 80 percent of the population of Africa depended on small-scale agriculture with minimal government assistance to survive, a proportion similar to that of the West two centuries before. In the two centuries since, Africans had been held back by a variety of forces, some of which were the choice of Africans themselves who preferred their own non-Western traditions that had evolved on their own with their own merits over thousands of years, and others were beyond African control. European colonialism, slavery, drought, and disease all played a role in Africa's development foundations prior to independence, as we have seen. It is difficult to know to what extent the blame of Africa's development problems can be placed on outside or inside factors.

What is patently obvious, however, is that nearly all the economic and governmental infrastructure that existed in Africa upon its independence from Europe had been set up exclusively to increase European power. The police, military, railroads, roads, ports, communication, resource exploitation, and government ministries served a purpose different from that needed by newly independent African countries. After independence, foreigners still controlled most of the economy for many years. Politicians thus accreted power unto themselves and their one-party states regularly to centralize control over the economy as a means of overcoming this colonial legacy.

Some leaders, feeling the demands of millions of unemployed and downtrodden citizens, sought massive outside assistance. Many received Soviet and Chinese help (economic, military, political), which exacerbated the Sino-Soviet rivalry that began to emerge in the late 1950s and lasted until the end of the Cold War, and others sought Western assistance. The superpowers used Africa as a large chess board to gain small victories in the Cold War. However, it was not as if Africans let themselves be used. They, in fact, had a much larger stake in this battle because they were the ones fighting and dying over it. The ANC, the MPLA, Derg, Lumumba, Kabila, Nkrumah, Amin, and other acronyms and names used the superpowers for their own purposes. These groups and leaders wanted to operate on the world stage. They had every interest in doing so precisely because they felt their causes were just in a generalized (i.e., not simply localized) sense. It behooved them to internationalize the struggle to gain allies, to legitimize themselves, and to increase their own power and prestige. If the people of their countries benefited, so much the better, but this usually did not occur.

Therefore, it was not uncommon to see many different nationalities fighting over small pieces of territory in Africa during the Cold War. Tens of thousands of Cuban doctors, nurses, teachers, politicians, and soldiers spread their influence across Africa. European, Rhodesian, and South African racist mercenaries employed by the CIA and other Western intelligence agencies were a common sight as well. Egyptians advised Algerians, Tunisians, Cubans, Sudanese, and Moroccans about revolution, while Tanzanians attracted revolutionaries and moderates from around the world to see how peaceful socialism could be, despite its lackluster economic achievements. And South African anti-apartheid rebels trained in the Soviet Union and Algeria, received Cuban aid, and elicited the sympathy of consumers from around the globe who launched a boycott of South African exports to end the racial segregation regime there. These stories continue in the pages following.

South Africa

The history of South Africa cannot be boiled down to the struggle between blacks and whites over apartheid. This system of imposed segregation and discrimination was only part of the wider complex history of a country that evolved in its creation unlike any other in Africa. The Afrikaners, English, and many African tribes, not to mention the immigrants from Asia and other continents that forged the new nation at the turn of the century, knew that conflict would continue with so many competing ethnic, regional, religious, and economic interests. With the institutionalization of the apartheid regime in 1948, the white population believed they had found the answer to the stability question.

Nelson Mandela and the African National Congress (ANC) responded to apartheid with accelerated militancy beginning in 1949. They used nonviolent resistance, especially with strikes in workplaces and schools, to which the Afrikaners responded with the Suppression of Communism Act in 1950, criminalizing all political dissent. The ANC then began its Defiance Campaign in 1952: 8,000 activists got themselves arrested breaking apartheid laws to overwhelm the justice system with their incarceration levels. In 1958, the new prime minister, the Nazi-trained Hendrik Verwoerd (1958–1966) instituted racial divisions across the country that officially separated blacks and whites. The ANC sought a "multiracial" future, however, not segregation or even black supremacy, and therefore viewed Verwoerd's plan as an entrenchment of discrimination. This indeed was Verwoerd's plan. Areas such as District 6, where people of all backgrounds lived in racial harmony prior to Verwoerd, were forbidden after 1958. Mixed-race families were separated from one another. Blacks and whites were not allowed to have sexual relations. Non-whites were required to apply for and carry a pass into any white areas. Many were arrested for violating these laws, which only escalated the tensions in this already tense country.

The March 1960 Sharpeville massacre by police that killed 69 people protesting the pass law added insult to injury. Mandela responded in 1961 by organizing a national strike, which ultimately failed. The ANC leader announced that violence was their only alternative now, as nonviolent resistance was met only with force by the apartheid regime. He created the Umkhonto we Sizwe (Spear of the Nation) with the combined assistance of the ANC and the Communist Party. Shortly after an 18-month bombing

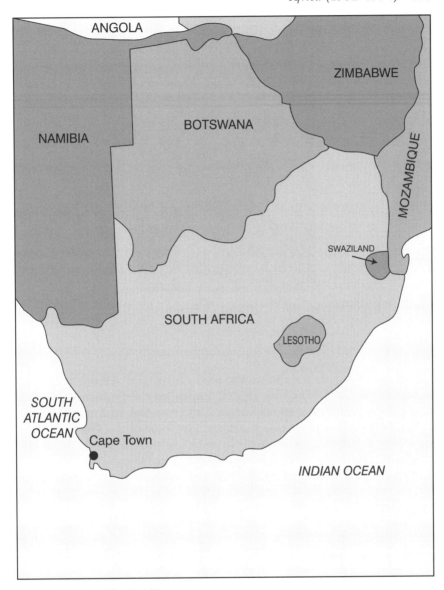

Figure 6.1 Map of South Africa

campaign to disrupt the economy began, Mandela left South Africa to collect support and training from other African states. He returned in 1962 and was soon arrested along with many other ANC members. He was sentenced to life imprisonment, and would serve 27 years before being set free. The first decade seemed hopeless, without much international attention or leniency for the black population in South Africa. A war in a former Portuguese colony would contribute to the coming winds of change, however.

Figure 6.2 Nelson Mandela (1918–) (Oistein Thomassen/Alamy)

Angola

The history of Angola was overlooked until a revolution overthrew the king of Portugal in 1974. The new regime dismantled the Portuguese empire, granting independence to its colonies in Africa and Asia. Its African colonies of Angola and Mozambique soon plunged into some of the worst civil wars the continent had ever seen. Angola in particular made headlines due to the rapid involvement of many different countries in the cause. The Angolan Popular Liberation Movement (MPLA) had emerged as an independence movement in 1956 under the leadership of the doctor-poet Agostinho Neto, a socialist supported by Moscow and Havana. The Soviets supported revolutionary movements in Africa and Asia to a much higher degree than in Latin America with the exception of Cuba and Nicaragua, as these two larger continents were under less U.S. influence during the Cold War. The Soviets and Cubans competed with the United States in several wars in Africa in the 1970s and 1980s, as Africa was seen as fertile territory for the acquisition of further influence for both sides.

Upon independence in 1975, the Cuban- and Soviet-backed MPLA quickly rose to prominence among the three revolutionary groups competing for dominance in Angola. The MPLA's opponents were the United States and the South Africa-backed National Front for the Liberation of Angola (FNLA), led by Holden Roberto, and the National Union for the Total Independence of Angola (UNITA), led by Jonas Savimbi. The South African military invaded Angola from the south through Namibia (not independent until 1980) in

1975 to support the FNLA and UNITA, eliciting the arrival of thousands of Cuban troops to drive the South Africans out. The Soviet-trained Cubans defeated the U.S.-backed South Africans in early 1976 and helped the MPLA achieve temporary victory and control over the government in Luanda. The civil war would continue until 2002, with stages of relative peace in between and additional incursions by the South Africans into the 1980s, leaving 300,000 dead Angolans and making this oil-rich nation the population with the highest amputee rate in the world. The issue of "blood diamonds" first hit international attention during this war as it became apparent that the UNITA and other anti-MPLA groups were using control over the diamond trade to finance their war.

In a surprising twist of fate, the total failure of the South African military and apartheid government to defeat the Cubans and the MPLA severely weakened the long-standing white supremacist system run out of Johannesburg. President Nelson Mandela, upon meeting Fidel Castro for the first time, referred to the Cuban leader as "my president, my brother" and pleaded with him to visit South Africa as soon as possible, making it clear just how important Cuba was in assisting the anti-apartheid cause through its support of the MPLA and the ANC. When Castro did arrive in South Africa in 1998, he was given a hero's welcome. He spoke to the South African parliament about the glory of the ANC's triumph over apartheid and was given thunderous applauses in between his remarks. As he slowly exited the hall, the parliament members of all races smiled widely as they danced, clapped, and sang the words, "Fi-del Cas-tro, Fi-del Cas-tro." The extent to which Cuba helped end apartheid can never be fully measured, and it must be coupled with the ANC's actions within South Africa and the international campaign to pressure the apartheid government into dismantling its system of racial discrimination. The day Nelson Mandela was released from prison in 1990, Angola and Cuba were not on the lips of international observers. Instead, people looked to South Africa with hope, embodied in the 72-year-old former lawyer who had now become the most famous person on the planet.

Egypt

Africa in the 1950s was an exciting if precarious place. This is the era of the giants of African nationalist leadership. Aside from Ghana's Kwame Nkrumah (1957–1966) in West Africa, North Africa had several notable leaders, chief among them was Gamal Abdul Nasser (1956–1970). In both cases, these leaders are considered the most important leaders in their countries' modern histories. However, Nasser distinguished himself for the global implications of his rule. Not only did he lead a successful revolt that ended 2,500 years of foreign rule over Egypt, he nationalized the Suez Canal and led the Middle East–wide anti-Israel movement and the Pan-Arabism movement. Though several of his endeavors failed, namely the elimination of Israel, his star nevertheless rose tremendously high. Timing was key to

Figure 6.3 Gamal Abdul Nasser (1918–1970) (Pictorial Press Ltd./Alamy)

his influence: The Cold War was hitting its peak in the 1950s, and thus his actions attracted the attention of both superpowers that were armed to the teeth with nuclear weapons. During the Cold War, the leaders of the developing world experienced a level of power and scrutiny from the outside world never before witnessed. Their actions now had meaning on a global stage, and leaders such as Nasser, Castro, Mao, and Ho, to name but a few, chose to use that new power to exert "Third World" power, which threatened the power of the West and sometimes promoted the power of the Communist Bloc.

King Farouk had ruled Egypt from 1936 to 1952 as part of a line of Turkish monarchs going back to Muhammad Ali's takeover of Egypt in 1805. Since then, the Ali dynasty had ruled Egypt with British assistance. In 1952, Nasser's Society of Free Officers (Dhobat el-Ahrar) overthrew Farouk and gained independence from England in one fell swoop. However, Farouk left the country with millions in treasure, a common act by departing tyrants in Africa and Latin America during this period. The new government was headed by the Revolutionary Command Council and, in 1953, declared Egypt a republic. Nasser also achieved Sudanese independence from Great Britain (Sudan had been ruled by Egypt and Great Britain since 1819) in gradual stages between 1953 and 1956, but attempts to unify the two countries proved problematic, in part due to religious and regional divisions. Southern Sudanese Christians feared northern Muslim dominance upon independence if unified with Egypt and, in the end, Sudan became an independent republic that has suffered from intermittent civil conflict over the past five decades. Millions have died, and many more have become both internal and external refugees, making Sudan, an oil-rich country, one of the most destitute places on the planet.

On July 26, 1956, seven months after Sudan gained independence, Nasser carried out his most (in)famous act. He nationalized the French- and British-owned Suez Canal, provoking military intervention by the French, British, and Israelis. The Canal served as the primary passage for Middle East oil headed to Europe and, as such, represented one of the most strategic locations in the world. In an uncharacteristic move by the United States, President Dwight Eisenhower (1953–1961) used the UN to pressure the three countries to back down within two days. Their withdrawal was a humiliation for Britain and France in particular, and while the French continued defending its colonial aspirations elsewhere in Africa, for the British, the Suez fiasco signaled the beginning of the end of its Empire in Africa.

Despite Egypt's military loss to Israel, Nasser emerged from the Suez Crisis as the larger-than-life hero of the developing world, and his years were characterized by extreme ups and downs. His main enemy was Israel, and the Arab world believed he would lead an invasion to crush the Jewish state eventually. Before he could launch his planned invasion in 1967, Israel bombed the Egyptian air force into oblivion on the ground and quickly took possession of the Sinai Peninsula, effectively cutting Nasser off at the knees. Nasser never got the chance to retaliate. He died in 1970, and power passed to his protégé, Anwar Sadat (1970–1981), modern Egypt's second-most important leader. Sadat was more moderate than Nasser, expelling all Soviet advisors and eventually reaching a peace agreement with Israel in the Camp David Accords of 1978, for which he was awarded the Nobel Peace Prize. However, this was after he launched an invasion of Israel in 1973 (the Yom Kippur War) and won back the Sinai, humiliating Israel in the process. His presidency helped to achieve a balance of power in the Middle East whereby the two strongest regional militaries, Israel and Egypt, were no longer at war. On the eighth anniversary of the Yom Kippur War, Sadat was assassinated by Islamic fundamentalists for his moderate stance toward Israel.

Sadat's legacy continued under his successor, Hosni Mubarak (1981–2011), who ruled for thirty years until the Arab Spring of 2011 that swept him from power in popular unarmed protest. Mubarak maintained peace with Israel during this period while receiving tens of billions of dollars in U.S. military aid, which helped him also maintain complete control over Egyptian political life.

Ghana

Although small by comparison to many African countries, Ghana has been an economic and political leader in the past century due to its natural and human resources. Named The Gold Coast by British colonizers, Ghana has been a major gold and cocoa producer for more than a century. By the time of independence in 1957, it enjoyed the highest level of prosperity in the

Figure 6.4 Kwame Nkrumah (1909–1972) (Bettmann/ Corbis)

tropics across the globe, and its founding father, Kwame Nkrumah, was also the main African nationalist leader. Nkrumah studied philosophy, economics, and sociology in the United States and spent time with leftists in London, which raised his consciousness about pushing for Ghanaian independence. He became an ardent activist within the Convention People's Party (CPP), which led to his imprisonment in 1949 by then-governor Charles Arden-Clarke. Yet, when the CPP gained thirty-four of thirty-eight parliamentary seats in 1951, the governor released Nkrumah and allowed him to enter his new post as prime minister. This was under a new platform of joint British-Ghanaian authority that still reigned supreme at this time as Ghana eased toward self-rule.

Nkrumah took a measured yet proactive approach to independence. He recognized the dangers of rapid transition while trusting in his government's ability to act alone. In 1954, he convinced the British to allow complete Ghanaian authority over the government and, by 1957, two grassroots parties, the CPP and the National Liberation Movement (NLM), competed in elections overseen by the British. This made total independence official on March 6, 1957, several years in advance of most African countries. Ghana's future looked positive, with strong cocoa and gold exports and the first sub-Saharan African-led independence movement. In 1958, Nkrumah invited 300 African delegates to the capital, Accra, for the All African People's Conference for an ideological discussion on the road the rest of Africa could take toward independence from Europe. Many future leaders and contenders for leadership across Africa attended. Yet, despite Nkrumah's anti-colonialist stance, he was known to have greatly admired Queen Elizabeth, and she admired him as well. He was invited several times to England, and was even awarded membership in Her Majesty's Most Honourable Privy Council.

Though beloved by most of his countrymen, trouble quickly began to brew over his political and economic policies. He marginalized all opposition quickly and created a one-party state (soon duplicated by most African nationalist leaders) that relied on patronage. This made both him and his CPP cronies wealthy as the country plunged into debt while the economy slumped. No longer did Ghana hold the coveted position of "most prosperous in the tropics"; instead, its socialist practices drove prices of all commodities down, including the all-important gold and cocoa, angering much of the population. This only widened the economic divide he had initially claimed to close with independence. In addition, like Castro and Nasser, Nkrumah supported rebel movements in neighboring countries, which angered the heads of state in Nigeria, Niger, Togo, and Cote d' Ivore, as a means of spreading his own prestige and influence.

In February 1966, a military coup supported by the CIA overthrew Nkrumah, in the process killing eight Soviet advisors. The next thirteen years witnessed two more coups and the rise to power of Jerry Rawlings, who provided relative stability to Ghana between 1979 and 2000. Rawlings was most known for his decision to reverse Nkrumah's state-run economic policies and moving Ghana toward neo-liberalism in the 1980s. This practice was followed by most of Africa and Latin America during this same period. By 1994, despite a long period of relative tranquility, ethnic violence broke out in the north, killing 1,000 people.

Algeria

Unlike Ghana and Egypt, the movement toward Algerian independence led to the deaths of 1 million people and lasted eight years. The French had lost several important colonies in the past, beginning with Haiti in 1803 and, by 1954, they had lost Vietnam and were slowly handing over sovereignty to Tunisia and Morocco, but none of these mattered as much as Algeria. The French had always considered Algeria as a French province. It was just across the Mediterranean and despite the 9 million Algerians in the majority, there were 1 million whites of various European backgrounds who were French citizens. The war began on All Saints Day, November 1, 1954, when the National Liberation Front (FLN) launched a series of coordinated minor raids on French army units. This revolt did not begin out of the blue, for the Algerians had suffered major French abuses in recent years, all the while being largely excluded from political and economic life in their own country. The FLN was composed of a variety of revolutionary tendencies, some Muslim fundamentalist, some socialist, but all with the same purpose: Algerian independence.

Both sides committed atrocities on a scale all too commonly seen in twentieth-century Africa. The FLN carried out bombings of Algerian and

French civilians in public places and other heinous tactics, while the French military became notorious for torturing suspects and massacring civilians. The intensity of the French *paras'* (soldiers') brutality was portrayed in the famous propaganda film *The Battle of Algiers*, which sought to illustrate the plight of the FLN in the face of French atrocities during this actual battle of 1957. The French rounded up thousands of poor Algerians in the Kasbah district of Algiers and many other places, torturing and killing untold numbers. This campaign did much to reduce the FLN's power and, when new oil discoveries promised high yields in 1958, the French became even more entrenched in Algeria.

The tide began to turn in the FLN's favor in May 1958 after a *pied noir* (French in Algeria) revolt against the status quo brought former French Prime Minister Charles De Gaulle back to power. The *pied noir* believed De Gaulle would crush the FLN once and for all, and instead he eventually handed the Algerians independence in 1962.

Independent Algeria faced several problems in spite of its recent victory over the French. Independence had been forged mostly in the fires of war and some intellectualism and diplomacy. The first President, FLN leader Ahmed Ben Bella (1962–1965), had spent most of the Revolution in prison and, therefore, was ill-prepared for the difficulties of running such a large, divided, and poor country. He was overthrown by his Minister of Defense Hourani Boumediene, who served from 1965 to 1978. The FLN regime lasted from 1962 to 1988 under the same three aspects that had won the Revolution: militarism, socialism, and Islam. It ran the economy along socialist lines that created both economic and population growth, causing the cities to swell. Debt also rose and, in the 1980s, so did ethnic and religious discontent. The minority Berber population and Islamic fundamentalists in particular felt repressed and excluded due to the FLN's efforts to limit group cohesion outside of its control.

In October 1988, riots erupted over price increases, and the army killed upward of 500 people. President Chadli Benjedid (1979–1992) then instituted a new constitution that loosened the FLN's control, and this led to a brief political opening that brought about both moderate and extremist parties in the 1991 elections. However, when the Islamic Salvation Front (FIS) party seemed poised to win, an FLN-led coup began a wave of anti-FIS repression. Throughout the 1990s, the FLN government battled with Islamic militants now under the name of the Armed Islamic Group. More than 100,000 died in this intermittent warfare, further diminishing Algeria's chances for a thriving future.

Nigeria

Though most of Algeria's ethnic tensions were minimal in the two decades after independence from France, Nigeria is a different story. Its divisions have been a mainstay of life ever since it embarked on its national experiment in the 1950s. It is also one of the world's top oil-producing countries, making its economic stakes high both nationally and internationally. It is also Africa's most populous country (158 million). It is divided into three rival regions, each of which contains multiple ethnic groups. The Muslim north is occupied by Hausa and Fulani peoples with traditionally less education, and they were given less attention by the British under colonialism. The Christian south is divided between the Yoruba in the west and the Igbo in the east. When the British granted independence in 1960 as part of a general pattern of British policy in Africa, the north received proportional representation, which represented a threat to the divided south.

In fact, all three regions operated semi-autonomously with ultimate authority vested in the Prime Minister and parliament in Lagos. With independence came an entrenched system of corruption based on bribery whereby political parties wielded power and siphoned government funds for themselves. Thus, the public's money paid for a system that perpetuated the very power of those stealing the public funds. The first political scandal hit right away: The Action Group government became notorious for its corruption between 1958 and 1962 when it was revealed it had diverted millions of dollars in contracts to businesses owned by Action Group party members.

However, the biggest challenge to the governmental system erupted in January 1966 when Igbo militants executed Prime Minister Sir Abubakar Tafawa Balewa (1960–1966) and other government officials in the western and northern regions. The army responded with a state of siege that quickly escalated into a civil war pitting the northern Muslims against the southern Christians. The Igbo coup leader, General Ironsi, claimed that his goal had been to overthrow the corrupt government. However, northerners suspected it was simply to increase Igbo and, therefore, Christian dominance. Ironsi ended the federation that had given semi-autonomy to all three regions and declared Nigeria unified on May 24, 1966. The northern-born General Yakubu Gowon then overthrew and assassinated Ironsi on July 29, 1966, reinstated the federation, and ran the country until 1975.

Though the coup appeared to resolve northern complaints about the January 1966 coup's termination of the federation, the Igbo-led coup only increased northern hatred of the Igbo. Muslims in the north killed thousands of Igbos living among them, driving most of the remaining Igbo into the east, causing a humanitarian crisis of epic proportions. The Igbo next announced their secession in the east under the banner of the new nation of Biafra, which was met with widespread repression by the Gowon government in what became known as the Nigerian Civil War (1967–1970). More than 1 million people died as international humanitarianism rose to heights never before seen in modern Africa, mostly providing aid to the suffering Igbos of the Biafra cause. The war ended in January 1970 along with the Biafra movement.

Gowon was seen as a source of stability in Nigeria despite his repressive tactics most evident in the Civil War. He was overthrown in 1975, and the new government soon led the way toward elections that brought Alhaji Shehu Shagari (1979–1983) to power in 1979. Shagari served a full four-year term but was overthrown in 1983 in a coup that was then followed by another in 1985, which instituted military rule until 1999 under various generals, most notably General Sani Abacha (1993–1998).

Kenya

The post-WWII era in Kenya was marked by an increase in population, violence, and nationalism that put this East African nation on the radar of many a Western observer. The Mau Mau rebellion in particular that lasted from 1952 to 1960 began initially due to the displacement of Kikuyu peoples by the influx of tens of thousands of newly arrived British subjects, many of whom were ex-soldiers. The Kikuyu resistance to these encroachments became known as the Mau Maus, but they did not represent all resistance to British imperialism in Kenya. Jomo Kenyatta, Kenya's founding father, headed the more moderate Kenya African Union (KAU) and enjoyed the most support from the Kikuyu peoples. However, others such as Bildad Kaggia and Fred Kubai favored insurrection, which Kenyatta openly opposed. Nevertheless, Kenyatta and 150 KAU cadre were jailed in 1952 while 100,000 Kikuyu farmers were forcibly removed by British colonial authorities from their lands in the Rift Valley. By 1958, the Mau Maus had killed thousands of Kikuyus loyal to the British and targeted whites only in small numbers. When the Mau Maus were largely defeated in 1958, the British enacted land and political reforms that sought to rectify some of the past injustices. Blacks were given more land and equal representation in parliament, a trend that was growing in other British colonies from East to West Africa.

During this period, the British aimed to create the Federation of Rhodesia and Nyasaland (modern-day Zimbabwe, Zambia, and Malawi). They were met with opposition from Malawi's founding father, the Nyasaland surgeon Hastings Banda and his Nyasaland African National Congress. All over British Africa, from Kenya to Nigeria to Ghana to Rhodesia and Uganda, Africans united in independence from Britain. The British faced the dilemma between giving independence to these poor countries with little infrastructure for national development and keeping up the expensive and hated colonial administrations. The danger of allowing quick independence without a slow transition was the inevitable power vacuum that could result in an invitation to Communist infiltration or, simply, a local despot.

Kenyatta himself was released in 1961, and Kenyan independence was granted two years later. As prime minister (1963–1964) and president (1964–1978), his plan was to maintain his moderate approach, which included easing white fears over black dominance and marginalization of the white population. His 1968 book entitled *Suffering without Bitterness* would have made Nelson Mandela proud in 1994 for advocating forgiveness and reconciliation. The transition to independence for all British colonies took two courses. Between 1951 and 1960, Ghana and Nigeria transitioned gradually over a period of several years before complete autonomy, whereas Kenya, Tanzania, Zambia, Malawi, Uganda, Rhodesia, Botswana, Lesotho, Swaziland, and Sierra Leone transitioned over a period of mere months or less between 1961 and 1968. The new leaders of the independent countries were largely friendly toward Britain and considered their former colonial master an ally. They did not base their nationalism on anti-British sentiments, unlike Algeria and the Congo with the French and the Belgians.

Independent Kenya stood out as an example of relative stability and prosperity by comparison to most of Anglophone Africa due to Kenyatta's leadership. He was considered by most to rule fairly, helping to distribute public funds to support infrastructure development, and galvanizing Kenyan nationalism in the process. However, this period also witnessed massive population growth that quickly flooded the major cities, and today the most impoverished people of the countryside vie for the unenviable distinction of most destitute with people living in Nairobi's slums.

Tanzania

Tanzania also gave birth to an exceptional leader in the form of Julius Nyerere (1964–1985), a moderate socialist intellectual and founding father like Kenyatta. He actually argued against European and North America–style democracy in Africa by pointing out how African independence was based on a unified opposition to European rule, not on a unified vision of Africa's future. This was different than the struggles carried out in the West in which parties emerged out of a need to represent ideological differences. Instead, the rivalries that existed in Africa (ethnic and religious primarily) were not dealt with prior to the realization of independence, and, therefore, the allowance of parties that would represent these factions would inevitably surpass the need to move forward as a unified nation. Nyerere advocated for a unified nationalistic push for economic growth as the only way forward for new African nations as a means of overcoming these divisions that became apparent in places such as Nigeria, Sudan, South Africa, Zimbabwe, the Congo, Rwanda, and Burundi.

Nyerere's political platform constituted a model whereby all interests would theoretically fall under the umbrella of the one-party socialist state that had the power and the interest to take all parties into consideration through the use of patronage. In practice throughout Africa, this provided a system whereby the only path to wealth and power was through the state. Still, Nyerere did not use this system to enrich himself or his allies, and he was respected and admired both within and outside Africa. Nyerere's main economic policy rested on collectivization, which ultimately plunged Tanzania's agricultural exports into the abyss, forcing the government to carry out structural adjustment programs in the 1980s. Nyerere also supported various armed revolts in Uganda, Mozambique, and South Africa in particular and even used Tanzanian troops to oust Ugandan dictator Idi Amin in 1979.

Uganda

Post-independence Uganda can be divided into two distinct eras. The first was dominated by two of the continent's most violent tyrants, Milton Obote (1962–1971, 1979–1985) and Idi Amin (1971–1979). Between them, they killed between 500,000 and 1 million people, wrecked the economy, and made Uganda one of the weakest states on the planet. It was plagued by poverty, disease, and violence during this period, and yet, the second era has been dominated by a more inspiring leader, Yoweri Museveni (1985–), whose National Resistance Army (NRA) overthrew Obote in 1985. In the first era, the state had a monopoly on violence, which it used at the whims of the dictator, whereas the second era has used force at times to combat Joseph Koney's Lord's Resistance Army (LRA) and Sudan and the Democratic Republic of Congo.

Obote was independent Uganda's first prime minister (1962–1966), but he quickly overthrew his own president in 1966 and served in that post until Idi Amin overthrew him in 1971. This first term as head of state was a socialist exercise in accreting all power unto himself through the use of force against all potential opponents. This empowered his army commander, Idi Amin, who carried out his dirty work. Still, the 1960s witnessed Uganda's rise as East Africa's strongest economy as tea, coffee, and cocoa exports increased. These economic benefits did not reach most of the population, however, and after a falling out with Amin, Obote was overthrown with little dissent among the military or the Ugandan people.

Amin was quick to root out all dissent in a manner even more ruthless than that of Obote. He armed loyalists who murdered large numbers of Acholi and Langi, the tribes loyal to Obote. He increased his brutality as his paranoia grew over potential plots against him. He ultimately left between 250,000 and 500,000 dead bodies in his wake by the time Tanzania invaded in 1979 (after Amin's troops had invaded northern Tanzania). He eventually found asylum in Saudi Arabia. Obote took his place and soon duplicated the level of barbarity meted out by Amin, until being overthrown by Museveni's NRA in 1985.

Although Amin and Obote stand out as particularly barbaric (and even mentally ill in Amin's case), there were several other African leaders during this period that exemplified the height of brutality in a similar manner. Joseph Sese Mobutu (1965–1997) of Zaire certainly ranks among these, as does Haile Mengitsu Mariam (1974–1991) of Ethiopia. Perhaps Amin's closest rival was the dictator of the tiny former Spanish colony, Equatorial Guinea. Francisco Macias Nguema ruled his country of 300,000 people as its first president after independence from 1968 to 1979 with complete contempt for them. His delusional sense of grandiosity led him to drive out the entire Spanish population (who owned most of the coffee and cocoa industries) and foreign laborers in a move similar to that taken by Amin in 1975 when the Ugandan dictator expelled all Asians to much acclaim in Africa. Like Amin, Nguema killed all opponents, real and imagined, reaching a total of 50,000, or one-sixth of the population. He also murdered large numbers of his own top government officials, destroyed the economy, and abolished all modern forms of education, instead compelling his people to view reality only in terms approved by him. His own nephew led a coup against him in 1979, after which the former dictator was executed.

The dictator of the Central African Republic, Jean-Bedel Boukassa (1966–1979), also deserves special mention here for the devastation he wrought on his country. He drained much of the nation's resources for his own personal whims and wasted millions of dollars more on poorly planned economic schemes as most of his people languished in poverty. Boukassa renamed his country the Central African Empire in 1976, and had himself crowned emperor. He murdered thousands of his opponents and relished in his fame and power on a scale far beyond his actual stature, all with French support. He used this support to build multiple large mansions in his home country while maintaining lavishly adorned homes in France and purchasing dozens of luxury cars, even as the vast majority of his people plunged further into destitution. The French eventually overthrew him and reinstalled former president David Dacko (1960–1965, 1979–1981) in 1979.

Somalia and Ethiopia: The Horn of Africa

The Horn of Africa is an arid region in East Africa with hardened people whose history of independence stands out within Africa. Ethiopia has been independent throughout its history with the exception of a five-year period in which Italian dictator Benito Mussolini took over the country from 1936–1941, and Somalia was rarely under the control of just one European master. The British held control over the north of Somalia from 1886 to 1941 and the Italians over the south from 1885 to 1941. That year, the British took over the entire colony, yet Somalia had preserved its own monarch throughout this period and maintained a strong amount of autonomy. Somalia was given its independence in 1960, but this was quickly overshadowed by conflict with its western neighbor, Ethiopia. Wars in the 1960s and 1970s that have not halted completely to this day brought the superpowers into the Horn of Africa's internal and cross-border affairs. Somali popular anger erupted after Somali Prime Minister Muhammad Ibrahim Egal (1967–1969) gave up claims to the Ogaden, a region in Ethiopia inhabited by Somalis. He was ousted in a coup in 1969 that brought Siad Barre (1969–1991) to power. The

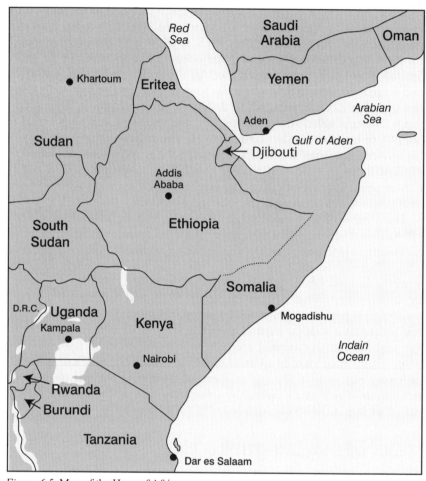

Figure 6.5 Map of the Horn of Africa

Soviets first supported Somalia between 1969 and 1977 but then switched to supporting Ethiopia in its quest to protect the Ogaden territory from a Somali invasion from 1977 to 1978. The United States supported Somalia in this invasion.

The Ethiopian Revolution of 1974 altered the course of the Horn in many ways. The revolt not only overthrew Africa's most beloved leader, King Haile Selassie (1930–1975), but initiated a terrible wave of repression under a Communist junta known as the Derg that ended the lives of more than 1 million people. The new leader, the Marxist Haile Mengitsu Mariam (1974–1991), killed 100,000 people from 1977 to 1978 in what has been dubbed the "Red Terror." Mengitsu's use of Cuban and Soviet troops also put the superpowers at loggerheads with one another as the United States decided to throw its support behind Barre's fight with Ethiopia from 1977 to

1978. In a move presaging the famine and war that would hit Somalia from 1991 to 1993, Mengitsu used starvation as a tool against the Tigray peoples, who rose up against him from 1983 to 1984, which led to the deaths of more than 1 million people. The famine in Ethiopia was the worst to hit modern Africa, and their plight soon became the focus of international attention as people from around the globe raised funds to send food aid, much of which was intercepted by Mengitsu. Mengitsu was finally overthrown by the Ethiopian People's Revolutionary Democratic Front in May 1991 after the Soviet Union had halted assistance to his regime as part of Mikhail Gorbachev's larger effort to liberalize the Soviet system under perestroika and glasnost. Of course, the Soviet Union itself dissolved in December of that year.

While Mengitsu was on his way to asylum in Zimbabwe in 1991, Barre was also on his way out of Somalia for eventual exile in Nigeria. A coup led by Muhammad Farah Aidid, a future warlord of ill-repute, demolished the Barre regime and plunged the country into civil conflict that has lasted to the time of this writing. The number of deaths since 1991 has reached 1 million, but a third of these were caused in the first year after the coup due to a great famine that killed 300,000, which ushered in the UN mission, Operation Restore Hope. The famine was exacerbated by the lack of infrastructure in place inside Somalia to distribute food, as there was no government to speak of, and multiple warlords commanded thousands of troops each. They were armed by the very Cold War era weapons provided the Somali military by Italy and the United States. The UN was oblivious to the dimensions of the problems lying ahead of it. The purpose of UN troops in Somalia was to ensure that the food aid reached starving Somalis and not warlords using the aid to force people to support them. The UN mission was declared a failure shortly after the infamous "Black Hawk Down" incident of October 3–4, 1993 that ended in 18 dead U.S. soldiers. Two of them were dragged through the streets of Mogadishu for the world to see on television and in the newspapers. It was under-reported at the time that the mission to rescue this company of just more than 100 soldiers led to the killing of more than 1,000 Somalis in Mogadishu and that the UN had killed thousands of Somalis over the course of its mission. Nevertheless, the United States withdrew its troops by March 1994, and the UN officially ended its mission the following year. It was difficult enough for many to accept that so many died in Somalia only to see the international community leave but, in April 1994, a disaster of even greater proportions hit the tiny country of Rwanda.

Zaire

After suffering the worst level of atrocities at the hands of its Belgian colonial masters over a period of eight decades, the Congo was finally a free state in 1960. Ironically, it had been called The Congo Free State under the man who had this enormous Central African colony conquered for his own personal possession from 1885 to 1908. Thus, when his descendant, King Baudouin I (1951–1993), lauded Leopold II and his successor in a speech given to the independent Congolese in June 1960, the new Congo prime minister, Patrice Lumumba, retorted with bitingly accurate criticism condemning Belgian colonialism. The Belgians did not expect one of their former subjects to dismiss their efforts to "civilize" the Congo because they believed in European supremacy over Africans. This much was obvious, but the level of devastation the Belgians meted out against the Congolese, especially under Leopold II, was actually known to all because Leopold's crimes had been exposed in the first international human rights campaign ever launched (in the early 1900s), which led to the end of his ownership of The Congo Free State.

Lumumba had only four years of schooling, but he had experience in the postal union, and he had written an anti-colonialist book entitled *The Congo, My Country* while incarcerated for embezzlement. After his release in 1957, he eventually became a member of the National Congolese Movement (MNC) and openly led the move for independence. He was also inspired by Nkrumah's call to action at the All-African People's Conference in 1958 in Accra, and the Belgians allowed black political movements to form in 1959. Though many political parties emerged along ethnic and regional lines (as predicted by Nyerere), the MNC was alone in pushing for Congolese independence as one nation. The Belgians finally held talks with Congolese groups in January 1960 in Brussels, where it was decided independence would officially begin June 30 of that year.

The Congo was not a country. The reader will remember that it was initially created as a string of 450 chiefdoms that individually agreed to Belgian annexation in the 1880s. This was the opposite from the way in which Western countries were formed. The United States was also created through conquest, but this took place by gradually spreading across the continent over the course of three centuries. The ethnic and regional differences would combine with political and international divisions to undo Congo's democratic experiment almost immediately.

When the MNC was victorious in the June elections and Lumumba was named prime minister, rivalries were already rampant across the country. Not only was President Kasa Vubu (1960–1965) opposed to Lumumba, but the army was run entirely by Belgian officers. Lumumba quickly resolved this problem and placed Joseph Sese Mobutu in charge of the army. Soldiers rose in protest over wages and soon ran rampant across the capital, attacking whites in the streets and causing the Belgians to intervene militarily. There were rebellions in other regions, including the copper mining district of Katanga, where rebel leader Moise Tshombe received Belgian assistance even as the UN intervened to stabilize the country.

The United States added itself to the fray soon enough. The Dwight Eisenhower (1953–1961) administration considered Lumumba a

Communist and authorized the CIA to "eliminate" him. The CIA paid an assassin $100,000 for the job, but he failed to reach Lumumba. Still, Belgian troops and Tshombe's rebels shot Lumumba and several associates in January 1961, ending the Congo's first attempt at democracy. They would not get another one for four decades. The next four years were still chaotic as Katanga was independent until 1963, and a leftist insurgency in eastern Congo led by Laurent Kabila erupted in 1964. This war brought the United States, South Africa, and Rhodesia into allegiance with the Congo military against Kabila and his Cuban guerrilla support unit led by Che Guevara. Che had thought of the Congo as the perfect place for a guerrilla insurgency that could spread throughout Africa. After six months, he and his Cuban comrades left dejected in 1965. The Congolese were not ideologically motivated, nor did they possess the discipline and skill necessary to succeed in guerrilla warfare. Che had no respect for Kabila, who rarely spent time with his troops and gave up rather easily and left for exile in Tanzania.

Mobutu emerged as the only leader capable of instilling a semblance of order in Congo, which he renamed Zaire after taking power from President Kasa Vubu in 1965. Mobutu ruled the country in a manner many other dictators emulated. He was known for his brutality but especially for wasting billions of dollars in international aid for his own luxuries and poorly managed state-run businesses and projects. He rose in stature briefly when he hosted the famous "Rumble in the Jungle" boxing match between Muhammad Ali and George Forman in 1974. Meanwhile, Mobutu became wealthy on international loans he would never pay back and was supported by France and the United States. These loan payments he ultimately placed on the backs of his people when he was overthrown in 1997.

Genocide as the new catchword

The end of the Cold War was supposed to be a time of renewal, a time of reconciliation, a time for peace and prosperity. The historian Francis Fukuyama dubbed it "The End of History," and U.S. President George H. W. Bush called it "The New World Order." Free trade across international boundaries would flourish, and nations would no longer fear catastrophe in this idealized world. However, the world soon realized that the superpower rivalry did not represent even a shred of the deep-seated divisions that had been brewing beneath the surface of many countries. Africa has been perhaps the saddest region on the planet since the end of the Cold War and, in part, this is due to the Cold War itself but is also due to factors inherent to Africa's culture and its pre–Cold War history.

In a way, the UN mission in Somalia from 1992 to 1995 was an attempt to use the world's weaponry for pure good after four decades of armament build-up during the Cold War. Yet, when the peacekeepers arrived, they soon discovered the difficulties of keeping misunderstood hatreds at bay. These mostly non-African UN troops had no comprehension of Somali history. They believed military technology, food, boots on the ground, good intentions, and a positive attitude would somehow win out over any situation. This is a principled stance. Principle, when dealing with millions of human lives in a country with a deep and complex history, is theoretical at best and hypothetical at worst. The principles must be linked to the concrete context in which people are attempting to solve a problem. Those lofty ideals were dashed so quickly in Somalia because all the money, advanced equipment, and heartfelt reasons for being there did not change the fact that no one understood how to fix Somalia. The lesson learned there was the opposite of the anti-genocide slogan used the world over since the Holocaust perpetrated by the Nazis: "Never Again."

In this case, the international community decided "Never Again" would they commit tens of thousands of troops to such a complex and violent situation in Africa. Therefore, when the Rwandan genocide erupted, the moral question was rarely asked: "What should we do to stop this?" Instead, Somalia had taught them to tread carefully, fence-sit and, most important, do not commit to sending too many troops and aid for fear of failure. Cynics may go so far as to accuse the international community of not wanting to risk white lives to save black lives, but this is certainly up for debate. However, the Rwandan genocide, discussed in depth in Chapter 9, did bring to a head this fundamentally moral debate question: What is the principled stance the international community should take when confronting an occurring genocide? The Genocide Convention of 1948 spelled out clearly that if genocide is occurring, the international community has the right to stop it. This rarely made sense to world leaders during the Cold War because any intervention to halt mass killings could be interpreted by one of the superpowers as interference in one side's sphere of influence. In the post–Cold War era, did the international community have to worry about stepping on one another's toes in this same sense? Ask yourself this question when reading the post–Cold War chapters in Part III of the book.

Discussion questions

1   What do you think explains the instability of places such as the Congo (Zaire), Algeria, Nigeria, Angola, South Africa, and Uganda?
2   What do you think explains the relative stability of places such as Tanzania, Kenya, and Egypt during this period?
3   What similarities and differences do you see with Latin America and Asia during the same period?
4   What differences do you believe divide the West from Africa's culture during this period? Do these differences explain anything significant? Explore these questions as far as you want.

Historical figures

Idi Amin (1925–2003)

Ironically made infamous by portrayals of his regime in two films (*General Idi Amin Dada*, 1974 and *The Last King of Scotland*, 2006), Idi Amin was perhaps the most brutal dictator in modern African history. He took power in a coup against Ugandan prime minister Apolo Milton Obote in 1971 and, until the end of his rule in 1979, he reportedly killed up to 500,000 people. He was known for delusions of grandeur and brutality against all opponents, suspected and real. He was ousted in revolution in 1979 and was provided a safe home in exile in Saudi Arabia until his death in 2003.

Frantz Fanon (1925–1961)

This Martinique-born psychiatrist and participant in the Algerian Revolution became famous for authoring several books advocating revolutionary thought and action in the developing world. Most well known is his *The Wretched of the Earth*, which is a must read for anyone who wishes to understand the arguments driving intellectuals toward anti-colonialism, revolution, and socialism in the 1950s and 1960s. Fanon died at the age of thirty-six from leukemia, but his legacy as one of the intellectual pillars of revolutionary tracts is permanently embedded into developing world history.

Jomo Kenyatta (1894--1978)

This Kenyan independence leader was imprisoned on trumped-up charges by British authorities for his anti-colonial advocacy as leader of the Kenya African Union (KAU), which the colonial administration equated with the Mau Mau rebels. However, this first president of Kenya openly spoke out against the Mau Maus and pushed for a moderate road to independence that sought equality between the whites and blacks in Kenya. Kenyatta represented a small group of African nationalists who sought a less radical approach to independence.

Patrice Lumumba (1925–1961)

Although only in office a matter of months, Lumumba's legacy as the first prime minister of the liberated Congo in 1960 has been felt for the past five decades. A former postal clerk and author with only four years of education, Lumumba was part of the growing trend of African anti-colonialist leaders from the Nkrumahist line of thinking that sought to galvanize public opinion through socialism and African nationalism. However, unlike Nkrumah, who presided over a smaller country with much more unification across ethnic and regional lines, Lumumba could never hope to bring together the disparate regions of the Congo under a unified concept of the Congo as a nation. His enemies included Europeans and Africans of many stripes, and he was assassinated in January 1961. This act effectively martyred Lumumba in the eyes of revolutionaries across the developing world.

Gamal Abdul Nasser (1918–1970)

No doubt the most important Egyptian leader of the modern era, Nasser led the Egyptian Revolution that overthrew King Farouk in 1952 and was president from 1956 to 1970. He established a one-party state apparatus that accreted all power to himself and his political and economic allies that remained in place through his two successors, Anwar Sadat (1970–1981) and Hosni Mubarak (1981–2011). He promoted the concept of pan-Arabism as a form of regional solidarity. He also led the regional effort to eliminate Israel (which did not succeed) and nationalized the French/British-owned Suez Canal in 1956.

Agostinho Neto (1922–1979)

The leader of the Angolan Popular Independence Movement (MPLA) and the first Angolan president, Neto's socialist movement, with support from Cuba and the USSR, formed one-half of the civil war that engulfed Angola and Namibia between 1975 and 2002. The other half was formed by Holden Roberto's FNLA guerrillas and Jonas Savimbi's UNITA guerrillas, along with Zaire, the United States, and South Africa. This war cost the lives of 300,000 and made Angola the country with the highest amputee rate in the world.

Kwame Nkrumah (1909–1972)

The godfather of African nationalism, Nkrumah's ideology of anti-colonialism spread throughout Africa due both to his intellectual writings and his leadership of pre-Independence and post-Independence Ghana from 1951 to 1966. Like all other African nationalists, Nkrumah spent time in prison for his anti-colonial activities. However, unlike the rest, he was led from his prison cell directly to the prime minister's office in 1951 after his Convention People's Party (CPP) won parliamentary elections. His reign instituted one-party socialist control over Ghana with the assistance of the Communist Bloc. The economy shrank dramatically during this period, and he was ousted in a coup sponsored by the CIA in 1966.

Julius Nyerere (1922–1999)

One of Africa's most important minds during the 1960s and 1970s, Nyerere distinguished himself among African leaders as a non-tyrannical progressive thinker while maintaining firm control over a one-party state in Tanzania.

He developed a unique style of "African socialism" in Tanzania based on his belief that Africans in general were predisposed to socialistic values. This did not equate to Soviet-style socialism based on the police state. Instead, it was based on the Arusha Declaration of 1967, which called for economic and social development based on the unique needs of Africans such as alleviating extreme poverty. He especially advocated rejection of foreign assistance due to its ability to make poor countries dependent on the interests of foreign entities.

Haile Selassie (1892–1975)

The emperor of Ethiopia from 1930 to 1975, Selassie was known as a staunch independence leader and defender of this only African country never to become a European colony (despite Italian rule from 1936 to 1941). Europeans and Africans respected and trusted him, and Allied powers helped him recover power by driving out the Italians in a joint effort with Ethiopians and Europeans in 1941. Rastafarianism in Jamaica considers Selassie their god from his original name Ras Tafari. He was overthrown in the Ethiopian Revolution in 1974.

Desmond Tutu (1931–)

The first black Anglican Archbishop of South Africa, he was awarded the Nobel Peace Prize in 1984 for his anti-apartheid activism. As Nelson Mandela advocated for a combination of armed and unarmed strategies to overthrow the apartheid system while serving his sentence behind bars, Archbishop Tutu led the international economic boycott movement aimed at weakening the government. He has also championed a wide variety of human rights issues in general, ranging from anti-racism to anti-sexism.

Further readings

Elkins, Caroline. *Imperial Reckoning: The Untold Story of Britain's Gulag in Kenya*. New York: Owl Books, 2005.
Fanon, Frantz. *The Wretched of the Earth*. New York: Grove Press, 2004.
Gleijeses, Piero. *Conflicting Missions: Havana, Washington, and Africa, 1959–1976*. Chapel Hill, NC: University of North Carolina, 2002.
Horne, Alistair. *A Savage War of Peace: Algeria 1954–1962*. New York: New York Review Books Classics, 2006.
Kramer, Mark, ed. *The Black Book of Communism: Crimes, Terror, Repression*. Boston, MA: Cambridge: Harvard University, 1999.
Mandela, Nelson. *Long Walk to Freedom*. London: Little, Brown Group, 1995.
Merideth, Martin. *The Fate of Africa: A History of Fifty Years of Independence*. New York: Public Affairs, 2005.
Osman, Tarek. *Egypt on the Brink: From Nasser to Mubarak*. New Haven, CT: Yale University, 2011.

Peterson, Scott. *Me against my Brother: At War in Somalia, Sudan, and Rwanda*. New York: Routledge, 2001.
Westad, Odd Arne. *The Global Cold War: Third World Interventions and the Making of our Times*. New York: Cambridge University, 2007.

Films

The Last King of Scotland. Dir. Kevin MacDonald. 20th Century Fox, 2007.
Lumumba. Dir. Raoul Peck. Zeitgeist, 2002.
The Battle of Algiers. Dir. Gillo Pontecorvo. Criterion, 2004.
The Color of Freedom. Dir. Bille August. Image, 2008.
Cry the Beloved Country. Dir. Darrell Roodt. Echo Bridge, 2011.

Online content

The National Security Archive: "Secret Cuban Documents on History of African Involvement" www.gwu.edu/~nsarchiv/NSAEBB/NSAEBB67/
East African Community: www.eac.int/
Columbia University Libraries African Studies: www.columbia.edu/cu/lweb/indiv/africa/cuvl/other.html
All Africa: www.allafrica.com
Economic Community of West African States: www.ecowas.int/
Third World Network: Africa: www.twnafrica.org/
Africa Expert.com: www.africa-expert.com/
Africa Renewal: www.un.org/ecosocdev/geninfo/afrec/

Part III
Globalization

7 Latin America and the Caribbean (1992–present)

Timeline

1992	Civil War ends in El Salvador, Abimael Guzman imprisoned in Peru
1993	Pablo Escobar killed in Colombia
1994	NAFTA begins, Zapatista Uprising in Mexico
1996	Guatemalan Civil War officially ends
1998	Hurricane Mitch hits Central America and the Caribbean
1999	Hugo Chavez assumes presidency in Venezuela
2000	Vicente Fox assumes presidency in Mexico, Plan Colombia begins
2001	Argentine debt and Presidential Crisis
2003	Lula assumes presidency in Brazil
2004	Jean Bertrand-Aristide overthrown in Haiti
2006	Evo Morales wins presidency in Bolivia
2008	Fidel Castro steps down as Cuban President, Raul takes over
2009	Mauricio Funes assumes presidency in El Salvador
2011	Daniel Ortega elected to a third term in Nicaragua

With the end of the Cold War, the major issues in Latin America became the Drug War, free trade (neo-liberalism), immigration, and the rise of the Left. All of these issues actually converged with a distancing of United States–Latin American relations and an increase in Latin American–Asian relations. Although Cuba remained Communist and totalitarian, every other nation has instituted democratic political structures. However, the trend toward leftism throughout the vast majority of countries has unsettled the United States, as hard-line leaders such as Hugo Chavez (Venezuela), Evo Morales (Bolivia), and Rafael Correa (Ecuador) have spread their influence, as have more pragmatic left-of-center politicians such as Luis Ignacio da Silva (Lula) in Brazil, Nestor Kirchner of Argentina, Michel Bachelet, and many others. The War on Terror has also risen in importance since the attacks of September 11, 2001, but they have had little overall impact in the region outside of U.S. security policies in Colombia and the U.S.–Mexico border.

Before diving into this chapter, let us flesh out our preconceived notions on this era with some discussion questions:

1 What assumptions do we have about the post–Cold War era in Latin America?
2 Are these assumptions founded on direct observation, readings, hearsay, television, movies? Explain.
3 What weight do we give to the sources of our information about Latin America during this period?
4 Do these ideas reinforce our preconceived notions or challenge them? Explain.

These questions should help us confront the legitimacy of what we think about Latin America during a time when the region is less linked to the West than ever before and as it extends its relations to Asia. Latin Americans continue to struggle for self-determination by using means that have worked in the past and by inventing new ones. The fact that left-wing ideologues still hold considerable sway in some countries says something about this struggle that is elusive to the outsider, unless that outsider visits Latin America's slums, universities, open-air markets, countryside, city squares, and public schools. If one does this and asks people questions about what they want, they will rarely encounter dogmatic anti-West slogans. Instead, they will find a wide range of perspectives. Some have prospered considerably under economic policies dislodged from U.S. oversight. Others are still confused about the causes of poverty in a region with five centuries of contact with Western civilization. They question whether Western notions of democracy, capitalism, and Christianity are really all they have needed to prosper. The ideologies from the Left and the Right tend to ring hollow to the unemployed who have seen nothing but poverty. At the same time, there has been a growth in the middle and upper classes over the past two decades. Some reason that this prosperity began with deregulation in the 1980s whereas others point to government assistance in homegrown businesses as the cause of Latin America's relative success, mostly in the past decade.

The end of the Cold War: Cuba

With the fall of the Berlin Wall in 1989 and the dissolution of the Soviet Union in 1991, many observers believed Cuba would cease to be Communist. Books such as Andres Oppenheimer's *Castro's Final Hour* made this argument twenty years ago and, despite reforms that have provided more freedom of movement and capital, the Communists still reign supreme. How did the Communist Party's power endure without the billions in annual Russian assistance? First, Castro announced that Cubans would have to tighten their belts. They lost their oil imports so they had to give up driving and ride bikes, walk, or take the bus. Economic output and standards of living plummeted for almost a decade. Cubans referred to this period as "The Special Period." However, the Cuban economy re-oriented itself toward its pre-revolutionary tourism roots and now hosts more than 2 million visitors per year, mostly from Europe, Canada, and Mexico, although many U.S. citizens skirt the travel ban and go there anyway.

The figure of Fidel Castro (1959–2008) is something entirely unique in Latin American and even world history. Not only did he outlast nine U.S. presidents between 1959 and 2008, he has survived numerous CIA assassination plots, two wars on Cuban soil, a missile crisis, and economic doldrums, all in the name of preserving his vision of revolution. The United States has struggled to deal with this defiant leader ninety miles from its shores in ways dissimilar to its dealings with other Communists. The United States actually fought wars against China and Vietnam and, despite their governments' still being Communist, the United States has economic and political relations with both but has neither with Cuba. Why? Part of this can be explained by the role of the Cuban exile community that resides primarily in Florida. There are 1.5 million Cubans in that state. Due to the electoral college in the United States, which gives all electoral votes in a presidential election to the candidate with even a slight majority, candidates must please this formidable bloc of voters who tend to vote the same. Therefore, any candidate who even mentions ending the five-decades-old embargo on Cuba will lose nearly all Cuban votes in Florida, not to mention the votes of nearly every foreign policy conservative in the country.

There is a reason why the exile community is so vehement in its opposition to restoring relations with Cuba. From their perspective, they lost their homeland. Anyone who goes to the Miami airport on any given day can see a microcosm of the impact of the Cuban Revolution on the Cuban family unit. One can witness hundreds of Cubans tearfully kissing and hugging their loved ones goodbye before some depart for Cuba and others stay in Miami, not knowing whether they will see one another again. The same scene plays out in the Jose Marti International airport in Havana. The Cuban people have been indefinitely divided in the wake of the Revolution. The exile community sees this as Castro's fault. Some Cubans on the island agree, while others lay the fault at the feet of the U.S. government and even the exiles themselves. Both have strong currents of truth. The recent reforms implemented by Raul Castro after Fidel stepped down in 2008 have included greater freedoms. Cubans regularly use cell phones and the Internet, and more small businesses have been permitted as well. It is still technically a dictatorship as of this writing, however.

Central America

In 1990, Nicaraguan president and Sandinista leader Daniel Ortega stepped down after open elections. It was revealed later that the victor, Violeta Chamorro, received $10 million in campaign assistance from the United

States. Her election ushered in a new era for Nicaragua, an era of free trade with stagnant growth and democracy, and freedom from war. The Nicaraguan people were tired of the wars that had ravaged their country over the past two decades, and many voted for Chamorro for the promise of relief. The Sandinista government had responded to the Contra threat in the 1980s with forced impressment of teenagers into the military, and thousands of them were killed as a result. Interestingly, it was the male population who voted for Chamorro in overwhelming numbers. She stated emphatically during her campaign that she was "not a feminist" as if to reassure male voters that her identity as a woman would not challenge their authority in a male-dominated society.

Today, Nicaragua is as divided as ever. Not only do the Miskito Indians on the Atlantic coast still feel completely separate and un-Nicaraguan, but the FSLN (referred to simply as "El Frente") is hated by a large portion of the population. However, the opposition is so divided that it cannot muster enough votes for a candidate to beat Daniel Ortega (1984–1990, 2007–), who had the electoral laws altered to allow himself to run for a third term. The 2011 elections were contentious, but Daniel Ortega won in the end.

Guatemala is perhaps the country with the most problems in Central America. Not only did they suffer a debilitating civil war that lasted from the coup that ousted Jacobo Arbenz in 1954 until 1996 that killed more than 200,000 people, they suffered from high crime rates, corruption, and ethnic tension. El Salvador's statistics are even worse, however, but there is less corruption and ethnic conflict. Two-thirds of Guatemala is Indigenous, and the vast majority of them are desperately impoverished. However, they do exercise a high degree of autonomy in certain places where traditions have been preserved. They were also the prime target of the military during the civil war. Literally hundreds of villages were wiped off the map during this period, and the dictator most responsible for these actions, Efrain Rios Montt (1982–1983) is completely free. He was ousted in a coup in 1983 but later held congressional office and was even leader of his party and Congress for a few years.

While Guatemala is considered divided both politically and culturally, the culture of Guatemala is what has provided the country with a vibrant tourism industry. This comes almost entirely from foreigners traveling to Mayan ruins and villages. Tikal in the north is the primary archeological site tourists visit, but the south provides quite a bit to see as well. The Mayan culture is alive and well despite the horrors they have experienced over the past five centuries, and their continuing struggle for self-determination rests on land and resource rights, which have always been major sources of contention between them and the state.

El Salvador, often overlooked but always making itself heard, is the most densely populated country in Latin America. At only 8,000 square miles, its 7 million people (not including 2 million in the United States) have made the country into the strongest economically in the region. The 1992 COPAZ peace accords allowed for both sides of the war to be reincorporated into society, which provided a means for ex-combatants to contribute to the future growth of the country rather than become a burden for the state. This was not the case in Nicaragua and Guatemala. Former Salvadoran soldiers and rebels were given land, education, job training, pensions and, most important, amnesty for all actions committed during the war.

This last act, although abominable to many who would like to see mass murderers and torturers behind bars, is a common feature of most cease-fires. That is, when neither side wins because each side is too formidable to vanquish, to stop the bloodshed, both sides agree to let matters rest as they are. There were many in the Salvadoran military known to have committed war crimes and went free, and there are a few in the FMLN who would have been in danger of serving long sentences as well for their crimes. Therefore, when the leader of the FMLN, Joaquin Villalobos, was given the opportunity to sign for peace under these conditions, he did so. Many former rebels fault him for this act, arguing that he could have held out for the punishment of at least a few of the worst military officers. However, El Salvador's peace accords have served as a model for other conflict resolutions around the world and, more important, they have had two decades of peace and democratic elections. In fact, for the first time ever, a left-wing candidate (from the FMLN political party) was elected president in 2009.

Today, El Salvador is plagued with gang violence comparable with Guatemala's despite its economic growth. This is also a result of the civil war but in a roundabout way. It began in the late 1970s, when military repression in El Salvador and an economic downturn caused many to flee northward to the United States. That flow increased dramatically during the 1980s as the war claimed more lives and displaced a fourth of the population. Although most refugees made it to California, hundreds of thousands ended up in refugee camps in Honduras, Guatemala, and Mexico. When they arrived in Los Angeles in the midst of the rise in gang violence there, Salvadorans found themselves threatened by African American and Mexican gangs and soon formed their own in self-defense. The Mara Salvatrucha, also known as MS-13, soon became a feared entity in the United States that has grown considerably since the 1980s. In the past decade, the U.S. government has repatriated many thousands of these gang members who ended up in U.S. prisons, thus placing the burden on the Salvadoran, Guatemalan, and Honduran states. MS-13 and their rivals now control much of the drug trade in Central America.

We can use the case of MS-13 to illustrate how the differences in U.S. immigration policies lead to different outcomes. For example, in the case of Cuba, because Castro is an official enemy of the United States, anyone leaving his island is given political asylum in the United States . Cubans are not considered "illegal immigrants," but the Salvadorans (and Guatemalans) fleeing the violence of U.S.-backed militaries in the 1980s were mostly forbidden from entering legally. They in turn lived lives of "illegal immigrants" and were, therefore, more subjected to the poverty that leads to gang violence than were the Cubans in Florida.

Peru

Mentioned little to this point in the book, Peru nevertheless has an important role in Latin American history. Not only is it the center of the largest Indigenous population in the hemisphere (Quechua and Aymara) and a significant tourist destination (Machu Picchu is the most visited archeological site in South America: 2,000–3,000 per day), but its politics are distinct from the rest of Latin America in several ways that are worth mentioning. Initially, Peru was the last holdout for royalist rule after the rest of mainland Spanish America had become independent. Nitrates and mining were Peru's and Bolivia's economic lifeblood throughout the nineteenth century, but Peru's longtime allegiance to Bolivia embroiled both in a war with Chile between 1879 and 1883 that cost Bolivia its only link to the coast and its nitrate fields in the Atacama Desert, not to mention Peruvian losses. The War of the Pacific drove a permanent wedge between Peru and Chile that causes great rivalry and even hatred to this day.

The twentieth century was a time of change in Peru. Prominent political philosophers whose influence spread beyond Peru, such as the Communist Jose Carlos Mariategui (1894–1930) and Victor Haya de la Torre (1895–1979), instigated reform agendas that fueled left-leaning movements between the 1920s and the 1990s. Mariategui was a Marxist, and Haya de la Torre was inspired by the Mexican Revolution's socialist and *indigenismo* foundations. *Indigenismo* as implemented in Mexico sought to incorporate the Indigenous population into the fabric of national society and was part and parcel of the Mexican Revolution's social reforms. Haya de la Torre witnessed these transformations in Mexico first-hand and founded the APRA political party as a result. APRA would prove important in Peruvian politics throughout the rest of the century but brought only one presidential candidate to power in Alan Garcia (1985–1990, 2006–2011).

In an interesting twist of political events, Peruvian army officers carried out a leftist revolution in 1968. General Juan Velasco (1968–1975) was sympathetic to Cuba and the Soviet Union, instituted widespread economic and social reforms, and carried out the second-largest *agrarian reform* (land redistribution) program in Latin America after Mexico. Nothing like this happened anywhere else. Both the successful and failed revolutionary movements throughout Latin America were decidedly anti-establishment and, therefore, would not be led by army generals. In Peru, it seemed as though the rules did not apply.

However, in another ironic twist of fate, due to the incomplete nature of the agrarian reform program in the poorest region of the country, the Upper Huallaga Valley, Peru would soon suffer from one of the worst terrorist insurgencies in Latin American history. The Shining Path rose up in this valley in 1980 as a result of the teachings of Abimael Guzman, soon to be known as Presidente Gonzalo. To finance their war, which included bombings, massacres of armed and unarmed opponents, and kidnappings, they controlled a large portion of the coca industry. Peru was the number-one coca growing country from the 1970s through the mid-1990s, and they sold most of it to Colombia, where it was processed into cocaine. The war between the Shining Path and the military would lead to the deaths of 69,000 (roughly an equal number were killed by each side). The Shining Path had a real chance of toppling the government at times, but once its leader was captured and imprisoned in 1992, the organization faltered. However, they are not entirely defeated as of this writing.

Peru's economy and political system suffered greatly during the war with the Shining Path. Inflation soared in the 1980s under Alan Garcia, tourism fell dramatically, and the country seemed destined for worse times. However, with the election of Alberto Fujimori (1990–2000), the economy improved, and the war ended, but at a cost. Fujimori, of Japanese descent, is currently serving a twenty-five-year prison sentence for corruption and authorizing the use of death squads against suspected dissidents and armed rebels. These actions took place in the process of rooting out the Shining Path's major players and members of the other rebel group, the Tupac Amaru movement, and reorienting Peru toward neo-liberal economic policies. When he tried to run for a third term, he was denied the opportunity, and soon federal authorities were hunting him down. He fled to Japan, then to Chile, where he was captured and imprisoned, then turned over to the Peruvians in 2009, making him the first democratically elected president to be convicted of human rights crimes in Latin America. Alejandro Toledo, an economic conservative and a Quechua Indian, succeeded him and presided over massive growth between 2001 and 2006 despite approval ratings in the single digits. Former president Alan Garcia won an election narrowly in 2006 over the leftist former army officer (another interesting twist attributed to Peruvian politics) Ollanta Humala. Humala moderated his leftist tone in the 2011 elections in which he defeated Fujimori's daughter, Keiko.

Free trade or neo-liberalism: Mexico

On January 1, 1994, the southern Mexican state of Chiapas became known to the world for an unexpected Mayan revolt initiated that day. It had been a tourist destination for decades, attracting foreigners and Mexicans alike to Mayan ruins at Palenque and Bonampak and the beautiful colonial towns situated high in the verdant forests. On this day, however, people watched their television sets with awe as 2,000 armed Mayans took control of seven cities and towns, including the center of cultural life in the state, San Cristobal de las Casas. Why did they rise up? The only other armed revolt with a strong Indian base was the Shining Path in Peru, but the Zapatistas of Chiapas were not terrorists. They did not target civilians. They did not assassinate politicians. They did not have a plan to take power in Chiapas, let alone in Mexico City. Their demands were different: they wanted self-determination.

Why on that date? NAFTA began that day and, unknown to most observers, "free trade" as it was posited between the three giants of North America meant that small Mexican farmers would compete in the same market with the giant agribusinesses of the United States and Canada. However, those countries' governments subsidize agricultural production, bringing prices down artificially, and they are highly mechanized and have other advantages as well. The small Mayan corn producers did not stand a chance against this new onslaught, the Zapatistas reasoned, and for this and the right to be treated as equals in Mexico, they rose up. Since then, the Zapatistas with their ski masks and red Mayan garb have become global symbols of resistance in a way similar to that of Che Guevara, albeit on a much smaller scale.

What has NAFTA done to Mexico? On the one hand, there are many more people in the middle and upper classes who hold considerably more wealth now than before. In fact, Mexico's overall GDP has more than doubled since 1994. On the other hand, half of the people whose livelihoods were in agriculture in 1994 have since sold their properties, and many of them headed to the cities or the United States. Some argue that this is the result of being outcompeted by U.S. and Canadian agribusiness, whose corn now dominates the Mexican market. Where U.S. products and stores had a small presence in Mexico before NAFTA, today they are omnipresent, from the smallest village to the largest cities. Walmart, McDonald's, Pizza Hut, KFC, and many more places common in the states attract millions of Mexican customers every year. Walmart has increased its presence to every corner of Mexico, even setting up shop within view of Mexico's most treasured archeological site, the 2,000-year-old city of Teotihuacan. In fact, as of this writing, Walmart in Mexico was embroiled in a nationwide bribery scandal. To illustrate the effects even further, the richest person in the world today is a Mexican, Carlos Slim, who was previously a minor billionaire but within less than two decades of NAFTA's initiation, was valued at $74 billion (in 2011).

Mexico's government also changed dramatically during this period. In 1994, a moderate PRI candidate was elected to office, and he soon implemented reforms that opened the political system to competitors. Ernesto Zedillo (1994–2000) presided over a 66-percent peso devaluation within weeks of coming to office in late 1994 as well, and this undermined people's faith in NAFTA. One unforeseen consequence by pro-NAFTA optimists was the massive rise in undocumented immigration from Mexico to the United States. The plan was initially sold in the United States as a means of reducing immigration, which had been increasing in the 1980s in part due to economic woes in Mexico and due to the Central American wars. Still, as of this writing, Latinos made up 14 percent of the U.S. population, making them the largest minority group.

By 2000, an opposition candidate was elected for the first time in seventy-one years. Vicente Fox (2000–2006) of the National Action Party

(PAN) represented the hopes of the Mexican people that democracy could finally hold sway after so many years of virtual dictatorship under the one-party system. Unfortunately, the Mexican Congress was divided three ways during Fox's tenure, a common problem throughout Latin America, and therefore his power was limited from the beginning. Still, a PAN candidate was elected again in 2006 (by the narrowest of margins). In fact, Felipe Calderon (2006–2012), a man of almost no experience in government, entered office under the shadow of his closest competitor and the man many still believe won the election, former Mexico City mayor Andres Manuel Lopez Obrador, or AMLO.

The country has been plagued with violence from the Drug War ever since Calderon took office, but Mexico's economy has ebbed and flowed as always. The Drug War only exacerbates the economic crisis that began in 2008 while ironically also infusing money into the economy. How is this possible? Thousands of people are killed every year due to the increased militarization of the Drug War. The Mexican military and police have dramatically stepped up the pressure on the dealers, causing them to respond with violence on a scale also witnessed in Central America, Colombia, and Peru in the past decades. This causes not only the population to flee Mexico for the United States but scares foreign tourists away and causes less trust for investors.

Conversely, the billions of dollars a year earned by drug dealers go mostly into the Mexican economy, as it does in other drug havens, and any withdrawal of those billions would surely impact the economy in a negative way if there were not sufficient reforms to cushion the blow. This helps explain the difficult situation all of the countries involved in the Drug War face but, of course, the costs of the Drug War surely outweigh the benefits. The violence carried out by the dealers is a result of the illegality of narcotics. Virtually every expert on the Drug War's economics and history has argued for a form of legalization or decriminalization along the lines of the Netherlands and Portugal to reduce the carnage. They realize the trend over time is that the black market nature of the drug industry leads to the continuous funding of gangs, rebels, terrorists, and even some governments.

The problems Mexico faces can be seen as part of the new era of globalization. Critics of free trade or neo-liberalism point to the unfairness of subsidized U.S. and Canadian agricultural products competing with Mexican products and the unbridled nature of capitalism to thrust its weight on the Mexican people. The overall effects on the economy of Mexico of these factors actually spell massive economic growth overall. However, economic growth does not mean the improvement of daily lives for the average Mexican person necessarily because that growth could be in part at the expense of or as a result of increased immigration and the War on Drugs, to name just two important factors. Immigration provides the number-one source of income to the Mexican economy due to the remittances sent home, but this also leads to the shattering of the Mexican family, the abandonment of farms and jobs in Mexico, and the lowering of wages in the United States for certain jobs. The effects of these combined cannot be easily factored into the overall economic growth numbers cited by economists who deem NAFTA a success.

As a symbol of the deep-seated distrust of U.S.-based, "Washington Consensus" or "Chicago School" free trade, many Latin Americans, Canadians, and U.S. citizens have worked to curb this growing trend. Indeed, the Free Trade Area of the Americas (FTAA) was defeated at the end of the twentieth century after a series of protests against it succeeded in convincing enough people that NAFTA extended across the Americas would not work. In response, the United States, Central America, and the Dominican Republic came up with a smaller version of NAFTA with CAFTA-DR in 2004. In addition, several Latin American countries have developed their own trade alliances. Mercosur (Brazil, Argentina, Paraguay, Venezuela, and Uruguay) and the Andean Community (CAN-Bolivia, Ecuador, Colombia, Peru, and Venezuela) are both examples of the intentions of South American nations to integrate their markets further. Most South American countries are also part of the newly formed Union of South American Nations, which seeks to solidify the broader integration of South America beyond economics.

Chile and Argentina

Like Mexico, Chile has been upheld as a paragon of free trade growth. In Mexico, part of the problem with orienting the economy toward free trade principles had to do with the fact that those in charge came from the ranks of those who had screwed it up. The PRI caused the debt crisis of 1982 due to fiscal ineptitude and corruption, and they oversaw the transition to neo-liberalism with NAFTA. In the case of Chile, Augusto Pinochet took the economy out of the hands of the state and allowed technocrats trained at the University of Chicago ("The Chicago Boys") to handle the economy along the lines dictated by Nobel laureate in Economics, the godfather of free trade, Milton Friedman. Although Chile suffered hard times in the early 1980s that led to a grassroots opposition movement that eventually caused him to step down in 1990, his plan eventually paid off. Investors from abroad and at home felt confident doing business in Chile under Pinochet, which explains why he has a divided legacy in the country and, indeed, in the region as a whole.

Pinochet's luck began to run out in 1996. While traveling in London, police arrested him on a warrant handed down from a Spanish judge accusing him of crimes against Spanish citizens. After his house arrest ran out and the charges were dropped, he returned to Chile where he died in 2006. Between his fall from power in 1990 and 2010, a coalition of the center Left that included socialists controlled the presidency, with Michelle Bachelet (2006–2010), Chile's first female president, in charge during the last four years. In 2010, this trend changed when Chileans elected conservative Sebastian Pinera (2010–). Throughout the post-Pinochet years, whether from the Left or the Right, Chilean presidents have maintained the free market policy orientation he initiated. However, the left-leaning presidents tried to also prosecute Pinochet for his human rights violations, and they set up a system to compensate the family members of his victims. Chile still stands out as the model for economic success in the post-1982 (i.e., debt crisis) era of transition from state-run, inward-looking economics to free trade in Latin America.

Contrast this with Chile's eastern neighbor, Argentina, whose debt crisis in 2001 was the worst of any Latin American country in history. Although the governments of Carlos Menem (1989–1999) and Fernando de la Rua (1999–2001) had maintained general free trade policies, they still artificially kept the peso pegged to the U.S. dollar, which caused major banking problems in 2001. After fears of Argentina's economic woes caused investor panic, billions of dollars left the country, plunging Argentina into a debt crisis that eventually led to de la Rua's resignation. After three more presidents stepped down in two weeks, and an interim government stabilized the situation, a new president, Nestor Kirchner (2003–2007), would reestablish financial confidence. His wife, Cristina Fernandez de Kirchner (2007–2011) took his place after his term ended. Both Kirchners were left-wing, and both represented a larger trend in Latin American politics that simultaneously contrasted with the more radical left-wing presidents such as Chavez, Morales, and Correa, while maintaining an alliance with them.

Venezuela

To the list of moderate left-wing presidents must be added Michelle Bachelet of Chile, Luis Ignacio da Silva of Brazil, and Mauricio Funes of El Salvador. These leaders' inclinations cannot be contextualized within the larger scheme without a comparison with Hugo Chavez of Venezuela (1999–2013). Chavez's story has been recounted by countless people, from both critics and admirers alike and the occasional "objective" observer. He ruled Venezuela and influenced Latin American politics for fourteen years, but he lost his battle with cancer in 2013 and, as of this writing, Venezuela was undergoing a transition. He instituted massive populist (social and economic especially) reforms by redistributing resources away from the rich and middle class toward the poor. This mainly came from oil revenues, which have traditionally benefited the whiter, wealthier Venezuelans. Many of these have either left the country outright or stayed to develop the opposition. In 2002, an opposition-backed coup overthrew Chavez for two days, only to see him restored by the military. The opposition has garnered considerable financial and political support from the U.S. government (especially during the George W. Bush years, 2001–2009) and from private U.S. organizations such as the National Endowment for Democracy. And although his brand of socialism influenced some Latin Americans, his radicalism also marginalized him.

Figure 7.1 Hugo Chavez (1954–2013) (Jeremy Sutton-Hibbert/Alamy)

Of particular annoyance to the United States, however, was Chavez's role in the Drug War. In short, U.S. leaders saw him as not cooperating enough. For one, he did not see the war in the same terms as the United States or his western neighbor, Colombia. While the United States and Colombia have used their resources to target left-wing guerrillas (FARC and ELN) and to spray coca fields, Chavez saw the problem as rooted in the consumption of drugs by U.S. citizens. The United States and Colombia also accused Chavez of colluding with the FARC.

Brazil

Post–Cold War Brazil contrasts considerably with its Cold War days, which is fitting because Brazil is a world apart from the rest of Latin America in many ways. As with most of Latin America, Brazil transitioned from despotism to democracy in the 1980s, but the dictatorship that ran Brazil from 1964 to 1985 behaved differently than most tyrannical regimes. Although it restricted many freedoms, it also began to open itself up to reforms in the mid-1970s, eventually paving the way toward its own demise in 1985. The *abertura* (opening) signaled the end of the dictatorship and the beginning of democratic and economic reforms. And while these reforms proved painful in the short term, they paid off in incredible dividends in the 2000s as Brazil formed part of the so-called BRIC countries of emerging powerhouse economies (Brazil, Russia, India, and China).

The figure that rose to prominence quickly for democracy and economics was Fernando Henrique Cardoso (1931–). Cardoso was a famous sociologist most recognized for his publications on "dependency theory," which criticizes Western capitalism as the cause of poverty in the developing world. Thus, when Cardoso was asked by President Itamar Franco (1992–1995) to be finance minister in 1993 after three ministers had failed as inflation soared to 2,700 percent, Cardoso had to adjust his theoretical perspective and apply it to reality. Cardoso introduced the Plano Real (Real Plan) as a way of slowly replacing the old *cruzeiro* currency with the *real* to end inflation. It largely worked, and Cardoso was then elected president for two consecutive terms (1995–2003).

His successor was his complete opposite and would rival Getulio Vargas for the prize as Brazil's most popular president. Luis Ignacio da Silva (Lula) was born in the poor Noreste (northeast) region of the country and worked as a lathe operator and union leader before entering politics. He rose to national recognition after leading protests against the dictatorship and failed in several presidential bids before achieving victory under his PT (Workers' Party) platform of populist reforms in 2003. His election caused celebrations in the streets unlike any Brazilian history, in part due to the extended hope from years of previous losses and in part because he represented a dramatic shift in Brazilian politics away from elites such as Cardoso and toward the common touch of a common person that would represent the common interests of Brazilians. Or so they thought. Although Lula indeed directed much-needed resources toward the poorest sectors of the country, he largely continued the policies of his immediate predecessor, Cardoso, in the economic realm. Free trade policies still dictated the structure of the Brazilian economy, with exports to Europe, China, and the United States increasing to gain much-needed revenues. In addition, Brazil has industrialized enough to increase both the middle class and the upper class, and the poor majority have seen a marked increase in their standard of living as well.

Indeed, Brazil has risen to the level of the essential nation, whose interests must be considered in all international economic and political discussions. The BRIC countries in general represent nearly half the world's population and are set to surpass the economic output of the G7 nations (United States, Canada, Australia, France, United Kingdom, Germany, and Italy) within the next two decades. Brazil has a diversified, industrialized economy that has been growing at a rate similar to the other BRIC nations and far ahead of the average for the G7. Brazil's coffee, oil, tourism, agri-business, mining, manufacturing, and high-tech industry form a strong economic base, and all indications point to the country's continuing ascendancy.

This has been true for most of Latin America as well, except for Haiti, Honduras, and Nicaragua in particular. Free trade reforms have suffered setbacks, to be sure, but overall growth has increased since the days of the debt-ridden economies south of the U.S. border, and the average Latin Americans are doing better than their parents' generation. In fact, in 2013, the World Bank announced that Latin America's middle class had grown to an average of 30 percent, up from 15 percent in 1990. However, this does not negate the fact that most of the population is young and still finding employment difficult. Indeed, more than half of Latin America is still poor, while the upper class has become wealthier and remains relatively small. By comparison to the United States, whose middle class is more than 70 percent of the population, Latin America appears to have a long way to go. Chile stands out as the great exception, with growth rates (despite its glaring disparity of wealth between the upper and lower classes) that could bring it into the "First World" by mid-century.

The drug war: The Andes and Mexico

After Escobar's death in 1993, it was assumed that cocaine trafficking would fall. However, the Cali Cartel soon replaced Escobar and expanded their reach into Europe through connections with the Sicilian mafia. Once the Cali Cartel was brought down in the late 1990s and Colombia produced both the most coca and cocaine, the United States and Colombia came up with Plan Colombia, This was a $7-billion program for diminishing the cocaine and heroin traffic coming from that country between 2000 and 2006. Seventy percent of the funds went to military aid that was used to fight the FARC and ELN guerrillas and other traffickers.

By the end of Plan Colombia, cocaine and coca production had fallen 50 percent in Colombia. However, it had increased in Peru and Bolivia, so that overall levels had not reduced at all. This has to do with the law of supply and demand. When the demand for drugs is constant, it does not matter if the supply in one part of the world reduces if the drugs can be produced elsewhere, and Bolivia and Peru have a long history of cocaine production. The law of supply and demand in the Drug War can be understood as the law of "Push Down, Pop Up," which is explained in great detail in Ted Galen Carpenter's book, *Bad Neighbor Policy*. In it, he explains how whenever efforts to eradicate drugs have worked somewhere, the supply of drugs remains the same overall due to consumer demand in the United States in particular. This happens because despite success in reducing coca and cocaine in Bolivia and Peru in the 1990s, for example, because coca can be grown and cocaine can be processed in Colombia, it grew there in the same period. This is why Colombia became the prime target for eradication during the first decade of the twenty-first century, and it is why it reappeared in Peru and Bolivia after Plan Colombia succeeded in reducing coca and cocaine production in Colombia.

As of this writing, the Drug War has extended into Mexico. Although Mexico was never completely peaceful, even during the PRI era, it was a place that outsiders felt safe to visit despite the corruption and crime experienced there at times. However, with the election of Felipe Calderon (2006–2012), Mexico began a trajectory toward war with drug dealers that has only led to mass death and a drop in tourism. Calderon, with no experience in command of the military or police, decided to dedicate his term to destroying the cartels that had been slowly growing since the 1970s. The cartels responded to violence with violence, making Mexico one of the most dangerous countries in the world. In fact, Juarez is the murder capital of the world, with more killings per capita than Baghdad, Iraq.

The controversy over the Drug War is linked to immigration as well. Immigration seems to come up in the political battleground every two years, whenever there is an election in the United States. In December 2005, the House of Representatives passed the Sensebrenner Bill, House Resolution 4437, which has a controversial section within it that makes all undocumented workers (illegal aliens) subject to felony prosecution, with a minimum sentence of one year in prison. This is a change from the past law, which made it a misdemeanor, with a maximum sentence of one year. Protests erupted in March 2006 in the streets of Los Angeles totaling more than 1 million people, making them the largest street protests in U.S. history for one city. People on the Left and the Right of the political spectrum were heavily divided.

Much of the fervor over illegal immigration had heated up earlier in 2005, when the self-declared "Minuteman Project" took it upon itself to guard a twenty-mile swath of the U.S.–Mexico border in April of that year. Nine hundred professed "patriots" stood watch over the Naco corridor that runs along the border on the Arizona side for one month, and they claimed at the end of the month that they reduced illegal crossings by 97 percent. This "triumph" was hailed by such notables as California governor Arnold Schwarzenegger and other conservatives. What they failed to notice was what the Border Patrol itself analyzed, which was that even though traffic slowed in the Naco area, it remained the same overall because the immigrants simply bypassed the Minutemen by going around their corridor.

If we apply the "Push Down, Pop Up" concept to immigration and the border, we can see how the current U.S. policy of blocking the border and punishing border crossers avoids the law of supply and demand. Until 1994, the two states with the most amount of illegal immigrant traffic were California and Texas, because these are the two most populous states in the country, and thus, there are more jobs in these states. Arizona was in third place at this time. However, in 1995, the Clinton administration instituted Operation Gatekeeper, which put up walls and beefed up border security in Texas and California more so than in Arizona and New Mexico, and the results were similar to what we have seen in the Drug War in South America. Since 1995, Arizona has moved into first place for illegal immigrant crossings, as California and Texas have moved into second and third place. Why? Because of the increased security in California and Texas, Arizona filled in the gap. In fact, it increased 20 percent overall across the border, with Arizona receiving fully 50 percent of the traffic. The debate over immigration reform not only divides people within the United States, it serves as a dividing line between the United States and Mexico and between pairs of economically disparate Latin American countries sharing a common border. Dominicans and Haitians, Mexicans and Guatemalans, Costa Ricans and Nicaraguans, Argentines and Bolivians, and Chileans and Peruvians are all engaged in similar debates over how to handle the immigration issues they face, and these debates are accompanied by the same vitriol, hatred, and racism seen in the United States.

Discussion questions

1   What is your stance on "free trade" in Latin America? Should there be more or fewer barriers? Is "fair trade" a better option? What areas of the international capitalist system do you find lacking in Latin America?
2   How should the Latin Americans and the United States deal with Cuba if it remains Communist? Should Latin Americans pressure the United States into reestablishing relations with Cuba? Should the United States pressure Latin Americans into breaking relations with Cuba? What ideas can you come up with?
3   What solutions can you think of to solve the problems of the Drug War? Is legalization of drugs an option? If not, is continuation of the war beneficial? Explain.
4   How should the United States and other Latin American countries experiencing large numbers of immigration from poorer countries handle this issue? Should more or fewer people be allowed in? Is there a work visa program you would advocate for? Should Berlin Wall–style walls be erected, as advocated by some people? What would the effect of that be on international relations? Explore as many options as possible.

Significant historical figures

Violeta Chamorro (1929–)

Representing a trend for Latin American women politicians, she first rose to prominence after her husband's assassination at the hands of the Nicaraguan dictator Anastasio Somoza's gunmen in 1978. Joaquin Chamorro is also one of the most significant Nicaraguans in history due to his opposition, both armed and unarmed, to the Somoza regime over several decades. It was Violeta who would win the coveted prize of president that would officially end the U.S. sponsorship of the Contra War against the Sandinista government (1979–1990) and, although her economic reforms are seen today as detrimental by most Nicaraguans, her presidency represented a major change in Central America. She was a female president (1990–1997) and a conservative and anti-feminist, and she eased Nicaragua away from its tumultuous, war-torn past toward a relatively stable democracy.

Hugo Chavez (1954–2013)

Despite his reduced influence in recent years, there can be no doubt that the most significant Latin American figure during the post-1992 era is Hugo Chavez. This is not a judgment on his abilities. It is a statement of fact. No other leader riled the United States more. No other leader's name has been uttered more often both in Latin American and U.S. political and economic circles. He rose to prominence in 1993 after a failed coup attempt against then-president Carlos Andres-Perez. Chavez's stated intentions were to abolish the corruption of the previous three-and-a-half decades of the two-party system that shared power between the Democratic Action and Christian Democrats. They had used oil wealth as political patronage to grease the wheels of power, but Chavez did the same ever since his first election victory in 1999. Overall, he represented what Fidel Castro did throughout the Cold War but on a smaller scale. He was a voice of defiance against the hegemony of the United States in the hemisphere for fourteen years.

Vicente Fox (1942–)

Although it cannot be argued that this president achieved much during his term from 2000–2006, he perhaps takes the prize for second-most significant figure in Latin America since 1992 for his victory over the longest-running political party in world history. The PRI had run Mexican politics for seventy-one years (1929–2000), during which time Mexico's population grew eightfold, industrialized, and introduced revolutionary reforms that inspired the Latin American Left, Right, and center throughout the century. However, its corruption and dictatorial powers became ever more unpopular between 1968 and 2000, making it easier for Fox to win under his PAN (National Action Party) platform of conservative nationalism. Fox was an astute politician who built up his base through a grassroots effort that culminated in an eleven-point victory over his PRI opponent, and although his legislative agenda was stalled due to a three-way split in the Chamber of Deputies (Congress), the PAN won again in 2006 with Felipe Calderon (albeit after a drawn-out contention of the results).

Lula (1954–)

Perhaps the most popular president in Brazilian history alongside Getulio Vargas, Luis Ignacio da Silva ran for president three times before being elected in 2003 to the first of his two terms (2003–2011). A former union leader and dissident working against the dictatorship that lasted from 1964 to 1985, Lula's brand of populism is not of the firebrand. However, he represents a larger trend of defiant left-wing Latin American politicians of a new brand that combines autonomy, independence, nationalism, social welfare, and capitalism. The fact that these leaders embrace a form of capitalism, which includes most of the left-leaning politicians in Latin America, signifies a broad-based initiative to move toward more pluralistic politics and cooperation within Latin America and with the United States.

Subcomandante Marcos (1957–)

As is often the case for Latin American leaders, Marcos's power is less direct than influential on a large scale. This spokesman for the EZLN (Zapatista Army of National Liberation, or Zapatistas) became known after the January 1, 1994 Zapatista uprising in the southern Mexican state of Chiapas. As the only known non-Indian of the group, who also spoke English, Spanish, and several Indian languages, he found reporters flocked to him for the story about the purpose of the uprising. His eloquence in explaining the Zapatista cause was enhanced by his masculine and unique appearance (ski mask, pipe, crossed bandoliers, and on horseback), quickly recognized the world over due to his astute use of the Internet. His image and name are symbols of the anti–free trade movement the world over, in a manner not unlike that of Che Guevara's use by revolutionaries and students during the Cold War.

Evo Morales (1959–)

Another leader considered within the "firebrand" category of socialists representing a "thorn" in the side of the United States, Evo Morales is also the first Bolivian president with a purely Indigenous background. What makes this most significant is that Bolivia has always had a majority Indigenous population. Morales is a former coca growers union leader to boot, making him a prime antagonist of the U.S. Drug War efforts in South America. Morales' MAS party (Movement to Socialism) represents a threat to the white elite of the eastern half of the country and has increased his power through populist reforms financed through natural gas and tin mining.

Carlos Slim (1940–)

The world's richest person as of this writing, this son of a Lebanese immigrant and Mexican national is worth more than Bill Gates, the long-running title holder of this prize. Slim's holdings extend from telecommunications to construction, the news media, financing, and the famous Sanborns restaurant/shopping center chains across Mexico. His meteoric rise to economic stardom began well before NAFTA but increased exponentially afterward. He is also known for his philanthropy, but nowhere close to Bill Gates, who donates more than half of his profits to charity.

Further readings

Bowden, Mark. *Killing Pablo: The Hunt for the World's Greatest Outlaw*. New York: Penguin, 2002.

Carpenter, Ted Galen. *Bad Neighbor Policy: Washington's Futile War on Drugs in Latin America*. New York: Palgrave Macmillan, 2003.

Castaneda, Jorge G. *Manana Forever? Mexico and the Mexicans*. New York: Knopf, 2011.

Collier, George, and Elizabeth Lowery Quaratiello. *Basta: Land and the Zapatista Rebellion*. Oakland, CA: Food First Books, 2005.

Gott, Richard. *Hugo Chavez and the Bolivarian Revolution*. New York: Verso, 2011.

Reid, Michael. *The Lost Continent: The Battle for Latin America's Soul*. New Haven, CT: Yale, 2009.

Skidmore, Thomas. *Brazil: Five Centuries of Change*. New York: Oxford, 2009.

Weitzman, Hal. *Latin Lessons: How Latin America Stopped Listening to the United States and Started Prospering*. Hoboken, NJ: Wiley, 2012.

Films

Even the Rain. Dir. Iciar Bollain. Image, 2011.

Amores Perros. Dir. Alejandro Gonzalez Inarritu. Lionsgate, 2001.

Y Tu Mama Tambien. Dir. Alfonso Cuaron and Carlos Cuaron. MGM, 2002.

Maria Full of Grace. Dir. Joshua Marston. HBO, 2004.

Cocalero. Dir. Alejandro Landes. First Run Features, 2007.

Intimate Stories. Dir. Carlos Sorin. New Yorker, 2006.

Online content

One Laptop Per Child (OLPC) in Colombia: www.ted.com/talks/nicholas_negroponte_takes_olpc_to_colombia.html

Jose Antonio Abreu: The El Sistema Music Revolution: www.ted.com/talks/jose_abreu_on_kids_transformed_by_music.html

TED talk: Violence in Mexico: www.ted.com/talks/lang/en/emiliano_salinas_a_civil_response_to_violence.html

TED talk: Rare Animal Trafficking in Brazil: www.ted.com/talks/juliana_machado_ferreira.html

8   Asia (1989–present)

Timeline

1990	Iraq invades Kuwait
1991	First Gulf War (Operation Desert Shield and Desert Storm)
1993	Oslo Accords
1994	Kim Il Sung dies
1995	Yitzak Rabin assassinated
1997	East Asian Economic Crisis begins, Hong Kong handed over to China
1999	Pervez Musharraf takes power in Pakistan
2000	Second Intifada declared by Palestinians
2001	U.S. Invasion of Afghanistan (Operation Enduring Freedom)
2003	Second Gulf War (Operation Iraqi Freedom)
2004	Yasser Arafat dies
2006	Israel-Hezbollah War, Saddam Hussein executed
2007	Benazir Bhutto assassinated in Pakistan, Saffron Revolution begins in Myanmar
2008	Beijing Summer Olympics
2011	Arab Spring begins, Osama Bin Laden assassinated in Pakistan
2012	Myanmar elections

Until five centuries ago, Asia held global prominence by a landslide. With empires in China in the east and the Ottomans in the west, it was quite a disappointment for Asia in the following centuries to experience a relative decline in the face of the industrialized West's conquest of most of the planet. However, post-1989 witnessed the return of Asia. This era can be divided into economic, political, and military struggles and, especially, success cases. Economically speaking, China, India, Singapore, Hong Kong, South Korea, Taiwan, and Japan especially rise tremendously within the world economic system. At the same time, the first Gulf War (1991), the Israeli-Palestinian conflict, wars in Afghanistan, Turkey's repression of the Kurds, and other forms of unrest have been the source of many a news headline.

Before embarking on what should appear to the reader as a daunting time period to cover, let us ask a few probing questions about our knowledge:

1   What events and images stand out when we think of post-1989 Asia?
2   What sources can we identify that created these thoughts?
3   How legitimate are these sources? Are they legitimate enough to assist us in engaging in an informed discussion?
4   If not, for what deeper reasons have we maintained these thoughts?

The pre- and post-1989 periods are often chosen to separate Asia into different eras for several reasons. The Cold War was effectively on its way to extinction after the Berlin Wall fell in 1989, and this had massive ramifications across the globe, including much of Asia. The Tiananmen Square massacre happened in 1989 as well. This event, though not pivotal in changing the Chinese government's attitude toward democracy, presented a stark example of the endurance of Communist tyranny in the world despite the coming end of the Soviet Union (which occurred in 1991). The world's treatment of China's repression at Tiananmen demonstrated that it would tolerate Communism when it was economically convenient. Contrast the U.S. ostracism of Cuba with its "Most Favored Nation" economic relationship with China, and you can see the double standards of U.S. foreign policy. While Cuba's treatment of dissidents is detestable, it is slight by comparison to the scale of repression meted out by the Chinese government even today. Asia's overall economic growth has largely overshadowed the world's focus on human rights in the region. Most important, it is the past two decades of buoyant economic growth across Asia that will go down in the history books as the main source of focus in this era.

The Four Tigers

The case of the Four Tigers fascinates observers because they were part of the underdeveloped world at the beginning of the Cold War and surged into the developed world by the end. Singapore, Taiwan, South Korea, and Hong Kong have all managed to leap in this direction in the past one to two generations and seem to be on a steady path of growth into the future. The creation of the Association of Southeast Asian Nations (ASEAN) by Indonesia, Malaysia, Philippines, Singapore, and Thailand in 1967 signaled the beginning of the region's move toward trade liberalization. It later incorporated Vietnam, Brunei, Myanmar, Laos, and Cambodia. The ASEAN today attempts to work as a unit to compete with the giants in the region (China and Japan). Singapore stands out head and shoulders above the other three, in particular due to the leadership of the founder and first prime minister of the country, Lee Kuan Yew (1965–1990). Singapore was the first country in history to transition from former colony, with its backward economic foundations, to developed country status in one generation. Initially part of Malaysia,

Figure 8.1 Lee Kuan Yew (1923–) (Asia File/Alamy)

a former British colony until 1957, Singapore gained its independence as a city-state in 1965. Its economy was on a par with the rest of Southeast Asia's at the time. This was one of the least developed regions in the world: Vietnam, Thailand, Indonesia, Malaysia, Burma, Cambodia, and Laos all lacked economic and political infrastructures conducive toward prosperity, mostly due to their colonial legacies left by the British (Burma and Malaysia; the French (Vietnam, Laos, Cambodia); and the Dutch (Indonesia). In the decade after WWII, these colonies became countries (with the exception of Thailand, which was never a colony).

It was due to the initiative, energy, and wisdom of leaders such as Lee Kuan Yew, assisted by U.S. private investment and an "Asian model" of development, inspired by the Japanese Ministry of International Trade and Industry (MITI) model, that these countries made their mark. Singapore's strong shipping and high-technology industries have made it one of the highest per capita income countries in the world (not to mention one of the most expensive) and a global economic player. Typical of Tiger leaders such as Yew and Korea's Park Chung Hee (1961–1979) was an authoritarian manner that stifled political dissent and drew criticism from the West and political opponents at home. Some argue that it was, in fact, the authoritarianism that made rapid growth possible. To convince U.S. investors such as Texas Instruments to invest large amounts of money in making semiconductors in Singapore, Yew had to make Singapore more conducive to manufacturing than his neighbors. Though the main incentive for U.S. businesses to send their production abroad is lower wages, the main concern is the potential for labor unrest. Therefore, Yew used force to prevent any inkling of strikes within his first few years in office. This extended to his treatment of suspected criminals and political opponents, many of whom suffered severe repression.

Yew helped spread the concept of the "off shore" business. As a small, underdeveloped city-state initially, Singapore had no infrastructure for Japan-like home-grown industries and, therefore, Yew had to rely on foreign companies establishing themselves in his country. By proving that Singapore was a worthy investment, Yew was able to contribute toward the trend in off-shore manufacturing that has spread throughout East Asia, not to mention developed the necessary funds to create the infrastructure for Singaporean companies.

Korea

Among these four exists a country divided in two that deserves a broader scope of attention than those of its three Tiger neighbors, namely for its role in the Cold War and its aftermath. Korea's modernization effort was actually initiated under Japanese imperial rule between 1910 and 1945. Despite the controversial nature of such recognition, it was Japan that put Korea on a footing to join the modern industrial world. However, after the Japanese surrender in 1945, the United States played a key role both in providing military training and security for the South Koreans against their northern neighbor and in bolstering the economy with billions of dollars in aid. This aid became especially important after the surprise attack from the North on June 25, 1950 that led to the U.S.-led UN invasion and occupation of Korea that lasted until 1953. In fact, the United States built bases and stationed 40,000 troops indefinitely in South Korea thereafter. The Korean War changed the entire trajectory of South Korean development, and after the cease-fire between South and North Korea was signed in 1953, the war did not officially end. As of this writing, it is still officially a cease-fire. The North Korean leader, the Stalinist Kim Il Sung (1948–1994), ruled over a relatively prosperous country that received most of its sustenance from the Soviet Union. By material standards, the North had stronger development than the South for most of the Cold War, until the reforms of one leader began to take hold in the 1970s and 1980s.

His name was General Park Chung Hee (President, 1963–1979), the man voted by the Korean people as the person they would most like to clone. His coup d'état in 1961 that overthrew Yun Bo-Seon ushered in a new era of economic development for South Korea that paved the way toward overtaking not only North Korea but most of the developing world. Its 1988 hosting of the Summer Olympics symbolized its upward mobility, as is often the case of this monumental event. President Park's plan was to utilize the Japanese MITI model in acceleration mode by essentially making himself the head of economic planning along with qualified and ruthless advisors to propel South Korea past the competition. As in Japan, South Korea would have its own automobile, ship building, and high-technology industries, and they built these with the assistance of the state in record time. By the 1990s, South Korea was flying past North Korea, which had recently lost its support from the USSR after its collapse and, by the 2000s, the comparison was obsolete. South Korea now enjoys a level of development similar to the other three Tigers and is poised to continue on this path.

While South Korean economics progressed, its politics lagged behind. Park ruled with an iron fist, jailing, torturing, and executing dissenters, as did his predecessors, most notably Syngman Rhee (1948–1960). Park was assassinated in 1979, and authoritarianism ruled the country with ups and downs through the 1980s and 1990s until a peaceful transition of power took place after the long-time opposition candidate, Kim Dae Jung, won the 1997 elections. Often referred to as "the Asian Nelson Mandela," Kim Dae Jong (1998–2003) won the Nobel Peace Prize in 2000 for his democratic rule, his respect for human rights, and his efforts to repair the North-South divide. South Korean politics still suffers some bumps in the road but is a long way from outright centralized authority.

In the North, however, it could not be more different. Kim Il Sung died in 1994, leaving his son, Kim Jong Il (1994–2011) to preside over one of the worst economic dives in history and a simultaneous bellicosity on the part of the North's leadership in its position toward the South and the United States. An indicator of the North's economic doldrums is the satellite imagery that demonstrates the contrast in nighttime electricity output and availability between the North and the South. The South is relatively well lit, while the North is virtually obscured. Meanwhile, the level of poverty experienced in North Korea is unparalleled in Asia, and indeed, outside of Africa. Malnutrition, starvation, and death from preventable diseases have run rampant. In addition, the world has held its collective breath a number of times due to his regime's insistence on developing nuclear weapons. His death in 2011 led to the rise of his son, Kim Jong-un (2011–). As of this writing, tensions between North and South had escalated to new heights as a result of Kim Jong-un's saber rattling shortly after coming to office, while at the same time there were ongoing international talks to reduce nuclear weapons proliferation in the North.

The Four Cubs plus One: China, Thailand, Malaysia, Indonesia, and Myanmar (Burma)

Although referred to as "Cubs," this group ironically contains some of the largest countries in Asia. By comparison to the so-called "Tigers," however, its economies are still not as strong on a per capita basis. China is clearly the largest economy of these four and is second only to the United States. Malaysia and Indonesia experienced relatively moderate growth during the past six decades, with further growth projected for the future, but lagged far behind their Tiger competitors for several reasons. One distinction between these two and their neighbors is the fact that they are Muslim, not Confucian or Buddhist, and some argue that the Islamic nature of these countries' governments has caused less cultural opening to the types of vibrancy in ideas witnessed in the Tigers. Like its neighbors in Vietnam, Laos, Burma, and Cambodia, the 17,000 island nation of Indonesia (the largest Muslim nation in the world at 200 million people) experienced decades of internal conflict and dictatorship.

Indonesia's Suharto dictatorship fell in 1997, the same year as Thailand set off an economic crisis that threatened the global economic system. The crisis began as a result of massive unchecked Thai real estate speculation that brought prices crashing in 1997. As with the Latin American debt crisis of 1982, investors pumped money into East Asian countries at an unprecedented rate because they had an artificially inflated level of trust that their investments would yield high returns. Initially, it was only the weaker economies of Thailand, Indonesia, Malaysia, and the Philippines that suffered, but the crisis eventually spread to the stronger economies of China, South Korea, and Hong Kong, undermining much of the global confidence that had been building in the East Asian markets for the past decade.

It all began in May 1997, when Singapore spent billions of dollars to help defend the value of the Thai Bhat after the real estate crisis was revealed in Thailand. Between July and August, the currencies of Thailand, the Philippines, Singapore, and Indonesia had all devalued. The International Monetary Fund (IMF) also began assisting these countries by providing loans based on economic restructuring. Thailand had devalued the Bhat and requested IMF assistance, the IMF was in the process of assisting the Philippines as well, and Singapore's dollar began to devalue. By the following year, the economies of the United States, Brazil, Japan, and South Korea took severe hits as well. South Korea was forced to open its economy even further as part of its agreement with the World Bank and the IMF. The structural adjustment programs experienced in East Asia were not unlike those forced upon African and Latin American countries in the 1980s. Fewer trade barriers, less governmental protectionism, and higher taxation at times with a reduction in social services for the short term were all common in East Asia during the late 1990s. However, the meltdown was not as large or far-reaching as was feared initially, but it did instill skepticism in East Asian economic models. This skepticism has subsided considerably with the post-1997 growth of the Asian economy in general, which now includes India, a relative newcomer (since the 1990s when Indian reformers implemented growth policies that have worked). Of course, the biggest success story is that of China, where the Communist Party still maintains absolute political control despite its capitalist opening three decades ago with Deng Xiaoping's reforms.

This reform process was not inevitable, as we see in Myanmar, situated between the Indian subcontinent and Southeast Asia. First called Burma by the British and later named Myanmar after a popular rebellion led the government to change the name, this medium-sized yet densely populated country is a police state. It has remained virtually closed economically and politically for the past five decades. Its neighbors have moved toward liberalization, however. Burma suffered from Communist insurgencies and Chinese intervention for the first fourteen years of its independence from Great Britain, until a military coup d'état brought a socialist dictatorship to power in 1962 under General Ne Win (1962–1988). The dictatorship became increasingly harsh as Ne Win exterminated his enemies, both violent and nonviolent until 1988, when another military coup instituted a new government under General Saw Maung, who led the country until 1992 and oversaw the name change to Myanmar.

The next two decades would catapult Myanmar onto the international stage. This began with the 1990 elections in which the National League for Democracy (NLD), led by Aung San Suu Kyi, won a majority of seats in parliament. The military rejected this move toward democracy and placed Suu Kyi on house arrest, where she stayed on and off between 1991 and 2010. Suu Kyi won the Nobel Peace Prize in 1991, an occurrence that brought renewed negative attention to the military dictatorship. Soon people around the world began reading about the widespread human rights abuses that had been taking place for three decades prior to the elections. People also learned of the several armed rebellions taking place against the government, namely the Karen movement, an ethnic minority-based insurgency. The Karen population has suffered widespread human rights abuses from the military government's scorched earth campaign in their homeland in the south of the country.

The year 2007 initiated a wave of protests that ushered in what appears to be a new era for Myanmar. The protests erupted soon after a major increase in fuel prices. The brutal repression of protestors by police was caught on tape for the world to see, and many reports of executions, torture, and mass imprisonment made their way into newspapers. The "Saffron Revolution," as this came to be known, helped spur a renewed international interest in Myanmar's fate, even to the point where Sylvester Stallone made his last Rambo movie about the country. Stallone's character fights the Myanmar military in the film, making sure to portray it as a ruthless dictatorship that threatens both Burmese and American citizens alike. Though films such as *Rambo* symbolized international views of the Myanmar government, serious efforts were under way to reform the system by locals such as Suu Kyi. She was released from house arrest in 2010 just in time to run for office in the 2012 elections. Her NLD party won a majority of seats in parliament, including one for herself, from which they hope to overturn the dictatorship's control.

China

Despite South Korea's professional Olympics display, nothing in the history of spectacles can compare to China's opening ceremonies of the 2008 Summer Olympics in Beijing. Indeed, the Chinese government made sure it would leave an indelible imprint on global consciousness when it planned how to open the games that summer. When Mexico hosted the Olympics in 1968 its intention was the same as China's: to demonstrate to the world that this was no "backward," "third world" country but a leader among developmentally advanced countries. However, China's example set the bar so high as to be unthinkable among even the most developed countries of the West, which Mexico did not even attempt.

The Olympics were symbolic of China's unprecedented consistent 9 percent growth rate achieved under who is undoubtedly the most important man in China's recent history after Mao Zedong. Deng Xiaoping was punished for his criticism of Mao's failed communist system in the 1960s but later rose to a position of authority after Mao's death in 1976. Although he never held the premier's office, he was the force that shifted China away from state-controlled economics to a newly invented Chinese form of socialist capitalism that has paved the way toward China's fast-paced growth. China is still considered part of the developing world due to the facts that nearly 200 million people still live in the direst of poverty and the vast majority of the technological ingenuity used in China came from the West. However, the fact remains that there are many more people that have been lifted out of poverty in China, and there is a large and growing middle and upper class. China and the United States are each other's number-one trading partners as of this writing.

However, the political system in China is still authoritarian and under the control of the Communist Party. Dissent is dealt with through intimidation, censorship, imprisonment, torture, and even extrajudicial killing. The Tiananmen Square massacre of unarmed students and the government's treatment of Tibetan separatists, not to mention the repression of the Muslim Wiegers of the north, is testament to this ongoing problem. However, it would be inaccurate to assert that the political system has not opened since Mao's death. Religious practices are almost entirely acceptable in China if the church is registered with the government. Unofficial churches are deemed suspicious and are dealt with harshly, however. This is seen by outsiders as an example of the Chinese government's brutality, but this is a rare occurrence.

In addition, the average Chinese person is more satisfied with his or her government than is the average U.S. citizen according to polling data. That is because despite the one party state in China, most Chinese see improvements occurring in their lives as a result of the government's economic opening. Society has changed in so many ways, from family life to one's own free time. For example, every city-dweller's life used to revolve around work units. The work unit was the site of your employment, your housing, and your leisure. There was no private space as it is understood today. It was nearly impossible to change employment. If one did, she or he risked not having a place to live. It was difficult to travel anywhere because you needed justification from your work unit supervisor, who was a Communist Party official. Now, people can travel at will, if they have the funds. The work unit is now largely a thing of the past. If one wants to rent or own a place to live, this is permitted just as in the West. If they want to have guests stay with them, no Party official will prevent this. Life is more or less free in China, but people stay out of politics. These freedoms have also arisen in the wake of the economic reforms. To be sure, many Chinese also see a reduction in their well-being as a result of this opening. The Chinese government used to guarantee employment, housing, education, and health care, and now that is in the past. The Communist system may have provided very little, but many saw this as stable by comparison to the new capitalist system because the government has virtually removed itself from oversight, leaving many at the mercy of the market. Whether this is sustainable only time will tell.

Israel and its neighbors

When considering Israel, it is important to think of its role in the world even more so than the country by itself. This is true of very few other states in history. The United States, China, and imperial Britain, France, Spain, Portugal, and the Netherlands all must be considered in this same vein but, in the modern era, Israel stands out as the nation with the highest amount of influence beyond its borders in proportion to its size. A nation of fewer than 8 million people, approximately the same as El Salvador, Israel's power to affect international relations is unprecedented. Israel has received more military assistance from the United States government than any other country since the 1960s. This assistance is symbolic of the fact that the U.S. government and a large portion of its population see Israel as an extension of the United States. This is facilitated by one of the most powerful lobbying firms in the United States, the American Israel Public Affairs Committee. This lobby helps to maintain a voice for Israelis and Americans who promote the protection of the State of Israel, with an eye especially on military, economic, and political support for Israel in the face of international opposition.

This opposition has been fervent since the end of the Cold War due to a number of controversial moves carried out by the Israeli government. The first volatile situation resulted from the 1993 Oslo Accords, signed by the Palestinian Liberation Organization (led by Yasser Arafat) and the Israeli government, led by Yitzhak Rabin (1992–1995), who was assassinated in 1995 by the Zionist Yigal Amir. This was supposed to set the stage for back-and-forth concessions on settlements and rights for both Palestinians and Israelis. However, unchecked Israeli citizens increased settlements in the Occupied Territories under the governments of Benjamin Netanyahu (1996–1999) and Ehud Barak (1999–2001). Palestinians carried out suicide bombings and other deadly attacks in Israel in response. The tensions spilled over to the breaking point between July and September of 2000, leading to the so-called "Second Intifada," a new Palestinian uprising that was met with increased violence from Israel.

This violence can also be traced to the failure of the 2000 Camp David peace process held in the United States at the initiative of President Bill Clinton (1993–2001). The main point of contention was the status of the holy city of Jerusalem and the sacred sites at the Temple Mount. Arafat had refused to negotiate over Palestinian sovereignty in East Jerusalem, the Dome of the Rock, and the Al Aqsa Mosque at the Temple Mount, and the talks ended with a rushed agreement that soon proved empty. In September that year, Israeli opposition leader Ariel Sharon visited the Temple Mount in the face of Palestinian protest. The Palestinians responded with a call for vengeance, and this soon escalated into a wave of attacks on both sides leading to thousands of deaths over the next few years. Israel then built a controversial wall to keep suicide bombers out of the country. This wall has been equated with the Berlin Wall by Israel's critics, and yet it has coincided with a marked decline in the suicide bombings.

In 2006, Israel launched an attack against Lebanon after Hezbollah rockets killed several Israeli soldiers. The war was largely one-sided, as Hezbollah rocket attacks on Israel proved ineffective and, within a month, the war ended, with thousands dead, massive damage in Lebanon, and no resolution of the conflict. The main issue concerning Israel as of this writing was its worry over Iran's potential nuclear weapons program. The Iranian president, Mahmoud Ahmadinejad (2005–), had not only called for the elimination of the State of Israel (interpreted as a call for its destruction by some and simply the loss of its status as a country by others) but he had made statements interpreted by many as denying the Holocaust. The UN and the International Atomic Energy Agency were in the process of debating Iran's future as of this writing.

The Arab Spring (2011–)

2011 began with the self-immolation of a young Tunisian man named Muhammad Bouazizi (1984–2011). He was a street vendor who had recently experienced police harassment and faced the loss of his meager business. His suicide touched off a wave of similar acts of protest against the long-term dictatorship of Zine El Abidine Ben Ali (1987–2011). This touched off the overthrow of the Tunisian government, followed by the Egyptian, and later the Libyan and Yemeni governments. The two major uprisings taking place in the Arab world on the Asian continent were in Yemen and Syria, and minor revolts were easily put down in Saudi Arabia and Bahrain. The Yemeni government of Ali Abdullah Saleh (1978–2012) faced mass protests from a population tired of dictatorship. As opposed to Libya's Qaddafi, Saleh used minimal violence (still several hundred were killed) to protect his regime and, in November 2011, agreed to elections and stepped down in 2012. Saleh was part of the old guard of Cold War–era dictators supported by the United States, of which Egypt's Mubarak (and the Saudi royal family and others in the Middle East) was also a part. Saleh presided over a volatile country divided between north and south with a strong rebel movement that threatened his rule at times prior to 2011.

The United States found it expedient to favor regimes such as those of Mubarak and Saleh in the same way it deemed it did in South Vietnam, South Korea, Pakistan, Saudi Arabia, Zaire, South Africa, Iran, Cuba, Haiti, Guatemala, El Salvador, Nicaragua, Argentina, Chile, Brazil, and many more during the Cold War. This followed from the belief that supporting strong, centralized dictatorships was preferable to leaders that represented the interests of their populations. Thus, these tyrants built up high levels of resentment among their populations toward themselves and their benefactors, the U.S. government. However, unlike during the widespread Islamic fundamentalist movements that erupted in Iran, Pakistan, Afghanistan, Lebanon, and Saudi Arabia beginning in 1979, which used violence and Islamic fundamentalism against their dictatorships and the United States, the Arab Spring has seen none of the anti-American violence of the past. These are widespread, mainstream movements and, with the exception of Libya and Syria, lack armed insurgent movements. It would appear a more auspicious beginning for stable democratic roots to be laid down for future generations.

Syria was still being contested as of this writing, with a massive bloodbath instigated by the government of Bashar Al Assad (2000–). As a sign of the changing times, Syria is in the headlines around the world every day, most of the international community has condemned the killings, and the UN is actively pursuing a peace process between the government and the rebels. Most analysts predict the end of the Assad regime is only a matter of time. The Arab Spring, as it has been called, represents an ongoing process of political opening and awakening in the Arab world the likes of which has never been witnessed there. These are truly historic times. Elections have taken place in Tunisia, Egypt, Libya, and Yemen and, although many are disappointed with their results, many more still have found hope beyond what they knew in 2010. Still, as a Tunisian friend tells me, as opposed to before, when everyone avoided politics and focused on soccer, now everyone focuses on politics. People are no longer intimidated about expressing themselves, and this is the first step in any hopeful situation.

Iraq

On August 2, 1990, with his army seemingly in tatters after eight years of war with Iran, Hussein invaded the tiny emirate of Kuwait in an attempt at annexation. The U.S. government soon elicited support from dozens of nations, including a UN resolution, to intervene and send a U.S.-led coalition of 700,000 troops to the Persian Gulf to expel Hussein from Kuwait. The United States began with a bombing campaign known as Operation Desert Shield that lasted several weeks. This paved the way toward the invasion, known as Operation Desert Storm. This drove the Iraqi forces from Kuwait in January of 1991. Desert Storm was officially over by February, but the next phase of conflict over Iraq began almost immediately, with the U.S. encouragement of a Shiite uprising against Hussein. The Iraqi leader received his captured military equipment from U.S. General Norman Schwarzkopf and then used it to crush the uprising. Hussein was thus able to put down this rebellion with brute effectiveness and, as such, further entrenched himself as absolute ruler of Iraq. The international community collaborated to marginalize this power through a dual regime of sanctions and weapons inspections during the 1990s.

The sanctions against Hussein limited Iraq's economic growth potential and reduced the amount of food and medicines necessary for the functioning of a society. This did not erode Hussein's hold on power, despite his military budget dropping to among the lowest on the planet by the end of the decade ($1.4 billion per year, compared to the U.S. budget of $800 billion). Weapons inspections under the UN Special Commission (UNSCOM) destroyed the entire Iraqi nuclear weapons program by 1991. UNSCOM also destroyed 95 percent of its chemical and biological weapons stockpiles by 1998. The end of the inspections came in December 1998 when UNSCOM complained of Hussein's obstruction of their work. This led to Operation Desert Eagle, a bombing campaign ordered by U.S. President Bill Clinton (1993–2001).

The end of UNSCOM in 1998 meant there was a four-year period in which no inspections were conducted in Iraq. After the attacks on the United States on September 11, 2001, many U.S. politicians conflated Hussein with the Al Qaeda terrorist organization responsible for the attacks, albeit with no proof. The desire for war in Afghanistan to destroy Al Qaeda and the Taliban was near absolute, and the U.S. invasion beginning October 7, 2001 succeeded rather quickly in overthrowing the Taliban regime. However, Al Qaeda and their Taliban allies still remained powerful in the region afterward. The U.S. President George W. Bush (2001–2009) quickly decided to shift U.S. hostilities toward Iraq and, by January 2002, was making the case that Iraq represented part of a tripartite "Axis of Evil" accompanied by Iran and North Korea.

The "Axis of Evil" speech made at the president's State of the Union address of 2002 made an impression on the U.S. public. Soon, battle lines were drawn between the pro-war crowd who sought to invade Iraq to "disarm" the Hussein regime and the anti-war crowd who demanded evidence that the Iraqi regime possessed weapons of mass destruction (WMD). The Bush administration made nearly 1,000 statements asserting that Hussein had WMD over the course of the following fourteen months, all of which turned out to be false. The UN agreed to resume weapons inspections under the leadership of Swedish diplomat Hans Blix in November 2002. The UN inspectors found no weapons of mass destruction and, as such, the Bush administration's attempt to elicit a UN resolution to support a U.S.-led invasion failed.

Operation Iraqi Freedom began on Mach 20, 2003 as a U.S.-led invasion that also contained forces from thirty other countries, most of which were non-combatants. The invasion quickly succeeded in overthrowing Hussein; however, the United States stayed in Iraq for nine more years battling rebels from both Shiite and Sunni factions. The war dead topped 100,000, and 3 million people were displaced. By 2012, U.S. combat forces exited Iraq, but 5,000 stayed behind as a skeleton presence.

The overall impact on Iraqi and U.S. society as a result of the Iraq invasion and occupation will never be completely understood. For the first time in its history, there is a culture of pluralistic democracy that has permeated Iraqi society. Although politics is still divided along regional, ethnic, economic, and religious lines to a degree, these divisions are not exploited by a monster sitting in the sole seat of power in Baghdad as was the case from 1979 to 2003. Whatever the costs, and they have been great, the death of the tyrant Saddam Hussein at the hands of hangmen in 2006 symbolized a hope for many that the degree of despotism experienced during his reign would never be repeated. However, the costs must also be considered. The amount of buildings and cultural artifacts destroyed caused irreparable harm. One in seven Iraqis was forced to leave homes amid the violence, and many were ·wounded and killed as well. In addition, the U.S. taxpayer is now responsible for $3 trillion in expenses related to the war as of this writing. George W. Bush's Defense Secretary Donald Rumsfeld estimated it would cost $50 billion on the eve of the invasion.

Pakistan/Afghanistan

After the Soviet withdrawal in 1989, the fates of Pakistan and Afghanistan (and, to a degree, those of Iran, Iraq, and Saudi Arabia) were intertwined. Aside from the fact that both nations have significant ethnic similarities (both have large numbers of Pashtun peoples), the international nature of the political and cultural conflicts occurring in Central Asia in general after 1989 combined with internal factors. Pakistan's Benazir Bhutto was constrained by the military and male-dominated world of Pakistani politics. She was forced to step down in 1990, only to reemerge and lead from 1993 through 1996. She and her husband were accused of corruption, and they sought exile for the next decade before returning in 2007 to run in the 2008 elections. She was assassinated on December 27, 2007, shortly after returning to Pakistan. Benazir's principal rival during her shaky regime was Nawaz Sherif, who ruled from 1990 to 1993 and from 1997 to 1999. He was overthrown by General Pervez Musharraf in 1999, and Musharraf ruled until 2008.

Musharraf rose to global prominence as the military dictator of Pakistan who assisted the United States in the War on Terror in the wake of the attacks by Al Qaeda on U.S. targets on September 11, 2001. Pakistan's role as ally against U.S. enemies in Afghanistan that had begun in the 1980s revived during this time and continued through the time of this writing, a decade

Figure 8.2 Benazir Bhutto (1953–2007) (Allstar Picture Library/Alamy)

after the attacks. The post-Soviet era witnessed the increasing rise of Saudi influence in Pakistan that had begun during the 1980s effort to support the growth of Islamic militancy there and in Afghanistan to expel the Soviets. The Saudi government sent hundreds of millions of dollars to Pakistan to build thousands of mosques that housed and educated millions of young Afghani and Pakistani men in the ways of the strict Wahhabi sect of Islam promoted by the Saudi state. This was taking place just as Afghanistan plunged into a civil war between competing mujahedeen factions and a younger generation of these Islamic students coming over the border from Pakistan. Many of the new fighters were the Afghani refugees living in Pakistan as a result of Soviet atrocities during the 1980s. At the same time, the Pakistani military was literally ten times larger in the 1990s than it was in 1979, almost entirely as a result of U.S. military aid.

When combined, the violent elements in both Pakistan and Afghanistan worked to create a volatile situation in Central Asia. The enormous Pakistani military (the dominant institution in Pakistani life), the millions of young men being trained in Wahhabism in Saudi-financed mosques in Pakistan, and the civil war among battle-hardened factions in Afghanistan all provided the conditions for enduring civil conflict in the region. This is what led to the rise of the Taliban and the Northern Alliance in Afghanistan, who fought each other just as ferociously as occurred between the mujahedeen and the Soviets in the 1980s. The Taliban controlled the government and most of the country between 1996 and 2001. Afghanistan had served as the so-called Golden Crescent between 1979 and 1996: The country with the highest opium and heroin production. After its decline there, Colombia and other countries filled in the void and began producing heroin. By 2002, production began reverting back to Afghanistan for reasons related both to the War on Terror and the War on Drugs.

The September 11, 2001 attacks occurred as Osama Bin Laden's Al Qaeda terrorist network had become fully entrenched within Afghanistan under the protection of the Taliban government of Mullah Omar. By October 7, U.S. forces had begun bombing Al Qaeda bases inside Afghanistan with the support of the Pakistani government and NATO. By the end of the year, the Taliban were on the run, and a new leader of Afghanistan had emerged in Hamid Karzai (2002–). As a result, the opium trade was no longer suppressed by the Taliban and was able to increase once again, just as it reduced in Colombia due to Plan Colombia, the U.S.-sponsored anti-drug effort there.

In the early days of the Afghan war, in November 2001, a U.S. citizen later called "The American Taliban" received tremendous U.S. media attention after being captured in Afghanistan fighting with the Taliban. The U.S. government released photos of a young man, John Walker Lindh, with a long beard and blindfolded and strapped to a stretcher. It charged him with twenty counts, including aiding the Taliban, which was against U.S. law. He was eventually found guilty of this last violation, but most Americans believed he was found guilty of the far worse crime of treason, and believed he should have received more punishment than twenty years in prison.

The details of the case showed that Lindh was not involved in any fighting against U.S. troops and that, instead, he had joined the Taliban in their fight against the Northern Alliance, in the months before the attacks on September 11, 2001. He ended up in U.S. hands as a result of the Northern Alliance's capturing him during a battle between the two Afghan sides that had been going on for a decade prior to the U.S. invasion. The law Lindh was convicted of violating—aiding the Taliban—was the result of the U.S. government's pre–September 11 policy forbidding anyone to give aid to the Taliban. However, in March of 2001, the George W. Bush (2001–2009) administration had given the Taliban $200 million as a reward for its near 100 percent success in eradicating the production and trafficking of opium and heroin production. The production of heroin has since risen dramatically in Afghanistan, as the Taliban and elements tied to the former Northern Alliance and the government of Hamid Karzai have been involved in extensive drug trafficking.

The conflicting nature of the Lindh case and the heroin trade in Afghanistan is symptomatic of greater problems in settling the Afghani dilemma. On the one hand, the United States and its allies (Pakistan, Great Britain, Canada, France, and many others) believe in staying the course there to preserve the gains achieved thus far: the ouster of the Taliban and the destruction of Al Qaeda training camps. However, as has been shown in analyses from top observers, including the foremost expert on the Taliban, Ahmed Rashid, Afghanistan has never been stabilized by outside powers and, in fact, those outsiders cause many of Afghanistan's problems. For example,

Pakistan's government politically supports the U.S. effort to keep the Taliban marginalized within Afghanistan. However, the Pakistani military is divided on this issue, as are the Pakistani people. When Kashmir is added to this discussion, it becomes even more complicated. When the border region of Baluchistan is added, it becomes ever grayer.

As of this writing, the trend over the past five years was to see a rise in U.S. military deaths as the result of a surging Taliban, which has caused some U.S. allies to seriously question the mission there, after eleven years of occupation and minimal gains. Ahmed Rashid was initially responsible for calling the world's attention to the atrocities of the Taliban in his 2000 book, *Taliban* but, by 2009, his book, *Descent into Chaos*, was a catalog of mostly failed U.S. policies in Afghanistan between 2001 and 2009, with a bleak outlook on the future possibilities of peace in the region. Rashid wrote his second book two years before the U.S. military launched a successful mission to kill the leader of Al Qaeda, Osama Bin Laden, inside Pakistan. He had been living there for at least five years in a compound next to a Pakistani military base in the city of Abbottabad. Rashid's latest book, *Pakistan on the Brink: The Future of America, Pakistan, and Afghanistan*, takes an even broader look at the consequences of poorly conceived international attention to the region.

India

At the end of the Cold War, India stood at a crossroads. It had maintained a closely monitored centrally planned economy since Independence in 1947 under the majority leadership of the Indian National Congress (INC) party but had experienced slow growth consistently along with a quickly increasing population. Though starvation rates had come under control through the Green Revolution, which also expanded the population tremendously, the economic growth rate of 3 percent was not enough to keep pace with that of the other emerging nations, especially those to the east, which were experiencing upward of 9 percent growth in their economies. Deng Xiaoping's reforms had begun a full decade before the Tiananmen Square massacre of 1989, and yet India still had not enacted the kinds of economic policy changes necessary to grow sustainably.

The Cold War and the ideals of post-colonialism drove much of India's (and the rest of the developing world's) economic policies. Classical economic philosophy, based on ideas about dependency theory and Keynesian economic protectionism (from the famous economist who had worked in India under the British Raj, John Maynard Keynes, 1883–1946) provided the basis for economic nationalism. The Asian, African, or Latin American nation that opened itself up for widespread Western investment during the Cold War was seen by many as "selling out" to exploitation, imperialism, or neo-colonialism. Thus, it was important ideologically to conform to economic nationalist pretenses that argued in favor of retaining national resources for the benefit of fellow nationals.

However, the economy had progressed rather slowly under the Nehru-Gandhi/INC inward-looking model. Nehru's economic policy centered on five-year plans based on a model created by the great Indian statistician, Prasanta Chandra Mahalanobis (1893–1972). The Indian government nationalized the banks, oil, coal, airlines and other major industries to work toward what Gandhi referred to as *Swadeshi*, or self-sufficiency. This philosophy led to the creation of what Indians referred to as the "License Raj" in which a vast bureaucracy controlled the structure of the economy. This detained growth to a minuscule level by comparison to that experienced by East Asia. As with the Latin Americans who had used the ISI (import substitution industrialization) model, Indians had been concerned that foreigners would profit from their natural resources to the detriment of the Indians themselves. However, as with Latin America, strict bureaucratic controls over the economy led to corruption and stagnation, and eventually both India and Latin America would abandon the ISI in favor of free market principles.

As with the East Asian Tigers and Cubs, it took the leadership of one politician in particular to change India's economic fate. However, India's example stood in contrast to its eastern neighbors in one crucial respect: it was a democracy. The fact that India was able to reach into the 9 percent growth realm by the 2000s without resorting to the authoritarianism of the East Asian nations demonstrates that perhaps absolute political control was not necessary to achieve unprecedented growth. The primary economic mastermind was Manmohan Singh, a Cambridge-educated economist who held a multitude of political posts between the 1970s and 1990s before being elected prime minister in 2004. Indian Prime PV Narasimha Rao chose Singh as his finance minister in 1991 to reverse a severe economic crisis brought about by inefficiency in the nationalized economy. Singh liberalized the economy by widespread privatization of previously state-run industries, as was the case with Latin American countries in the 1980s.

Singh decided to follow the East Asian example of opening up to foreign companies that had the capital necessary for developing India's economy at a rapid pace. Outsourcing, already popular in East Asia and Latin America, arrived in India with a boom in the 1990s. However, unlike East Asia, India established semi-skilled labor in the form of call centers and the like, which helped provide considerable funds eventually for the growth of high-technology firms in the 2000s. Bollywood, the center of Indian cinema production, produces more films than Hollywood, albeit with a smaller per-film budget. As India is several decades behind East Asia in its reform agenda, its per capita and overall wealth (measured in gross domestic product or GDP) is still behind the Tigers and some of the Cubs. However, its 9 percent GDP growth means that its economy is nearly doubling every two decades.

Though its economy has left the Cold War far behind, its geopolitical situation has not. The conflict with Pakistan over Kashmir rages as of this writing, with both sides fighting over the previously unresolved zone to the north of both countries. Both sides have developed formidable nuclear arsenals and have threatened to use them. The India-Pakistan nuclear conflict sometimes hangs by a thread, and it is perhaps more of a threat than any other inter-state rivalry on the planet, including North and South Korea, or Israel and Iran. The United States and the UN have been involved in tempering the heated exchanges between both sides for decades, and these have helped to reduce tensions at times; yet, fighting breaks out between Pakistanis and Indians within Indian-occupied Kashmir (most often) and across the India-Pakistan border (from time to time).

Turkey

Situated geographically, politically, culturally, and economically at an historical crossroads between Eastern and Western Civilization, the developed and developing world, and the continents of Europe and Asia, Turkey's definition of nationalism is still being defined both in the eyes of its inhabitants and outside observers. In the tradition of Ataturk, Turkey's government and military remain separated from its religious institutions, which are predominantly Islamic. This has helped Turkey be considered at the top of the Muslim world's standards for civil rights, with some glaring exceptions. The two situations that have caught most international attention since the end of the Cold War are the Kurdish question and Turkey's request to be part of the European Union. In both cases, Turkey's nationalism is under scrutiny. On the one hand, the Kurdish people of the east belong to a minority that resides in five different countries (Turkey, Iraq, Syria, Iran, and Armenia), and there is an ongoing insurgency (the Kurdistan Worker's Party) that the Turkish government has used U.S. military aid to brutally suppress since 1984.

The Kurdish population, much like the Armenian population in Turkey during WWI, has suffered extreme forms of discrimination and mass murder at the hands of the Turkish military. It is this type of sledgehammer approach to internal ethnic and political problems that has prevented Turkey from entering into full-fledged membership in the European Union. The politics of the Armenian genocide also play a role in Turkey's international reputation, for the Turkish government continues to deny that genocide ever took place. Westerners see this as tantamount to denying the Jewish Holocaust at the hands of the Nazis. Turkey's trade with the West is indeed extensive but, as of this writing, Turkey was not considered part of the European Union, although it was a part of NATO, and its trade with Europe had decreased, while its trade with Asia was on the rise. This was no doubt an indication of Europe's dire financial crisis that had crippled much of the continent's economic growth between 2008 and 2013, whereas Asia's economic outlook never seemed brighter.

The UAE, Bahrain, and Qatar: Small but significant

The small city-states in the preceding subtitle stand out in comparison to their neighbors in the Arabian Peninsula in several important ways. Not only are they wealthier on a per capita basis, but they are more cosmopolitan, progressive, and safer for foreigners. Unlike the rest of the Arab world, the United Arab Emirates have cooperated to use their oil wealth since Independence from the United Kingdom in 1971 to form the richest per capita group of nations in the world. They are technically seven monarchies (Abu Dhabi, Ajman, Dubai, Fujairah, Ras al-Khaimah, Sharjah, and Umm al-Quwain) with a president as chief of state in the capital, Abu Dhabi. Also unique to the UAE is its majority foreign-born population, which is mostly South Asian, Arab, and Iranian. The economic growth experienced in the UAE surpasses even Singapore, with its abundance of oil wealth fueling construction, a welfare state, and immigration on an unprecedented scale. Many foreigners also attend university there, and major international conferences and sports competitions take place in Abu Dhabi and Dubai.

Bahrain is another small monarchical city-state with a reputation for being open to visitors of all stripes, in particular because alcohol consumption is legal. Therefore, Arabs from surrounding countries travel to Bahrain for a chance to let loose. Qatar is also receptive to outsiders and is currently the wealthiest country per capita in the world. With just 2 million people, it is home to the Al Jazeera network, which reports on news from around the world. In particular, it is known for being equally critical of all sides, including both Arab and Western countries. They have incurred the criticism of U.S. officials and Arab governments when the station covers issues unflattering to their governments. The station became prominent especially during the U.S. invasion of Iraq in 2003, when it covered events from the perspective of the Iraqi people as opposed to most U.S. news stations, which presented a highly sanitized version of events, mostly from the perspective of U.S. troops and pro–United States Iraqis. In fact, U.S. news stations reprimanded U.S. reporters who presented the war in critical terms and, in one case, the U.S. military bombed the Al Jazeera station in Baghdad, killing one of its reporters.

The last story brings us to a broader point made by the late Edward Said in his monumental study, *Orientalism*. Though it could be considered a stretch to assert that the Al Jazeera reporter was killed by accident, it was no accident that the U.S. government invaded Iraq based on perceptions of that country that did not conform to reality. That is, the U.S. government did not simply "think" they were in the right. They "knew" there were WMD in Iraq that threatened the United States. When it was discovered that no WMD existed in Iraq, George W. Bush did not apologize, withdraw troops, or deny that he was right in ordering the invasion. No institution of justice brought him or anyone else to trial for killing thousands of people needlessly. This is not opinion. It is fact. The justification used to invade Iraq in 2003 proved to be false, and there is zero room for doubt about that now. The fact that the Iraqi people and the Arabs and other concerned international citizens who opposed the war have no legal recourse to call for justice or to undo the effects of the U.S. invasion symbolizes a form of perception among many Westerners that people of the East are inferior. Said sees Western perspectives of the East as perpetuated throughout history by notions of people in the Middle East in particular as brutish, sexually depraved, violent, wasteful, and the like. This has resulted from centuries of Western portrayals of Middle Eastern peoples in negative terms, especially in terms that contrast them to the West.

In a way, the book you read now is an attempt to find reasons for people in the West to care about people outside the West and to see other human beings as they see themselves. The reader can see certain political or economic or cultural systems as better or worse than others, but for there to exist a detachment between the humanity of one group of people and another is what all learned people should seek to mend. If nothing else, let us read this book with the intention of realizing how to bring the peoples of the Earth closer and closer together, not further and further apart, as certain flavors of nationalism, racism, classism, sexism, and regionalism have done throughout history.

Discussion questions

1   What do you think best explains the economic divergence between the poor and the rich countries of Asia in the past several decades?
2   Do you believe Asia more so than the West will shape the world of the twenty-first century? Explain.
3   Develop two lists of points arguing the pros and cons of the speed at which many Asian nations are growing economically.
4   Compare and contrast the pre–Cold War regions of Asia to their post–Cold War eras: the Middle East, Southeast Asia, the Indian Subcontinent, Central Asia, East Asia.

Historical figures

Mahmoud Ahmadinejad (1956–)

The president of Iran since 2005 as of this writing, this controversial figure served as the new Middle Eastern bogeyman for the West, and Israel in particular, in the wake of the overthrow of Hussein in Iraq in 2003. Ahmadinejad was a known participant in the kidnapping of the U.S. embassy personnel from 1979 to 1981 and, after assuming the presidency, denounced the existence of the State of Israel. The main problem with Ahmadinejad has been the concern over Iran's possible development of nuclear weapons.

The UN and the International Atomic Energy Association have attempted, without success, to determine whether Iran's nuclear program is purely for energy purposes, which is what Ahmadinejad claims. As of this writing, tensions were at their peak between Israel and Iran.

Yasser Arafat (1929–2004)

While the jury was still out on whether he was poisoned to death, Arafat's legacy both as revolutionary leader of the Palestinian people and the sometimes enemy of Israel and the United States is not in doubt. Egyptian by birth and education, Arafat rose to prominence initially in 1959 when he founded the Fatah political party, which still holds considerable power in the Palestinian territories within the State of Israel. Fatah went hand in hand with his Palestinian Liberation Organization, which carried out attacks against Israel in response to the occupation of Arab lands, particularly in Gaza and the West Bank. Arafat later became the president of the Palestinian National Authority from 1994 to 2004, until his death. Arafat symbolized the more secularized version of Arab "terrorism" that drew inspiration in part from (and inspired) revolutionaries in the developing world and from its opposition to Israel's violence against Palestinians.

Benazir Bhutto (1953–2007)

Pakistan's first female head of state, Benazir inherited the political legacy of her executed father, Zulficar. Benazir's election symbolized great hope for women and progressives in general around the world. However, her two truncated terms (1988–1990, 1993–1996) were largely fraught with tensions with her rival Nawaz Sherif and the military, both of which considered her ill-prepared and a threat to the traditional power structures in Pakistan. Benazir was in fact quite moderate, did not push hard for reforms and, indeed, was the first head of state to recognize the rule of the Taliban in Afghanistan. Her assassination in 2007 has been blamed by most observers on the lack of security provided by then-president General Pervez Musharraf (2001–2008).

Aung San Suu Kyi (1945–)

This Burmese Nobel Peace Prize laureate (1991) has been a politician and peace activist most of her life in rebellion against the military dictatorship of her country. Just before her party, the NLD, won a clear majority in the 1990 elections, she was placed on house arrest, where she remained for most of the next two decades until her final release in 2010. Two years later, she was elected to a seat in parliament in the nation's first relatively free and fair election, which she played an enormous part in bringing to fruition.

Park Chung Hee (1925–1979)

Unlike the rest of the historical figures listed here, General and President Park has two legacies, each in the extreme. He not only represented the "old guard" traditional strongman style of East Asian authoritarianism, but he created a South Korea with economic prosperity to the degree that most citizens revere the former leader. Park's heavy hand was part of a tireless effort to bring South Koreans out of the poverty that had put them on a par with much of the developing world. Within a generation, South Koreans reversed this trend and were in the developed world, competing with U.S., European, and Japanese car manufacturers, for example, a feat no other formerly developing country can claim. Park's philosophy was that political progress could wait while economic progress could not and, in this way, he put the cart before the horse, but it worked, until his assassination in 1979.

Saddam Hussein (1937–2006)

This former dictator of Iraq (1979–2003) was known as the most ruthless dictator on the planet in the last two decades of the twentieth century. Initially an assassin for the Ba'ath Party, he eventually became president in 1979 and invaded Iran the following year. The Iran-Iraq War (1980–1988) claimed the lives of upward of 1 million people. In 1991, the UN sponsored a mission to remove him from Kuwait, after which his power was marginalized to within Iraq's borders. He increased the police-state structures within Iraq throughout the following twelve years until being overthrown in a U.S.-led invasion in 2003. He was later captured by U.S. forces and hanged by Iraqi authorities.

Osama Bin Laden (1957–2011)

This Saudi-born millionaire led the international terrorist organization known as Al Qaeda for two decades until his assassination by U.S. troops in Pakistan in 2011. Although he first gained experience in the anti-Soviet jihad in Afghanistan during the 1980s, he later formed Al Qaeda as a Wahhabi Sunni-based group opposed to Israel's foreign policy and the U.S. military's presence in the Muslim holy land of Saudi Arabia in the wake of Saddam Hussein's invasion of Kuwait. After declaring jihad and carrying out attacks on U.S. and other foreign targets in the 1990s, he fled to Sudan and then to Afghanistan, where his organization planned the attacks on the United States on September 11, 2001, for which he became most well known. These attacks, which killed 3,000 people, ushered in the U.S.-led War on Terror, which can be argued to have shaped much of the first two decades of the twenty-first-century world.

Manmohan Singh (1932–)

As with many of the other historical figures listed in this chapter, former Indian Finance Minister and Prime Minister Singh was responsible for transforming his country's economy. As finance minister, he reversed the state-run economic model to allow for massive privatization. This allowed the Indian economy to engage with the emerging markets associated with globalization. Although initially unpopular with both dominant parties within India's government, Singh's market-based solution to Indian poverty proved successful for growing a middle class and increasing the upper class. As prime minister, he has continued these policies.

Lee Kuan Yew (1923–)

Founder and first prime minister of the city-state of Singapore, he led the country from developing- to developed-world nation within one generation. He is considered even more of a visionary than China's Deng Xiaoping, the man responsible for China's economic miracle, as he almost single-handedly orchestrated Singapore's success. Although an authoritarian politically, a legacy that lasts to this day, Lee solidly established a culture and infrastructure conducive toward sustainable export-led growth that has made Singapore the envy of East Asia.

Mohammad Yunus (1940–)

Another recipient of the Nobel Peace Prize, Mohammad Yunus is considered the father of the micro-lending revolution, about which we will learn more in Chapter 12. Bangladeshi by birth, Yunus founded the Grameen Bank, which has given micro-loans to mostly women for the past four decades in an innovative effort to reduce global poverty. Grameen Bank's micro-loans and those of many other banks in its wake have helped spark a revolution in small business growth throughout the developing world.

Further readings

Bhutto, Benazir. *Reconciliation: Islam, Democracy, and the West*. New York: Harper Collins, 2008.

Corn, David, and Michael Isikoff. *Hubris: The Inside Story of Spin, Scandal, and the Selling of the Iraq War*. New York: Broadway, 2007.

Demick, Barbara. *Nothing to Envy: Ordinary Lives in North Korea*. New York: Spiegel and Grau, 2010.

Fishman, Ted. *China Inc.: The Relentless Rise of the Next Superpower*. London: Scribner, 2006.

French, Patrick. *India: A Portrait*. New York: Vintage, 2012.

Mearsheimer, John J., and Stephen M. Walt. *The Israel Lobby and US Foreign Policy*. New York: Farrar, Straus, and Giroux, 2008.

Jacques, Martin. *When China Rules the World: The End of the Western World and the Birth of a New Global Order.* New York: Penguin, 2012.

Rashid, Ahmed. *Descent into Chaos: The U.S. and the Disaster in Pakistan, Afghanistan, and Central Asia.* New York: Penguin, 2009.

Schuman, Michael. *The Miracle: The Epic Story of Asia's Quest for Wealth.* New York: Harper, 2010.

Films

Slumdog Millionaire. Dir. Danny Boyle. 20th Century Fox, 2009.

Gaza Strip. Dir. James Longley. Typecast Pictures, 2002.

Reel Bad Arabs: How Hollywood Vilifies a People. Dir. Sut Jhally. Media Education Foundation, 2012.

Lions for Lambs. Dir. Robert Redford. United Artists, 2008.

Vietnam: Long Time Coming. Dir. Jerry Blumenthal, Peter Gilbert, and Gordon Quinn. FACETS, 2007.

No End in Sight. Dir. Charles Ferguson. Magnolia, 2007.

Control Room. Dir. Jehane Noujaim. Lionsgate, 2004.

Syriana. Dir. Stephen Gaghan. Warner, 2006.

They Call it Myanmar: Lifting the Curtain. Dir. Robert Lieberman. New Video Group, 2012.

Online content

ASEAN: www.asean.org

China News (authorized by Chinese government): www.china.org.cn

TED talks:

India on National Geographic: http://travel.nationalgeographic.com/travel/countries/india-guide/

Jacques Martin: Understanding the Rise of China: www.ted.com/talks/martin_jacques_understanding_the_rise_of_china.html

Hans Rosling: Asia's Rise: How and When: www.ted.com/talks/hans_rosling_asia_s_rise_how_and_when.html

Anil Gupta: India's Hidden Hotbed of Invention: www.ted.com/talks/anil_gupta_india_s_hidden_hotbeds_of_invention.html

Rory Stewart: Time to End the War in Afghanistan: www.ted.com/talks/rory_stewart_time_to_end_the_war_in_afghanistan.html

Sam Richards: A Radical Experiment in Empathy: www.ted.com/talks/rory_stewart_time_to_end_the_war_in_afghanistan.html

Patrick French on Indian Democracy: www.youtube.com/watch?v=U-YJEDxJE8g

9   Africa (1994–present)

Timeline

1994	Genocide in Rwanda, Refugee crisis in Zaire, Apartheid ends, Nelson Mandela becomes president of South Africa
1995	UN withdraws from Somalia
1996–1997	First Congo War
1997	Joseph Sese Mobutu overthrown in Zaire, first sub-Saharan African (Kofi Annan) named Secretary General of the UN
1998–2002	Second Congo War
1999	End of sixteen years of military rule in Nigeria
2001	UN peacekeepers help end civil war in Sierra Leone, Kabila assassinated in DRC
2001	African Union (AU) created
2002	Ceasefire in Sudanese north-south Civil War
2003–present	Darfur Genocide
2006	Ethiopia invades Somalia
2007	Slavery abolished in Mauritania, ex-Liberian president Charles Taylor indicted by International Criminal Court
2008	Kenya election riots
2010	South Africa hosts World Cup
2011	Arab Spring, South Sudanese Independence

Africa in our imagination

1   What assumptions do we have about Africa since 1994? Do we have more concrete details or mostly vague notions in our minds?
2   What sources do we draw upon for our understanding of Africa since 1994?
3   How legitimate are these sources?
4   Do we gain something from using these sources over others? What is the effect of these sources on our mindset?

Perhaps unlike any other continent, Africa has a definite image in everyone's mind. "The Dark Continent" is a term that means something, whether accurate or not. Not everyone shares the same image, but there is definitely something that means Africa for each person who knows that Africa exists. This is because the explanations non-Africans receive about Africa come mostly from non-Africans in a simplified way, consumable by people who really do not factor Africa into their own daily lives. We all certainly feel moved by stories of suffering emanating from Africa, but they appear as events we could never imagine happening in our own regions. This is not a true image of Africa, and we perpetuate this imagery for a variety of reasons, only some of which have to do with the Africans themselves. Central images about Africa we conjure up come directly from the electronic box sitting in our living rooms projecting content filtered by the combined efforts of uninformed and informed people. When producers and directors from the West combine with people knowledgeable about Africa, there may be some truth in their portrayals, but the images will be shaped to yield better ratings; thus, the profit motive will inevitably and tremendously alter our perspective.

This can happen even in instances of the most forthright efforts to reveal honest portrayals of Africa. For instance, the U.S. investigative program "Frontline" aired a gripping special in 2004 on the genocide in Rwanda that stands out as the definitive documentary on the event. A two-hour blow by blow depiction revealing the horrors made up almost exclusively of actual footage and interviews, with fact-based narration, made this program particularly authentic and meaningful. It can even be said to have honored the victims by showing the world just how awful the Hutus were to the Tutsis. However, it left out so many important truths that, when excluded, leave the uninformed viewer with some false notions of the causes and effects of the genocide. The fact that the Tutsis and the Hutus had fought each other for decades before 1994, in Rwanda and Burundi, where hundreds of thousands had died in civil wars and smaller genocides, was not mentioned. This was important because hundreds of thousands had already died, making this not the out-of-the-blue mass killing spree portrayed in the film. The fact that the Tutsis pursued the Hutus into Zaire in 1996 and killed tens of thousands of Hutus, the vast majority of whom had nothing to do with the 1994 genocide, was not mentioned. That the Tutsi-led government in Rwanda was the main player in the following decade of wars in the Congo was never mentioned either. These Congo Wars from 1996 to the present have killed 5 million people, and the Rwandan Tutsis, although not exclusively to blame by any means, played a central role in fomenting the violence.

The reasons for these events are so complicated that only large volumes can treat them fairly, and although it is better for viewing audiences to have some knowledge than none at all, in practice, stories about Africa such as the "Frontline" episode lead to distorted views on issues we cannot comprehend fairly without in-depth knowledge. In the case of Rwanda, the viewer leaves feeling something concrete about the people there: Hutus are bad because they killed 800,000 Tutsis and moderate Hutus indiscriminately, and Tutsis are simply innocent victims of genocide. The victims of the Tutsis themselves before and after do not factor into the viewer's mind because he or she will probably never delve deeper than the two-hour program he or she just watched. This is not really a criticism of the program, because it performed a service to the world for illustrating in such stark detail what did occur in those fateful months.

These programs unfortunately portray Africa as a violent place in need of assistance, but some argue that the economy suffers from these negative portrayals. The post–Cold War era has been marked by waves of famine, disease, and war, to be sure, but African economics and politics have changed radically during this time. Most governments are in transition away from dictatorship toward electoral democracy, albeit with deeply entrenched problems. Most countries have experienced economic growth, whereas others have stagnated or even slid backward slightly. Countries such as Kenya, Ethiopia, Egypt, Sudan, Rwanda, Nigeria, South Africa, Angola, and Ghana have expanded their economic bases as the wider phenomenon of urbanization and improved agricultural techniques have enhanced along with extended links to international trading partners in Europe, Asia, and the United States. Most of these have also suffered from internal conflicts.

Conversely, the Democratic Republic of the Congo (DRC), Niger, Zimbabwe, the Central African Republic, Malawi, Somalia, and others have suffered tremendous economic setbacks. In addition to viewing Africa's two separate economic categories, we can see it in two political categories: One group of nations is just now beginning to transition to independence, whether from white rule or outright colonial or monarchical rule, while the other group is in its second or third generation of independence from colonial rule. Nearly all African countries suffer from a lack of political and economic equity, but the strides that have been made in the past twenty years by such a relatively poor continent that also suffers from the highest level (by far) of HIV, malaria, and tuberculosis are admirable, to say the least.

Countries that fit into the first political category would be Zimbabwe, South Africa, Angola, Mozambique, and Swaziland, all southern African countries. Swaziland is the last standing monarchy on the continent and suffers the distinction of being the most destitute country per capita in the world, with an average life expectancy of thirty-one, and 40 percent of the population is HIV-positive. Mozambique and Angola gained independence from Portugal only in 1975, then suffered from civil wars until the 1990s, and only now are they beginning to live with a semblance of stability, albeit on the verge of absolute poverty. Zimbabwe and South Africa experienced white minority rule both during their colonial and independence eras, and this was undone only recently. South Africa gained independence from Great Britain in 1910 and experienced higher economic growth than the rest of Sub-Saharan

Africa as the apartheid regime kept the majority black population completely disenfranchised until it ended in 1994. Zimbabwe gained independence in 1980, when Robert Mugabe's Zanu party took power. However, Zimbabwe has gone in a completely different direction than South Africa. Though South Africa has its problems, it is the dominant player in Sub-Saharan Africa; it is industrialized; and its political leaders have promoted multi-racial equality (relatively) since the end of apartheid. Conversely, Zimbabwe has been led by a dictator who has worked to marginalize the white minority since independence ended that country's version of apartheid, which also privileged the white minority until independence.

The second group of countries, such as the DRC, Rwanda, Nigeria, Algeria, Egypt, Libya, Nigeria, Kenya, Uganda, Tanzania, Ghana, and others have enjoyed independence since the 1950s and 1960s, but the results vary tremendously. Egypt, Ghana, Tanzania, and Kenya have been relatively stable despite several episodes of civil conflict since independence from Great Britain, whereas Algeria, Sudan, Somalia, Nigeria, the DRC, Rwanda, Libya, and Uganda have suffered horrible wars both within their borders and with their neighbors since independence from their European overseers. The period since 1994 has seen tremendous change in some countries and continuity with others.

Somalia

The events of October 1993 that eventually led to the pullout of UN troops by 1995 only set the stage for a greater problem both in Somalia and the wider region. The first effect of the UN intervention was to establish a new post–Cold War UN mission, established by UN Secretary General Boutros Boutros Ghali, in which nations would cooperate to stem the rising tide of failed states by providing humanitarian aid with boots on the ground. Prior to this time, a UN armed intervention could have elicited the negative response of either of the superpowers or their allies. In addition, with the end of the Cold War, nations were freer to utilize their large militaries built up for Cold War purposes to supposedly "do good." However, Operation Restore Hope also proved that humanitarian interventions can be sticky affairs fraught with prejudices, ineffectiveness, lack of cooperation, corruption, and outright human rights abuses. The intervention killed thousands of Somalis and, in the end, the mission utterly failed, and twenty years later, Somalia still has no government.

Since UN troops left, perhaps 600,000 have died as a result of conflict, starvation, disease, and poverty. More recently, Somalia has spawned a new breed of international pirates who have plagued the Indian Ocean, stirring up media attention due to their high-profile targets, and the international terrorist organization, Al Qaeda, operates there freely. In 2006, Somalia's long-standing enemy, Ethiopia, invaded Somalia from the west, occupying the country with U.S. assistance in an effort to control the political scene there. This failed as well, and Ethiopia soon withdrew. Somalia and the DRC are perhaps the only two countries during this period that can be considered "basket cases" in the sense that there seems to be little hope for long-term change amidst massive suffering.

Rwanda

The case of Rwanda, however, represents both suffering on the widest scale per capita in Africa and one of the best success rates thereafter. As with the case of the Jewish population in the wake of the Holocaust, the ethnic Tutsis of Rwanda, after suffering the loss of three-fourths of their numbers at the hands of Hutu *Interahamwe* extremists, responded with vigor to the threat. Much like the Israelis, the Rwandan Tutsis have also used force beyond its borders to defend itself from aggression. The analogy between these two small states fits into a wider phenomenon in which ethnic minorities have struggled for millennia. In cases where autonomy is an option, these minorities have opted to arm themselves to the teeth to defend what they have left, using their expansion of influence as a buffer against another genocide.

The horrors of the genocide have been detailed at great lengths in many articles, books, international studies, and films, but no amount of retelling can bring to light the true depth of destruction wrought on Rwanda between April and July 1994. There are deep roots of the conflict that had been raging in various ways both before and since Rwandan and Burundian independence in 1961. Before the installment of first German and then Belgian colonialism, Rwanda and Burundi were kingdoms under Tutsi control over Hutus. Tutsis were only 15 percent of the population who were distinguished by their lighter skin, higher cheekbones, and tallness by comparison to the Hutus, but there was much intermingling between the two nonetheless. Wealth in Rwanda was tied to one's possession of cattle and, in the 1920s, the Belgians determined to officially separate the two ethnic groups based on the amount of cattle one owned. Tutsis were those possessing ten or more cattle, and Hutus possessed less. The Belgians forced every citizen to carry an identity card, which was then continued after independence and utilized by the Hutu to find and kill Tutsis in the hundreds of thousands between April and July of 1994. The trigger for the genocide occurred on April 6, 1994, when Rwandan president Juvenal Habyarimana (1973–1994), a Hutu, was killed in a plane crash in Kigali. Hutu extremists and the Tutsi rebel group the Rwandan Patriotic Front (RPF) operating under the leadership of Paul Kagame are both suspected of shooting the president's plane out of the sky, but no evidence has surfaced to support either conclusion.

The Hutu-dominated military and their militia groups known as the *Interahamwe* immediately took to the airwaves to call for the elimination of the Tutsi population. The historical roots to the Hutu-Tutsi ethnic violence are covered in Chapter 3, but it is important to remember how the Belgian official division between the two, which included requiring the carrying of identity cards indicating one's ethnicity, laid the foundation for the genocide. The RTLM radio station used by the Hutu extremists had been calling for anti-Tutsi violence for months before April, constantly referring to the Tutsis as their oppressors that had to be wiped out. They had been rehearsing their plans well in advance by practicing killing thousands each day. They had the names and locations of the Tutsis and moderate Hutus and were able to identify them by their identity cards: 80 percent of the Tutsi population died this way. The day after Habyarimana's plane crash, the *Interahamwe* executed ten Belgian UN peacekeepers and the prime minister and began the systematic killing. By April 11, the French, U.S., and Belgian governments had evacuated nearly all of their citizens from Rwanda, and tens of thousands lay dead already. The RPF had also begun their operation to stop the genocide and take the capital.

The civil war that raged between 1990 and 1993 was also an important precursor to the 1994 genocide. Paul Kagame had actually been within striking distance of the capital in 1993 (prior to the ceasefire) and had made the decision not to take it over, reasoning that the RPF's mission was not to overthrow Habyarimana but to pressure him to allow for the return of Tutsi refugees living in Uganda and Burundi. These refugees had been driven into Uganda and Burundi in 1959 by Hutus bent on eliminating the Tutsi presence in Rwanda. Kagame and his mother were among these refugees. From Uganda in 1990, with the assistance of the revolutionary leader and president Yoweri Kaguta Museveni (1986–1996, 2001–2011), the RPF mounted a powerful insurgency against the Hutu government. The RPF gained major victories between 1990 and 1993, thus reinforcing the Hutus' desire for violence against the Tutsis. The Arusha Accords signed in Tanzania in 1993 were intended to end the civil war and allow for a peaceful transition toward Tutsi and Hutu coexistence in Rwanda. The *Interahamwe* sought to prevent this and to eliminate the Tutsis once and for all.

The Hutus did not target armed rebels during the genocide. They deliberately killed unarmed Tutsis on a scale previously unimagined in human history. It was the most intense slaughter ever, with 800,000 perishing in just three months in a country of 8 million and mostly through the use of small arms (rifles, handguns, machetes). The international community looked on in horror and yet did virtually nothing even as the UN's commander of forces in Rwanda, Lt. General Romeo Dallaire (Canada), pleaded for massive intervention. His book, *Shake Hands with the Devil*, tells his perspective of the genocide.

Three months into the killings, the RPF entered Kigali and drove the Hutu government from power, ending the genocide. However, one of the worst humanitarian crises of the twentieth century was about to unfold, as the Hutu *genocidaires* (people who committed the genocide) spread word to

Figure 9.1 Paul Kagame (1957–) (Kevin Moran/Alamy)

their Hutu brethren that the RPF would commit genocide against them now that they were in power, driving nearly 2 million refugees into neighboring Zaire (later the DRC). Thus, just as the Rwandan Tutsis could breathe a sigh of relief after suffering so much loss, the Hutus, most of whom had not participated in the genocide, were now subjected to their own peril in the refugee camps.

However, in the wake of the genocide, Paul Kagame emerged as vibrant leader of a devastated country that put Rwanda back on the map. Aside from instigating the Congo wars, which is addressed below, his leadership, first as vice president (1994–2000) and then as president (2000–) has brought Rwanda into a new age of economic prosperity and political stability in ways unseen throughout Africa. Not only has GDP grown steadily with economic diversification through micro-lending, government-supported training, and international assistance, but Rwanda's parliament is nearly 50 percent women, a unique situation for any country in the world.

The Congo Wars

The refugee crisis that resulted from the RPF's ending the genocide in Rwanda dumped 2 million Hutus into Zaire, mostly in the eastern Kivu region. Thousands died every week for months after their arrival in July 1994 from exposure, disease, hunger, and abuse. The international relief effort was odd, because there was virtually none during the genocide, and yet the refugees in Zaire received thousands of aid workers whose agencies and governments spent billions of dollars. The French even sent 5,000

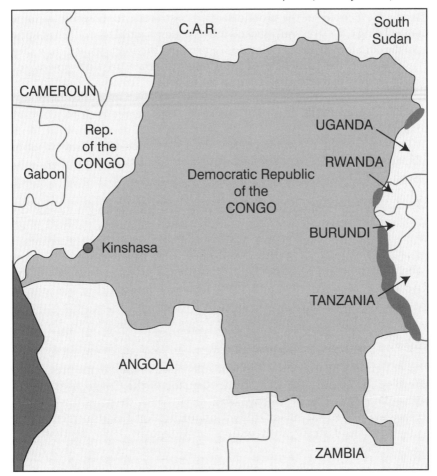

Figure 9.2 Map of the Democratic Republic of Congo

troops to assist the Hutus' escape after providing them with political and military support both during the 1990–1993 civil war and on the lead-up to the genocide. Even with this tremendous effort, the death toll of the Hutu exodus made this the worst humanitarian crisis of the 1990s after the genocide in Rwanda, and it touched off the Congo Wars that lasted from 1996 to 2002. And despite their official end in 2002, the violence continues as of this writing.

The complicated nature of the Congo Wars, also referred to as "Africa's World War" by Congo expert Gerard Prunier, makes this section particularly challenging for observers to comprehend. At the same time, this complexity should reveal just how we cannot view Africa in simplistic terms. The stories emanating from the DRC since these wars began in 1996 have shocked the world, and yet shock value obscures why these horrors have occurred, making the people on the ground seem monstrous as opposed to rational human beings. We are, thus, sucked into a conundrum: Do we focus on the tragedies in all their details? Or, do we examine the interests and how they played out on the battlefield of the Congo to come up with generalized human lessons that will enable humanity to benefit from historical analysis in an honest manner? The former can cause readers to act. The latter can cause readers to think. It is your choice to what degree each affects your conscience.

The war actually began long before the 1994 genocide in Rwanda when rebel troops under Laurent Kabila took up arms against the dictator of Zaire, Joseph Sese Mobutu (1965–1997) with Cuban assistance. The quick defeat of Kabila's forces in 1965 was followed by three decades of corrupt rule but relative internal stability as Mobutu served as a counterweight against the rising tide of socialism in Africa. He was heavily supported by the United States, South Africa, and France. Mobutu had also assisted the Habyarimana government in Rwanda in their suppression of the RPF insurgency between 1990 and 1993 and provided military assistance to the *genocidaires* in the Kivu region between 1994 and 1996, making him a thorn in the side of the new RPF-dominated government in Rwanda. By 1996, with the help of Rwanda, Uganda, Zimbabwe, and Angola, the same Kabila from the previous revolt restarted his insurgency under the banner of the Alliance of Democratic Forces for the Liberation of Congo after years of exile. Within a year of fighting, he overthrew Mobutu and placed himself in the presidency, renaming the country the Democratic Republic of the Congo, thus ending what is known as The First Congo War.

Rwanda played the major role in supporting Kabila's insurrection and had placed itself strategically within the Congo by 1996. In that year, Rwanda had begun an effort to root out the *Interahamwe* militias in Zaire, killing tens of thousands of Hutu *genocidaires* and civilians alike. They had also established a proxy army of Congolese Tutsis, or Banyarwanda, to carry out some of these operations, stirring up anti-Rwanda sentiment in the Congo. At the same time, Rwandans were seen as too powerful within the new administration in Kinshasa, the capital of the DRC, and eventually a clash broke out between Rwandan Tutsis and Kabila's government in 1998. Thus began the Second Congo War. The ensuing conflict pitted Uganda, Rwanda, and Burundi against the DRC, Angola, Chad, and Zimbabwe, but the fighting all took place in and over control of the DRC and its resources. By 2001, an estimated 3.1 million people had died as result of the conflict.

What made these wars different from the other major wars of the twentieth century were the indirect casualties. Most had died as a result of displacement and diversion of resources to the war effort. Disease, hunger, and exposure-related deaths all skyrocketed after 1996 in an otherwise impoverished country that had been pillaged of its resources and money by colonial powers, European and Asian corporations, and Mobutu and Kabila.

There were also hundreds of thousands of rapes, tortures, and other atrocities that did not end lives but devastated them nonetheless. However, what made this war similar to other conflicts was the presence of the incentive to fight over resources.

During the Cold War, it was uranium for nuclear missiles that drew attention to the Congo (Congolese uranium was used for building the atomic bombs that fell on Japan in 1945). During the Congo Wars, it was gold, diamonds, and coltan, a mineral used for video game consoles, computers, and cell phones, the value of which climbed considerably during the war, as it occurred during the so-called "dotcom boom." All of the more than twenty competing armed groups (militaries and their proxies from all nations involved) fought for control over these resources and carried out atrocities against the civilian population whenever threatened by one of their competitor armies. Thus, the people who suffered the most were (and are) the villagers who happened to live in regions dominated by armed groups. Europeans also fought over these riches during the colonial period. Witness the Boer Wars fought over gold and diamonds. Witness Leopold II's Congo Free State atrocities over rubber profits. And the examples go on and on. Seen in this light, the recent Congo atrocities fit into a broader history of tragedy that many, outsiders and insiders alike, have created. By the end of the Second Congo War in 2002, Kabila had been assassinated (in 2001) by a member of his personal guard, and his son Joseph (2001–) had taken over the presidency with little prospects for creating lasting change.

The years since then have led to the deaths of a further 2 million people due to the chaos unleashed by the Congo Wars. UN peacekeepers, international political and economic advisors, and the International Criminal Court have been added to the ranks of the relief organizations and various armed groups that remain in the DRC after the wars have officially ended. In a situation such as this, one must ask, "How is the DRC to improve its situation?" Time and again, historians who examine the Congo see its problems as rooted in colonialism primarily. The Portuguese robbed the soil of its native inhabitants and sold them into slavery beginning more than five centuries ago, and the Belgians killed millions in their effort to raise themselves to the economic levels of their European counterparts who had also benefited financially and technologically from their overseas conquests. The Congo has also never been a unified country. It has always been a vast region divided ethnically and ideologically, and any efforts to unify the country have inevitably led to despotism, exploitation, and war.

And yet, there are people who care tremendously about this place. The natural and human resources are also sources of beauty. It is the home to the second largest river basin in the world, the Congo River Basin, and the flora and fauna there are almost unmatched. The culture is vibrant, with music, art, literature, and food of enviable quality. In short, the war should not define the DRC.

Blood diamonds: Angola, the DRC, Sierra Leone, and Liberia

The issue of "blood diamonds" has recently come to world attention in part due to the acclaim of the film by the same name. However, the film itself could never convey the complexity of how diamonds came to fund rebel movements in Africa in the 1990s. It began when the Angolan anti-Communist rebel movement UNITA lost its long-running support from the United States and South Africa when the Cold War ended. It had been fighting the leftist MPLA government for two decades by the mid-1990s, when it turned to dominating the diamond industry in Angola to finance its ongoing war.

In 1991, Sierra Leone witnessed the uprising of the Revolutionary United Front (RUF), led by Foday Sankoh. The RUF eventually moved into the diamond-producing zones and enslaved large portions of the population, demanding a constant flow of diamonds to fund their war. Former rebel leader and Liberian president Charles Taylor (1997–2003) supported the RUF with the aim of uniting the two countries under his and Sankoh's rule. Upward of 70,000 people lost their lives, and 10,000 had their limbs chopped off by the RUF before the UN intervened with 17,000 troops to defeat the rebels in 2001. By 2002, international pressure led to a worldwide effort to regulate the sale of diamonds to prevent their use to fuel conflicts. Militias, rebels, and militaries in the DRC have also been using diamonds (along with gold, coltan, and other minerals) to fund their efforts since 1998, but regulation there has been scant by comparison to Sierra Leone, which has had a constitutional government in control since 2001.

Uganda

The former British colony that suffered under the worst despot perhaps in African history (Idi Amin, 1971–1979) has begun to hit its stride in recent years after decades of oppression and war. The post–Cold War era has been dominated by the long-standing president Yoweri Museveni (1986–). This is despite international condemnation over Uganda's role in the Congo Wars and the existence of a waning insurgent group known as the Lord's Resistance Army (LRA), headed by Joseph Koney. Koney has been fighting against the Ugandan government for more than twenty years now and is known for kidnapping large numbers of children and indoctrinating them into the ranks of his army. The atrocities committed by the LRA defy imagination, as not only are children the primary victims of kidnapping, but they are forced to kill their own family members, and they have been known to dismember and disfigure their victims. The death count of the LRA is relatively low by comparison to wars in neighboring countries, but they have been accused of killing up to 60,000 people nonetheless.

Museveni has been recognized in part for making significant gains in marginalizing the LRA and the areas of political equity and economic growth. He helped Uganda turn its HIV infection rates around from the highest level in Sub-Saharan Africa to the lowest and enhanced women's liberation efforts, even making a woman his vice president (Specioza Kazibwe). In addition, like nearly every Latin American country, he cooperated with the International Monetary Fund in the 1980s to overturn the reigning state-centered economic structures that had brought about Uganda's financial woes. The structural adjustment program Museveni agreed to meant a reduction in state spending and selling state-run enterprises, an unpopular move for the poor. However, like Mexico in the 1980s, Uganda was at the mercy of international lenders who refused to continue funding their economy without the promise of being paid back in full over the long run, which is what the structural adjustment programs ensure.

Sudan

Although Sudan has been embroiled in civil wars for three decades, events since 2003 in the oil-rich North African nation have caused global concern. In fact, Sudan should be considered as more in line with the scale of suffering and war experienced by the DRC: More than 2.5 million have been killed, and nearly 6 million have been displaced. Moreover, like the DRC (and unlike Rwanda in 1994), the wars in Sudan are on multiple fronts with regional, national, and international interests. The first conflict raged from 1983 to 2002 between the Muslim north and the Christian south and was largely religious and ethnic in nature. The ceasefire of 2002 paved the way for southern Sudan to vote for secession in 2011; however, a new war began in 2003 in the western province of Darfur when rebels took up arms against the Khartoum government in the capital over the government's lack of attention to the area's problems.

The war in Darfur is largely a series of massacres carried out by proxies of the government of Omar al-Bashir (1989–) called the *Janjaweed* militias. Of course, Bashir denies these accusations, but he has been indicted in the International Criminal Court for backing the *Janjaweed*. More than 400,000 people have been killed in Darfur since 2003 by these militias, and although global activism has pressured the international community in general to denounce their actions as "genocide," very little has been done as of this writing to stop the killings. One major obstacle to halting the *Janjaweed* is the support of China for Bashir in the UN Security Council. China has received access to Sudan's oil fields and has refused to denounce the Khartoum government's crimes. We have only to review what we know of the Congo Wars or even the U.S./U.K. intervention in Iraq to understand China's incentive to defend Bashir. As of this writing, there are more than 20,000 African Union peacekeeping troops in Darfur whose job it is to prevent the killings, but they do not fight the *Janjaweed* and instead take on more of an "observe and report" mission. As with Rwanda, the genocide in Darfur has also led to severe problems for Sudan's western neighbor, Chad, which has received hundreds of thousands of refugees. However, the difference here is crucial: Unlike the Hutus fleeing the Tutsi victims of genocide in Rwanda, the Darfur refugees are the victims themselves of genocide and are now suffering as victims of displacement.

Nigeria

When Nigeria is in the headlines, it is rarely good news. The same divisions that plague Sudan plague Nigeria but thankfully without the same level of violence. The Muslim north holds the majority of the population while the Christian south holds a minority but still maintains a high level of influence in national affairs. A recent story involving this division held international attention when a woman was condemned to be stoned to death for having sex out of wedlock. In this case, the woman (Safiya Husseini) had been divorced from her husband but, under Sharia law, this warranted a specific type of death penalty that caught the attention of the world. Sharia had been adopted in twelve Nigerian states at the time of Husseini's trial in 2002. Her eventual acquittal was no doubt in part the result of international pressure, but it is also indicative of the growing integrity of the African justice system in general. Under dictatorial rule, which was the norm in Africa for the first two generations of independence, these courts would not have gained international attention, and they would have been subject to the dictator's whims as opposed to the "rule of law."

The post–Cold War era did not begin this way at all. Sharia law was barely an issue, and a dictator who would place a permanent stamp on Nigerian history initiated a five-year reign of corruption and terror. His name was General Sani Abacha, and he seized power in a coup in 1993 but died in office in 1998. This period was marked by Abacha's repression of all dissent. He targeted political opponents, both real and imagined, by leveling spurious charges at them leading to long imprisonments and even death. He broke strikes by oil workers with brute force, causing the largest employment sector to submit to his rule. When the Ogoni people of the oil-producing Niger Delta region, along with other activists, rose in protest against both the unequal distribution of oil revenues to non-oil-producing regions and the environmental impact of oil production on the Delta, Abacha sent in troops. Dozens of activists were killed, and nine Ogoni were given the death penalty for their role in instigating the movement. The "Ogoni Nine" case led to worldwide condemnation that fell on deaf ears. Unlike most African dictators, Abacha set up a system to create a democratic façade for his one-man rule by establishing five political parties that would simultaneously select him as their candidate. He died in 1998 before this plan could take effect, however, and a new crisis of succession took place.

Abacha was followed by another general, Abdulsalami Abubakar (1998–1999) who opened up the political process to dissenters to pave the way toward democracy. He released imprisoned dissidents and oversaw free and fair parliamentary and presidential elections in 1998 and 1999. Former Abacha opponent General Olosegun Obasanjo (1999–2007) won the presidency outright and initiated what appeared to be a new openness in Nigerian politics. However, previously subdued ethnic divisions soon erupted in violence in 2000 over the north's shift toward Sharia law as Muslims targeted uncooperative Christians, killing hundreds in the process. In 2002, hundreds more died in Muslim-Christian clashes in Lagos on the eve of Obasanjo's 2003 reelection, which was condemned by his opponents as fraudulent. Parts of Nigerian society seemed to be disintegrating as ethnic, regional, political, and economic factors drove them apart. Oil was a major driving force in all of this tension: As one of the world's top producers, Nigerian oil served to increase the wealth of a small elite, and the resulting poverty of millions of people only exacerbated the country's problems. Criminal and ethnic violence plagued much of the country as well and, due to the public's lack of trust in the police and the military, militia and vigilante groups began to form along ethnic, religious, political, and regional lines, further spreading the violence. One vigilante group known as the "Bakassi Boys" rounded up and killed upward of 3,000 alleged criminals in their state of Anambra, earning them a prize by Nigerian journalists for reducing crime to the lowest levels in the country.

By 2007, with ethnic violence at its peak, Nigeria marked its second peaceful transition of elected civilian government when Umaru Yar'Adua took the presidency (2007–2010). His presidency would be marred by more ethnic violence and the rise of Islamist insurgencies aimed at turning Nigeria into an Islamic country. At the same time, these problems were linked to access to oil and the rise and fall of world oil prices. Yar'Adua died in office in 2010 and was succeeded by Goodluck Jonathan (2010–).

Zimbabwe

Unlike Nigeria, but like South Africa, Zimbabwe's colonial past contained a white minority controlling most of the economy living within a black majority that shared only in the small remnants of the nation's wealth. This was the case two decades after independence from Britain in 1980, when Robert Mugabe came to power. However, unlike South Africa, whose black leadership made reconciliation with the very white minority that had brutalized the black majority for three and a half centuries a central priority of their new vision for South Africa, Zimbabwe's leader did not hold to this position for very long. The difference between both countries is indeed stark. In one case, you have blacks and whites working together for a new future. In the other, you have a worsening and deepening race war driven by the dictator's dedication to punishing the white population for the legacy of colonialism, all political opposition, and the rest of society's ills.

The post–Cold War era in Zimbabwe has been dominated by Robert Mugabe (1980–), the eighty-seven-year-old despot with a socialist background who never came close to implementing socialist reforms. Although at first conciliatory toward the white minority population during the 1980s, he crushed his black political opponents by massacring thousands and imprisoning tens of thousands and eventually targeted white property in the 1990s and 2000s. As of this writing, most white farmers had been removed from their land, many of whom were physically abused and even murdered in the process of expropriation.

The land issue is inextricably linked to Zimbabwe in a manner unique in Africa because the history of the country is rooted in the land allocation differences between the white and black populations dating back to the 1890s arrival of the first white settlers. The British government allowed its citizens to grab land already inhabited by indigenous Shona and Ndebele Africans, pushing the natives from their traditional lands to provide a foundation of economic growth for future white generations at the expense of the black population. British officials established the Land Apportionment Act to distribute land between the races and, by 1931, the 1 million blacks were given 29 million acres, and the 48,000 whites were given 48 million. The largest cash crops were tobacco, corn, and cotton, and the white population would benefit disproportionately from the rise of these on the market. This is yet another important example of how colonialism laid the foundation for inequality in many places around the world.

As with Kenya in the post–WWII era, more whites entered Rhodesia throughout the 1950s and 1960s. They were given black farms, and more blacks were pushed into reserves. Thousands of black farmers were forcibly removed from their farms in this way in the years prior to Mugabe's rise to power in 1980. As such, when Mugabe's rule came into question in the 1990s, he used this history to justify divisions between the white minority and the black majority to gain more popularity. The whites became scapegoats for his ill-conceived method of governance but, at the same time, the history of the white destruction of the black population's traditional way of life and the enrichment of the white population as a result were indeed very real. Whatever abuses suffered by the white Zimbabwean population in the past twenty years must be considered in relation to this abusive history suffered by the blacks for a century at the hands of the white population.

However, this cannot dismiss Mugabe's increasing abuses or his mismanagement of the economy. And there is a long list of abuses, indeed. The most recent headlines on Zimbabwe concentrate on the record-high inflation rates, which have reached the highest on the planet (25 million Zimbabwe dollars to the U.S. dollar). However, in the decade before hyperinflation, the land issue became central to Mugabe's Zanu-PF party platform for a number of reasons. In the mid-1990s, veterans from the Rhodesian War (1972–1979) that led to Mugabe's rise to power in 1980 began protesting loudly over their lack of governmental support. The protestors were veterans with disabilities who pointed out how uninjured veterans among the Zanu-PF elite had received large pensions and plots of land from Mugabe's government. By 1997, Mugabe capitulated to the war veterans' demands and agreed to pay them and to provide them all with plots of land. Where to get the land? He announced he would take over 1,503 white farms without compensation to their owners, claiming that the British government, not Mugabe's government, should compensate the farmers for any losses.

The argument came across crassly to the once-colonial masters who had violently taken land from black Africans across east, southern, and west Africa over the course of more than a century. From Mugabe's perspective, his actions were inherently moral and just. By 1998, international and domestic opposition to land seizures led him to ease up briefly to discuss a more just form of land reform with international donors. The donors agreed only to assist in a land reform program whereby their funds assisted people in buying farms. They specifically opposed using their funds for forcing people off their land. Mugabe agreed and then went back on his word and ordered the seizures to continue. This weakened overall confidence in the economy, as his supporters invaded white farmlands, and this began a long period of decline in agricultural output. This country had once exported its products and now depended on imports as its population descended into extreme poverty.

What exacerbated the economic doldrums was Mugabe's support for Laurent Kabila's revolutionary government in the DRC, especially during the Second Congo War (1998–2002). Mugabe was motivated by an agreement with Kabila to give Zimbabwe companies privileged access to the DRC's cobalt, diamond, and timber resources. Considerably more could be said about this aging yet still forceful leader. As Mugabe ages, Zimbabweans hold their breath about the future leadership, which could just be an extension of Mugabe's Zanu-run government that has been in place since 1980. The neighboring country of South Africa is an example of an alternative method for dealing with post–white minority rule.

South Africa

The main political party of post-apartheid South Africa is the African National Congress (ANC). It is what everyone is talking about, and it is indicative of the nature of the transition away from white rule in the post-1994 era, because the ANC is the only organization the majority black population and their white ANC allies have pinned their hopes on for almost a century, since the ANC was formed in 1912. Naturally, Nelson Mandela would become president after the end of apartheid. He and the

ANC won the historic 1994 elections, and his term represented a model for the transition away from dictatorship and civil war toward reconciliation that many other countries have learned to use in the wake of their own conflicts. Perhaps only a figure such as Mandela, recognized the world over for his ability to forgive and even work with his former oppressors, had the star power to ease South Africa in its transition period. He led with the concept of "National Reconciliation" to make the white population feel more at ease with the new racial equality culture, as many feared a Mugabe-like anti-white racist state in the wake of the ANC's rise to power. Although Mandela succeeded in easing this transition, economic and civil problems exploded during his presidency as crime surged and whites maintained their privileged economic status and a new class of wealthy blacks allied to the ANC emerged. After he stepped down in 1999 at the age of 81, there emerged two powerful leaders, Thabo Mbeki and Jacob Zuma, from the younger generation of ANC activists who had helped lead the resistance in the 1970s and 1980s. Mbeki served two terms as president from 1999 to 2008, resigning just months before he was to stand for a third term amid major scandals and schisms within the party.

The problems for the ANC began with controversial economic policies begun under Mbeki. His GEAR (Growth, Employment and Redistribution) program (at first fully endorsed by his future rival and deputy president Jacob Zuma) had the aims of attracting investment from abroad, increasing savings at home, and general fiscal austerity. Though this increased overall GDP growth, it left out large portions of society that had always suffered from a lack of education, sanitation services, and medical treatment, and employment. With the HIV rates reaching record numbers and the urbanization rate accelerating, the poor felt their economic woes even more so as the number of millionaires increased. Accusations surfaced that ANC officials had accepted kick-backs after a 1999 series of arms deals worth $5 billion. In 2005, deputy president Zuma was forced out over allegations that he had been one of these officials, and this allegation caused a rift in the ANC. The discussion on the streets centered on whose side ANC followers would take between Zuma and Mbeki. Zuma followers saw him as the scapegoat for the ANC's corruption scandals, and his image became distorted as a champion of the poor who would overturn the GEAR program if elected.

By 2008, Zuma emerged as the new ANC leader, and Mbeki was seen as out of date. After Mbeki was pressured to step down in September 2008, the prominent ANC activist and official Mosiuoa "Terror" Lakota created a new party out of the ranks of the ANC called Congress of the People (COPE) to stand in the 2009 elections against the ANC and Jacob Zuma. The ANC won nearly 70 percent of the vote, but the COPE initiative still represented a possibility of change that came from within the ANC, and this can be seen as a positive step toward more transparency and pluralism that could reduce cronyism. Despite these problems, South Africa is seen as a leader among the African nations with a more sophisticated national dialogue than most. They did not go the route of Zimbabwe, marginalizing the white population in the wake of the ANC victory in 1994, nor have political contests turned violent as of yet. South Africa's hosting of the 2010 FIFA World Cup also represented the country's rise on the world stage as it was the first African country to receive this honor.

Kenya

Last, we look at one of the most politically stable African nations in the post–Cold War era. Recently, Kenya has made headlines especially in the United States, in part due to the fact that the father of President Barack Obama (2009–) was Kenyan. For Africans, the U.S. President's African heritage means that for the first time there is a real link between the highest levels of U.S. power and the African people. Of course, the global economic downturn has meant reduced U.S. assistance for Africa since Obama came to office.

Kenya has also become world-renowned for having the very best marathon runners in the world. Kenyan runners often take the top prizes in the most prestigious international competitions, most notably the Boston, Chicago, London, and New York City marathons. Much like baseball in the Dominican Republic and soccer in Brazil, running represents Kenya's national pastime and serves as a springboard for many Kenyans seeking prosperity. Kenya has also gained international attention through The Greenbelt Movement (GBM), led by Wangari Maathai, whose efforts to reduce greenhouse gases, increase soil integrity, add more green spaces, and empower women has gained her worldwide notoriety.

Still, aside from Kenya's stability, violence on a level not seen there since the Mau Mau rebellion of the 1950s hit the country after the contentious elections of 2008. Mwai Kibaki (2002–), the incumbent president, had originally represented a new day for Kenyan democracy when he replaced the long-time dictator Daniel arap Moi (1978–2002). However, by 2007, his opponents had achieved enough popular support to give him a serious run for the presidency. When the Electoral Commission of Kenya announced that Kibaki had won a narrow victory in December 2007, supporters of opposition candidate Raila Odinga called the results fraudulent, which led to a wave of violence between Odinga and Kibaki supporters and between police and demonstrators, leading to the deaths of more than 1,000 people by April 2008. That month, former UN Secretary General Kofi Annan mediated a power-sharing arrangement between both camps, ending the violence but leading to the largest-ever Kenyan government, thus causing massive increases in spending just to maintain government officials' salaries.

Kenya has also been at the center of many development projects that illustrate the difficulty of coordinating between international

Figure 9.3 Wangari Maathai (1940–2011) (Jeremy Sutton-Hibbert/Alamy)

non-governmental organizations (NGO), national governments, local governments, and the people affected by the programs. One example of this challenge is the effort to provide updated housing to slum dwellers in Nairobi, the capital. To many who live in the slums, which are essentially tightly packed shacks built with corrugated metal, sometimes wood and other materials by their occupants, their current existence is better than the countryside. The growth of African, Asian, and Latin American cities, in the past four decades in particular, is mostly attributed to rural-to-urban migration by former farmers seeking steadier work. The various groups seeking to aid slum dwellers believe no one would prefer to stay in the slums if provided with better housing. However, the slum dwellers in Nairobi are skeptical about the NGOs' ability to provide this housing because they have been promised improvements in the past by the Kenyan government, only to be disappointed. If private interests get involved as well, there are added problems. In the case of the Nairobi slums, most were excluded from the new housing projects, and those selected to receive new housing were forcibly evicted from their homes and had to fend for themselves for indefinite periods of time. This conundrum of how to promote development is buttressed by a considerable amount of theory set forth by academics with high levels of education and perhaps little practical knowledge. However, as this small example illustrates, theory cannot account for the simple everyday problems that crop up when attempting to implement concrete plans. These theories, discussed further in Part IV, rarely take into account the ever-changing feelings of human beings.

Arab Spring

The two World Wars, the Russian and Chinese Revolutions, the Cuban Missile Crisis, and the fall of the Berlin Wall mark perhaps the six most significant events of the twentieth century. The Arab Spring of 2011 could be considered the twenty-first century's first event on a par with these six, and indeed, the world has yet to see the final results of this widespread movement. The fact that the center of this movement has been in Africa has not made headlines, however, as it is portrayed as a Muslim or Arab phenomenon. The year 2011 began literally with a flare. The young vendor Muhammad Bouazizi set himself on fire in Tunisia as the highest act of protest against what many deemed to be a corrupt political system that had lasted for twenty-three years under president Zine al-Albidinl Ben Ali (1987–2011). It was January 4, and the Tunisian people immediately rose in unarmed revolt in what has been labeled "The Jasmine Revolution" against Ben Ali, causing his resignation within days. Little did the world know, but Bouazizi's act and Ben Ali's response quickly sparked revolts across the Arab World.

Within weeks of Ben Ali's departure from power, millions of Egyptians from all across the country openly resisted the thirty-year presidency of Hosni Mubarak (1981–2011). The Egyptian leader had dominated political life through a repressive yet restrained state apparatus and maintained peace with Egypt's long-time rival, Israel. However, many viewed Mubarak as a dictator who limited freedoms and stole from public coffers. His estimated wealth was $80 billion. During his presidency, he would routinely receive $2 billion a year in U.S. military funding as a means of keeping Egypt as an ally in the Middle East and preventing it from attacking Israel. The Nobel Peace Prize winner and former head of the UN's International Atomic Energy Agency (IAEA), Muhammad al-Baradei, helped lead the non-violent protests in Cairo, as did intellectuals, politicians, students, workers, business owners, and even many elements from within Mubarak's own political and military circles. After three weeks of protests that shut the country down, Mubarak stepped down on February 11, a truly significant event and date due to Egypt's leadership role in the Arab World.

Still another scenario was playing itself out in Libya where armed revolts took place against the forty-two-year dictatorship of Muammar Qaddafi. Here is a leader unique in the world: He was both a socialist revolutionary and a Muslim firebrand that supported fundamentalist Islamic terrorism in the 1980s against both the United States and Europe. After the population rose in defiance of his regime in February 2011 Qaddafi ordered his troops to use brute force against armed and unarmed rebels and civilians alike. Under UN auspices, NATO decided to intervene militarily in Libya to establish a no-fly zone that would protect the Libyan people from being massacred in certain areas. Within months, Qaddafi was captured and assassinated, ushering in a new era in Libyan politics. Yemen and Syria also experienced uprisings against their long-term dictatorships, covered in Chapter 8.

Disease: A symptom of poverty

The three main diseases killing the largest number of people on the planet are AIDS, malaria, and tuberculosis (TB). Africa has one-seventh of the world's population but half of its disease victims. This disproportion has been attributed to a lot of different explanations. Some in the West assert that this is due to the backward nature of Africans, an essentially racist explanation only enhanced by the very real fact that many Africans do not understand the nature of preventing infection from these diseases. However, many non-Africans around the world are just as ignorant about disease and, therefore, this explanation cannot do much to help us understand the high death toll in Africa. Simply witness the deaths of millions of Americans who do not understand that smoking, overeating, and inactivity are just as deadly as infectious diseases. In fact, many Americans do not believe the scientific evidence linking smoking to lung cancer.

In the developed world and among the wealthy of the developing world, these three main diseases are treatable by modern medicine. Even HIV can be kept at bay with an anti-retroviral cocktail due to the massive effort by noble researchers who have been studying this disease since the first infections occurred in the early 1980s. Even so, the more educated have become more responsible in recent years by following Uganda's three-point ABC (Abstinence, Be faithful, and Condoms) plan for prevention. Although the Ugandan government (and most African countries) is exceptionally brutal toward homosexuals, their plan accommodates all lifestyles and has been taught for the past three decades in the West to people in high school and through public health campaigns. Malaria can be prevented through avoiding exposure to malaria-carrying mosquitoes, especially at night, and through taking anti-malaria drugs. The drugs are prohibitively expensive for most Africans and, therefore, millions of mosquito nets have been distributed by governments and aid organizations to families in need. However, many more have to live without either drugs or netting and, as a result, suffer from contracting the disease several times throughout their lives. Many die as a result, and children and the elderly are especially susceptible.

TB presents a different problem than most infectious diseases because there are multiple resistant strains that have evolved in response to the antibiotics given to patients down the years. The drugs for all three of the major diseases are prohibitively expensive in their current state; however, there has been a largely successful movement afoot in the past decade to pressure pharmaceutical companies to provide these drugs at much-reduced prices to countries most affected. Surprisingly, the U.S. administration of George W. Bush (2001–2009) took the lead in providing money to combat AIDS in Africa and the Caribbean. The five-year $15 billion aid package was the largest ever allocated by any government, even on a per capita basis, for this AIDS prevention and treatment. However, five years of war in Iraq cost the United States $3 trillion. In other words, the United States was willing to spend 200 times more on invading a country under false pretenses than it was on helping millions of people survive the AIDS epidemic: 200 times more people's lives could have been saved if the money for invading Iraq were spent on this, the worst global epidemic in the history of the world.

Discussion questions

1   What do you think explains Africa's current status as the poorest and most unstable continent in the world?
2   What are the fundamental changes that have occurred in Africa since the end of the Cold War, and what do you think are the reasons why these changes have occurred?
3   What is the logical, objective argument against Robert Mugabe's land expropriation campaign against the white population, considering the fact that Europeans did just that all over Africa during its conquest and colonization of the continent and on a much larger scale than Zimbabwe?
4   What makes Africa unique in a positive way? That is, what can other continents learn from Africa to apply to their own lives?

Historical figures

Kofi Annan (1938–)

The former Secretary General of the United Nations (1997–2006), this Ghanaian was the first UN official to be awarded the Nobel Peace Prize (2001) for his global efforts to stem the rising tide of violence, particularly in Africa, the Balkans, and the Middle East. However, in his pre–Secretary General days at the UN, he also presided over the decision to reduce UN forces in Rwanda during the genocide in 1994, which his critics will never let him live down. He was also known for his advocacy of placing the UN more in touch with the common problems of people suffering in the developing world.

Muhammad Al Baradei (1942–)

This Egyptian intellectual was head of the UN International Atomic Energy Agency (IAEA) from 1997 to 2009 and won the 2005 Nobel Peace Prize for his diligent efforts to limit the proliferation of weapons of mass destruction (WMD). He emerged as an outspoken critic of the U.S. effort to invade Iraq in 2003 due to the absence of evidence of WMD there and later gained prominence for his efforts to accurately discern the extent of Iran's nuclear ambitions. He was a top leader of the protest movement that led to the ouster of Egyptian president Hosni Mubarak in 2011.

Omar al-Bashir (1944–)

This president of Sudan since 1989 has overseen not only a decade of civil war between his Muslim-dominated government in the north and the Christian south during the 1990s, which killed 2 million and displaced 5 million, but he is wanted on war crimes by the International Criminal Court for his role in promoting genocide in the western province of Darfur, which has killed 400,000. The case of Darfur has received major media attention since the mid-2000s in part due to Western celebrities and politicians who have highlighted the plight of the Darfur citizens, terrorized by the Bashir-backed *Janjaweed* militias suppressing a revolt in the province through massacres, mass rape, and outright destruction of thousands of villages.

Muhammad Bouazizi (1984–2011)

Although his name will only now start to appear in history books, this former Tunisian street vendor will go down in history as the person who lit the spark for the revolution that hit the Middle East in 2011. After being denied a permit to continue vending on the streets of Tunis and being abused by police, on January 4, 2011, Bouazizi set himself on fire in protest against the corruption of the Tunisian government. His public suicide in the age of instant global communications quickly caused a great stir in the Muslim world, first triggering the overthrow of the long-standing Tunisian government and then spreading to Egypt, Libya, Syria, and Yemen.

Alhaji Aliko Dangote (1957–)

The richest man in Africa, this Nigerian businessman has a net worth of $14 billion as of 2011. Mr. Dangote's wealth has multiplied in recent years with increased distribution in mobile technologies, cement, and other products and services. What makes him stand out is that unlike in past years where the richest Africans were white South Africans, Mr. Dangote is black, which has brought pride to many Africans.

Laurent Kabila (1939–2001)

Initially the leader of a guerrilla army fighting a socialist revolution in Zaire in the 1960s, Kabila's failed insurrection caused him to lay low for three decades until the Rwandan government supported his renewed rebellion from 1996 to 1997 against longtime dictator Joseph Mobutu (1965–1997). Kabila's victory honeymoon did not last long, as his Rwandan backers soon supported his overthrow and possibly his assassination in 2001. Both his days as rebel commander and national president of the Democratic Republic of the Congo (1997–2001) witnessed massive suffering across the countryside, with upward of 3 million perishing from violence, displacement, malnourishment, and disease by 2001, and a further 2 million died in the decade afterward.

Paul Kagame (1957–)

This president of Rwanda since 2000 is seen today in two different lights, each of which are valid. The first view contends that he ended the genocide against his people, the Rwandan Tutsis, when his rebel group, the Rwandan Patriotic Front (RPF) overthrew the Hutu-dominated government there in July 1994, after the Rwandan army and *Interahamwe* militias had killed 800,000 people. His leadership of the Rwandan government, both as vice president and president, has been acclaimed as a major African success story due to the increased economic and political stability the country has witnessed but also for Kagame's stance on national reconciliation. However, it was also under his leadership that the Rwandan military and government has supported massive human rights abuses in the Democratic Republic of Congo since 1996.

Wangari Maathai (1940–2011)

Dr. Maathai was the first woman from East and Central Africa to earn a PhD (University of Nairobi, 1971), and she won the 2004 Nobel Peace Prize for her work in resisting environmental degradation in Africa. The GBM has planted tens of millions of trees as a means of reducing both environmental problems and greenhouse gases, and this has provided a foundation for the reduction of poverty—in particular for women—in Africa. She has become a world-renowned author, speaker, and advisor, not to mention a politician in Kenya.

Naguib Mahfouz (1911–2006)

Known for his controversial novels that tackled subjects set deep within the national psyche of Egyptian society, Mahfouz won the Nobel Prize for Literature in 1988. He wrote more than fifty novels during his long life, some of which were banned at home and abroad for their alleged blasphemy against Islam. He also became involved in government ministries and the film industry.

Nelson Mandela (1918–)

By far Africa's most famous person in history (alongside another South African leader, Shaka Zulu), Nelson Mandela began his anti-apartheid activism as leader of the ANC in the 1950s. He was imprisoned for twenty-seven years for these acts, during which time the ANC struggled to end apartheid. Mandela's release in 1990 represented the beginning of the end for apartheid, which officially terminated in 1994, the year Mandela was elected as president. He received the Nobel Peace Prize in 1993 and served as president from 1994 to 1999. His ANC political party has dominated political life in South Africa since 1994.

Hosni Mubarak (1928–)

The Egyptian president from 1981 to 2011, he was known as the first Egyptian president to preside over lasting peace with Israel after his predecessors, Gamal Abdul Nasser and Anwar Sadat, led the wider anti-Israel movement in the Middle East between the 1950s and 1970s. Sadat actually signed the peace accords in 1979 that began this peace but was assassinated in 1981. Mubarak was overthrown in a mass nonviolent uprising in February 2011 in the wake of the Tunisian uprising of January that year.

Robert Mugabe (1924–)

He first rose to prominence as an intellectual and activist promoting independence from Great Britain in the 1960s and then led the Zanu revolt against the white-dominated government of Ian Smith in the 1970s before winning election as president in 1980. After the dictators Milton Obote (Uganda) and Joseph Sese Mobutu (Zaire) were ousted in 1985 and 1997, respectively, Mugabe stands out as the last in an old breed of African tyrants running their countries into the ground.

Further readings

Campbell, Greg. *Blood Diamonds: Tracing the Deadly Path of the World's Most Precious Stones*. Boulder, CO: Westview, 2004.

Gourevitch, Phillip. *We Wish to Inform you that Tomorrow We Will Be Killed with our Families: Stories from Rwanda*. New York: Picador, 1999.

Hunter, Susan. *Black Death: AIDS in Africa*. New York: Palgrave Macmillan, 2003.

Johnson, R.W. *South Africa's Brave New World: The Beloved Country since the End of Apartheid*. New York: Penguin, 2009.

Kinzer, Steven. *A Thousand Hills: Rwanda's Rebirth and the Man who Dreamed it*. Hoboken, NJ: Wiley, 2008.

Maathai, Wangari. *The Challenge for Africa*. New York: Anchor Books, 2010.

Mahajan, Vijay. *Africa Rising: How 900 Million African Consumers Offer More than You Think*. Upper Saddle River, NJ: Pearson, 2008.

Merideth, Martin. *The Fate of Africa: A History of Fifty Years of Independence*. New York: Public Affairs, 2005.

Merideth, Martin. *Mugabe: Power, Plunder, and the Struggle for Zimbabwe's Future*. New York: Public Affairs, 2007.

Steidle, Brian. *The Devil Came on Horseback: Bearing Witness to the Genocide in Darfur*. New York: Public Affairs, 2007.

Sterns, Jason. *Dancing in the Glory of Monsters: The Collapse of the Congo and the Great War of Africa*. New York: Public Affairs, 2011.

Films

Hotel Rwanda. Dir. Terry George. MGM, 2005.
Sometimes in April. Dir. Raoul Peck. HBO, 2005.
Frontline: The Ghosts of Rwanda. Frontline. PBS, 2005.
Invictus. Dir. Clint Eastwood. Warner, 2010.
The Constant Gardener. Dir. Fernando Meirelles. Universal, 2006.
A World of Conflict: One Man, One Year, Twenty Wars. DVD included within Kevin Sites' book, *In the Hot Zone: One Man, One Year, Twenty Wars.* New York: Harper Perennial, 2007.
Without the King. Dir. Michael Skolnik. First Run Features, 2008.
Mugabe and the White African. Dir. Lucy Bailey and Andrew Thompson. First Run Features, 2010.
Blood Diamond. Dir. Edward Zwick. Warner, 2007.
Bamako. Dir. Abderrahmane Sissako. New Yorker, 2008.
Darfur Now. Dir. Ted Braun. Warner, 2008.
Dreams of Dust. Dir. Laurent Salgues. Film Movement, 2008.

Online content

The Greenbelt Movement: www.greenbeltmovement.org/index.php
International Criminal Tribunal for Rwanda:www.unictr.org/
The African National Congress: www.anc.org.za
Partners in Health: www.pih.org
Africa Book Centre: www.africabookcentre.com
Africa Confidential: www.africa-confidential.com/news
Africa Focus: Sites and Sounds of a Continent: www.uwdc.library.wisc.edu/collections/AfricaFocus
National Security Archive: "The US and the Genocide in Rwanda in 1994": www.gwu.edu/~nsarchiv/NSAEBB/NSAEBB117/index.htm
Save Darfur: www.savedarfur.org/
World Bank: Publications and Documents: www.worldbank.org/reference/
UN World Health Organization: Country Reports: www.who.int/countries/en/
Southern Africa Regional Poverty Network: www.sarpn.org.za/

Part IV
Development

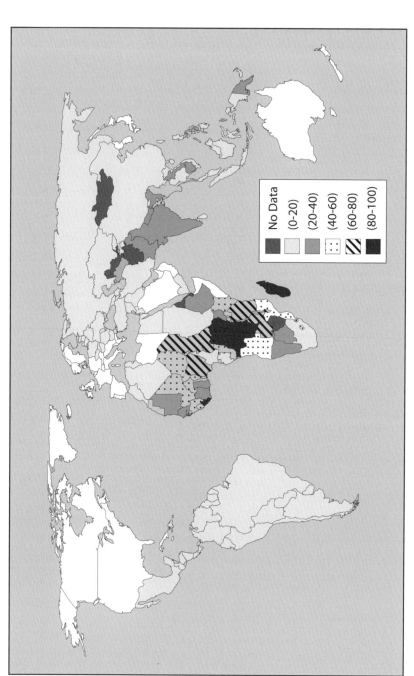

Figure 10.1 World Bank map on poverty headcount ratio, $1.25/day

10 Views from below

Critiques of colonialism, imperialism, and capitalism

The preceding map and statistics on the following pages are strong indicators for the divergences that exist among the different countries of the world. What is apparent is that places such as Central America, parts of South America, Sub-Saharan Africa, and South Asia in particular suffer from lower levels of health and economic prosperity than those in the rest of the world. What are the causes of this divergence? People have been attempting to answer this question since time immemorial, usually with abysmal results because it is too difficult to answer with one perspective. Unfortunately, language itself is a constant barrier toward understanding reality in general, and this question in particular is one of the most problematic to analyze. The immense number of factors that need to be considered to formulate a comprehensive explanation seem too daunting to assume through the work of theory. However, many people think they have figured it out, and their voices are what this part covers. Before covering the theoretical perspectives on the causes of progress and inequality, let us probe our previously held ideas about this topic.

- Prior to reading this book, was there an author or school of thought that informed your ideas about the causes of inequality, underdevelopment, and socioeconomic progress?
- If so, what are the main argument's foundations?
- Were they legitimate?
- If not, what do you think helped perpetuate those ideas in your head?

This chapter will cover some of the prominent voices that have advocated for a bottom-up perspective of development and, at the end of the chapter, there is a list of links about each perspective to allow students to expand upon what I provide here. *The point of Part IV is that there is a debate, not any degree of certainty, about the causes of development and underdevelopment.* Despite the assertive and unequivocal language utilized by the authors surveyed in this part about how some nations thrive and others do not, it should become readily apparent that each version is a theory, with both incredible insight and some drawbacks. This is, of course, my own analytical

Table 10.1 Infant mortality rates per 1,000 births of Asia, Africa, and Latin America, 2011

United States	6.4	Dominica	10.7
World:	36.9	Dominican Republic	20.9
Afghanistan:	72.7	Ecuador	19.6
Albania	12.8	Egypt	18.0
Algeria	25.6	El Salvador	13.1
Angola	96.4	Equatorial Guinea	79.6
*Antigua and Barbuda	6.4	Eritrea	46.3
Argentina	12.6	Ethiopia	51.5
Armenia	15.6	Fiji	14.1
The Bahamas	14.1	Gabon	49.3
Bahrain	8.6	The Gambia	57.6
Bangladesh	36.7	Ghana	51.8
Barbados	17.7	Grenada	10.3
Belize	14.5	Guatemala	24.2
Benin	67.9	Guinea	78.9
Bhutan	42.0	Guinea-Bissau	98.0
Bolivia	39.3	Guyana	29.4
Botswana	20.3	Haiti	52.9
Brazil	13.9	Honduras	18.2
*Brunei Darussalam	5.6	India	47.2
Burkina Faso	81.6	Indonesia	24.8
Burundi	86.3	Iran	21.1
Cambodia	36.2	Iraq	30.9
Cameroon	79.2	*Israel	3.5
Cape Verde	18.2	Jamaica	15.7
Central African Republic	108.2	*Japan	2.4
Chad	97.1	Jordan	18.0
Chile	7.7	Kazakhstan	25.0
China	12.6	Kenya	48.3
Colombia	15.4	Kiribati	37.7
Comoros	58.8	North Korea	26.3
Dem. Rep. of Congo	110.6	*South Korea	4.1
Republic of Congo	63.8	Kuwait	9.3
Costa Rica	8.6	Kyrgyz Republic	27.0
Cote d'Ivoire	81.2	Laos	33.8
*Cuba	4.5	Lebanon	8.0
Djibouti	71.8	Lesotho	62.6

Liberia	58.2	Seychelles	11.9
Libya	12.8	Sierra Leone	119.2
Madagascar	42.8	*Singapore	2.0
Malawi	52.9	Solomon Islands	18.4
*Malaysia	5.6	Somalia	108.3
Mali	98.2	South Africa	34.6
Marshall Islands	22.1	South Sudan	76.0
Mauritania	75.6	Sri Lanka	10.5
Mauritius	12.8	St. Lucia	13.8
Mexico	13.4	St. Vincent and the Grenadines	19.5
Micronesia	33.5	Sudan	56.6
Mongolia	25.5	Suriname	26.0
Morocco	28.2	Swaziland	69.0
Mozambique	71.6	Syrian Arab Republic	13.2
Myanmar	47.9	Tajikistan	52.8
Namibia	29.6	Tanzania	45.4
Nepal	39.0	Thailand	10.6
Nicaragua	21.6	Timor-Leste	45.8
Niger	66.4	Togo	72.9
Nigeria	78.0	Tonga	13.2
Oman	7.3	Trinidad and Tobago	24.5
Pakistan	59.2	Tunisia	13.9
Palau	14.3	Turkey	11.5
Panama	16.7	Turkmenistan	44.6
Papua New Guinea	44.8	Tuvalu	25.1
Paraguay	19.1	Uganda	57.9
Peru	14.1	*United Arab Emirates	5.6
Philippines	20.2	Uruguay	8.7
*Qatar	6.4	Uzbekistan	41.5
Romania	10.8	Vanuatu	11.4
Russian Federation	9.8	Venezuela, RB	12.9
Rwanda	38.1	Vietnam	17.3
Samoa	16.0	West Bank and Gaza	19.7
Sao Tome and Principe	58.2	Yemen	57.0
Saudi Arabia	7.9	Zambia	52.7
Senegal	46.7	Zimbabwe	42.8

Source: World Bank

*Countries with infant mortality less than or equal to that of the United States position after having reviewed the literature of this topic as honestly as I can. I have included only what I consider to have the most valid arguments.

Throughout most of history, the preferred method of analysis rested upon the supernatural. Whether a hunter-gatherer tribe tens of thousands of years ago or a group of average urban citizens in the eighteenth century, people tended to look to the sky for divine explanations about the causes of problems and solutions. Regionalism, racism, and sexism also played important destructive roles in determining perceptions of the world. Thus, the question of why millions of people of African and Indigenous American origin deserved to be enslaved was in fact not questioned by supporters of slavery because it was "God's plan," for example. Some protested this system, and often they used Biblical passages to condemn slavery. The belief that non-Westerners are poor because they have somehow failed is a perspective that still holds favor among many in the developed world. However, it is fortunately on the decline.

It was not until the age of Enlightenment when large groups of people began to question this supernatural method of belief. Scientific thinking gained a foothold between the sixteenth and nineteenth centuries. Copernicus, Galileo, Newton, and Darwin, to name a few, validated the notion that analysis needed rationally-based modes of observation. The nineteenth century was the golden age of science, and there soon emerged theories about both the physical and the social universe. Around the same time in which Darwin expounded his theory of natural selection, social theorists such as Karl Marx, Friedrich Engels, Auguste Comte, and many others analyzed human history and current events to advocate for new models of organizing society.

Karl Marx and Friedrich Engels: Marxist theory

From *The Communist Manifesto*, 1848, pp. 2–3:

> The history of all hitherto existing societies is the history of class struggles.
>
> Freeman and slave, patrician and plebeian, lord and serf, guild-master and journeyman, in a word, oppressor and oppressed, stood in constant opposition to one another, carried on an uninterrupted, now hidden, now open fight, a fight that each time ended, either in a revolutionary reconstitution of society at large, or in the common ruin of the contending classes...
>
> Our epoch, the epoch of the bourgeoisie, possesses, however, this distinct feature: it has simplified class antagonisms. Society as a whole is more and more splitting up into two great hostile camps, into two great classes directly facing each other—Bourgeoisie and Proletariat...
>
> The discovery of America, the rounding of the Cape, opened up fresh ground for the rising bourgeoisie. The East-Indian and Chinese markets,

the colonisation of America, trade with the colonies, the increase in the means of exchange and in commodities generally, gave to commerce, to navigation, to industry, an impulse never before known, and thereby, to the revolutionary element in the tottering feudal society, a rapid development.

The feudal system of industry, in which industrial production was monopolised by closed guilds, now no longer sufficed for the growing wants of the new markets. The manufacturing system took its place. The guild-masters were pushed on one side by the manufacturing middle class; division of labour between the different corporate guilds vanished in the face of division of labour in each single workshop...

Modern industry has established the world market, for which the discovery of America paved the way. This market has given an immense development to commerce, to navigation, to communication by land. This development has, in its turn, reacted on the extension of industry; and in proportion as industry, commerce, navigation, railways extended, in the same proportion the bourgeoisie developed, increased its capital, and pushed into the background every class handed down from the Middle Ages.

The rest of the *Manifesto* elaborates on the foregoing points. The splash made by Karl Marx (1818–1883) and Friedrich Engels's (1820–1895) 1848 tract, not to mention Marx's three-volume study, *Das Kapital* (1867), still reverberates throughout the world. For better or worse, Marx had more effect on the world than any other author of the social sciences. His class-based analysis provided not only the foundation for much of the leftist explanations for the next century and a half but inspired the rise of Communism, which took the lives of 60 million to 100 million people in the twentieth century.

According to Marx and Engels, the elites and the bourgeoisie (middle class) have become wealthy through conquest, colonialism, imperialism, and exploitation of the peasantry and the working class (the proletariat). Their logic followed that this system must be overturned to provide the order for a more just world. It is difficult to argue with the premise, if not the solution. The premise rests on history, which clearly demonstrates that the elites drove the power systems that came to rule the world through wealth, which controls political power. However, it fails to provide an appealing reason about why this is wrong, for one, and how overturning it in favor of a classless society run initially by a "dictatorship of the proletariat" would improve the situation. Of course, history showed after Marx and Engels that whenever this system was put into place, the consequences were disastrous. The sheer volume of barbarity meted out against hundreds of millions of people (killed, imprisoned, subjected to totalitarian conditions) in the Communist world in the twentieth century rivaled that carried out by the Nazis.

Aside from its political consequences, Marxist analysis was able to permeate many legitimate forms of inquiry. It can be found in the lenses of leftist analysis, which focuses on the subaltern, a term used by Antonio Gramsci to describe those sectors of society with less of a voice than the elites and middle class. This includes women, minorities, the working class, rural and urban poor, less developed countries, and other less privileged sectors. As such, it is customary for authors of the Right wing or even the mainstream to accuse their opponents of having a Marxist bias, as if they were in fact, pro-Communist. It is important to distinguish between Marxist analysis and Marxist politics/economics/social planning, and the like. The former is a school of thought that focuses on exploitation by elites of the subaltern. It could be argued that without Marxism as a precursor, the social sciences would lack foundation. At the same time, it could be argued that the world did not need Marx and Engels to understand exploitation, as can be seen by the Indian movement for independence led by Mahatma Gandhi (and many others).

Anti- and post-colonialism

Marx and Engels's *Manifesto* coincided with an outbreak of revolutionary fervor throughout Europe in 1848, and these continued intermittently over the next few decades. The Russian Revolution of 1917 witnessed the climax of their inspiration in the form of Vladimir Lenin's Bolshevik Revolution in October of that year. Thus began the first and longest-lasting experiment in the formula set to paper by Marx and Engels. Others would follow, to the dismay of a third of humanity who lived under Communist tyranny across Eurasia, parts of Africa, and Cuba. However, as the developing world comprises more than 70 percent of the planet's population, it made sense that there would emerge a diversity of revolutionary movements over the course of the twentieth century. The best-known icons of revolution are Mao, (China), Ho (Vietnam), Gandhi (India and South Africa), Nehru, (India), Che (Latin America and Zaire), Sukarno (Indonesia), Mandela (South Africa), Nasser (Egypt), Nkrumah (Ghana), and a few others. Some of these were also great theoreticians of revolution, and they sought to espouse what they viewed as the causes of inequality along the way. Collectively, these wide-ranging leaders fall under the concepts of anti-colonialism and post-colonialism, according to scholars who study this phenomenon. I will survey only a few of the prominent voices here.

Mahatma Gandhi: The ultimate anti-colonialist critic

Speaking in Jamshedpur in 1925:

> [M]y ideal is that capital and labour should supplement and help each other. They should be a great family living in harmony, capital not only looking to the material welfare of the labourers but their moral welfare also—capitalists being trustees for the welfare of the laboring classes under them.

While at the same time an unabashed advocate of Western Civilization's finest cultural aspects, Mahatma Gandhi (1869–1948) critiqued colonialism and modernization in general for what he perceived as their lack of humanity and disconnection from the needs of the majority for the benefit of the minority. From Britain's use of force to subdue its colonies to railroad transportation and manufactured clothing, Gandhi advocated for traditionalism over modernization, as he saw modernization occurring by force from British colonialism. Like Marx and Engels, Gandhi approached the problem systemically: The entire premise of British colonialism had to be challenged to release the Indian people from its grip. Unlike Marx and Engels, Gandhi did not advocate for a violent overthrow of the system. In the end, while Gandhi is revered in India, his economic philosophy, which was anti-technological (clothing, transportation, food, etc.) plays no role in modern India's growth, which has reached 9 percent in the past two decades due to outright capitalist models of development.

An example of Gandhi's attempts to move India away from the modern, capitalist direction it was moving is found on pages 494 to 496 in his autobiography, *An Autobiography: The Story of My Experiments with Truth* (1927), in which he provides a dialogue between himself and a mill owner. The discussion revolved around Gandhi's promotion of the use of the spinning wheel as a means of empowering people both to make their own clothing and not remain dependent on the capitalist market and employing the poor:

> "I can understand your grief, but I can see no ground for it. We are not conducting our business out of philanthropy. We do it for profit, we have got to satisfy the shareholders. The price of an article is governed by the demand for it. Who can check the law of demand and supply? The Bengalis should have known that their agitation was bound to send up the price of Swadeshi cloth by stimulating the demand for it."
>
> I interrupted: "The Bengalis like me were trustful in their nature. They believed, in the fullness of their faith, that the mill-owners would not be so utterly selfish and unpatriotic as to betray their country in the hour of its need, and even to go the length, as they did, of fraudulently passing off foreign cloth as Swadeshi." ...
>
> "but I am engaged in the revival of the spinning wheel."
>
> "What is that?" he asked, feeling still more at sea. I told him all about the spinning wheel, and the story of my long quest after it, and added, 'I am entirely of your opinion; it is no use my becoming virtually an agent for the mils. That would do more harm than good to the country. Our mills will not be in want of custom for a long time to come. My work should be, and therefore is, to organize the production of handspun cloth, and to find means for the disposal of the Khadi thus produced. I am, therefore, concentrating my attention on the production of Khadi. I swear by this form of Swadeshi, because through it I can provide work

to the semi-starved, semi-employed women of India. My idea is to get these women to spin yarn, and to clothe the people of India with Khadi woven out of it. I do not know how far this movement is going to succeed, at present it is only in the incipient stage. But I have full faith in it. At any rate it can do no harm. On the contrary to the extent that it can add to the cloth production of the country, he it ever so small, it will represent so much solid gain. You will thus perceive that my movement is free from the evils mentioned by you."

Gandhi's position, though certainly from a place of compassion for India's poor as they existed under British colonialism, is not informed by the global nature of market competition and instead is motivated by an ideal, which was noble but not realistic. The version of development for Gandhi is completely opposite of that which worked in East Asia and Latin America, and it is even more divergent from what is envisioned by India's leaders today. The traditional method of producing one's own goods as opposed to engaging in a consumer society would have made India perpetually impoverished, according to the capitalist and Marxist mindsets alike.

Raul Prebisch: The roots of dependency theory

In 1949, the Argentine economist, Raul Prebisch (1901–1986) assessed the problem of development in the Third World in a revolutionary manner. Poor countries such as his had been caught in a cycle of exporting large quantities of unfinished goods, or raw materials, to the rich countries to finance the purchasing of manufactured goods from those rich countries. The "value added" by manufacturing goods meant that countries that exported raw materials would always fall behind the rich countries that produced those goods.

Prebisch's analysis led to the broad theoretical realm known as "dependency theory," which encompasses world-systems theory and Marxist analysis as well. Dependency theorists believe traditional capitalism led to an unequal balance of power between the rich or "core" countries, which had been profiting off the "periphery" or poorer countries, and this process was in need of repair. This perspective was opposite from Max Weber's advocacy of modernization theory, which asserted that the developing world was behind due to its cultural backwardness. Dependency theory, conversely, blamed Western-style capitalism, with its origins in conquest and imperialism and pushed for a solution to this historical problem. Dependency theory has formed the underpinning of much of the bottom-up, leftist analysis of international economics and development theory. Prebisch's ideas also reformed Latin American and some African and Asian economic models with import substitution industrialization (ISI). Third World countries, inspired by ideas of economic nationalism, created state-run businesses that kept wealth within their own countries: As opposed to exporting only raw materials, they produced these and manufactured goods for internal consumption.

ISI worked in Latin America until the 1982 debt crisis brought it crumbling down. Until then, countries such as Mexico and Chile experienced sustained growth rates that financed rapid development throughout Latin America. By 1982, the inefficiency of ISI became glaringly clear when many governments failed to repay their debts, and soon countries were forced to sell off (privatize) state-owned businesses to repay and renew their loans. This process of privatization, or undoing ISI, led to the rise of the "free trade" agreements such as the North American Free Trade Agreement (NAFTA), the Free Trade Agreement of the Americas (FTAA, now defunct), and the Dominican Republic-Central American-US Free Trade Agreement (CAFTA-DR), signed since the end of the Cold War. Dependency theory has thus been under severe scrutiny by economists since the 1980s because although it informed ISI models, which created tremendous growth in some countries, it also caused irresponsible spending and corruption. In addition, the developing countries that have reduced or eliminated trade barriers have largely seen their economies grow.

Under economic nationalism, in oil-rich countries such as Nigeria and Mexico, the state took out massive international loans and spent money with no oversight. When the price of oil dropped in 1982 and 1986, for example, Mexico and Nigeria, respectively, did not have the oil revenue necessary to service their debts and, therefore, suffered cutbacks in social spending and employment previously funded by the oil sector. The Cold War–era dependency theory model that led to economic nationalism thus allowed for temporary "good times," but its centralized nature meant the public's money (and the public, not the government officials, had to pay off those debts) was spent by officials not beholden to the people. Economic nationalism, therefore, went by the wayside in the 1980s. However, it reemerged in a more open manner in the 2000s in response to globalization. There are many state-centered businesses throughout the developing world that have combined state ownership with private ownership, particularly in the natural resources industries. The combination has allowed for a dialogue between the state and private sectors that has promoted massive growth in the areas of oil and natural gas especially.

Frantz Fanon: Diagnosing the problem

The Martinique-born psychiatrist who died at thirty-six after writing several books and serving in the Algerian Revolution has become one of the most-known anti-colonialist authors of the twentieth century. Frantz Fanon's (1925–1961) cynicism and hostility were similar to those of Guevara (both were doctors), and his defiance toward colonialism and promotion of independence for all colonized peoples resembled those of Gandhi. Che was *the* revolutionary icon; more of a symbol than a creator of ideas, unlike Gandhi and Fanon. As seen on the third page of Fanon's most famous book, *The Wretched of the Earth* (1961), the act of colonization did not benefit the Africans specifically because of the attitudes of the Europeans toward the Africans and the institutions they created to control their territories:

> The colonized world is a world divided in two. The dividing line, the border, is represented by the barracks and the police stations. In the colonies, the official, legitimate agent, the spokesperson for the colonizer and the regime of oppression, is the police officer or the soldier. In capitalist societies, education, whether secular or religious, the teaching of moral reflexes handed down from father to son, the exemplary integrity of workers decorated after fifty years of loyal and faithful service, the fostering of love for harmony and wisdom, those aesthetic forms of respect for the status quo, instill in the exploited a mood of submission and inhibition which considerably eases the task of the agents of law and order. In capitalist countries a multitude of sermonizers, counselors, and "confusion-mongers" intervene between the exploited and the authorities. In colonial regions, however, the proximity and frequent, direct intervention by the police and the military ensure the colonized are kept under close scrutiny, and contained by rifle butts and napalm...
>
> The colonized's sector, or at least the "native" quarters, the shanty town, the Medina, the reservation, is a disreputable place inhabited by disreputable people. You are born anywhere, anyhow. You die anywhere, from anything. It's a world with no space, people are piled one on top of the other, the shacks squeezed tightly together. The colonized's sector is a famished sector, hungry for bread, meat, shoes, coal, and light. The colonized's sector is a sector that crouches and cowers, a sector on its knees, a sector that is prostrate. It's a sector of niggers, a sector of towelheads. The gaze that the colonized subject casts at the colonist's sector is a look of lust, a look of envy.

The contrast between the colonized and the colonizer comes across in stark, black-and-white terms. His perspective is that the colonizer benefits from the unequal relationship with the colonized and that the colonized lose out in this deal. This seems self-evident and yet, according to some of the authors discussed in Chapter 11, colonial repression is not a relevant factor in explaining the divergence in wealth between the developed and the developing worlds. Some authors believe the West is culturally superior to the rest of the world and thus, the Africans, Asians, and Latin Americans were lucky to receive the benefits of Western civilization. Fanon and the other authors in this chapter, however, argue that modernization in the West occurred as a result of exploitation of the developing world, which suffered as a result.

Immanuel Wallerstein: World systems theory

The father of world systems theory, Immanuel Wallerstein is perhaps the gold standard among leftist academic theoreticians who study development theory. Wallerstein delineates his views in a multi-volume work (and many others) that represents his magnum opus, entitled, *The Modern World System* (1970). These four extensively detailed books analyze the development and results of the world system from the sixteenth to the twentieth centuries.

Wallerstein's world systems theory states that imperial European nations (the core) created a system of inequality between themselves and their colonies (the periphery) through the extraction of the resources of Africa, Asia, and Latin America. Thus, their wealth and the divergence between the West and the developing world occurred during the phase of European imperialism in the Americas, Africa, and Asia. During this phase, wage labor in agriculture and skilled labor developed in the "core" states (northern and western Europe specifically) whereas coerced unskilled labor developed in the periphery, (Latin America, Africa, Asia). At the same time, the semi-periphery (Spain and Portugal) channeled resources and bullion from their own periphery in the Americas to the core states. In other words, the Spanish and Portuguese extraction of wealth from the Americas went into the banks of northern and western European countries that were then able to finance their own economic advancement during the Industrial Revolution. The unit of analysis for Wallerstein is economic and comes in many forms and should not focus on the states themselves primarily. Markets for mining, sugar, weapons, cotton, coffee, and all other traded commodities are the units of analysis. He is perhaps the most articulate academic critic of the global capitalist system.

Taken from his 1972 article, "The Rise and Demise of the Capitalist System" (taken from *The Essential Wallerstein*, p. 86):

> The three structural positions in a world-economy—core, periphery, and semi-periphery—had become stabilized by about 1640. How certain areas became one and not the other is a long story. How certain areas became one and not the other is a long story. The key fact is that given slightly different starting-points, the interests of various local groups converged in northwest Europe, leading to the development of strong state mechanisms, and diverged sharply in the peripheral areas, leading to very weak ones. Once we get a difference in the strength of the state-machineries, we get the operation of "unequal exchange" which is enforced by strong states on weak ones, by core states on peripheral areas. Thus capitalism involves not only appropriation of surplus-value by an owner from a laborer, but an appropriation of surplus of the whole world-economy by core areas. And this was as true in the stage of agricultural capitalism as it is in the stage of industrial capitalism.

Wallerstein sees his world systems theory as less ideological than the extremism of the authors on the Left and the Right in general. What is important to him is that students of history realize that the way in which we understand history has been established by human beings narrating a mostly top-down story of cause and effect that does not necessarily draw upon logical scientific-based reasoning. His theory of examining history through the dominant economic and political systems that have driven action resides in his fundamental disagreement with traditional historical narration. As he states in his article, "World-Systems Analysis" (taken from *The Essential Wallerstein*, p. 148):

> History and social science took their current dominant forms at the moment of fullest unchallenged triumph of the logic of our present historical system. They are children of that logic. We are now however living in a moment of transition wherein the contradictions of that system have made it impossible to continue to adjust its machinery. We are living in a period of real historical choice. And this period is incomprehensible on the basis of assumptions of that system.
>
> World-systems analysis is a call for the construction of a historical social science that feels comfortable with the uncertainties of transition, that contributes to the transformation of the world by illuminating the choices without appealing to the crutch of a belief in the inevitable triumph of good. World-systems analysis is a call to open the shutters that prevent us from exploring many arenas of the real world. World-systems analysis is not a paradigm of historical social science. It is a call for a debate about the paradigm.

Wallerstein's often obscure, intellectualized language also keeps him firmly within the ranks of academia and firmly at arms distance from the mainstream reader. One author who has been able to communicate more effectively with the mainstream follows next.

Noam Chomsky: Anarchist theory

This MIT linguist became the most published critic of capitalism and U.S. interventionism in the world in the second half of the twentieth century. For that reason he is included here, but his critique is more activist than academic and is focused on a variety of areas that include and go beyond the causes and consequences of inequality. He is someone who largely agrees with the authors listed in this chapter (although he would not advocate for Marx's and Engel's vision for the future). Chomsky's books range across a wide spectrum of topics but always start from the premise that the citizens of the West should use the same standards for viewing themselves as they use to view non-Westerners. Perhaps more than any other author listed here, Chomsky concentrates on how nationalism allows people to live with illusions about the world, such as the causes of inequality, that then foment the citizenry to justify and support the use of force in other countries.

Though most of his books concentrate on both economic and political events, all of his books see "the system" as a problem on a global scale. *Manufacturing Consent* (co-authored with Edward Hermann, 1988) is his most famous book, and there are more than 100 other books and thousands of articles and speeches that can be accessed online. Some books that critique capitalism and globalization are *Profit over People: Neoliberalism and Global Order* (2011); *World Orders Old and New* (1996); and *Year 501: The Conquest Continues* (1999), and though popular among left-leaning professors and students, his ideas have not spread to mainstream politics.

An example of the type of language he uses, which elicits visceral responses from critics, follows here from page 138 of *World Orders Old and New*. Here he explains the role of Western loans to the developing world: "The crushing Third World debt results primarily from the collapse of commodity prices in the early 1980s combined with monetarist financial policies in the West." He then cites an economist's analysis of this to support his statement, and then follows with, "The loans, granted to our favorite dictators and oligarchs so that they could purchase luxury goods and export capital to the West, are now the burden of the poor, who had nothing to do with them, and the taxpayer at home." Chomsky is referring to a history unknown in most of the West, namely that the United States and Europe have supported countless authoritarian leaders in the past century, many of whom have wrecked their economies while taking out massive loans from the rich countries, leaving their countries' citizens to pay the debts after they leave office. Mobutu of Zaire, Pinochet of Chile, Suharto of Indonesia, and many others are examples of dictators supported by the West's dollars and governments. From reading Chomsky, however, one would not conclude that this history is complex. In fact, he portrays U.S. support for these dictators as negative across the board. However, there were both positive and negative economic consequences among these cases. Therefore, the sledgehammer language Chomsky uses does not necessarily apply all the time, and the reader is led to see the role of the West in blanket negative terms as a result.

That said, it would not necessarily be irresponsible of him to portray the system in such stark terms if indeed the consequences are bad enough to warrant change, and if qualified economists agree with his assessments. Chomsky cites Melvin Burke and Michael Meacher to support the preceding argument that the developing world's loss means the developed world's gain. For Chomsky, the "neo-liberal" path of development means that "…in sub-Saharan African, children are to die by the hundreds of thousands each year to ensure compliance with the noble principles of economic liberalism." On page 139, he sums up his beliefs:

> Only the willfully blind can fail to see the mechanisms at work. . .What is really happening is brought out by a closer analysis of the UNDP

figures on the rapidly growing gap between rich and poor. . .In 1960, the GNP ratio between the countries with the richest 20 percent of the world's population and those with the poorest 20 percent was 30:1; by 1989, it had reached 60:1.

Many intellectuals do not read Chomsky's critique of the global capitalist system or U.S. interventionism abroad because he is not a specialist in these areas. However, Chomsky is mentioned in this book because he is perhaps the most successful academic who has transcended his own discipline and reached out to readers of other disciplines. At the same time, though many of his books may sell only a few thousand copies, he has published so many books and articles, and given so many interviews and speeches that his message is constantly being renewed and added to the discussion in a manner that he is seen as the leading voice among those who dissent against the current capitalist mode of thinking.

David Korten: Anti-corporatism

David Korten does not have as much notoriety as Chomsky; however, his most well-known book, *When Corporations Rule the World* (1995), is a pillar of the modern anti-corporatism movement. This former Harvard Business School professor and long-time activist comes from an angle similar to Wallerstein's by advocating a "whole-systems" approach to the problems associated with global capitalism, as stated on page 21 of his book: "Whole-systems thinking calls for skepticism about simplistic solutions ..." Like all other authors from this chapter, it is his social conscience that drives his activism, as he points out with this statement from the same page: "The point of departure of *When Corporations Rule the World* is the evidence that we are experiencing accelerating social and environmental disintegration in nearly every country of the world ..." Thus, he starts from the premise that the situation is dire enough to warrant rethinking the way we view economic development.

By contrast, the authors discussed in Chapter 11 advocate for the perspective that capitalist development is the primary goal of all societies because it is inherently good. Korten derides the grotesque extravagances created by the capitalist system by pointing out how the rich live. From the subsection entitled, "A Different World" on pages 113 to 114:

> Forbes prefaced its 1993 listing of the 400 richest people in America with an article on the struggle of the very rich to make ends meet in today's economy. In one year's time, the price of a one-kilo tin of beluga malossol caviar had increased by 28 percent to $1,408. A Sikorsky S-780 helicopter with full executive options had increased 8 percent to $7 million. And a suitable night's hotel lodging in New York was up 15 percent to $750. Theirs is a different world.

On page 115, he then illustrates just how different the worlds are between the rich and the poor, a point made above by Wallerstein as well:

> Nike, a major footwear company, refers to itself as a "network firm." This means that it employs 8,000 people in management, design, sales, and promotion and leaves production in the hands of some 75,000 workers hired by independent contractors. Most of the outsourced production takes place in Indonesia, where a pair of Nikes that sells in the United States or Europe for $73 or $135 is produced for about $5.60 by girls and young women paid as little as fifteen cents an hour. The workers are housed in company barracks, there are no unions, overtime is often mandatory, and if there is a strike, the military may be called to break it up. The $20 million that basketball star Michael Jordan reportedly received in 1992 for promoting Nike Shoes exceeded the entire annual payroll of the Indonesian factories that made them.
>
> When asked about the conditions of the plants where Nikes are produced, John Woodman, Nike's general manager in Indonesia, gave a classic Stratusdweller response. Although he knew that there had been labor problems in the six Indonesian factories making Nike shoes, he had no idea what they had been about. Furthermore he said, "I don't know that I need to know. It's not within our scope to investigate."
>
> The Nike case is a striking example of the distortions of an economic system that shifts rewards away from those who produce real value to those whose primary function is to create marketing illusions to convince consumers to buy products they do not need at inflated prices. It is little wonder that many managers, like the Nike manager who avoided contact with Indonesian workers, prefer to avoid talking to too many people outside the elite circles.

This extended section of *When Corporations Rule the World* should provide the reader with a sense of the kinds of arguments used by those authors who are critical of the capitalist model as an exploitative and unjust system that perpetuates inequality. At the same time, it must be pointed out that the alternatives put forth by authors such as Chomsky, Korten, and Wallerstein seem beyond implementation and as a whole, academic in nature. The one theory, Marxism, which was attempted by many, proved destructive beyond comprehension in most cases, as was proven in the USSR, China, Cambodia, Vietnam, Laos, North Korea, and Ethiopia in particular. That is not to say that theories partly informed by Marxism, anti-imperialism, anti-colonialism, or anti-capitalism could not lead toward a form of more equitable and sustainable growth than the current global economic system, however. Chapter 12 introduces a few authors who have at least come up with some minor solutions to the problems inherent in this system.

Discussion questions

1 What do you think of the possibilities of Marxist doctrine for improving the lives of people in the developing world? Provide examples to support your answer.
2 Which of these authors do you believe to be the most effective at explaining the causes of underdevelopment? Please elaborate.
3 Do you see any of these authors providing a useful mindset for envisioning methods of creating economic progress and social justice simultaneously? Explain.

Further readings

Chomsky, Noam. *Understanding Power: The Indispensable Chomsky*. New York: The New Press, 2002.
Fanon, Frantz. *The Wretched of the Earth*. New York: Grove, 2005.
Gandhi, Mohandas K. *An Autobiography: My Experiments with Truth*. Boston: Beacon, 1993.
Korten, David. *When Corporations Rule the World*. San Francisco: Berret-Koehler, 2001.
Marx, Karl. *Das Capital*. 3 volumes. New York: Penguin, 1992.
Wallerstein, Immanuel. *The Modern World System*. 4 volumes. Berkeley, CA: University of CA, 2011.

Online content

Marxism content website: www.marxists.org
Gandhi speeches website: www.mkgandhi.org/speeches/speechMain.htm
Immanuel Wallerstein's website: www.iwallerstein.com
David Korten's website: www.davidkorten.org
Noam Chomsky's (unauthorized) website: www.chomsky.info

11 Views from above

Advocates of economic liberalism

- Before reading from the pro-capitalist perspective, please examine your own ideas about Western civilization's effects on the developing world.
- What were your thoughts on the effects of the West on the developing world prior to reading this book?
- Has this book changed your ideas about this? Explain.

The main belief that unites the authors in this chapter is that Western-style modernization is inherently better than all alternative methods of existence. Capitalism, in its purest theoretical form, as advocated by Adam Smith, Comte, and Max Weber, or in the form carried out by governments in practice, with all its flaws, is what is most needed to create a better world. The results for them are quite clear: Wherever societies and governments have used capitalist economic models, you find advanced economies and democratic freedoms to a much higher degree than those practicing either socialistic or dictatorial models (sometimes they are combined). The following three figures represent the scholarly founders of this school of thought.

The founders: Smith, Comte, and Weber

Adam Smith (1723–1790), Auguste Comte (1778–1857), and Max Weber (1864–1920), all men with classical European educational training and the founders of their own schools of thought (capitalism, positivism, and sociology), were the most important voices contributing to the understanding of development of their day. Adam Smith's theory was explained in his 1776 classic work, *The Wealth of Nations*. This book is considered as gospel to advocates of Western-style economic growth. From the first page, Smith speaks of the primacy of "the skill, dexterity, and judgment" of the nation's labor force and the employment rate in deciding economic growth:

> The abundance or scantiness of this supply, too, seems to depend more upon the former of those two circumstances than upon the latter. Among

the savage nations of hunters and fishers, every individual who is able to work is more or less employed in useful labour, and endeavours to provide, as well as he can, the necessaries and conveniences of life, for himself, and such of his family or tribe as are either too old, or too young, or too infirm, to go a-hunting and fishing. Such nations, however, are so miserably poor, that, from mere want, they are frequently reduced, or at least think themselves reduced, to the necessity sometimes of directly destroying and sometimes of abandoning their infants, their old people, and those afflicted with lingering diseases, to perish with hunger, or to be devoured by wild beasts.

Thus, Smith paints a portrait not unlike what many in the West view today of the developing world. However, unlike a common Western perspective of poverty being attributed to idleness today, Smith points out that those who stop working in poor countries will suffer from a lack of community support and die. However, in the more prosperous nations, as he continues on the same page, this is not the case, because the sum of what is produced overall is enough to support everyone well:

Among civilized and thriving nations, on the contrary, though a great number of people do not labour at all, many of whom consume the produce of ten times, frequently of a hundred times, more labour than the greater part of those who work; yet the produce of the whole labour of the society is so great, that all are often abundantly supplied; and a workman, even of the lowest and poorest order, if he is frugal and industrious, may enjoy a greater share of the necessaries and conveniences of life than it is possible for any savage to acquire.

Smith ascribes this divergence to Western-style capitalism, which was facilitated by geography. He points out how those nations near great navigable waterways such as the Mediterranean Sea and the Ganges, Nile, and Yellow rivers provided the foundations for commerce. However, it was the Mediterranean that had international commerce that thrived and spread across that region for future generations. It was in places without such waterways that he saw backwardness, as he explained on page 16:

All the inland parts of Africa, and all that part of Asia which lies any considerable way north of the Euxine and Caspian seas, the ancient Scythia, the modern Tartary and Siberia, seem, in all ages of the world, to have been in the same barbarous and uncivilized state in which we find them at present.

This has also become part of the analysis of contemporaries such as Thomas Sowell and economist/activists such as Jeffrey Sachs, whom we cover later.

Smith's ability to fuse grand theory with specifics makes his *Wealth of Nations* a guidebook for future generations to follow. On page 43, he explains how labor supply and demand shapes the behavior of owners and managers:

> When in any country the demand for those who live by wages, labourers, journeymen, servants of every kind, is continually increasing; when every year furnishes employment for a greater number than had been employed the year before, the workmen have no occasion to combine in order to raise their wages. The scarcity of hands occasions a competition among masters, who bid against one another in order to get workmen, and thus voluntarily break through the natural combination of masters not to raise wages.

Farther down the same page, he explains how incentive allows for people to climb the socioeconomic ladder, whether upper or lower class:

> When the landlord, annuitant, or monied man, has a greater revenue than what he judges sufficient to maintain his own family, he employs either the whole or a part of the surplus in maintaining one or more menial servants. Increase this surplus, and he will naturally increase the number of those servants.
>
> When an independent workman, such as a weaver or shoemaker, has got more stock than what is sufficient to purchase the materials of his own work, and to maintain himself till he can dispose of it, he naturally employs one or more journeymen with the surplus, in order to make a profit by their work. Increase this surplus, and he will naturally increase the number of his journeymen.

This also fit into Smith's broader philosophy of why western European nations such as England were situated to spread capitalism. And while he writes of the rest of the world by comparison to the West, his direct experience in Africa, Asia, and Latin America was absent. This was typical of academics prior to the twentieth century, when modes of transportation were limited.

A philosopher whose ideas especially caught on in the developing world, and specifically in Latin America, was Auguste Comte, the French philosopher of positivist theory. Comte advocated for viewing the world and organizing society along scientific lines. The observable must be chosen over the metaphysical, religious, fictitious, assumed world. The concept of "order and progress" was central to his ideas. Political and social order needed to be established to provide the means for economic progress. In fact, the Brazilian flag has the words "Ordem e Progresso" emblazoned across the front in honor of Comte's slogan, and Comte's gravestone in Paris is honored with a message of gratitude from the Brazilian people.

As indicated by this honor, positivism was often used in Latin America by dictators who enhanced their nations' material progress at the expense of social and political justice. A classic case was Mexican dictator Porfirio Diaz (1876–1911), who provided massive economic growth mostly to the upper classes while the majority poor remained destitute, lacking social services and suffering at the hands of his police and military forces. He had himself elected seven times before finally being overthrown in the biggest revolution to ever hit the Western Hemisphere. The Mexican Revolution from 1910 to 1920 took the lives of 1 million Mexicans, and the reforms instituted by the revolutionaries sought to reverse the inequality that resulted from Diaz's positivist policies.

Max Weber created an up-to-date theory of modernization in the twentieth century upon which rest the arguments of the cultural determinists in the following century. He coined the term *Protestant ethic* to illustrate the role of the Protestant sect of Christianity in fomenting capitalist growth. This philosophy compares the economic development of majority Protestant countries such as England, Germany, and the United States to majority Catholic countries such as Spain, Portugal, Italy, and France, not to mention those in the developing world. The results and reasons are obvious to cultural determinists from Weber to Sowell: The Protestant Ethic of hard work, thrift, delayed gratification, and trust in your fellow Protestant community members to do the same has created systems conducive to prosperity. To illustrate the powerful influence of cultural determinism on scholars as it flows from Weber, one need only read the anthology edited by Lawrence Harrison (author of *Underdevelopment is a State of Mind*, 1985) and Samuel Huntington (author of *The Clash of Civilizations*, 1996), entitled, *Culture Matters: How Values Shape Human Progress*, 2000. This book includes chapters by twenty different authors examining how this plays out across the globe.

Milton Friedman and the Chicago School of Economics

Friedman won the Nobel Prize in Economics in 1984. He is the founder of the Chicago School of Economics, which is a school of thought advocating for nearly unfettered capitalist economic growth. He is also a controversial figure: Not only is he revered by capitalists around the world for the economic growth generated by governments that have followed his model, but he is demonized by many for the social consequences of that same model. He became most infamous for advising the dictatorial regime of Augusto Pinochet of Chile (1973–1990), which came to power through a bloody military coup that overthrew the democratically elected Marxist president Salvador Allende (1970–1973), murdered 3,000 people, and tortured tens of thousands more. The Chicago School philosophy rests on a lowering of taxes, government deregulation, privatization of state industries, and massive cuts in social spending to unleash market forces.

The controversy lies in whether Friedman's advice caused both greater economic growth overall while also causing greater inequality and human rights abuses. The overall gross domestic product (GDP) of the countries he advised certainly did increase, but so did national debts and military spending, while social spending was cut. This occurred often as the result of International Monetary Fund and World Bank loans that were issued on condition of massive social spending cuts and privatization of state businesses, which led to losses in government revenues that had paid for social programs. South Africa, Russia, and Chile are often used as test-cases for the Chicago school, for in each case, wealth has grown along with military spending as social spending has decreased.

Friedman (1912–2006) is often contrasted with the world-renowned economist John Maynard Keynes (1883–1946). Keynes got his start working as an administrator in India under the British Raj as a young man. There he formulated his ideas that would later become famous round the world. He became the main advocate of the government-regulated economy, especially in times of crisis, and is therefore considered the antithesis of Milton Friedman, who has become the main advocate for laissez-faire economics. Keynes was the person most responsible for the creation of the World Bank, and his ideas were largely adhered to in the West and the developing world to a degree throughout the first three decades of the post–WWII era. However, with the economic problems of the 1970s (associated with wars and the oil crises, especially) and the rise of two Friedman-inspired chief executives, in Washington, DC (Ronald Reagan) and London (Margaret Thatcher) in the 1980s, Keynesian economics was largely abandoned. Friedman's deregulation model that urged governments to shift away from social spending and economic nationalism to unleash market forces created the era of globalization that has led us to this point in time. However, in 2008, Keynesianism made a return as governments worked to rejuvenate private industry in the wake of the global financial crisis. The Friedman-Keynes divide is a perfect example of how it is folly to assume a one-size-fits-all theory of development.

Jared Diamond: Geographical or cultural determinism?

Now the most read advocate of "geographical determinism" for his Pulitzer Prize–winning book, *Guns, Germs, and Steel* (1997), Diamond's theory rests on the idea that individual nations, peoples, cultures, and the like are not as responsible for their development as the geographical hand that was dealt them. However, he could be considered a cultural determinist as well because he believes that a society's behavior is shaped by their geography, and although *Guns, Germs, and Steel* specifically aims to destroy racial arguments of causation when determining why majority white societies have more prosperity than majority non-white societies, Diamond does see the geographically given tools possessed by Westerners as being more sophisticated, civilized, or advanced, and the main cause of their progress in relation to the rest of the world. His theory rests on several undisputable facts:

1   The first domestication of crops and animals took place in the Fertile Crescent in the Middle East 11,000 years ago;
2   This led to the growth of civilization in that region first, which included food production, writing, government, leisure time, the arts, technology (weaponry included), and the acceleration of disease cycles due to living close to livestock;
3   The spread of civilization's elements were facilitated in Eurasia by the East-West axis of that continent, which provided for an ease of movement across large spans of space, especially when compared to both Africa and the Western Hemisphere, each of which have a North-South axis.
4   In 1492, the Spanish were able to utilize the tools at their disposal (guns, germs, and steel) that resulted from geographical luck to conquer the Native Americans of the Western Hemisphere. Though European germs did not assist in the conquest of Africa and much of Asia in the nineteenth century, European wealth, guns, ships, and other technology did.

What is disputable is his central assumption that conquest pushed down the non-Western regions while uplifting the West, leading to the great divergence that Diamond refers to in the form of "Yali's Question." Yali, a native New Guinean friend, asks Diamond why whites have more "cargo" than New Guineans. The fact that Diamond assumes Western conquest and colonization of non-Westerners such as New Guineans to be a cause of inequality and wealth for different groups runs up against many cultural determinists, such as Lawrence Harrison et al. in *Culture Matters*. The authors therein argue that it was the ingenuity of Westerners, not the use of force against non-Westerners, that led to the rise of the West. Thomas Sowell, introduced below, asserts that imperialism added very little to the overall economic progress of Europeans. Diamond would agree that Western civilization was superior, but he would include that it was the result of geographical luck and that this luck also pushed down others in the process.

He also professes the need for advanced societies to learn from the devastation wrought by man-made environmental disasters of past societies in his monumental study, *Collapse* (2005). Diamond uses stark examples of cases where humans ignored environmental realities and depleted their own resources on such a large scale as to elicit either complete downfalls or massive conflicts. Easter Island, the Ancient Maya, Greenland, Haiti, and Rwanda take center stage in this book as illustrations of what can happen when populations do not exist in tune with their environmental resources. Easter Island is located 4,000 miles off the coast of Chile and is best known for its giant elongated stone heads that captivate tourists every day. However, what many also notice is the absence of trees. Research has yielded various theories about the disappearance of the Easter Island civilization that built these heads, but it is commonly accepted that its inhabitants depleted the island of its resources somehow. Similarly, the Maya of southern Mexico and northern Central America flourished for 1,000 years until abandoning their great pyramidal cities in the ninth and tenth centuries AD. Hieroglyphs show that many battles between the city-states took place during this period, which Maya experts believe was brought on by environmental degradation exacerbated by the increase in population over the centuries. The traditional Maya of today try to rotate their land usage by leaving large portions of land fallow for years at a time to allow for soil rejuvenation to occur. If this process is sped along, soil depletion rates increase at a rate higher than is sustainable for continuing yields into the future.

The Nile River Valley is a perfect example of historically rooted successful traditions that we do not see in the Ancient Maya world. For 4,000 years, the Nile River has naturally flooded farm lands for a short period, providing nutrients and water to the soil, after which the water has receded, allowing for the growth of crops. With population growth rates in this area, however, the prospect of man-made alterations is not far off. And population growth around the Nile's source in Rwanda has proven to be a factor in exacerbating conflict in that country in the second half of the twentieth century especially. The genocide of 1994 took place in an environment where the population density is among the highest on the planet, and despite one-eighth of Rwanda's population being killed in 1994 and perhaps another one-eighth dying in the two years afterward in both Zairian refugee camps and further battles between the Hutus and Tutsis, the population of that tiny country has increased 20 percent from its pre-genocide levels due to high birth rates and an accelerating economy. Though another genocide seems unlikely, there is no escaping that environmental stress due to a high population density cannot help reduce conflict in Rwanda. The general trend around the planet is an increasing birth rate in the developing world and a reduction in the developed world. Countries such as Italy have even begun to reduce its overall population, as young people decide against both marriage and procreation.

Diamond's latest book, *The World until Yesterday: What Can we Learn from Traditional Societies?* (2012) delves further into this topic by explaining how modern societies can both learn from and teach developing nations. Although Diamond reveals his affinity with the traditional society of Papua New Guinea, his overall message is that the West points the way forward. Diamond is an advocate of Western-based capitalist development, yet his intimate field work over four decades with traditional societies in Papua New Guinea in particular gives him a perspective unlike the majority of the cultural determinist authors contributing toward this discussion. Diamond is more firmly rooted in the geographical determinist position than perhaps any other author, which detracts from his legitimacy in the eyes of many social scientists who see modern historical trends as more important in shaping development.

Michael Schuman: The Asian work ethic

Schuman's perspective on the role of culture in creating Asia's economic boom fits him in with the rest of the authors covered in this chapter; however, in one respect, he differs considerably. While recognizing Western Civilization's contribution to Asian economic philosophy, he has a tremendous admiration for Asian culture as a thing unto itself. Unlike Niall Ferguson discussed below, Schuman downplays Western influence by focusing on how individuals and cultures have worked to make Asian progress stand out in the world. It is not Weber's Protestant ethic but an "Asian work ethic" that has created an economic boom there. However, unlike the rest, Schuman focuses specifically on Asia and does not contrast the continent much to Latin America or Africa, although he does ask the reader to consider that the Asian work ethic and stability within Asian countries helped it advance when Africa, specifically, did to a much lesser degree. His book, *The Miracle: Asia's Quest for Wealth* (2010) walks the reader through the recent economic histories of Japan, the four Tigers (Singapore, South Korea, Hong Kong, Taiwan), the four Cubs (China, Malaysia, Indonesia, Thailand), and India by focusing on the biographies of the leaders who created the economic reforms that led to the astronomical growth we have seen in Asia since WWII.

Singapore's Lee Kuan Yew (1923–) and China's Deng Xiaoping (1904–1997) stand out as particularly effective and visionary leaders who catapulted their nations into the stratosphere of economic growth. The biographical approach differs from the rest of the authors in this chapter and is likely the result of the author's journalism background. The others considered here are PhDs in the social sciences mostly and, therefore utilize the tools of academia. Schuman's stories are effective in conveying the importance of culture as a main factor driving development. How else do we explain the widespread Asian model of development utilized by the leaders in all ten nations? This Asian model is based on strong government oversight and assistance in guiding private industry. This differs tremendously from both the traditional capitalist West and the Communist East. The personal approach is often not respected within academia because it is seen as biased, subjective, or un-intellectual. However, no authors lack considerable bias in approaching such a "big history" issue as the causes of development and underdevelopment. This is a deeply personal topic because it goes to the heart of human desires and survival.

Niall Ferguson: Mainstream pro-West intellectual

Considered more of a popular historian now that several of his books have become bestsellers, Niall Ferguson has become perhaps one of the most influential voices within this growing movement of cultural determinism. His most-well-known book illustrated this perspective clearly and contributed greatly to the overall debate over this topic. In *The Ascent of Money* (2009),

Ferguson demonstrates how financial institutions, from the Medici family in early Renaissance Florence to the current banking houses around the world, have provided the essential foundation for economic growth in the modern age. The first two pages of his Introduction present a question and a series of answers to the reader:

> Angry that the world is so unfair? Infuriated by fat-cat capitalists and billionaire bonus bankers? Baffled by the yawning chasm between the Haves and the Have-nots-- and the Have-yachts? You are not alone. Throughout the history of Western Civilization, there has been a recurrent hostility to finance and financiers, rooted in the idea that those who make their living from lending money are somehow parasitical on the 'real' economic activities of agriculture and manufacturing. This hostility has three causes. It is partly because debtors have tended to outnumber creditors and the former have seldom felt very well disposed towards the latter. It is partly because financial crises and scandals have occurred frequently enough to make finance to be a cause of poverty rather than prosperity, volatility rather than stability... Despite our deeply-rooted prejudices against 'filthy lucre', however, money is the root of most progress... Far from being the work of mere leeches intent on sucking the life's blood out of indebted families or gambling with the savings of widows and orphans, financial innovation has been an indispensable factor in man's advance from wretched subsistence to the giddy heights of material prosperity that so many people know today.

Thus, he asserts that prosperity as we know it today is the height of human achievement. And his perspective is widely heard. He is not only a Harvard historian with several important bestselling books in his repertoire, but he is also more in tune with the so-called twitter generation. This translates into a more effective style of communication with what should be the main target audience of all college professors: our students. For example, he is fond of using the term *the six killer apps of prosperity* as a catch phrase for illustrating the difference between Western Civilization and "the Rest." The West is Europe, the United States, Canada, Australia, and New Zealand and those influenced by the West, while "the Rest" is the developing world. His six killer apps are central to his latest book, *Civilization: The West and the Rest* (2012), in which he presents a detailed argument that explains how western Europe was able to leap past the rest of the world in a short period of time.

These six apps are competition, science, property rights, medicine, the consumer society, and the work ethic. He proceeds to explain in chapters aligned with these apps just how all six combined within Western civilization to develop the modern world. Competition emerged among the small states of Western Europe, as various kingdoms sought an edge over their rivals and, therefore, developed more sophisticated weapons, merchandise, and methods of governance. This was not the case with any other region on the planet: The Russians, Ottomans, Chinese, Aztecs, and Incas, to name the notable large states between the fifteenth and sixteenth centuries, all dominated their spheres of influence and, therefore, less competition was fomented there.

This reached into the realm of science as well. All the larger states had scientific discoveries, but scientists within imperial states served the sovereign, not humanity as a whole and, therefore, any scientific research that threatened the power structure would be limited or even eliminated. In Western Europe of the sixteenth and seventeenth centuries, a wide variety of scientists from different backgrounds were able to explore the heavens and the Earth, albeit sometimes with negative backlash from the Catholic Church, and were eventually able to challenge conventional wisdom successfully and lead to the anti-deferential attitude of the Enlightenment.

The Enlightenment led to advances in medicine as well and, as Ferguson points out, much of the breakthroughs came at the hands of Westerners operating in the developing world. Many anthropologists and historians point out how traditional societies had no need of Western medicine prior to their arrival in the modern age by asserting that Africans, Latin Americans, and Asians had long life expectancies and even their own effective medicinal practices. This Ferguson denies by generally asserting that life spans were low and that traditional societies relied on witchcraft and herbal remedies alone, which were ineffective. The problem with this discussion is that the amount of data that needs to enter into any assessment of the merits of either his or the opposite side's arguments is too complex to be generalized in his book. He uses only a handful of examples to support his contention that life in Africa was less healthy than that of the West around the time of colonization in the late nineteenth and early twentieth centuries, and though this may be true, the reader is expected to take his word for it without much explanation. Still, his delineation of the rise of disease prevention and eradication efforts carried out by scientists and governments demonstrates without question that Western Civilization has given a tremendous gift to the world. Perhaps of all his killer apps, medicine is the least controversial.

He also points to the very blatant example of Japan as a concrete example of the first non-Western country to modernize. All six of the killer apps emerged in Japan among nationalists, and the adoption of European mode of dress among Japan's elite symbolized how superior they believed the European way of life to be. From this view, Ferguson invites us to see how clear cut the issue is: There is no debate about whether the Western method of development is superior, because the most non-Western of societies adopted Westernization when confronted with its offerings. This is indeed difficult to argue with, considering how quickly Japan was able to rise economically and then militarily to the point of near dominance over East Asia during the first half of the twentieth century. The fact that so many other Asian countries then followed in Japan's footsteps after WWII to reach high economic growth rates of their own supports Ferguson's point further.

The non-mainstream neoconservative academics: Harrison, Landes, and Sowell

Ferguson appears to be mostly reiterating in more popularized fashion what David Landes, Lawrence Harrison, and Thomas Sowell have been explaining for decades. All three authors in this section write for a less mainstream, more academic audience than Ferguson and, as such, provide more detail and receive less attention. They are no less ideological or controversial. David Landes's monumental and detailed study, *The Wealth and Poverty of Nations* (1998), is a much more dense read and is written in classical historical fashion, rather than for a popular audience, unlike Ferguson, and Harrison was the most blatant with his title, *Underdevelopment Is a State of Mind*. Harrison's beliefs of cultural determinism were formed after his stint with the United States Agency for International Development in Haiti, the poorest country in the hemisphere and one of the poorest in the world. His perspective was black and white in terms of where he believed the problem lay: It was the cultural backwardness of the Haitians, not French imperialism or U.S. interventionism, that caused Haiti's economic doldrums.

Harrison is adept at presenting clear-cut differences between countries with his paired examples of similar nations that diverged due to cultural differences. He compares Haiti to the Dominican Republic, Argentina to Australia, Barbados to Haiti, and Spanish culture to British culture, for example. He elaborates on the last example clearly on page 143 of his book:

> One particularly important consequence, in my view, of the set of values and attitudes flowing from Spanish individualism is the failure of the Spanish-and Latin America—elite to develop a sense of noblesse oblige. The histories of Barbados and Australia make clear, I think, that the noblesse oblige of the British aristocracy, doubtlessly related to the concept of fair play, had much to do with the progressive evolution of those two societies.

His critique of Spanish culture comes from other authors, presumably so he does not appear alone in what could come across as political incorrectness. On page 142, he cites Henry Wells, author of *The Modernization of Puerto Rico—A Political Study of Changing Values and Institutions* (1969), who uses a list of "four fundamental value premises" of Spanish culture:

1   *fatalism* ("life is shaped by forces beyond human control");
2   *hierarchy* (society is naturally hierarchical; one's position depends on one's birth);
3   *dignity* ("the person has the intrinsic worth or integrity," but this has nothing to do with the rights, initiative, enterprise, or equality of opportunity); and
4   *male superiority* (from which flow authoritarianism, paternalism, and machismo).

There are two aspects of his critique we need to consider here. First, if the reader is presumably familiar with Spanish culture as it occurs in Spain or in Latin America, that reader can interpret the validity of Harrison's and, by extension, Wells's words. Second, if the reader is not familiar with said culture, he or she is supposed to receive a negative message. This is where we must raise several questions:

- What are the possible cultural attributes possessed and spread by the Spanish?
- Is Spanish culture monolithic? Are there not also Catalans and Basques in Spain who also spread their cultural values in the Americas? Do they not have cultural attributes worthy of recognition?
- Are there also non-economic values that the Spanish spread in the Americas that might be of value to Latin Americans and visitors alike?
- Last, what is the purpose of claiming cultural superiority of some and cultural inferiority of others?

Of course, Ferguson, Landes, and Harrison, among many others, are part of a broader group of authors who laud primarily the accomplishments of the British people. The person who has probably written the most about this is Thomas Sowell, the world-renowned economist and preeminent scholar on the connection of race and culture to economic development. Sowell is informed by Smith and Weber and his own analysis of the effects of human migrations throughout history. In this manner, it becomes apparent how different peoples' cultural attributes and drawbacks have spread through their interactions, whether they be through force or persuasion. In his trilogy of books covering this topic (*Race and Culture* [1995]*; Migrations and Cultures* [1997]; and *Conquests and Cultures* [1999]), Sowell focuses on the ways in which some cultures, such as the British, Japanese, Germans, and Jews, thrived, while others, such as the Africans, Slavs, and Indigenous peoples of the Americas, primarily did not.

One aspect beyond a fondness of British cultural power that unites all of these culture-based theorists is that their perspectives seem to be informed by an assumption that capitalistic development is inherently sustainable and beneficial. That is, none of these authors entertains the possibility that capitalism will eventually drain the planet of its resources, exacerbate climate change, artificially increase the planet's population through genetically modified foods, pesticides, fertilizers, and other chemically-altered methods, not to mention the fact that money itself is not a "real" thing in the sense that wheat and meat are real. In addition, the current economic growth is entirely supported by financing and, as of this writing, the global debt was approximately $32 trillion and counting. The idea that this endless trend toward financing development based on loans that may or may not be paid off is sustainable should be questioned by these authors. The global economic crisis that has devastated millions of people since 2008 has done nothing to change the attitude of these authors, much as the downfall of Communism did nothing to change the minds of die-hard Communists about what they considered to be the superior system put forth by Marx and Engels.

In addition, it is apparent that these authors' interactions are with upwardly mobile people from the developing world, rather than those who still struggle at the bottom. These authors come from the perspective opposite that of scholars who spend considerable time learning the traditions and languages of the people of poor countries. Anthropologists, political scientists, sociologists, economists, historians, journalists, and medical professionals who have lived among the average Africans, Latin Americans, and Asians tend not to express as much admiration for the European powers' actions in the developing world nor to express such disdain for the cultures of the developing world as do most cultural determinists, who seem to view little if any value in them. The exceptions in this chapter are Schumann and Diamond, perhaps because they have spent considerable time learning the cultures and languages of the people they study.

It is obvious from all of the authors' use of language and attitude in their pages that the true nature of underdevelopment as it is lived on a daily basis, with all of the struggles and texture that entails, is merely proof that capitalism must accelerate to include them. They largely assume that to be poor is bad and is the fault of the poor or the governments in charge of the poor, rather than colonialism, imperialism, or capitalism. They do not entertain the possibility that many poor people would consider themselves much happier than people living these upwardly mobile lifestyles, whether in the West or not. Many traditional societies have resisted modernization for centuries and many Westerners who venture to traditional areas never want to return to their modern societies. It is because these traditional societies have more to offer than mere "advancements" in technology, medicine, weaponry, or pastimes. There is a texture to the way of life of every group of people and place on the planet, and it cannot always be measured in terms set by the World Bank or the World Health Organization.

Discussion questions

1   Which author do you find the most compelling? Explain.
2   Compare and contrast one author from Chapter 10 and one from this chapter and provide examples to support each side. Try to come to a conclusion about which author you agree with most.
3   Is there something missing from the perspectives of the foregoing authors? What is it? How would you address this issue differently?

Further readings

Ferguson, Niall. *The Ascent of Money: A Financial History of the World.* New York: Penguin, 2009.

Ferguson, Niall. *Civilization: The West and the Rest*. New York: Penguin 2012.

Harrison, Lawrence E., and Samuel P. Huntington, ed. *Culture Matters: How Values Shape Human Progress*. New York: Basic, 2000.

Landes, David. *The Wealth and Poverty of Nations: Why Some are so Rich and Some are so Poor*. New York: Norton, 1999.

Schuman, Michael. *The Miracle: The Epic Story of Asia's Quest of Wealth*. New York: Harper Business, 2010.

Smith, Adam. *The Wealth of Nations*. New York: Simon and Brown, 2009.

Sowell, Thomas. *Conquests and Cultures: an International History*. New York: Basic, 1999.

Weber, Max. *The Protestant Ethic and the Spirit of Capitalism*. New York: Renaissance Classics, 2012.

Online content

Adam Smith website: www.adamsmith.org

Max Weber journal: www.maxweberstudies.org/

Ayn Rand website: www.aynrand.org

Milton Friedman's 1970 *NYT Magazine* article: www.colorado.edu/studentgroups/libertarians/issues/friedman-soc-resp-business.html

Lawrence Harrison articles: http://spectator.org/people/lawrence-e-harrison/article.xml

Niall Ferguson on TED Talk: www.ted.com/talks/niall_ferguson_the_6_killer_apps_of_prosperity.html

Jared Diamond on TED Talks: www.ted.com/talks/jared_diamond_on_why_societies_collapse.html

Samuel Huntington webpage, Foreign Affairs Journal: www.foreignaffairs.com/author/samuel-p-huntington

Lawrence Harrison webpage, The American Spectator: http://spectator.org/people/lawrence-e-harrison/all

Thomas Sowell webpage: www.tsowell.com/

12 Idealism

Views of progress for the future

As we embark on the last part of this book, please reflect upon your own ideas about how to address the problems of poverty in the developing world.

* What ideas do you have about how to alleviate extreme poverty?
* Are these ideas informed through your readings of history or from other disciplines?
* Does this book help you see the problem of underdevelopment in a different light? Explain.

This last chapter will not attempt to summarize the book to this point but instead will provide students with alternative views to the more ideological ones discussed in the previous two chapters. As with Chapters Ten and Eleven, I have provided a list of links at the end of the chapter for students to follow so as to learn more about the authors discussed here. Authors such as Jeffrey Sachs, economist and author of *The End of Poverty*, will be discussed along with doctor and anthropologist Paul Farmer, author of many books and subject of Tracy Kidder's best-selling *Mountains Beyond Mountains*. Muhammad Yunus's Nobel Peace Prize–winning achievements with the micro-loan movement that has swept across the developing world over the past four decades will also be covered, along with several other important authors. What I hope for this chapter is that students will walk away from the end of the book with a strong sense of the complexity of the major issues people of the developing world have faced throughout history and a sense of hope for the future. The aforementioned authors are all academics who recognize the problems of underdevelopment, but they also provide their own prescriptions for solutions, with an eye on the concerns of the impoverished people living in Asia, Latin America, and Africa.

As the reader will notice, I give no space to unqualified political or media pundits in this book. There is a reason for that: Unfortunately, most of the discussion about policy that the general public is exposed to occurs on the airwaves already by people with a political axe to grind. In the United States, people from Bill O'Reilly to Keith Olberman and many others are paid millions of dollars to increase their television station's ratings and in turn to rile up the Republican and Democratic parties in favor of a narrative about a plethora of policies, including that of development. This occurs even though serious analysis of development receives zero attention in the mainstream TV stations. Instead, the public hears people arguing about either increasing or decreasing foreign aid or whether to support or not support an invasion of the next enemy of the United States depending on the party's line at a given time. This leaves the uninformed yet voting public believing they actually know something about development, when in fact it takes tremendous in-depth research to make an informed decision. This takes concrete examples, direct observation, discussion with those being affected, the coordinators of policy implementation, and a strong background in the academic theoretical perspectives gained from decades of historical observation, which includes as many other comparative examples as possible. This is such a monumental task as to be impossible for one person to explain, let alone the largely ignorant media and political talking heads, most of whom possess not the slightest of qualifications to address the matter seriously. Human lives are at stake, which is why we are reading this book in the first place. Who can say whether the following academic/activists can help, but at least they are out there trying.

Daren Acemoglu and James Robinson: The inclusive institution

Although their book title sounds negative in tone, *Why Nations Fail* (2012) is both a history of what has and has not worked and a positively inclined guidebook for potential success. Acemoglu and Robinson focus on the importance of "critical junctures," historical events where populations are forced into making decisions at times of great change. These include disease outbreaks, wars, innovations in science and technology, and political/social/economic revolutions. The aftermath of these events helps shape the likelihood of either a positive or a negative direction for political and economic institutions. The authors argue both that these institutions must be inclusive and that the political authority be centralized and respected as legitimate by the populace. In other words, a corrupt central authority will not do, nor will political and economic institutions that seek to extract wealth unfairly from the population.

The authors astutely use comparative examples to illustrate their point. They use Nogales, Arizona (USA) and Nogales, Sonora (Mexico), twin cities that reside on either side of the U.S.–Mexico border as a microcosm that proves their point. They have similar demographics and similar cultures but are starkly different in their economic development. The Mexican Nogales population suffers from malnutrition, a lack of education, and a high crime rate, while the U.S. Nogales has high standards of public health and education and a low crime rate. The difference for the authors is in the governments of each nation. The Mexican government has not created the institutions necessary for positive growth, while the U.S. government has provided for better conditions. The same can be said for the difference between Botswana and Sierra Leone, for example. In both countries, mineral resources in the form of diamonds make up the foundation of the economies. In Sierra Leone, diamonds have been its main source of turmoil, while in Botswana the government has created institutions that allow the diamond industry to provide its citizens with a relatively high degree of economic growth, and the country is known for being among the most stable politically, economically, and socially in Africa.

Acemoglu and Robinson's focus on the power of individual actors in shaping the political and economic futures of nations is essential here because they provide explicit examples of the ways in which these leaders set up institutions that were either extractive or inclusive. The contrast between Botswana's leaders and those of most of Africa is instructive. We can see this within the same country as well, as is the case between the leadership styles of Mao Zedong and Deng Xiaoping. Both governments were Communist, and yet, under Mao, China suffered totalitarianism that extracted (even as it claimed to provide for all) and, under Deng, China underwent a process that created the fastest-paced sustained growth rate ever witnessed in the developing world. In addition, totalitarianism would be an inaccurate word to describe the post-Mao Chinese government, for Deng decentralized the power of the government away from the Maoist model in which all important decisions emanated from one person.

Why Nations Fail claims to demolish the previous explanations of the divisions between the haves and the have-nots that are based on Marxism (and other anti-capitalist explanations), geographical determinism, and culture. Acemoglu and Robinson see individuals and organizations as fundamental actors that respond to major events (the critical junctures) in either constructive or destructive ways as essential for understanding both the past and the present of humanity's economic development. As opposed to Diamond's bleak prognosis that geography has dealt a bad hand to the majority of the planet or Ferguson's belief that Western civilization points the only way forward, Acemoglu and Robinson show that individual leaders can affect drastic change no matter what their geographical assets or their cultural background.

Jeffrey Sachs and Paul Collier: Elite advocates for the poor

Jeff Sachs is perhaps the most recognized name of this chapter. He is considered a top international economist with numerous claims to fame, including his work extricating Bolivia from hyperinflation and what seemed like a permanent debt crisis there in the 1980s; his numerous books; and his leadership of the UN Millennium Project. His book, *The End of Poverty* (2005), is highly acclaimed around the world. Its basic premise is that fixing poverty's structural problems would be relatively simple with the assistance of the developed world. These problems include prevention and treatment for the most deadly diseases (malaria, AIDS, and tuberculosis), providing start-up funds at the grass-roots level to provide for a foundation of economic growth, the construction of roads, the improvement of technology, investment in sound government, and other elements.

Though many see this as no different from what has been done in the past with little impact, in reality this is a major change. As of now, governments have provided a large portion of their aid in the developing world to largely corrupt governments that have not used the funds for effective implementation of projects. Once they leave office, the public is saddled with the debt, much of which was stolen by dictatorships such as Mobutu in Zaire, Mubarak in Egypt, and many others. Mubarak's wealth is estimated at $70 billion. His government was receiving $2 billion per year in U.S. military aid in the last years of his thirty-year reign (1981–2011). This is not to imply that he took U.S. military funding for himself: It is to illustrate the level of wasted money flowing to dictatorships that could otherwise be using this funding for the improvement of their countries' economies. As Mubarak received military funding from the United States, he apparently made considerable amounts of money for himself through massive corruption. Therefore, we are led to question whether the money he received from the United States facilitated his corruption to make him one of the world's wealthiest people in a relatively poor country.

Sachs also points out that aid has been a fraction of what it should be. To end poverty, the developed world, which represents 20 percent of the planet, should supply approximately one-half of 1 percent of its income to the poorest in the developing world, which represent 20 percent of the planet. Put in other terms, about 1 billion people live in relative wealth, while 1 billion people live on the brink of outright destitution. The "bottom billion" to borrow a term from another development theorist, Paul Collier, would need only one two-hundredth of the top billion's income to create sustainable growth. Again, this is a theoretical perspective based on economic models that take into account many factors, but what could not be predicted for its full effect was the global recession that began in 2008, three years after Sachs's book came out.

However, the details he presents are enticing. If we want to prevent malaria to acceptable levels (as low as possible), it would cost the developed world only $3 per person per year, which is fifteen times what was spent in 2005. The volume of lives saved could reach into the millions every year. The costs for preventing and treating malaria rely on both mosquito nets and medicinal treatments. These two seemingly easy remedies would cost too much for the average destitute person to afford, especially if they must provide these for their families. This is where the wealthy countries could lend a hand even more so than now. As of now, mosquito nets are provided to millions of families by generous governmental and non-governmental donations. However, they have to be replaced when ripped, and people must be taught how to use them. Sending truckloads to villages across Africa is not enough. Sachs's plan is oriented toward the foundations of development: As opposed to treating the symptoms of poverty, the world must treat the causes.

Dr. Paul Collier, the Oxford economics professor, is another academic of elite background working on this problem. His best-seller, *The Bottom Billion: Why the Poorest Countries are Failing and What Can be Done about It,* has won him great acclaim for his straightforward approach that denies both leftist and rightist absolutist approaches. Though most of the developing world has indeed pulled itself out of "absolute poverty," a term referring to those living on $1 or less per day, Dr. Collier points to four "development traps" that have kept one-seventh of the population there. The first trap is conflict, which on average costs $64 billion per year per conflict. Specifically, civil wars are the most typical conflicts around the world today, and the vast majority take place among the bottom billion. Collier also looks to dependence on natural resources, being a landlocked country with bad neighbors, and poor governance in a small country all as development traps from which the world community must work to extract these bottom billion.

The bottom billion should be contrasted with middle-income countries in the developing world. Middle-income countries made crucial economic reforms over the past half century and are climbing quickly out of poverty. These include, but are not limited to, China, India, Botswana, Egypt, Vietnam, Indonesia, Malaysia, Bangladesh, Mexico, Argentina, Brazil, Chile, and many more. Middle-income countries had wars and economic doldrums in the past but have largely left these behind. The bottom billion, conversely, are either just recently getting started after years of conflict and/ or corrupt governments or are still mired in conflict. These include Bolivia, Haiti, Zimbabwe, Angola, Sierra Leone, the DRC, Central African Republic, Burundi, Rwanda, Malawi, Zambia, Afghanistan, Turkmenistan, Niger, Sudan, Somalia, Liberia, North Korea, and many more. Of course, within all of these same countries there are a minority that possess a high degree of wealth and, in some cases, such as Rwanda, Liberia, and Sierra Leone, concrete steps have been made to improve the governments and economies in the very recent past.

Collier's title may seem negative in tone, but his perspective is decisively forward-thinking and practical in nature. He sees very little use for violent revolutions, which statistically do not improve the lot of the countries in the bottom billion. Nor does he believe in outright capitalist orientation, which opens the possibility of exploitation of fragile societies with large supplies of highly prized resources and commodities. Collier is motivated by his personal concern for those living in both the poorest countries and the rest of the world. He has spent considerable time researching in Africa in particular, and his work there shines through in his tone.

Collier's platform for development follows that aid should be given to bring the greatest numbers of people out of poverty. He points out how too much of the aid goes to the middle-income countries because they are considered more likely to advance; however, they are not the countries with the most need. The European Commission, for example, has been giving money in the form of grants to middle-income countries because they can be counted on to use the money well, but they do not provide much to those of the bottom billion, who are seen as a wild card. The World Bank, where Collier used to work, has been giving loans mostly to the bottom billion, which means they must pay the money back with interest, and much of this money goes to governments that then use the money to entrench themselves through military spending.

Collier is not a fan of "aid" on a continual basis but instead calls for the developed world to centralize efforts to improve the lot of the bottom billion by getting all organizations on the same page to coordinate assistance. This means an international charter governing how funds are used. If the funds are used improperly, such as to support corrupt governments, the international community will enforce the charter. Preferential treatment must also be given to exports from countries of the bottom billion who currently compete with countries of middle-income countries for the same markets. The latter group has a several-decade head start over the former, thus giving them a perpetual competitive advantage. This also involves providing technical assistance from abroad, not a popular notion among many aid organizations that see this as an imposition from the developed world. However, Collier points out that many technically trained personnel from the bottom billion countries have immigrated to the developed world, leaving a dearth of qualified people in these countries.

In addition, the products being sold must be reconsidered. As the bottom billion sell mainly primary materials such as coffee, bananas, rice, and other agricultural products, there is little chance for advancement above their current economic state, even with preferential tariffs in the international market. What they need is diversification, and with technical assistance from the developed world, this becomes possible. Collier takes special interest in providing assistance in post-conflict countries where there are serious reforms being made. That is where the new leaders are not corrupt and have a pragmatic vision for development devoid of leftist or rightist dogma. He notes how this aid must be maintained for at least a decade. And as he shows with the example of Sierra Leone, it is possible for international military interventions to help ensure that reforms take place. Collier's perspective contrasts greatly with most non-governmental organizations, which oppose the use of international law enforcement and military interventions. Collier makes no bones about this, for as he points out, the world's concern over terrorism has led to an international effort to enforce laws eliminating loopholes that allow for money to flow to terrorists, despite the major difficulties involved, not to mention the major U.S.-led military interventions in Iraq and Afghanistan.

Unfortunately, the Iraq invasion has left a bad taste in the mouths of many who have learned the wrong lesson that intervention in general is wrong. Collier calls for foreign military intervention in the four following situations: "expelling an aggressor," "restoration of order," (especially "in a collapsed state") "maintaining post-conflict peace," and "preventing coups." The greatest example he notes is the comparison between Somalia and Rwanda. In Somalia, the deaths of eighteen U.S. troops on October 3, 1993 led to the U.S. withdrawal from that country and the refusal of U.S. and UN military intervention in Rwanda to prevent the genocide there that took 800,000 lives in 100 days. In other words, the international community must be willing to work smartly to carry out its stated agenda of reducing poverty, especially if it hopes to meet the Millennium Development Goals set for 2015.

Dr. Paul Farmer: Doctor to the poor

> Paul Farmer is a superb physician, a penetrating anthropologist, and a prophet of social justice. He combines an unflinching moral stance— that the poor deserve health care just as much as the rich do—with scientific expertise and boundless dedication. He has saved the lives of countless destitute patients in Haiti, Peru, and Russia, and he has shown that effective health services, even complex medical regiments, can be put in place in impoverished communities.
> (Jeffrey Sachs, *Natural History,* taken from back cover of Farmer's *Pathologies of Power*)

One who has worked with Sachs and the Millennium Project is Paul Farmer, the subject of the international bestseller, *Mountains beyond Mountains,* by Tracy Kidder. Farmer grew up poor himself, always with a keen eye for injustice. He earned both his doctorate in anthropology and his degree in medicine, making him a PhD and an MD and, as such, he is in a unique position to have both the theoretical perspective of an academic and the practical perspective of a medical expert. He has spent considerable time in Haiti since the 1980s, opening a free clinic in Cange called Zamni Lasante and then co-founding Partners in Health (PIH) in 1985.

His timing in Haiti was perfect for developing an analysis of the causes of poverty. The long-standing dictatorship of the Duvaliers (first Papa Doc, 1957–1971, then Baby Doc, 1971–1986) had wrought havoc on both the society and the economy of Haiti, all with the assistance of rich countries such as the United States and France, to name a few. In this time, they killed upward of 60,000 people, imprisoned and tortured many more, and further enriched the elite and themselves, and when Baby Doc was overthrown in 1986, he left with a fortune as his people were left to pay off the debts his government had acquired. Farmer sees the result of the exertion of power by elites, both today and throughout history. Sometimes, this power is exercised directly against the poor majority, and sometimes it is through the assistance of foreign powers assisting the elite of another country. It is also the result of long-standing power structures that make it difficult for change to take place. As he notes on page 19 of his book, *Pathologies of Power: Health, Human Rights, and the New War on the Poor*:

> Pathologies of Power suggests that a broad biosocial approach, when anchored in careful examination of specific cases, permits a critical reassessment of conventional views on human rights. To make the case, I link detailed case histories of individual to broader analyses of health and human rights. . . As noted, human rights discussions have to date been excessively legal and theoretical in focus. They seek to define rights, mandate punishment by appropriate authorities for the violators, enforce international treaties, and so on. A focus on health alters human rights discussions in important and underexplored ways: the right to health is perhaps the least contested social right, and a large community of health providers – from physicians to community health workers – affords a still-untapped vein of enthusiasm and commitment. Furthermore, this focus serves to remind us that those who are sick and poor bear the brunt of human rights violations. In making this argument, I draw freely on the critiques that a doctor to the poor is well placed to make.

Thus, although Farmer knows his history, his experience as a physician in the poorest reaches of the world and his leadership in a medical aid organization are what make Farmer different from others on the Left with a similar ideology. He is a forceful advocate for the poor, whom he has served for nearly three decades. He likes to ask people who claim the task of ending poverty is too difficult, "Is that the beginning of the conversation or the end of it?" This question is an indication of where he is coming from, which is in the field itself. If he is not in Haiti, he is in Russia, or Rwanda, or Peru, or another country suffering from acute outbreaks of infectious diseases, and he addresses them as a systemic problem. For example, he tells the story of a Haitian man about whom someone in a village far from his clinic in Cange told him years ago who was suffering from AIDS. It took hours to walk there, up and down mountains with little water, and when Farmer arrived, he saw a man reduced to half his normal weight, dying with his family all around. His plan was in line with the structure of PIH, which is to provide a structure for recovery: He would need medicines, but his family would also need money to provide for his loss of income during his illness to prevent them from slipping into destitution as he recovered.

This is what happens to many who become sick: They lack drugs, they can no longer provide for the family, and whether they die or do not, the family is left with nothing. This further subjects other members of the family to other problems, such as illness, starvation, crime, or other problems. Therefore, PIH seeks to look at the entire situation, respond in kind, and provide a sustainable development program both on the individual and the community level. Farmer is happy to show before and after pictures of this particular patient, who eventually doubled his body weight with PIH's assistance, and his family was also maintained. This provided him with a foundation upon which to return to providing for his family.

Farmer is concerned about fixing our priorities as a species, as indicated in the following paragraph from page 146 of *Pathologies of Power*, which looks at the conundrum of tuberculosis treatment and the disease's connection to poverty:

> Ironically enough, some who understand, quite correctly, that the underlying causes of tuberculosis are poverty and social inequality make a terrible error by failing to honor the experience and views of the poor in designing strategies to respond to the disease. What happens if, after analysis reveals poverty as the root cause of tuberculosis, tuberculosis control strategies ignore the sick and focus solely on eradicating poverty? Elsewhere, I have called this the "Luddite trap," since this ostensibly progressive view would have us ignore both current distress and the tools of modern medicine that might relieve it, thereby committing a new and grave injustice. The destitute sick ardently desire the eradication of poverty, but their tuberculosis can be readily cured by drugs such as isoniazid and rifampin. The prescription for poverty is not so clear.

Of all the sources consulted for this book, Dr. Paul Farmer has the most credibility for me. In this case, I actually met Farmer at a speech he gave in Kansas City in 2006. Unlike the majority of the authors who write about Asia, Latin America, and Africa, Farmer spends the bulk of his time either on these continents or studying and working to solve the most serious problems their poor suffer through every day. The fact that he speaks Haitian Creole after having lived among the Haitians shows how much he cares. That he and PIH also build free hospitals and clinics, train and hire medical personnel from the countries where they operate, and advocate for the poor locally, nationally, and globally illustrates that he is doing more than just about anyone on the planet to solve the problem of inequality, rather than just analyze it. One major success was their pressuring of pharmaceutical companies to provide inexpensive HIV treatment drugs to the poor in Africa and Latin America. Another is the recent appointment of the co-founder of PIH, Jim Yong Kim, to head the World Bank. Farmer has even been nominated for the Nobel Peace Prize, but his political inclinations will probably prevent this from happening anytime soon.

Kevin Sites: Highlighting the effect of war

> The most destructive result of the war has been the phenomenon of night commuting, in which rural families, out of fear of LRA abductions, leave their homes each night and walk miles to protected urban areas,

where they spend the night, then return to their homes the next day. An estimated fifty thousand Ugandans make this journey every day, and it has wreaked havoc on their communities by disrupting their planting and harvesting cycles, children's education and family cohesion.

The preceding quote comes from Kevin Sites's 2007 book, *In the Hot Zone: One Man, One Year, Twenty Wars*. Journalists are among the most important authors we have in the study of developing countries, as they often have the resources to spend more time in country and have more access to important people. Journalist Kevin Sites recently spent one year traveling the world with the mission of reporting on all of the world's major conflicts. Though other journalists have covered these same wars, no others immersed themselves within these wars so intensely on a planet-wide level. He reported from Iraq, Somalia, the DRC, Uganda, Sudan, Lebanon, Israel, Syria, Chechnya, Afghanistan, Colombia, Nepal, Kashmir, Sri Lanka, Myanmar, and others, all of which have all been suffering prolonged conflicts for years and sometimes decades. We have to ask, what effect does this warfare have on the economic growth potential of each country? Why is this not mentioned more often by scholars (other than Paul Collier) as part of the overall picture of what causes inequality in the world?

Somalia has been without a functioning central government since 1991, when President Siad Barre (1969–1991) was overthrown. The resulting warfare and famine set Somalia down the path of disunity and increasing poverty, not to mention the loss of upward of 1 million people over the past two decades. The DRC is the poorest country per capita on the planet and has suffered not only under Belgian colonialism (1884–1960) and the dictatorship of Joseph Sese Mobutu (1965–97) but under two civil wars (1996–1997, 1998–2002) and widespread militia atrocities sponsored by the DRC government and neighboring countries since 1996. Five million people have died in the past seventeen years to make the DRC the site of the highest death toll on Earth since WWII. Sudan, which recently divided into two parts (Sudan and South Sudan) has been embroiled in intermittent civil wars for decades, with the most recent conflicts between north and south and the genocide in Darfur, not to mention Sudan's role in the conflicts of Uganda and the DRC. Sudan's death toll is close to 3 million and, despite its oil exports that largely go to the government in Khartoum, the majority of its citizens suffer unrelenting poverty. The following excerpt from page 94 of *In the Hot Zone* illustrates what these wars mean to the average citizen:

In a circle of twenty SPLA fighters, I ask them to raise their hands if they have lost an immediate family member in the fighting. Every hand goes up.

"Sometimes they would bomb four or five times a day," Colonel Makuac says, "and then into the night. We didn't have any antiaircraft guns, so we shot at them with our AK-47s and RPGs. We brought a lot of them down," he says of the Russian Antonov planes the government used against them.

Most of the men here say they joined the SPLA because of the atrocities committed against them by Arab tribal militias known as Janjaweed. The SPLA claims the militias are sponsored by the government, a charge the Janjaweed denies.

SPLA Sergeant Tihong Garang says that ten of his family members were killed when the Janjaweed attacked his village, including six children. "They looted everything," he says, "raped the women and shot the children. After— they burned it all down."

The details are important to keep in mind: We can see, in each aspect of this small part of one interview with a small group of Sudanese men, just how the economic development, not to mention the physical well-being of the population, would be adversely affected by this type of situation. This fighting has set Sudan back considerably. The people have to rebuild. They have lost family members who would otherwise contribute economically. The country is seen as unstable for investment. And, most important, the morale of the population is the opposite of what is necessary for economic progress. Why is this element not central to scholarly focus when trying to understand the divergence between rich and poor nations? Are we to assume these wars are mere hiccups in the otherwise uninterrupted economic development of these countries?

Iraq has suffered not only under the tyranny of Saddam Hussein between 1979 and 2003 but under the U.S.-led invasion/occupation and the various insurgencies that combined have caused more than 100,000 deaths and displaced more than 3 million people. This war has certainly brought U.S. and other international funds to Iraq, but what effect does the loss of human life and the displacement of millions of people have on development? Does it assist it? Does it reverse it? Likewise, without Lebanon's internal and international strife since the 1970s, what would its economy be like now? Although it is over now, the Sri Lanka civil war that lasted from 1983 to 2009 and ended with the government's destruction of the Tamil Tigers' resistance caused tremendous economic problems in a country that depends on tourism, tea, and textiles, all of which were affected adversely by the war. Likewise in Afghanistan, Yemen, Chechnya, Nepal, Myanmar, Colombia, and Syria, there have been conflicts with high numbers of deaths and refugees and loss of property. In all of these cases, there is economic destruction, a loss of international and domestic confidence in economic viability, and a buildup of debt, either by the nations themselves or the intervening nations.

The causes of these nations' problems are historical to be sure, but the past four decades have shown that both warmongering leaders and the international community have also caused newly created problems that seem quite difficult to reverse. What is the effect of these new problems on the future of development in these countries? Can we point to simply culture, corporate exploitation, class warfare, racism, or imperialism as the culprits? Or do the actions of tyrants, intervening countries, international economics, and ethnic conflicts as they occur as the result of decisions made by individuals make more sense as units of analysis to understand the causes of their problems? In other words, perhaps grand theories of causation have less import than the details of what is actually happening in real time as we can observe them. Scholars of development theory would have us look to institutions, culture, geography, class, and race to see concrete trends that point the way toward explaining why some nations progress economically while others do not. However, why can we not examine the role of warfare itself as an element that stalls or reverses economic development?

At the same time as we must consider conflict as a major source of economic underdevelopment, it is imperative that we consider the scale of violence in the developing world over the course of modern history. Is it growing, as many people think? Or is it in fact drastically declining, as is proven by the two prominent voices on this topic: Harvard psychologist Stephen Pinker and international relations expert Joshua Goldstein. These two men simultaneously produced nearly clear-cut studies documenting the decline in violence as measured globally in modern times. Pinker starts further back in time than Goldstein, but both concentrate on the post–WWII and the post–Cold War eras to demonstrate beyond a shadow of a doubt that the world is much safer now than it has ever been. Pinker uses a psychological argument: People have become more civilized and averse to violence over time and, therefore, less inclined to go to war or murder one another. Goldstein uses the international community and, in particular, the history of the UN to demonstrate that international peacekeeping has caused a dramatic decline in global conflict. Goldstein concentrates mostly on the developing world to highlight a number of cases in which the UN and the international community in general have used a variety of pressures and military interventions to gradually reduce the outbreaks of war and the death tolls of the wars that do break out. Both Goldstein and Pinker provide ample evidence to demonstrate that the developing world is much less violent than it used to be, despite the images most people in the West receive about Asia, Latin America, and Africa.

Kevin Bales: Ending modern slavery

Although most do not know it still exists, there is slavery throughout the world. It does not come in the form of the outright legal ownership of another human being, but the absolute control of one human being by another for the purposes of extracting the worth of another's labor is still intact in places such as Thailand, Brazil, India, and Pakistan. Thai sex workers are inadvertently "sold" by their parents after being told of job opportunities for their daughters in Bangkok. Brazilian charcoal producers are coaxed deep into the rainforest and held under armed guard for little to no pay. Pakistani families are held in perpetual debt servitude to produce bricks for working off loans that pass from generation to generation. Bales describes his experiences with Pakistani brick workers on pages 151–152 of his book, *Disposable People: New Slavery in the Global Economy*:

> In spite of the risk, the children work on: their families need their help to get by . . . The value of their work means that as I visited many brick kilns across the state of Panjab, I found only a handful of children who attended the local school. . . For the children of the brick kilns the work is long and hard, but hard work and diligence don't guarantee success. . . Virtually all of the families making bricks are working against a debt owed to the owner of the kiln. These debts pose a special danger for the children. Sometimes, when a kiln owner suspects that a family will try to run away and not pay off their debt, a child might be taken hostage to force the family to stay . . . The debt owed to the owner of the kiln does not end if the father of the family dies. Instead it passes to his wife and sons. A boy of thirteen or fourteen can be saddled with a debt that he will carry for many years, perhaps his entire life.

These are the types of labor that hold people coercively to a "master" illegally throughout the world. There are activists that have been working to end these modern forms of slavery, and chief among them is Kevin Bales. He claims that there are still 27 million slaves, and his books are not leftist polemics against corporate abuses or Western imperialism. He provides a wide range of case studies that illustrate the detailed ways in which people are forced into slavery from across the world, and the book culminates in a recipe for ending this scourge.

What is most relevant to Bales is the impact of extreme poverty. When people reach the point where they are on the brink of survival, which is the case for approximately one-seventh of the planet today ("The Bottom Billion," to use Paul Collier's term), they seek out means to alleviate their situation in which they are made to pay with their freedom. Bales's solution in part rests on consumption habits: If people in the developed world would vote with their wallets, purchasing items not made by slaves, they would reduce the power of the slaveholders. The international community must also take a more active role by acknowledging that slavery still exists and then ensure the enforcement of anti-slavery laws. Sex trafficking has been pursued with great vigor in the past decade, but more needs to be done. Although Bales's dream may seem far-fetched, it is important to point out that at one time, Great Britain was the largest slaveholder on the planet, and yet it became the nation responsible for ending legal slavery altogether in the early to mid-nineteenth century. Bales' efforts are another example of an academic translating his analysis of the causes of inequality and putting them into action to help solve the problems resulting from that inequality. Though they may not free all 27 million possibly in slavery today, they can be considered as at least productive rather than simply as academic.

Muhammad Yunus: The micro-lending revolution

This Bangladeshi-born economist and Vanderbilt professor won the Nobel Peace Prize in 2006 for his role in fomenting a revolutionary move toward economic development and liberation for the world's poor. This movement began in the 1970s with the idea that providing small loans to mostly women in the impoverished nation of Bangladesh was the best solution for ending poverty. The Grameen Bank, run by Yunus and his allies, provided this service through soliciting funds from the same donor pool from which charities draw their funds (i.e., developed countries and the rich of developing countries). The major difference is that unlike charities, the Grameen Bank provides its donors with a near-100 percent return because the money is technically a loan. However, unlike traditional banks, there are no interest payments.

Yunus' plan was to provide a means by which the most vulnerable populations—women—could change their economies through empowerment. Loans of 100 dollars or so provided seed money for women and some men to open small businesses in Bangladesh (and later many others). The women were considered more important, more reliable, and more efficient targets for these loans. Women are most in need of economic liberation due to the historical trends that have placed women in roles subservient to those of men across the world. It is well understood in social science circles that a solid indicator of a nation's development is the manner in which it treats its women. In other words, the better women are treated in general, the better the nation's economy tends to be, wherever you go. In addition, women have been found to repay their loans at a rate of nearly 100 percent because they see a direct link between this money and their family's well-being. In his book, *Creating a World without Poverty*, Yunus points out how men have been known to use portions of their money selfishly, whereas women tend to not have this inclination and are, therefore, more economically viable as a target for micro-lending.

The success of Yunus' revolutionary approach is unprecedented. Not only has Bangladesh developed rapidly in the past twenty years in particular, but Grameen Bank and other micro-lending institutions have spread to the rest of the developing world. Literally hundreds of millions of people, mostly women, have been assisted with these programs. Yunus' success is based on both an historical understanding of the causes of underdevelopment and a potential solution. By focusing primarily on women, he recognizes the way in which gender discrimination has kept many nations from advancing economically. The gender link could be considered as part of the culture argument advocated by Landes, Harrison, Huntington, et al. because there is a stronger semblance of gender equality in the more developed nations. However, this is not always the case, of course: Rwanda's parliament is 50 percent women, for example. At the same time, Yunus's method could be considered as further recognition of the debt richer nations have to poorer nations, which might fall in line with the likes of Farmer and Chomsky, whose criticisms of unabashed capitalism and imperialism are well documented.

Yunus's method and theory have at least proven to work on a grand scale. The focus on women as the primary targets of assistance as a form of empowerment demonstrates both his humanity and his intellect. In addition, unlike the traditional charities, where donors do not expect to see a return, micro-lenders see the recipients of their donations as equals who have a mutual stake in the development process as both sides expect yields on their relationship. This cannot be said so categorically about the neo-liberal economic model proposed by the Chicago School of Economics and the so-called "Washington Consensus" that has assisted both in the massive economic gains of many nations and in continuation of inequality in the developing world, not to mention the increased militarization and debt crises that often come with such programs.

The United Nations Millennium Development Goals

The Millennium Development Goals (MDG) is a list of targets for reduction of poverty and economic growth in the poorest countries established by a collection of countries in 2000. These are:

1   eradicate extreme poverty and hunger,
2   achieve primary universal education,
3   promote gender equality and cmpower women,
4   reduce child mortality,
5   improve maternal health,
6   combat HIV/AIDS, malaria, and other diseases,
7   ensure environmental sustainability, and
8   develop a global partnership for development.

As the reader can see, even after all of the authors listed previously, there are broad-based efforts with international-level resources such as those provided by the UN that are at work on solving the problem of poverty. This effort should demonstrate at the very least that the historical causes of poverty and wealth are only one aspect of the more important cause, which is what to do about it right now. The critics of capitalism, imperialism, and colonialism have led many to anger and hostility toward those forces. Why not? They are justified in their anger because there were atrocious deeds perpetrated against vulnerable populations for the greed of a minority of individuals. However, imperialism was not limited to the Westerners who have sat atop the world for the past two centuries. The Mongols, Chinese, Ottomans, Aztecs, Incas, Zulus, and many others throughout history have utilized conquest to subjugate peoples, so are we to blame only those who happen to be the latest beneficiaries of conquest? Is that fair? And, what if only a portion of their (the West's) wealth is due to those conquests? The fact that the weight that we can place on factors of causation is so difficult to measure should give us pause when considering how much blame to place on imperialism, despite its very real role in causing the imbalance we see in the past two centuries especially.

Are the same critics of the West equally critical of the destructive power of Maoist and Stalinist policies in China and Russia, respectively? It also seems partly counterproductive to praise Western culture as the decisive factor of a limited materialistic version of "progress" despite the incredible economic, social, and technological advances emanating from it. There are a multitude of negative aspects of Western imperialism that are only too obvious to even the casual reader of history. Slavery, the destruction of Indigenous cultures, and rampant industrialization causing a host of environmental problems that are literally impossible to undo or reverse are but a few of the most important examples of this; however, these also occurred under all other forms of imperialism, especially under Chinese and Russian Communism. We have to learn an important lesson from these concrete events while acknowledging the positive aspects of Western civilization, but we must also acknowledge the contributions of non-Western cultures, which is something rarely mentioned by the cultural determinists.

Post–Millennium Development Goals

The preceding authors and the UN as an institution promoting the MDG seem to have the most valid positions on development theory because they are active in searching for solutions rather than searching for someone or something to blame or praise. However, it may be time to consider that theory is what has both caused the problems we now deal with and blinded us to observing the world as it is. Theory is what motivated Gandhi, but it also motivated Mao, and neither demonstrated that their theories could solve humanity's greatest ill, which is poverty. The latest trend in understanding the development gap is to approach the problem scientifically, systematically, and without theoretical bias. The developing world has sought to add their voice to the UN's MDG by submitting their plan for Sustainable Development Goals (SDGs), which arose from the Earth Summit 2012, also known as Rio +20, which was held in Rio de Janeiro, Brazil in June 2012. This calls for environmental protection and sustainable plans for growth that incorporate the needs of developing countries.

The Rio +20 SDGs demonstrate the growing power of developing countries on the world stage, and it teaches us how we need to be flexible in our understanding of how development occurs. The most notable analysts contributing toward non-theoretical perspectives on development are Abhijit Banerjee and Esther Duflo, the authors of *Poor Economics: A Radical Rethinking of How to Fight Global Poverty*. Banerjee and Duflo strike a strong balance between data analysis and field work to come up with a list of categories to use to both survey and address the problems of poverty in a variety of countries. They also take apart some of the theories presented by advocates of development aid and its opponents. Each side assumes too much about the effect of aid, which is difficult to measure due to other internal circumstances such as war, weather, politics, and resources. The generalized view either in favor or against aid to poor countries thus limits our ability to discern the real impact of aid or its absence unless its usage is analyzed intensely.

To flesh out why challenging theoretical perspectives is important, the authors of *Poor Economics* use Rwanda and India to raise the question of the effect of aid. Both countries have experienced rapid growth in the past two decades, but Rwanda has received considerable international aid, whereas India has received virtually none. Was Rwanda's aid responsible for its massive growth? If so, what explains India's similar growth rates during the same time period? The authors use micro- and macro-economic analysis to explain how countries can pull themselves out of poverty. Instead of the MDGs, Banerjee and Duflo founded the Jameel Poverty Action Lab, or J-PAL, to coordinate development research across the globe. They pioneered the use of randomized controlled trials (RCTs) that use factors such as loans, grants, vaccinations, school attendance, family size, employment, food consumption, and mosquito netting, to name a few, in analyzing the weight of such factors in determining development and poverty.

RCTs showed how to weigh the effects of incentives in driving behavior that led to improvements in development. One example of this was in Udaipur, India, where two different types of immunization camps were set up. These were chosen randomly to control for the factor of incentive. In one group, immunizations were free with no extra incentive, whereas in the other, they were free with the incentive of a gift of lentils. The latter group was twice as likely to get the immunizations. It would seem to those in the developed world that something as important as immunizations for one's child would not need an added incentive. However, as the authors point out, and this is a reason why aid by itself cannot be used as a single factor of analysis, the people did not always trust clinics due to a number of factors. First, most Indians placed some trust in unofficial "Bengali doctors" or traditional healers without medical credentials to provide them with inexpensive medical care. Second, free, government-run clinics have a reputation for having unreliable hours, and as such, if a parent considered taking the day off from work to travel with their children to the clinic, they risked a whole day's pay plus the cost of transportation and food for nothing if they found the clinic closed.

The example of immunizations in Udaipur highlights the problem of simply throwing money at the problem (or ignoring the problem altogether) without examining human behavioral tendencies in specific locations. That is, people in Udaipur behave differently than in Calcutta, and likewise Kenyans have different concerns than Nicaraguans, and so on, throughout the world. The authors of *Poor Economics* find that cultural, environmental, political, and social factors have to be considered on a case-by-case basis in the areas being examined to find the best solutions to ending poverty. This makes solving the problem more difficult than the ideologues of Chapters Ten and Eleven would prefer. Aside from the example of immunizations in Udaipur, Banerjee and Duflo also found that low-cost health-based efforts to provide free de-worming and durable mosquito netting to families in the water-borne illness and malaria zones of the developing world represented highly efficient ways of helping the poor out of poverty. Their website (www.pooreconomics.com) highlights their past and present work, and it is likely that this type of scientific methodology will be utilized by development workers and policy makers in the coming decades, rather than the ideologically based ones of the not-so-distant past.

Discussion questions

1   Which author's approach do you prefer the most and why?
2   Which author's approach do you see as the least appealing or effective and why?
3   Do you believe these authors have left out any crucial factors? Explain.

Further readings

Acemoglu, Daron, and James Robinson. *Why Nations Fail: The Origins of Power, Prosperity, and Poverty*. London: Crown Business, 2012.

Bales, Kevin. *Disposable People: New Slavery in the Global Economy*. Berkeley, CA: University of California, 2004.

Banerjee, Abhijit, and Esther Duflo. *Poor Economics: A Radical Rethinking of the Way to Fight Global Poverty*. New York: Public Affairs, 2011.

Collier, Paul. *The Bottom Billion: Why the Poorest Countries are Failing and What Can be Done about it*. Oxford: Oxford, 2007.

Farmer, Paul. *Pathologies of Power: Health, Human Rights, and the New War on the Poor*. Berkeley, CA: University of California, 2004.

Goldstein, Joshua. *Winning the War on War: the Decline of Armed Conflict Worldwide*. New York: Penguin, 2011.

Kinzer, Stephen. *The Better Angels of our Nature: Why Violence has Decline*. New York: Penguin, 2012.

Sachs, Jeffrey. *The End of Poverty: Economic Possibilities for our Time*. New York: Penguin, 2005.

Sites, Kevin. *In the Hot Zone: One Man, One Year, Twenty Wars*. New York: Harper Perennial, 2007.

Stiglitz, Joseph. *Globalization and its Discontents*. New York: Norton, 2002.

Stiglitz, Joseph. *Making Globalization Work*. New York: Norton, 2007.

Yunus, Mohammad. *Creating a World without Poverty: Social Business and the Future of Capitalism*. New York: Public Affairs, 2009.

Online content

Rio +20: Sustainable Development Goals: www.uncsd2012.org/content/documents/colombiasdgs.pdf

Esther Duflo on TED Talks: www.ted.com/talks/esther_duflo_social_experiments_to_fight_poverty.html

Poor Economics: www.pooreconomics.com

Ngozi Okonjo-Iweala on TED Talks: www.ted.com/talks/ngozi_okonjo_iweala_on_aid_versus_trade.html

Paul Collier on TED Talks: www.ted.com/talks/paul_collier_shares_4_ways_to_help_the_bottom_billion.html

Kevin Bales on TED Talks: www.ted.com/talks/kevin_bales_how_to_combat_modern_slavery.html

Jacqueline Novogratz on TED Talks: www.ted.com/talks/jacqueline_novogratz_on_an_escape_from_poverty.html

Jared Diamond on TED Talks: www.ted.com/talks/jared_diamond_on_why_societies_collapse.html

Paul Farmer:

Partners in Health: www.pih.org

World Bank Data: http://data.worldbank.org/

60 Minutes story: www.cbsnews.com/video/watch/?id=4069409n

Jeffrey Sachs website and articles: www.earth.columbia.edu/articles/view/1804

Acemoglu and Robinson, Why Nations Fail website: http://whynationsfail.com/

Muhammad Yunus' Grameen Bank: www.grameenfoundation.org/join-us?gclid=CP6eqe7y57QCFUOK4AodET8AYw

Appendix

Twentieth-century deaths from major conflicts, repression, genocides, and interventions in the developing world

1910–1920	Mexican Revolution: 1 million
1915	Turks commit genocide against Armenians: 1–1.5 million
1927–1937, 1931–1945	Japanese occupation of China: 20 million
1943	East Bengal famine caused by British government: 1.5 million
1944–1945	Vietnam famine caused by French: 1–2 million
1945–1949	Chinese Civil Wars: 3–6 million
1946–1975	Vietnamese wars with the French and the United States: 2–4 million
1947–1948	India–Pakistan Partition: 1 million
1948–1958	Colombian era of violence: 200,000
1949–1976	Mao Tse Tung's rule in China: 30–60 million
1950–1953	Korean War: 2–4 million
1954–1962	Algerian Revolution: 1 million
1954–1996	Guatemalan genocide and Civil War: 200,000
1959–1975	U.S. wars in Cambodia and Laos: 1 million
1962–1985	Ugandan dictators Milton Obote and Idi Amin repression: 500,000–1 million
1965–1997	Suharto's genocide against dissidents in Indonesia and the East Timorese: 700,000–1.2 million
1967–1970	Biafra genocide, Nigeria: 1 million
1971	Bangladesh: 300,000–3 million
1972	Burundi Tutsis commit genocide against Hutus: 100,000
1974–1987	Ethiopian dictator Mengitsu kills 1.1 million
1975–1979	Khmer Rouge in Cambodia: 1–2 million
1975–2002	Angolan Civil War: 300,000
1977–1990	Nicaraguan Revolution and Contra War: 80,000
1979–1989	Soviet occupation of Afghanistan: 1 million
1980–1992	El Salvador Civil War: 70–80,000
1980–1992	Peru Civil War: 69,000
1980–1988	Iran/Iraq: 1 million

1983–2005	Sudan: 2 million
1983–2009	Sri Lankan Civil War: 200,000
1989–2003	Liberian Civil Wars: 200,000
1990–1991	Iraq, Desert Shield, and Desert Storm: 100,000
1991–2001	Sierra Leone: 70,000
1992–present	Somalia: 1 million
1994	Rwanda Hutus commit genocide against Tutsis: 800,000
1996–present	Congo Wars (in and around the Democratic Republic of Congo): 5 million
2003–present	Darfur, Sudan: 400,000
2003–2011	Operation Iraqi Freedom: 100,000–600,000

Glossary of terms

AIPAC: American Israel Public Affairs Committee

ANC: African National Congress

APEC: Asia Pacific Economic Cooperation

AU: African Union

Afrikaner: South Africans of non-British European origin, mostly Dutch and German

Agrarian Reform: Programs to redistribute land more equitably throughout the developing world, mostly during the twentieth century, under left-leaning regimes

Al Qaeda: International Islamic fundamentalist terrorist organization, responsible for the attacks in the United States on 9/11/2001, among many others

The Americas/American: Geographical and cultural term referring to the Western Hemisphere

The Andes: The longest mountain chain in the world, which runs through seven countries (Venezuela, Colombia, Ecuador, Peru, Bolivia, Chile, and Argentina)

Apartheid: Afrikaner term for "separateness" that dictated racial segregationist policies in South Africa during the Cold War

Arab Spring: The eruption of popular uprisings leading to the widespread challenging of long-running dictatorships throughout the Arab World, beginning in 2011

Arawak: Indigenous group of the Caribbean, first encountered by Columbus

Atlantic Charter: Generalized freedom platform announced by Allied leaders Roosevelt and Churchill during WWII

Ayatollah: Shi'ite Islamic religious leaders of Iran

Aztec: Dominant empire of Central Mexico from 1325 to 1521

Ba'ath: Secular, Socialist party of Syria and Iraq

Bantu: The predominant ethnic group of sub-Saharan Africa

Berber: Indigenous African ethnicity of a small portion of the lighter-skinned population of North Africa

Biafra: Igbo Independence movement of Nigeria

Blood diamonds: Also known as "conflict diamonds," a term to describe diamonds mined and sold to fund wars in West Africa, the Congo, and Angola.

Bourbon: Spanish imperial family that ruled much of the Americas from 1700 to 1826

Bourgeoisie: Marxist term for the middle and upper classes

Brahman: The Indian elite caste

Brazil wood: This produced a reddish dye that became the main resource coveted by Portuguese colonists in Brazil in the sixteenth century

(British) East India Company: British imperial trade company that operated throughout Asia during the colonial era

Buddhism: The dominant religion of Asia, originating in India with the teachings of Siddhartha Gotama (563–483 BC), the Buddha, 2,500 years ago

CCP: Chinese Communist Party

COPAZ: Commission for the Consolidation of Peace (Peace accords for El Salvador and other countries)

CPP: Convention People's Party (Ghana)

Caliphate: A region under an Islamic ruler (caliph), prominent until the twentieth century

Cape Horn: The southern tip of South America

The Cape of Good Hope: The southern tip of Africa

Caste system: The Indian social hierarchical system ranging from the Brahmans to the Untouchables

Caudillo: Regional strongman in Latin America

Coca: Traditional Andean leafy bush used for thousands of years as a medicinal plant that is also used to make cocaine

The Columbian Exchange: The results of the many exchanges between the Old and New World in the wake of Columbus' first voyage

Confucianism: The main undercurrent of Chinese cultural traditions stemming from the teachings of Confucius (551–479 BC)

Conquistadors: The Spanish conquerors of the New World

Corvée: Forced labor system often used in the developing world before, during, and after colonial-style slavery

Cultural Revolution: Period of Mao's power reconsolidation in China from 1966 to 1976

DMZ: Demilitarized zone, used in divided countries suffering from civil war and foreign interventions, especially the two Koreas and the two Vietnams

Dependency Theory: This argues that traditional capitalism created wealth for industrialized countries at the expense of underdeveloped countries

Derg: Communist dictatorship in charge of Ethiopia, 1974–1987

Dirty War: The torture, murder, and imprisonment carried out by Latin American military governments during the Cold War

To disappear someone: Term invented in Latin America during the Cold War to describe how military governments abducted, imprisoned, and usually murdered dissidents and suspected dissidents, leaving little to no record of their "disappearance"

Domino Theory: U.S. President Dwight D. Eisenhower's (1953–1961) term to assert the need for the United States to intervene in places such as Vietnam to prevent the subsequent crumbling of regimes to Communist rebellions

(Dutch) East India Company: Dutch imperial trading company that operated in East Asia and the South Pacific primarily during the colonial era

EZLN: Zapatista Army of National Liberation (Mexico)

FARC: Revolutionary Armed Forces of Colombia

FLN: National Liberation Front (Algeria)

FSLN: The Sandinista National Liberation Front (Nicaragua)

Fertile Crescent: Land in the central Middle East where agriculture and civilization first began, 11,000 years ago

Force Publique: Belgian colonial security forces in the Congo, responsible for the deaths of millions

The Four Cubs: China, Indonesia, Malaysia, and Thailand

The Four Tigers: South Korea, Singapore, Taiwan, and Hong Kong

Genocidaires: The general term for the Hutus who carried out the Rwandan genocide

GBM: The Green Belt Movement (Kenya)

GIA: Armed Islamic Group (Algeria)

Glasnost and Perestroika: Soviet Premier Mikhail Gorbachev's programs of economic and political opening and restructuring that eventually led to the dissolution of the USSR

Great Leap Forward: Mao's failed development program from 1958 to 1961 that led to the deaths of tens of millions

Green Revolution: Scientific approach to agriculture using pesticides and chemical fertilizers that led to widespread reductions in hunger and massive environmental and health consequences and tremendous increases in populations in the developing world

Hapsburg: The Spanish imperial family from 1516 to 1700 that ruled much of the Americas

Harappan: Ancient Indus Valley civilization that possibly thrived from 3100 to 1700 BC

Hezbollah: Lebanese Shi-ite fundamentalist terrorist organization

Hinduism: Dominant religion and culture in India, with multiple roots dating back 5,000 years

The Horn of Africa: East African region containing Somalia, Ethiopia, Eritrea, and Djibouti

Hutu: The majority ethnic group in Rwanda and Burundi, and the group that perpetrated the Rwandan genocide against the Tutsis in 1994

IAEA: International Atomic Energy Agency

INC: Indian National Congress, Gandhi and Nehru's Independence movement party

ISI: Import substitution industrialization, an economic model in which developing world nations created manufactured goods for internal consumption to reverse poverty resulting from their traditional unequal relationship with developed countries

Inca: The empire that dominated the Andes from 1438 to 1532

Indigenismo: Latin American political movement promoting Indigenous pride

Indus Valley: Region in modern India and Pakistan in which ancient civilizations thrived beginning possibly 5,000 years ago

Inquisition: The imperial Spanish and Portuguese religious court system

Interahamwe: Rwandan Hutu militias responsible for much of the 1994 genocide

Intifada: Popular uprising in the Occupied Territories of Israel

Iran/Contra Scandal: Also known as "Arms for Hostages," this scandal stemmed from U.S. weapons sales to Iran to finance the arming of the Nicaraguan counter-revolutionary forces in Central America

Islam: Dominant religion of West and Central Asia, along with North Africa and Indonesia, stemming from the words of the Prophet Mohammad (570–632 AD)

Jainism: Indian religion based on nonviolence that inspired Mahatma Gandhi

Janjaweed: State-supported militia carrying out genocide in Darfur, Sudan

Junta: Latin American military government

KAU: Kenyan African Union

KMT: Kuomintang, also known as the Chinese Nationalist Party

Khmer Rouge: Cambodian Communist regime that carried out the 1975–1979 genocide

Khoisan: Minority traditional tribe throughout Southern Africa

Kibbutz: Israeli collective farm

Kikuyu: Prominent Kenyan tribe

Kongo: Name of the kingdom of what is now the western Congo during the colonial era

Kurd: Ethnic minority in Turkey, Iran, Iraq, Armenia, and Syria

LRA: Lord's Resistance Army (Uganda)

Liberation Theology: Catholic sect initiated in the wake of Vatican II to orient clergy toward "a preferential option for the poor"

"The Liberator:"   Simon Bolivar's nickname for ending Spanish colonialism in the five new nations of Colombia, Venezuela, Ecuador, Bolivia, and Peru

The Lost Decade: The economic decline in Africa and Latin America during the 1980s

MAS: Movement to Socialism, Bolivian President Evo Morales' party

MDG: Millennium Development Goals

MNC: National Congolese Movement

MITI: Ministry of International Trade and Industry (Japan)

MPLA: People's Movement for the Liberation of Angola

Manila Galleons: The giant Spanish ships that sailed between Acapulco, Mexico, and Manila, Philippines from the sixteenth to nineteenth centuries to trade silver and gold for porcelain, silk, spices, and other Asian goods

La Matanza: Massacre of 10,000–30,000 peasants by military in El Salvador in 1932

Mau Mau: Kenyan rebel movement

Maya: Dominant group of ethnicities and the ancient civilizations of southern Mexico, Yucatan, and northern Central America

Mercosur: Trade bloc among Argentina, Brazil, Paraguay, Venezuela, and Uruguay

Mesoamerica: Pre-Columbian Mexico and Central America

Mesopotamia: The region between the Tigris and Euphrates rivers (Iraq, Syria, Iran, Turkey), where civilization first began

Mestizo: The race of people born of Spanish and Indigenous unions in Latin America

Micro-Lending: Concept of providing small business loans to people in the developing world

Middle Passage: The slave voyage across the Atlantic from Africa to the Americas

Modernization Theory: Term promoted by Max Weber to explain how societies can attain economic, political, and cultural progress

Mongols: North Asian tribe that conquered Asia and Eastern Europe in the thirteenth century

The Mothers of the Plaza de Mayo: The Argentine Mothers of the Disappeared

NAFTA: North American Free Trade Agreement

NRA: National Resistance Army (Uganda)

NLF: Northern Liberation Front, also known as the Vietcong, or VC

NVA: North Vietnamese Army

Nama and Herero: Indigenous Namibian groups virtually annihilated by German imperialism

Nationalization: The shift in a business's status from privately owned to state-owned

New Spain: Spanish colonial realm encompassing its Caribbean and North American continental holdings

New World: The Western Hemisphere

Non-Aligned Movement: Movement of developing world countries that arose during the Cold War to assert influence as an alternative model to that posed by the two superpowers

OECD: Organization for Economic Cooperation and Development

Occupied Territories: The areas seized and controlled by Israel outside its original 1948 borders but residing technically inside the boundaries of other countries: the West Bank, the Gaza Strip, East Jerusalem, and the Golan Heights

Ogaden: Border region between Somalia and Ethiopia claimed by both but residing within Ethiopia's border

Old World: The Eastern Hemisphere

Oligarchy: Rule by a small elite

Olmec: First civilization to emerge in the Americas, approximately 3,500 years ago, in Mexico and Central America

Operation Ajax: The CIA overthrow of the Iranian Prime Minister Mohammad Mossadegh in 1953

Operation Desert Storm: UN intervention in Iraq and Kuwait, 1991

Operation Enduring Freedom: U.S.-led intervention in Afghanistan between 2001 and 2013 as of this writing

Operation Iraqi Freedom: U.S.-led intervention in Iraq, 2003–2011

Operation Restore Hope: UN intervention in Somalia, 1992–1994

Operation Success: The CIA overthrow of Guatemalan President Jacobo Arbenz in 1954

Ottoman: Name of the empire that dominated the Middle East for six centuries ending after WWI

PIH: Partners in Health

PKI: Indonesian Communist Party

PKK: Kurdish Workers Party

PLO: Palestinian Liberation Organization

PNI: Indonesian National Party

PRC: The People's Republic of China, the official name of mainland, Communist China

Pan-Arabism: Concept of widespread Arab World solidarity promoted primarily by Egyptian President Gamal Abdul Nasser

Paras: French military in Algeria

Pashtun: Prominent ethnic group in Afghanistan and Pakistan

Pathet Lao: Laotian Communist regime

Peninsular: Someone born in the Iberian Peninsula living in the Americas

Persia: Traditional name for Iran

Phalange: Maronite Christian-based Lebanese armed group fighting with Israel against the PLO and Hezbollah during the 1975–1990 Civil War

Pharaoh: Term referring to ancient Egyptian rulers from 3100 to 30 BC

Pied noir: French nationals living in Algeria

Positivism: The scientific ordering of society, a concept promoted by the French philosopher Auguste Comte

Proletariat: Marxist term for the lower classes

RPF: Rwandan Patriotic Front

RUF: Revolutionary United Front (Sierra Leone)

Rainbow Nation: Term used by Nelson Mandela to describe his intention to unite all the different racial groups of South Africa under one broadly-defined banner of nationalism

Raj: System of British colonial rule in India from 1858 to 1947

Rastafarianism: Jamaican religion that began in the 1930s believing Ethiopian ruler Haile Salassie to be the incarnation of God on Earth

Repartimiento: Forced labor obligation system of colonial Latin America

SAVAK: Secret police of the Shah of Iran, 1953–1979

SCO: The Shanghai Cooperation Organization, originally the Shanghai Five when founded in 1996, coordinates security between its six members: China, Russia, Kyrgyzstan, Kazakhstan, Uzbekistan, and Tajikistan

Satyagraha: Gandhi's philosophy, translated as "truth" or "soul force"

Scramble for Africa: Term describing the manner in which Europeans divided and then conquered Africa from the 1870s to 1910s

Shah: Term for king in Persia (Iran)

Shi'ite: Minority sect of Islam (although they are the majority in Iraq and Iran)

Shining Path: Terrorist organization of Peru

Shogunate: Japanese system of rule by regional chiefs (shoguns) from 1192 to 1867

Songhay: Name of a fifteenth-century empire of the Niger River Valley

Southern Cone: Southern half of South America: Chile, Argentina, Paraguay, and Uruguay

Special Period: Era when the Cuban economy tightened its belt in the decade after the disintegration of the USSR

Stalinist: Term referring to the types of harsh totalitarian methods originally used by Josef Stalin but applied by other Communist governments in Asia and Africa

Sultan: Term for a king in the Islamic world

Sunni: Majority sect of Islam

Taiping: The rebel group led by Hong Xiuquan from 1850 to 1864, and his rebellion that led to the civil war in China that took the lives of 20 million people

Taliban: Afghan Islamic fundamentalist organization

Tamil Tigers: Tamil Nationalist rebel force in Sri Lanka

Taoism: Prominent Chinese philosophy stemming mainly from Laozi's (fifth–fourth century, BC) *Tao Te Ching*

Tudeh: Iranian Communist Party

Tutsi: The minority ethnic group in Rwanda (and Burundi), the primary victims of the Rwandan genocide at the hands of Rwandan Hutus

UFCo: United Fruit Company

UNSCOM: United Nations Special Commission (Iraq WMD inspections, 1991–1998)

UP: Popular Unity, Chilean President Salvador Allende's (1970–19-73) political party

Vedas: The four sacred texts of Hinduism

Viceroy: Colonial ruler representing the Crown's interests in European colonies

Viet Minh: Ho Chi Minh's original rebel force that opposed both the Japanese and the French between 1941 and 1954

Vietnamization: Term used by the U.S. government under the Nixon administration (1969–1974) to describe the transfer of responsibilities for defending South Vietnam to the South Vietnamese military and government

La Violencia: The era of violence in Colombia that killed 200,000 people

Wahhabi: Fundamentalist Sunni branch of Islam founded by Muhammad ibn Abd al-Wahab (1703–1791)

World-Systems Theory: Theory devised by Immanuel Wallerstein arguing for a systems-based approach to understanding history rather than a focus on individual states, in particular for analyzing how capitalism benefited the "core" countries at the expense of the "periphery" and "semi-periphery"

Zanu: The Zimbabwe African National Union

Zoroastrianism: Believed to be the first monotheistic religion originating in Persia in the sixth century BC by the prophet Zoroaster

Index

Abacha, Sani 212–13
Abubakar, Abdulsalami 213
Acemoglu, Daren 260–1
Afghanistan: Drug War in 189–90;
  effects of conflict in 269;
  globalization in 187–91; nationalism
  in 110–12
Africa: ancient 58–63; Arab Spring
  in 219; blood diamonds in 210;
  Britain in 62–9, 72–3, 214, 224;
  China and 131, 211; Cold War
  and 130–1, 134–6, 149–50, 203,
  209–10; colonization of 39; Cuba
  and 131, 134; disease in 13, 202,
  216, 220, 262–3; East 68–9; Europe
  and 12–13, 59–75; France in
  65–9, 73–4, 139–40; globalization
  in 200–24; historical figures 74–5,
  151–3, 221–4; Horn of 145–7;
  images of 201; imperialism in 39,
  58–75, 130, 209; independence
  in 71, 131, 139–40, 143, 202–3;
  infant mortality rates 230–1; Islam
  in 11–12, 59, 211–12, 219; maps
  of 11, 146; nationalism in 129–53;
  the Netherlands in 62; overview of
  1–5, 10–13; Portugal opening 60–1;
  reality, imagination and 1–4; Russia
  and 131, 134, 146–7; Scramble for
  67, 74; slavery and 60–2, 68–70;
  southern 62–5, 74; Sub-Saharan
  12; timelines 58, 129, 200; U.S.
  and 134, 137, 146–9, 201, 203,
  208, 210–11, 217, 219–21; West
  68; WWI and 71–2; see also specific
  countries
African National Congress (ANC) 64,
  132–3, 135, 215–17, 223–4
agrarian reform 162

Ahmadinejad, Mahmoud 185, 195–6
AIDS 13, 216, 220–1
Alexander the Great 40, 51, 59
Alfonsin, Raul 94
Algeria 130, 139–40, 151, 203
Allende, Salvador 92–3, 97, 248
Al Qaeda 187–8, 190, 197
American Israel Public Affairs
  Committee 184
Amin, Hafizullah 110
Amin, Idi 144–5, 151
anarchist theory 240–2
ANC see African National Congress
Angola: globalization in 202, 210;
  nationalism in 130, 134–5, 152
Angolan Popular Liberation Movement
  (MLPA) 134–5, 152
Annan, Kofi 217, 221
anti-colonialism 234–6
anti-corporatism 242–3
apartheid 132–3, 135, 203
Arab-Israeli War 113
Arab Spring 137, 185–6, 219, 222
Arafat, Yasser 114, 184, 196
Arbenz, Jacobo 89, 160
Argentina: Evita in 93–4, 98–9;
  globalization in 167; independence
  of 29; Kirchner in 157, 167;
  nationalism in 93–4
Arias, Oscar 97
Aristide, Jean Bertrand 85
Armenian genocide 45, 193
Aryans 41–2
The Ascent of Money (Ferguson) 252–3
ASEAN see Association of Southeast
  Asian Nations
Asia: ancient civilizations of 39–41;
  Cold War and 103–4, 109–13, 116–
  24, 177, 179, 191–2; colonization of

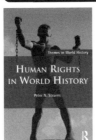